CBAP®/CCBA® Exam Prep

By Barbara A. Carkenord, CBAP, PMP

RMC
Publications, Inc.

CBAP®/CCBA® Exam Prep

By Barbara A. Carkenord, CBAP, PMP

Printed in the United States of America

First Printing

ISBN 978-1-932735-59-8

Library of Congress Control Number: 2012936160

RMC Publications, Inc.

Phone: 952.846.4484
Fax: 952.846.4844
E-mail: info@rmcproject.com
Web: www.rmcproject.com

I dedicate this book to Rita Mulcahy.

Even though I only spoke with Rita a few times, she is a constant presence in my work. I feel she is looking over my shoulder. In addition to helping me earn my PMP certification through her training and exam prep book, Rita developed a learning system that has helped tens of thousands of project managers improve their careers and their personal effectiveness. She built a company of smart, dedicated people who provide the highest level of customer service and support to their students. She built an amazing legacy by relentlessly pushing people to excel.

I am humbled by her impact and hope to bring her high-quality educational success to the business analysis profession.

Acknowledgements

The following people made invaluable contributions to this book.

I would like to give special recognition and thanks to my editor, Mary. More than I ever expected from an editor, Mary really dove into business analysis. With little prior exposure to the *BABOK® Guide*, she studied intently to learn the content, terminology, and idiosyncrasies of business analysis. Answering her insightful questions about the details of each task and technique helped me understand how to better explain these concepts. She clearly is an excellent business analyst in addition to being an excellent editor!

Editor

Mary Lofsness, PMP

Production Editor

Whitney Thulin

Content Reviewers/Contributors

Clinton Ages

Sonja Almlie, PMP

Tom Burke, MS, CBAP

Laurie Diethelm, PMP

Kathleen Hass, PMP

Deborah Kaufman

Anton Mueller, CBAP

Eric Rudolf

Table of Contents

About the Author

Barbara A. Carkenord, CBAP, PMP
Practice Director and Trainer—Business Analysis

Barbara A. Carkenord has over 25 years of experience in business analysis, and is one of the founders of the Business Analysis training industry. Barbara has an MBA from the University of Michigan, is a Certified Business Analysis Professional™ (CBAP®) and a certified Project Management Professional (PMP)®. She is also the author of the worldwide best-seller *Seven Steps to Mastering Business Analysis*, and is a frequent speaker at industry conferences and chapter events. An active IIBA® member, she was a core team member of the *BABOK® Guide* creation committee and contributed to the book, *Managing Business Analysts*. In 2010, Barbara was named Small Business Woman of the Year by the Georgia Women in Technology Association.

Barbara possesses detailed knowledge and experience in many analysis tools and techniques. She develops and delivers business analysis training using proven techniques and real-world experience. Barbara's areas of expertise include business analysis, software design, quality assurance, and project management. Her experience covers many industries including insurance, banking, and manufacturing.

About RMC Project Management, Inc., and RMC Publications, Inc.

Founded in 1991 by Rita Mulcahy, RMC Project Management is the innovator in project management training and professional development. Over the last 20-plus years, hundreds of thousands of project managers in over 50 countries have utilized one of our professional development resources, classes, or e-Learning courses to expand their project management knowledge and further their careers. Today, RMC offers a wide range of innovative classes and products for beginning and advanced project managers—as well as those seeking a project management or business analysis certification.

When people ask what makes RMC different than other companies, our answer is threefold: 1) we minimize the number of hours needed to learn, 2) we maximize knowledge delivery and retention in everything we do, and 3) we communicate knowledge that is immediately applicable by project managers in the real-world. This simple, yet powerful philosophy has turned RMC into one of the fastest-growing training organizations in the world.

Welcome to my *CBAP®/CCBA® Exam Prep* book. Preparing for a business analysis certification exam will challenge you, increase your knowledge, and enhance your career! Committing yourself to working toward certification shows character and ambition and I am honored to accompany you on your journey. Business analysis is an exciting new profession. You are one of the early adopters of a skill set that will grow increasingly valuable as our organizations continue to develop more complex systems and products. Business analysis is a broad discipline and certification requires you to have a broad base of knowledge. In studying for your exam, I expect to introduce you to new ways of performing business analysis which will increase your effectiveness. My goal is to bring this knowledge together with your existing experience and help you prepare to pass a business analysis certification exam. It won't be easy, but nothing worth doing is easy.

Barbara A. Carkenord, CBAP, PMP
Director of Business Analysis
RMC Project Management

Free Updates   Purchase of this book includes access to updates regarding the CBAP® and CCBA® exams, as well as additional tricks, tips, and information to help you prepare for your exam. Access this information at www.rmcproject.com/baprep.

We Need You to Help Us Stop Copyright Infringement   As the publisher of the best-selling PMP exam prep book on the market, RMC is also, unfortunately, the most illegally copied. It is true that many people use our materials legally and with our permission to teach exam preparation. However, from time to time, we are made aware of others who copy our exam questions, Tricks of the Trade®, and other content illegally and use them for their own financial gain.

If you recognize any of RMC's proprietary content being used in other exam prep materials or courses, please notify us at copyright@rmcproject.com immediately. We will do the investigation. Please also contact us at the e-mail address above for clarification on how to use our materials in your class or study group without violating any laws.

Contact Us   We love to hear your feedback. Is there anything in this book that you wish was expanded? Is there anything on which we focus too much? Did we miss something? Please send us an e-mail at baprep@rmcproject.com.

Tricks of the Trade® for Studying for Your Exam

Is Business Analysis Certification for Me?

Why would you decide to spend hours applying for, studying for, and taking a difficult exam? There are many reasons to earn a business analysis certification:

- Increase your knowledge of business analysis practices. Even if you have been working as a business analyst for many years, you can always learn more analysis techniques. Learning industry standards introduces you to additional proven tools and techniques.
- Demonstrate you are disciplined and have the ability to complete a difficult project. Earning a certification is a significant personal achievement.
- Improve communication with your peers. Using a common terminology increases meaningful communication with professionals in the discipline and allows professionals to share ideas and best practices.
- Advance your career. A business analysis certification builds your personal résumé and shows you have industry knowledge.
- Increase your earning potential. An International Institute of Business Analysis™ (IIBA) salary survey found that certified business analysis practitioners earn, on average, 10 percent higher salaries than those without a certification.
- Increase your opportunities. A certification may help you more rapidly advance your career.
- Be a leader in your organization. A certification may give you credibility in your organization; you can help your company better define your role and hire other people who are effective business analysts.
- Manage your career. Staying current with best practices and technology and continuously improving your effectiveness are the best ways to maintain economic security in an ever-changing world.

These are all good reasons for you to invest the time required to achieve business analysis certification!

When you achieve your CCBA® or CBAP® certification, you can say you have passed an international exam designed to prove your knowledge of business analysis. The exams focus on situations you might encounter in your work rather than just asking you to reiterate information you have learned. Passing a certification exam proves your knowledge and experience in the application of the art and science of business analysis. The certification is a way to set yourself apart.

Types of Business Analysis Certification

International Institute of Business Analysis™ (IIBA) currently offers two business analysis certifications:

- Certificate of Competency in Business Analysis™ (CCBA®)
- Certified Business Analysis Professional™ (CBAP®)

The CCBA® designation is intended for:

- Full-time business analysts with three years of business analysis experience. You will have the opportunity to pursue CBAP® certification in the future as you gain more experience in business analysis.
- "Hybrid" business analysts, who spend part of their time performing business analysis work and part doing something else (such as project management or testing). The CCBA® certification recognizes your competency in the business analysis components of your role.

The CBAP® designation has been designed for:

- Full-time business analysts with at least five years of extensive business analysis experience. Having a CBAP® certification indicates that you can walk into any business situation and effectively analyze business needs.

One of the goals of IIBA is to elevate the profession of business analysis. Achieving a business analysis certification demonstrates that you are a significant member of that profession. Business analysts are valuable problem solvers and help their organizations identify new projects and successfully implement solutions to business needs.

Qualifying to Take the Exams

To earn an IIBA business analysis certification, you must meet the requirements as outlined by IIBA. The current requirements are described in the following tables.

Certification of Competency in Business Analysis™ (CCBA®)

General Education	Business Analysis Education	Business Analysis Experience	Breadth of Experience	References
High school education or equivalent	21 hours professional development in the last four years	3750 hours (as defined in the *BABOK® Guide*) in last seven years	900 hours in two of the knowledge areas or 500 hours in four of the six knowledge areas	Two references from a career manager, client, or CBAP® recipient

Certified Business Analysis Professional™ (CBAP®)

General Education	Business Analysis Education	Business Analysis Experience	Breadth of Experience	References
High school education or equivalent	21 hours professional development in the last four years	7500 hours (as defined in the *BABOK® Guide*) in last ten years	900 hours on four of the six knowledge areas	Two references from a career manager, client, or CBAP® recipient

Business analysis certification acknowledges that you can perform business analysis work because you have the knowledge and experience deemed necessary by IIBA. IIBA verifies your *knowledge* through an exam; it verifies your *experience* through your application.

A Guide to the Business Analysis Body of Knowledge® (BABOK® Guide) Version 2.0 is the industry standard. You must complete the online application documenting your work experience within each knowledge area as defined in the *BABOK® Guide*. To do this, you must have a high-level understanding of the *BABOK® Guide* knowledge areas. This chapter will help you gain that high-level understanding.

About the Exams

Are You Ready for Your Exam?

The goal of this book is to get you ready to take your exam, but you should already have some experience in the following areas:

- Developing business analysis plans for yourself and others
- Eliciting and analyzing requirements
- Categorizing or classifying requirements
- Modeling and diagramming requirements
- Communicating and presenting requirements
- Working on teams using various methodologies (Examples include waterfall development methodology, agile team, iterative development project, Six Sigma® process improvement)
- Facilitating formal and informal elicitation sessions with multiple stakeholders
- Delivering requirements to a technical team who used them to design and build a solution
- Helping your organization smoothly implement a significant change

If you don't have this experience, you may need to brush up on your understanding in these areas. Pay special attention to the Apply Your Knowledge activities in this book. If you find that many of the concepts and terminology presented in this book are new to you, you will benefit from additional business analysis training before preparing to take your exam.

If you have already been accepted to sit for a certification exam, IIBA has approved your work experience and your professional development hours (formal business analysis training). This indicates you have the knowledge and skills to be a Certified Business Analysis Professional™. Now you just have to pass the exam!

To pass these exams, you must understand the *BABOK® Guide* terminology and be able to apply it to your experience. Most people who fail the exams do so because they are not familiar with the terminology used in the *BABOK® Guide*. This book will provide you with definitions for the *BABOK® Guide* terminology, with examples and exercises to help you learn the concepts behind each term.

If you have not yet applied for certification, see our application help on www.rmcproject.com/baprep.

What Are the Exams Like?

The CCBA® and CBAP® exams each contain 150 multiple choice questions with four answer choices per question. Each exam must be completed in 3.5 hours. The questions are selected randomly from a database of questions. The questions will jump from topic to topic and often cover multiple topics in a single question. You will be able to mark questions for review and go back to them if you are unsure of the answers. IIBA does not release the passing score or your individual results. When you take an exam online, you will be notified immediately that you either passed or failed! (If you fail you will be told how far you were from passing.)

Both exams test on the six knowledge areas presented in the *BABOK® Guide*, even though you do not have to document experience in all of them.

Exam Questions

The following table breaks out the percentage of questions currently on the exams in each knowledge area.

Questions on Exams				
	CCBA®		CBAP®	
BABOK® Guide Knowledge Area	Number of questions	Percentage	Number of questions	Percentage
Business Analysis Planning and Monitoring	30	20%	29	19.33%
Elicitation	20	13.33%	21	14%
Requirements Management and Communication	24	16%	24	16%
Enterprise Analysis	23	15.33%	23	15.33%
Requirements Analysis	29	19.33%	29	19.33%
Solution Assessment and Validation	24	16%	24	16%

Questions about material in the *BABOK® Guide* Introduction, Underlying Competencies, and Techniques chapters will be interspersed among questions associated with related knowledge areas.

> *IIBA occasionally makes changes to aspects of the exams, including qualification requirements, the application process, and the breakdown of questions in each knowledge area. For the latest information, please visit www.iiba.org and read your authorization notice carefully. Any differences between what is listed here and what is communicated by IIBA should be resolved in favor of IIBA's information.*

The following diagram indicates my assessment of the level of difficulty of each knowledge area. For many people the most challenging areas are Business Analysis Planning and Monitoring and Enterprise Analysis. Make sure you study these two areas carefully, as well as any knowledge areas that are unfamiliar to you.

BABOK® Guide Knowledge Area	Level of Difficulty
Business Analysis Planning and Monitoring	Most difficult
Enterprise Analysis	
Requirements Management and Communication	↓
Solution Assessment and Validation	
Requirements Analysis	
Elicitation	Least difficult

Be aware of the following for the exams:
- Both exams test knowledge, application, and analysis. This makes the exams more than a test of memory. You must know how to apply the information in this book to analyze typical business analysis situations. Do not expect the exams to have all straightforward, definition style questions.
- The CCBA® exam contains more questions on definitions and specific elements from the *BABOK® Guide* than the CBAP® exam. Since people sitting for the CCBA® exam have less experience, there are fewer situational questions.

- Most acronyms will be spelled out (e.g., the exams will use the full term "work breakdown structure" rather than WBS). You may see a few common acronyms like BA (business analyst) or PM (project manager).
- You will not see any graphics, diagrams, or models on the exams, but will be required to know about specific types of diagrams (e.g., entity relationship, swimlane, and workflow diagrams). You will need to know when you would use each type.
- Most people feel uncertain about several of the questions on the exams. Do not get anxious if you don't know the answer to every question.
- Many people need only about two hours to answer every question and then take the remaining time to review the answers about which they were unsure.
- For people heavily involved in project management, there are some points that may seem out of synch with PMI's approach. In preparing for either of these exams, you will need to step back from that approach and look at this material with a fresh perspective to overcome some of the overlaps and discrepancies. I will point these out along the way.

The exam questions have been designed by psychometricians (professionals who specialize in writing questions). The questions are challenging and require the test taker to *know* the material rather than just memorize it. Be prepared for the following types of questions so you won't be caught off guard when you are taking your exam.

1. **Questions with more than one item in each choice.** Example:

   What is needed to Define a Business Case?
   A. Solution scope, business need, assumptions and constraints
   B. Solution scope, requirements, assumptions and constraints
   C. Business analysis approach, business need, assumptions and constraints
   D. Business analysis approach, solution scope, and requirements

   Answer: A

   For these types of questions, use the process of elimination to rule out incorrect answers. In this example, if you know that a business analysis approach can't be developed without a business case, you can immediately rule out two of the answer choices.

2. **Questions where each answer shows a flow or process.** Example:

   The tasks in the Elicitation knowledge area should be performed in order. The correct order is:
   A. Conduct, prepare, document, confirm.
   B. Document, prepare, conduct, confirm.
   C. Prepare, conduct, document, confirm.
   D. Prepare, document, conduct, confirm.

   Answer: C

   Some test takers find it useful to think of their answer before they read the choices. Be sure to carefully consider each of the items in the answers.

3. **Situational questions.** These questions require you to have experience applying business analysis to specific situations. Example:

You have joined a new company and are learning about their business. After observing a business process and interviewing the domain SME who performs the process every day, you have an idea about how to improve the process. What should you do NEXT?

    A. Draw a workflow diagram of the process.
    B. Meet with the domain SME's manager and make your recommendation.
    C. Write a business case for the change.
    D. Schedule time to observe the next business process.

Answer: A

This is a challenging question because each of the answers is a valid step. To answer the question correctly, you need to put yourself in this situation. Since you have just joined the company, it is possible your recommendation has already been tried. If finding a process improvement was this easy, someone would have already done it! Your best choice is to diagram the process to make sure you really understand it before making recommendations or writing a business case for a change. The second best choice would be to observe the next process, as it may have an impact on your recommendation.

4. **Questions with two or more right answers.** Questions that appear to have two, three, or even four right answers are a challenge to test takers. A few questions will list choices that all could reasonably be correct, or that less-experienced or less-qualified business analysts are likely to choose.

As you go through questions and review the answers in this book and in RMC's *PM FASTrack° Exam Simulation Software for Passing the CBAP° and CCBA° Exams*, look for instances where you think there is more than one right answer and try to figure out why you think multiple choices are correct. I have intentionally included questions like these in our products for business analysis exam preparation. The explanations provided for each question will help you understand why your right answer may not be the *correct* answer.

Look again at the previous question. All four of the answers could be correct, depending on the details of the situation. But we have only the details provided in the question. Be careful not to assume anything else; evaluate the question based only on the information provided.

5. **Questions about the roles involved in business analysis work.** Much business analysis work involves communication with stakeholders, so understanding the roles of stakeholders and how they work with you is critical. Example:

Which stakeholders are involved in planning the business analysis approach?
    A. Sponsor, project manager, operational support, implementation SME
    B. Business analyst, project manager, domain SME, operational support
    C. Business analyst, project manager, operational support, domain SME
    D. Sponsor, project manager, business analyst, implementation SME

Answer: D

The easiest way to prepare for these questions is to learn the meanings of each task and the stakeholder roles. If you understand the work being described you'll be able to match tasks to stakeholders when answering a question. I'll talk more about this in the next section.

6. **Questions where terminology is important.** Example:

Interface analysis is:
A. A structured analytical technique for identifying the root cause of a problem.
B. The identification and design of external connections required by the solution.
C. A description of software components which can "plug and play" automatically.
D. A description of how competitive forces in the industry impact each other.

Answer: B

To correctly answer this question, you must understand all of the terms in the answer choices. In this example, the word *interface* has basically the same meaning as *external connections*, so knowing these two terms would give you a strong clue to the correct answer.

7. **Questions with a new approach to a known topic.** There will be instances where you understand the topic, but have never thought about it in the way the question describes. Example:

After a project is closed, the requirements:
A. Will be immediately used on another project.
B. Should all be archived.
C. Should be stored based on the requirements management plan.
D. Are virtually useless.

Answer: C

Many business analysts don't realize that requirements may be reused on future projects and must be stored based on their requirements management plan.

8. **Questions that require memorization.** (I'll point these out to you along the way.) Example:

What is a SMART objective?
A. Specific, measurable, achievable, relevant, timebounded
B. Satisfactory, measurable, accurate, routine, timebounded
C. Specific, monetary, accurate, routine, timeframed
D. Supportive, monetary, achievable, realistic, textual

Answer: A

How to Use This Book

I have developed this exam prep book to help you learn the industry best practices for business analysis by explaining the *BABOK® Guide* in an accessible, relaxed way. It includes examples, exercises, and activities to make your study active. This doesn't mean you don't have to read the *BABOK® Guide*! Use this book as your primary resource and I'll suggest how best to use the *BABOK®*

Guide as a reference. First we'll look at how this book is organized, and then dive into the *BABOK® Guide*, and finally you'll build a study plan for moving forward.

Overview of This Book

One of the first things you may notice about this book is that I present the six knowledge areas in a different order from that of the *BABOK® Guide*. As presented in this book, each knowledge area chapter builds on the information covered in the previous chapter. Business analysis, as you will see, is *not* sequential in nature, which can make studying for your exam difficult. To increase your understanding, I have included diagrams and explanations in this book showing when you would perform tasks and how they are related to each other.

How This Book Is Organized

Each chapter in this book includes the following sections:

- Chapter Title (with a reference to the corresponding *BABOK® Guide* chapter number).
- Quicktest—A list of key terms used in the chapter. Refer back to this list when you are finished with each chapter to test your knowledge of the chapter content and to review what is most important. These terms are listed randomly so you will get practice jumping from one topic to another.
- Introduction to the Knowledge Area—An overview of the content of the chapter.
- The <XYZ Knowledge Area> in Action—A story describing one of my experiences with work described in the knowledge area.
- Barb's BA Themes—There are four core themes that run through the *BABOK® Guide*. I'll introduce them to you in the next chapter. At the beginning of each chapter, I'll discuss how the themes are involved in that knowledge area.
- Things to Know for the Exam—A list of key concepts you are likely to be tested on.
- Introduction to the Tasks of the Knowledge Area—An overview of the tasks and how they are related to each other.
- Knowledge Area Tasks—(in the same order as presented in the *BABOK® Guide*) For each task you will find:
  - An introduction to the task.
  - A table summarizing inputs, outputs, and techniques.
  - The business analyst's responsibilities for this task.
  - A description of the detailed work included in the task.
  - Techniques, presented in alphabetical order. Techniques critical to the understanding of the task will be discussed in detail. To see where each technique is covered, refer to the Tasks/ Techniques Reference Sheet on page 38. Over the course of this book you will learn about every one of the 34 techniques in the *BABOK® Guide*!
  - Case study exercises (See a description of the case study below). Be sure to complete each exercise *before* you read my answer, to make sure you really learned the material.
  - Apply Your Knowledge practice activities. These are designed to help you to think about how your work fits into the tasks and techniques of the *BABOK® Guide*. Use these activities to apply your knowledge of the task or technique to a situation you have encountered. The more you can relate the tasks and techniques to your experiences, the easier it will be to answer questions on your exam.
  - Summary of the task.
- Summary of the chapter.
- Practice Exam for the chapter.

Workforce Tracking Case Study

Exercises in the book are designed to give you practice with specific business analysis tasks and techniques. Many of the examples and exercises use a case study involving a Human Resources (HR) department at a large, multi-national organization. This fictional company has over 20,000 full and part time employees along with contractors and consultants. There are three projects underway in the HR department:

1. Worker Profiles: This project will give workers the ability to update their profiles (address, phone number, contact info) directly via a secured website and allow candidates to apply for open positions on a public website. This will decrease the time HR administrators spend entering data, decrease errors, and allow for more timely updates.

2. Worker Equipment Tracking: This project will give employees the ability to request new PCs and office equipment and to schedule repairs via a secured website. Currently, a "middleman" secures equipment for employees. Elimination of this intermediary will get employees the equipment they need sooner.

3. Payroll: This project will enhance the payroll system to automate the tax processing for six countries outside the United States. Currently, non-US tax processing requires a significant manual effort.

You will be given more details about the case study in exercises throughout this book.

Symbols Used in This Book

 Extra insight to help you better understand business analysis

 Advanced topics that may appear on the CBAP® exam

 Examples and exercises specific to the Workforce Tracking case study

 Places where I recommend you read the *BABOK® Guide* standard description because it provides a good explanation or review of the topic

Overview of the *BABOK® Guide*

The *BABOK® Guide* is an important resource. You should plan to read it at least once before you take your exam. But that doesn't mean you have to read it in order or all in one sitting! As you study for your exam, I recommend that you first read each chapter in this book, and then read the corresponding knowledge area chapter in the *BABOK® Guide*. This will help reinforce the tasks and techniques of the knowledge area. If there is something in the *BABOK® Guide* you don't understand, be sure to add it to your study plan for further review or research.

Since the *BABOK® Guide* is a reference, become familiar with its organization so you can quickly find information when you need it. The more you refer to the *BABOK® Guide*, the more comfortable you will become with the format.

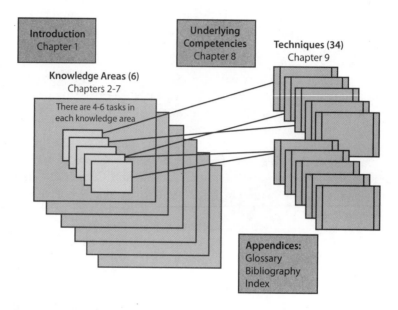

How the *BABOK® Guide* Is Organized

The *BABOK® Guide* is divided into knowledge area chapters and tasks within in each chapter. There are also several appendices, most important of which is the glossary. Get in the habit of looking up a word whenever you are unsure of its definition or usage.

Chapter 1 is the Introduction and contains important foundational concepts you'll need to know to get started with your exam preparation. It briefly describes each knowledge area and explains how the guide is structured.

Chapters 2 through 7 define the following six knowledge areas. Within each knowledge area there are four to six tasks.

- Business Analysis Planning and Monitoring
- Elicitation
- Requirements Management and Communication
- Enterprise Analysis
- Requirements Analysis
- Solution Assessment and Validation

Chapter 8 outlines Underlying Competencies for business analysis. These competencies, such as communication skills, business knowledge, and problem solving skills, are important in business analysis, but aren't unique to the business analysis profession. This book will address many of these topics within the knowledge area chapters, rather than covering them in a separate chapter. Most test takers do not need additional explanation of these items. Be sure to read this chapter in the *BABOK® Guide* at some point during your study. This is a pretty easy chapter, so you might want to save it for a day when you need a little break. Exam questions about Underlying Competencies will be incorporated into the knowledge area questions.

Chapter 9 describes most of the business analysis techniques referenced in the knowledge areas. These techniques are powerful analysis tools that business analysts use every day. A task can use many techniques and a technique can be used by many tasks. See the Tasks/Techniques Reference Sheet on page 38 of this book. There are a few additional techniques that are described only in the discussion of the task in which they are performed. Once again, exam questions about business analysis techniques will be incorporated into the knowledge area questions.

The appendices of the *BABOK® Guide* include a glossary of terms, an index, and a bibliography of references used to develop the standard. These bibliography references are recommended by the authors of the *BABOK® Guide*. You may want to consult additional resources on topics that are unfamiliar to you.

 Its clean organization makes the *BABOK® Guide* a great reference manual. Take a look at the table of contents now. It is easy to look up a task, technique, or a definition when you need one.

Nothing Is Perfect

One of the criticisms of the *BABOK® Guide* is that it is biased toward software development projects. As you learn about each task, be sure to consider it from both a software perspective and a non-software perspective (e.g., business process reengineering). A second criticism is that the task descriptions often assume you are working on a project with a project manager and well-defined team. As you know, not all business analysis work is performed on a project. Enterprise Analysis tasks, for instance, are often done before a project is initiated. A *project* is not a *requirement* of business analysis work!!

There are some sections of the *BABOK® Guide* that are very clear and well-written. Rather than trying to improve on a good thing, I will point you to those sections as appropriate. There are also a few inconsistencies and editing errors. The *BABOK® Guide Version 2.0* was written entirely by volunteers. Having been a volunteer on the *BABOK® Guide* writing committee from the beginning, I can tell you about the challenges we faced in developing this professional standard from scratch!

Inconsistencies or errors in the *BABOK® Guide* do not release you from understanding the best practices for business analysis. I will point out these inconsistencies so you are aware of them, and will not let you skip understanding the material. Please be patient with IIBA and the *BABOK® Guide* authors when you discover imperfections. Like our work on requirements, we can never attain perfection, but if we successfully communicate, we have accomplished our goal. Each new version of the *BABOK® Guide* will improve. Maybe you will be inspired to get involved and join the review or writing committee!

Assess Your Understanding of the *BABOK® Guide* Concepts

Now that you have a sense of how to use this book and the *BABOK® Guide* to study, let's take a look at the knowledge areas, tasks, and techniques covered in both books. This will also provide a good opportunity for you to identify gaps in your knowledge and experience so you can figure out where to focus most of your study time and energy.

If you already have experience performing a task or technique, you only need to familiarize yourself with the terminology used by IIBA before taking your exam. If you have not used a task or technique, you'll want to learn the task or technique and try it out. This book provides activities and examples of how you gain experience by actually performing the work. Once you've assessed your knowledge and experience in the knowledge areas, you can use this information to develop a personalized study plan. We'll walk through an example study plan in the next section.

Know the Knowledge Areas

The bulk of the *BABOK® Guide* and this book cover the six major knowledge areas. Below are brief introductions to each knowledge area and tables listing the tasks and examples of relevant experience for each knowledge area. The lists are not exhaustive. They are intended to give you a general idea of the type of work included in the tasks. As you read the lists, indicate in the table your level of knowledge/experience for each task.

Business Analysis Planning and Monitoring

Business Analysis Planning and Monitoring describes the tasks necessary to plan for and monitor effective business analysis work. Planning is extremely important because business analysis work is complex and time consuming. Business analysis plans describe how you will perform your communications, analysis, and requirements management. This knowledge area also describes the work to measure and monitor business analysis performance.

BABOK® Guide **Business Analysis Planning and Monitoring Tasks**	**Work Experience Have you ever...**	✓ **I have never done this**	✓ **I have done this!**
Plan Business Analysis Approach	Helped your team decide how work would be done, worked in a waterfall environment, worked in an agile environment, helped the project manager decide how to plan work		
Conduct Stakeholder Analysis	Identified people who would be impacted by your work, identified people who would be impacted by a change, considered how a person would react to a change, assessed a person's attitude toward a project, identified a person's communication style		
Plan Business Analysis Activities	Made a to-do list for yourself, made an activity list and given it to your project manager, worked with your manager to set up tasks and milestones to get work done, created a work breakdown structure (WBS)		
Plan Business Analysis Communication	Developed a communication plan for your stakeholders, considered how best to communicate with an individual or group, decided on communications frequency, decided on how formal your communications needed to be		
Plan Requirements Management Process	Planned how you would capture and document requirements, used a requirements management tool, decided which requirements categories you would use, used a standard template for requirements		
Manage Business Analysis Performance	Kept track of your time and compared it to your estimates, recommended improvements to your organization's requirements templates, tools, or processes, asked your stakeholders for feedback on how you were doing, conducted a debrief or lessons learned session to discuss ways to improve future work		

Elicitation   Elicitation involves researching, asking questions, listening, and discovering to obtain information (primarily requirements) from stakeholders and from existing documentation.

BABOK® Guide **Elicitation**	**Work Experience** **Have you ever...**	✓ I have never done this	✓ I have done this!
Prepare for Elicitation	Developed questions to ask a stakeholder, determined where you would meet with a stakeholder, set up a requirements workshop		
Conduct Elicitation Activity	Conducted an interview, moderated a meeting or workshop about requirements, reviewed existing business documentation looking for requirements, reviewed software application user manuals, conducted a focus group, sent out a questionnaire or survey about requirements, discussed how systems work together, discussed how information is exchanged between two organizations or systems, discussed the look and feel of a software screen, website, or report, researched business processes or the industry, researched competition, learned a software application used in your organization, reviewed the history of user problems, reviewed customer complaints		
Document Elicitation Results	Reviewed and revised notes made during an interview, recorded notes during a meeting or workshop, made notes when reviewing a document, video or audio recorded a conversation, drawn a workflow diagram of a business process		
Confirm Elicitation Results	Shown a stakeholder your refined notes and asked if you had understood him or her correctly, given a presentation of your understanding or findings after an interview, given a document to a stakeholder with your analysis conclusions and asked him or her to review it for accuracy		

Requirements Management and Communication   Requirements Management and Communication knowledge area includes tasks that are performed throughout business analysis work. Managing and communicating requirements includes traceability, packaging and communication.

BABOK® Guide **Requirements Management and Communication**	**Work Experience** **Have you ever...**	✓ I have never done this	✓ I have done this!
Manage Solution Scope and Requirements	Received approval of requirements, baselined requirements, identified requirements that were not in scope and communicated this issue, resolved conflicts about requirements, presented requirements for approval, tracked problems with requirements		
Manage Requirements Traceability	Linked requirements to other requirements or to test cases, built relationships between requirements, confirmed that each requirement was addressed in the solution, made sure each requirement was tested, used links to find the impact of a change to requirements, assessed the potential impact of a requirements change, used a requirements management tool to trace or link requirements		

BABOK® Guide Requirements Management and Communication	Work Experience Have you ever…	✓ I have never done this	✓ I have done this!
Maintain Requirements for Re-use	Kept requirements after a project was complete to use for a future change, carefully named and defined requirements so that another analyst could use them, used requirements developed by another analyst, shared requirements with another project		
Prepare Requirements Package	Documented requirements to present to a stakeholder, organized requirements into a document with a table of contents and/or index, decided which requirements had to be reviewed by which stakeholders, discussed how best to present requirements to a particular stakeholder, presented requirements using different formats (text, graphic, table) to make them easier for a stakeholder to review and understand, grouped requirements together to make them easier to review, participated in the creation of a request for proposal (RFP)		
Communicate Requirements	Presented requirements to stakeholders to get their feedback and approval, talked with a stakeholder about requirements to confirm your understanding, sent notes or documents containing requirements to a stakeholder to confirm their understanding, given formal presentations of requirements and recommendations, given presentations to implementation stakeholders (software developers, builders, architects) to help them understand the work required of them, shared requirements with testers or QA professionals		

Enterprise Analysis   Enterprise Analysis includes tasks that usually initiate business analysis work and that help to determine solution goals. These tasks are totally focused on business needs. When you work with business stakeholders to define their problems, opportunities, and expectations for solutions, you are performing enterprise analysis.

BABOK® Guide Enterprise Analysis	Work Experience Have you ever…	✓ I have never done this	✓ I have done this!
Define Business Need	Discussed a problem or a business opportunity with a business person, talked with a marketing person about a new product idea for your company, spoken to an external customer about a complaint or suggestion, observed a problem with an existing system or process		
Assess Capability Gaps	Discussed a missing function in an existing software application with a user, observed processes, compared a business process to a vendor software package, performed gap analysis		
Determine Solution Approach	Thought about how a business problem could be solved, spoken with a business person about how a process could be changed, spoken with a technical person about how a problem could be fixed, brainstormed about a process improvement, brainstormed about how the company could offer a new product or service		

BABOK® Guide **Enterprise Analysis**	**Work Experience Have you ever...**	√ I have never done this	√ I have done this!
Define Solution Scope	Facilitated a conversation about what will be included in a process change, discussed how a new software application would fit into your organization, discussed who would be involved in the definition of a new process, drawn a context level data flow diagram to show the boundaries of a solution, drawn a use case diagram to show what would be included in a new software system, listed processes to be included in an analysis project, identified "out of scope" items in a requirements document.		
Define Business Case	Discussed the costs or benefits of a change to the business, researched costs of purchasing a software package, or hardware, or equipment, estimated the cost/time required to implement a business change, estimated the time to be saved by a process change, measured the time or cost required to perform a business process		

Requirements Analysis   Requirements Analysis is the heart and soul of business analysis. The tasks in this knowledge area involve creating detailed requirements; using techniques like process modeling and data modeling. Requirements are analyzed, prioritized, organized, modeled, and reviewed for completeness and accuracy.

BABOK® Guide **Requirements Analysis**	**Work Experience Have you ever...**	√ I have never done this	√ I have done this!
Prioritize Requirements	Discussed the relative importance of different requirements with a stakeholder, made a list of requirements assigned priority rankings like High, Medium, or Low to a list of requirements, discussed the best order to perform technical development with a developer or architect, explained to a business stakeholder how the solution could be built or implemented in phases		
Organize Requirements	Categorized requirements by type (e.g., business or technical), sorted requirements by business area or stakeholder, split requirements into separate documents for different implementation stakeholders		
Specify and Model Requirements	Drawn a data model, process model, workflow diagram, use case diagram, decision tree, decision table, class diagram, or sequence diagram, made a list of requirements in a table or spreadsheet		
Define Assumptions and Constraints	Written a list of conditions under which a project will be completed, documented a technical constraint, discussed limitations of the new technology for solving a business problem, discussed a business limitation, listened to stakeholder concerns about a proposed solution		

BABOK® Guide Requirements Analysis	Work Experience Have you ever…	✓ I have never done this	✓ I have done this!
Verify Requirements	Asked another business analyst or a stakeholder to review your requirements, reviewed the requirements of another business analyst, made sure your requirements complied with organizational standards, invited QA people to review your requirements		
Validate Requirements	Conducted a meeting to review your requirements, attended a requirements review session for another project team, made sure the solution described by your requirements would solve the business problem as intended		

Solution Assessment and Validation   The last knowledge area covered in the *BABOK® Guide* is Solution Assessment and Validation. It describes the tasks business analysts perform to make sure the solution meets business needs and is smoothly introduced into the business with minimal disruption.

BABOK® Guide Solution Assessment and Validation	Work Experience Have you ever…	✓ I have never done this	✓ I have done this!
Assess Proposed Solution	Reviewed ideas for solving business problems to help recommend one over another, conducted a workshop for the stakeholders to brainstorm on solution ideas, developed a formal comparison of two or more solution options, reviewed vendor package offerings to determine whether they would solve the current business need, developed an RFP to solicit a vendor proposal, developed a scoring system to evaluate vendor proposals		
Allocate Requirements	Made sure each requirement was included in the solution idea, helped to assign individual requirements to a release or iteration of an project, categorized requirements by business department or job function, identified who would work on each requirement, determined how each requirement would be satisfied, helped the team determine what to do first based on dependencies, constraints, and value, helped with the planning of the implementation schedule		
Assess Organizational Readiness	Considered how well the organization and individual stakeholders within the organization would accept a change, considered all of the impacts of a change on the organization, listed all of the possible ramifications of a change, considered how different stakeholders would accept the change (based on their culture, location, knowledge of the effort)		

BABOK® Guide Solution Assessment and Validation	Work Experience Have you ever...	✓ I have never done this	✓ I have done this!
Define Transition Requirements	Helped decide how to prepare the organization and stakeholders for a change, designed or developed training materials for employees on a new system, helped decide when to roll out a change, developed an implementation or rollout plan, worked with the business people helping them learn a new system, worked with the technical people to convert data to a new system, helped to update employee job descriptions to support a new business process		
Validate Solution	Reviewed a new system or change to determine if it was going to help the business, reviewed test results to make sure the outputs were as expected, assisted with user acceptance testing of a software change, assessed problems before implementation to find a solution or workaround, assessed problems to decide if they were serious enough to delay implementation		
Evaluate Solution Performance	Talked with a business person about how new production systems were working, worked as a help desk or customer service person answering questions and solving problems, looked for improvement possibilities by observing day-to-day operations of a business, measured the time to accomplish a task and compared it to the estimated time, conducted a debriefing, lessons learned session, or retrospective on a project after implementation		

Know the Tasks

As you have seen, each knowledge area includes from four to six tasks. The tasks are the most important part of the *BABOK® Guide*, so this is where you should focus your study. Let's look at the format in which each task is presented. Open your *BABOK® Guide* to the task Define Business Need (Task 5.1). Each task starts out with its name and a brief purpose of the task—one or two sentences. Then there is a longer Description section which includes a graphic showing the inputs and outputs. The Inputs section lists each input with a brief description of how it is used in the task. Many exam questions will ask you what is needed to perform the task.

Next you will find the Elements section, which sometimes includes other diagrams to more fully explain a concept. This section describes the task in detail by breaking it down into smaller topics. Some elements are lengthy, while others are very short. Don't be fooled into thinking that a longer description means one element is more important than the others. Be sure you understand each element, but don't try to memorize them. They are provided to aid in understanding of the task. I have not recreated each of the elements in this book because many of them are straightforward and clearly presented in the *BABOK® Guide*. I have instead provided some additional supporting material about each task along with examples to help you better understand the elements. Finally, you will see lists of Techniques, Stakeholders, and Outputs. These are brief descriptions of how each is related to the task. Each technique has a reference number so you can easily refer to a more detailed discussion of the technique in Chapter 9 of the *BABOK® Guide*.

TRICKS OF THE TRADE® Most tasks only have one output and the names of tasks were carefully selected. Understanding the name of a task will help you understand its inputs and outputs, rather than trying to memorize them. Although task names are always singular (e.g., Assess Proposed Solution), they can be performed many times during a project.

Where's the Diagram of the *BABOK® Guide*?   I have not provided you with a diagram of the tasks with their inputs and outputs because I don't think reviewing such a diagram is useful. If you want one, there are many available from other sources. In my opinion, the value of a diagram is in the analysis and research needed to create it. If you like the idea of a diagram, draw one. I would recommend drawing a data flow diagram of the inputs and outputs of each task for one knowledge area first. This will show you task dependencies and places where the tasks are related. I will warn you that these diagrams are complex (and if you try to draw one big diagram with all of the tasks, it is very complex). Don't get stuck drawing pretty pictures (that's called "analysis paralysis"). Focus instead on learning and understanding. If this technique is useful to you, sketch the diagrams but don't worry about making them perfect.

Do I Need to Memorize?

No! If you understand each task and why it is performed, you will be able to think of the inputs, outputs, elements, and stakeholders, because they are logical components of the task. One of the best ways to remember the tasks is to focus on the verb at the beginning of each task name. For instance, when the task name starts with Assess or Evaluate, you know one of the inputs is the thing being evaluated (e.g., *Assess Proposed Solution*) and another input must be the criteria upon which to evaluate. And the output will always be the evaluation or assessment! When you are asked (directly or indirectly) which of the following is an input or output of task xyz, you should be able to reason out the correct answer if you understand the task.

Know the Techniques

A significant part of the *BABOK® Guide* is dedicated to techniques. Techniques are specific, structured tools to help you accomplish the tasks. Take a quick look at the *BABOK® Guide* Table of Contents for Chapter 9. You will see a list of 34 techniques.

To answer exam questions about which techniques would be useful in a particular task, you must know the purpose of each technique. Be sure to *understand* the uses, and advantages and disadvantages of each technique. You should not have to memorize them.

Think about walking through the power tool department in a large hardware store. There are hundreds of tools, some of which you have used, but many of which you've never seen before! If you decided to retile your bathroom, you would probably get a book or take a class to teach you how to use the tools for tiling. The analysis techniques in the *BABOK® Guide* are your power tools. Some you will use frequently, others only occasionally, some never. But when you have a specific need, you should be aware there are applicable tools you can learn to use. For purposes of the exam, you need to know why each one is included in the business analysis toolkit. It will help if you have experience using each technique. This book includes practice ideas to give you some of that experience.

Use the following worksheet below to do a quick assessment of your knowledge of the techniques. I have given you three options here: never heard of it, heard of it but never used it, or have used it. Of course, the more experience you have with these techniques, the less you will have to study them. I'll give you practice ideas for key techniques so you can get the experience you need to feel confident answering questions. (Don't spend too much time on this. Quickly check the appropriate column for each technique. It will give you an idea of which techniques you need to focus on as you read and study this book.) The techniques in bold are highlighted in the *BABOK® Guide*, indicating they are used by a majority of business analysts. There will be more test questions on these.

Techniques	√ Never heard of it	√ Heard of it but never used	√ Used it
Acceptance and Evaluation Criteria Definition			
Benchmarking			
Brainstorming			
Business Rules Analysis			
Data Dictionary and Glossary			
Data Flow Diagrams			
Data Modeling			
Decision Analysis			
Document Analysis			
Estimation			
Focus Groups			
Functional Decomposition			
Interface Analysis			
Interviews			
Lessons Learned Process			
Metrics and Key Performance Indicators			
Non-functional Requirements Analysis			
Observation			
Organization Modeling			
Problem Tracking			
Process Modeling			
Prototyping			
Requirements Workshops			
Risk Analysis			
Root Cause Analysis			
Scenarios and Use Cases			
Scope Modeling			
Sequence Diagrams			
State Diagrams			
Structured Walkthrough			
Survey/Questionnaire			
SWOT Analysis			
User Stories			
Vendor Assessment			

Developing Your Personal Study Plan

How Do We Learn?   Studies have shown that if you visit a topic three times, you will remember it. Therefore, you should read this book once and skim through it two more times, focusing most on the type of work with which you do not have experience or the concepts you have trouble understanding.

Neurologists and scientists who study human learning patterns know that we learn something new by relating it to something we already know. These connections in our brains allow us to attach the new information to existing information and make the new information accessible. Whenever you come upon a new concept, term, topic, etc. try to find a connection with something you already know.

For example, when I first saw the task name Allocate Requirements (you'll learn this one in Solution Assessment and Validation), I had no idea what work it described. I had to learn what was included in the task and how it related to what I already knew. I had used a spreadsheet template on one of my projects, showing which requirements would be included in each phase (we had called it the design area scope). Once I was able to make the connection, I was comfortable answering questions about the task. Now, whenever I see the task name Allocate Requirements, I picture my spreadsheet in my mind and can recall what the task name means.

Build Your Plan   Your personal experience will determine how best to study for your exam. Here are some suggestions for developing a study plan.

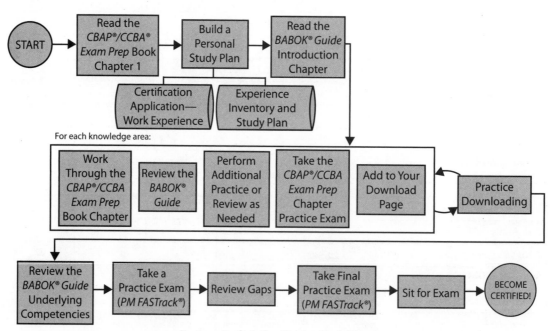

Business Analysis Certification Study Plan

If you can review and understand this diagram, give yourself credit for understanding a workflow diagram (described in the Process Modeling Technique 9.21)!

Read on to learn about the download page and other things to include in your study plan.

Use Your Experience to Learn Business Analysis Best Practices   Review your check marks in the knowledge area tasks and techniques tables starting on page 12. If you have little or no experience in a task or technique, list it in the table below (My Practice Plan). Many of these tasks and techniques can be easily practiced on your own or with a study group. Exercises and Apply Your Knowledge activities in this book will give you direction on how to practice. It may also be helpful for you to think about a business where you see opportunities for improvement. This could be your employer, a company with whom you do business as a customer, your place of worship, a professional association, or a club.

For the tasks and techniques you have never used, develop a practice plan describing how you will practice each one. Incorporate these practice opportunities into your overall study plan. When completed, this practice plan should give you an overall picture of how much you'll need to study. You can also use this table to record your progress.

Example Practice Plan		
Task or Technique I Need to Learn	**What will I do?**	**Complete?** ✓
Sequence Diagrams (9.28)	Draw one of these for the Workforce Tracking case study	✓
State Diagrams (9.29)	Draw one of these for my current project	
Allocate Requirements (7.2)	Use my last project (already implemented) to make a list of solution components and tie them to the major requirements.	

My Practice Plan		
Task or Technique I Need to Learn	**What will I do?**	**Complete?** ✓

My Practice Plan		
Task or Technique I Need to Learn	**What will I do?**	**Complete?** ✓

Great news! By creating this practice plan, you are practicing the Enterprise Analysis task of Assess Capability Gaps! You are assessing your own gaps in experience and knowledge. Check that one off of your list!

Practice Exams   At the end of each chapter, I have included practice questions related to the chapter content. The practice questions can benefit your study by testing your knowledge of the material you have just learned. Each question includes the correct answer and an explanation of why it is correct.

Some people take these practice exams before they develop their study plan or read the chapter, to identify gaps in their knowledge. You may choose to create a score sheet on which to capture your results. Your score sheet might include columns for each attempt and a column to record notes about what you learned.

Example Score Sheet				
Question Number	**Answer (First Time)**	**Why I Chose the Wrong Answer**	**Answer (Second time)**	**Why I Chose the Wrong Answer**
1.				
2.				
3.				
4.				

Download Sheet   Lots of test takers find it useful to design a "download sheet." Your download sheet is usually a page of handwritten notes of things you want to reference during the exam to help you answer questions. It is both a study tool and a help during the exam. You can't take any notes into the exam with you, but you will be given blank paper or a dry erase pen and a small whiteboard upon which you can make notes. You will "download" these notes from your memory when you start the exam (usually during the tutorial or exam startup). This download sheet is useful for several reasons. I used one when I took the PMI PMP® exam and it really helped! I wish I had heard of a download sheet before I took the CBAP® exam!

Benefits of a Download Sheet   You design your download sheet based on your personal test-taking strengths and weaknesses. For example, if you have trouble memorizing the tasks from one of the knowledge areas, you may want to make up an acronym or poem with the first letters of the knowledge areas to remind you. Since you design it yourself, your download sheet will meet your unique needs.

To be able to download your content quickly on the day of your exam, you should practice downloading it for several days before the exam. This is great practice in remembering things and realizing which areas you are struggling with the most. It took me several attempts before I could remember everything I wanted to have on my download sheet. After awhile, I noticed that some items were easy to download, and I realized I didn't need to waste space on my sheet anymore because I had permanently learned them!

When you arrive at the exam, you may be anxious and hesitant to answer the first question. If you start by downloading your memory joggers, you will have information to reference as questions pop up. These notes give you confidence to start the exam, knowing you can refer to your notes whenever you need them. As you read questions and answers during the exam, you may make additional notes.

As you work through this book, make notes for your download page. In the next chapter, I have included a Business Analysis Terms Reference Sheet that you may want to consider when creating your download page (page 40).

Study Time   IIBA recommends three to four months study time, spending eight hour per week reading the *BABOK® Guide* and other resources. Since you are not memorizing, and instead learning, you should not have to rush to take the test before you forget all that you have learned. But you will be more successful if you take the exam relatively soon after studying, because the terminology and concepts will be fresh in your mind.

How to Use This Book in a Study Group   To get your study group started, pick someone to lead the discussion of each chapter (preferably someone who is not comfortable with the chapter). Have everyone read the chapter in this book and the *BABOK® Guide* knowledge area before the meeting. Each time you meet, review topics you do not understand and review the Quicktest terms or the *Hot Topics* flashcards, if you have them. Most study groups meet for one-and-one-half to two hours per chapter. Either independently or with your study group, do further research on topics with which you do not feel confident.

Each member of the study group will need his or her own copy of this book and the *BABOK® Guide*. Use the case study exercises and practice activities provided. Make sure you are not violating international copyright laws by creating any derivative works from this copyrighted book.

If you are leading or teaching a structured business analysis exam preparation course using RMC's products, I encourage you to contact RMC for information on our Corporate Partnership program. Partners may be allowed to create slides or other materials using content from this book. I also encourage you to contact RMC about other tools we offer for study groups and independent instructors, or to learn how to receive quantity discounts on this book, RMC's *PM FASTrack® for Passing the CBAP® and CCBA® Exams Simulation Software* (CD or downloadable) and *Hot Topics Flashcards for Passing the CBAP® and CCBA® Exams*.

Other Materials to Use to Study

In addition to reading the *BABOK® Guide*, here are a couple other resources you may find useful.

PM FASTrack® Exam Simulation Software
for Passing the CBAP® and CCBA® Exams
PM FASTrack® allows you to filter questions by knowledge area and keyword—and also includes enough questions for three complete exams for each certification!

Other features of this product include free question bank updates for people with Internet connections, and exam reporting and archiving functionality. In addition, all questions are cross-referenced back to *CBAP®/CCBA® Exam Prep, Premier Edition*, or the *BABOK® Guide Version 2.0*, so you may quickly and easily return to this book and work on your weak areas. Why be surprised when you take the actual exam? Find your gaps before the exam finds them for you!

Available in both CD ROM and downloadable formats.

Hot Topics Flashcards for Passing the CBAP® and CCBA® Exams
In audio, flip book, or mobile format. These flashcards feature the most important and difficult-to-recall CBAP® and CCBA®-related terms and definitions. They are an excellent study tool for people with busy schedules. You can use them at the office, on a plane, or in your car, adding instant mobility to your study routine.

CHAPTER 2

Business Analysis Key Concepts

Before we jump into Enterprise Analysis, there are some business analysis fundamentals you need to learn. These key concepts and terms are used throughout the book and will be critical to your understanding of the material. Terminology is extremely important in business analysis. The vocabulary used in the *BABOK® Guide* provides the industry a standard language. One of the values of a worldwide, industry certification is the development of a common language which we can use to communicate with business analysts anywhere.

 Review the Introduction Chapter of the *BABOK® Guide* (pages 1–6) now to get familiar with the core definitions.

What Is Business Analysis?

Let's make sure we agree on the definition of business analysis. Business analysis work can be performed by anyone with any title. To simplify references, we refer to people who do this work as *business analysts*.

IIBA has defined business analysis work as:
> …the set of tasks and techniques used to work as a liaison among stakeholders in order to understand the structure, policies, and operations of an organization and to recommend solutions that enable the organization to achieve its goals.

This is a great definition because it includes *relationship-building* as a liaison role, talks about the importance of *learning the business*, and encourages business analysts to *recommend* changes that will help an organization better meets its goals. Be sure you understand each word in this definition and its implications.

Barb's BA Themes

I have identified four overriding themes that drive all business analysis work. Understanding these themes will help you see how the knowledge areas work together, and help you learn how tasks in one knowledge area are dependent on tasks in other knowledge areas.

The purpose of this diagram is to help you understand how the knowledge areas are connected, not to show everything inside each knowledge area. I have intentionally made this diagram relatively simple. I've seen lots of diagrams showing tasks from the *BABOK° Guide*, and most of them look like spaghetti! The business analysis standard is a very complex set of tasks and interrelationships among tasks, but don't let yourself get too bogged down in the details right away. Get a high-level understanding of the fundamental themes and then learn the details.

Let's review the business analysis themes graphic. The knowledge areas are represented as columns. The order of the knowledge areas (left to right) is the order in which I recommend you study them (and the order I've presented them in this book). Enterprise Analysis is first because a business need, which is defined in Enterprise Analysis, should drive everything we do. Notice that Business Analysis Planning and Monitoring is presented last. Does this seem odd to you? Many people find Business Analysis Planning and Monitoring a difficult knowledge area because they don't have experience developing formal business analysis plans. I believe it is easier to learn the other knowledge areas before Business Analysis Planning and Monitoring. Once you understand the tasks and techniques of the other areas, the Planning chapter will be a bit of a review because it requires you to think about how you will perform all of the other tasks.

The themes are presented horizontally across the knowledge areas. They are:
* The Planning Theme
* The Business Case Theme
* The Requirements Theme
* The Solution Theme

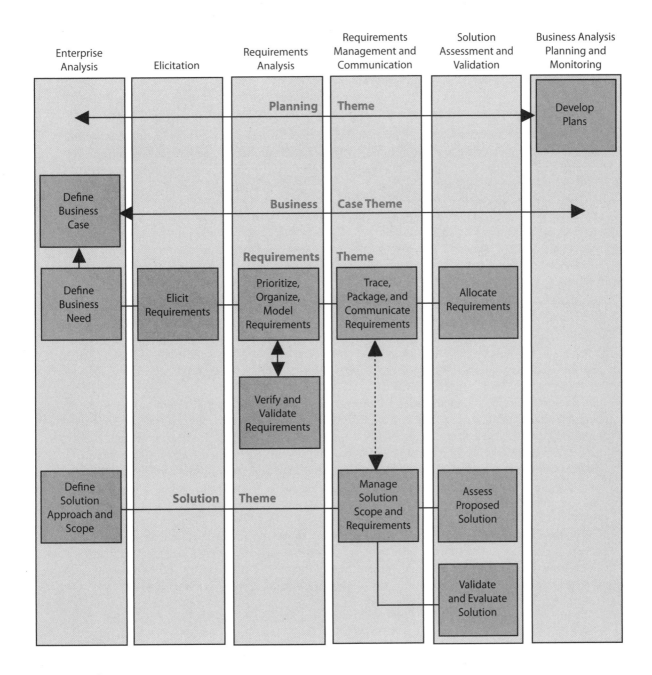

The Themes

I'll use this diagram at the beginning of each chapter to set the stage for the chapter and describe how these themes apply to the knowledge area being presented. Let's look at each of the themes.

The Planning Theme

Before diving into the details of an assignment, a business analyst should plan his or her work. You will learn about the three plans that are created in the Business Analysis Planning and Monitoring knowledge area: the business analysis plan, the business analysis communication plan, and the requirements management plan. The plans are developed using organization standards, solution characteristics, stakeholder characteristics, and analysis techniques. During planning you make lots of decisions about how you will approach each assignment. The arrow running from the Business

Analysis Planning and Monitoring knowledge area to the other knowledge areas and back to planning illustrates that the plans are used in every other area to guide your work. The plans will be updated as you perform tasks in the other knowledge areas and as new information is uncovered. The plans are inputs to every other knowledge area.

The Business Case Theme

The business case is the basis for all work and the success criteria upon which the solution is judged. The business case describes the business need, the proposed solution, and the expected value of the change. It includes both tangible and intangible costs and benefits of the proposed solution. It provides the context within which we will perform our analysis work. The business need and the business case are inputs to many tasks in the other knowledge areas. The horizontal arrow here illustrates that you must be constantly referring back to the original need and justification for the change as you are doing detailed business analysis work. If at any point, you learn something that changes the business case, you must revisit this deliverable with your team.

The Requirements Theme

You will learn many things about requirements as you prepare for your exam. This is the area where even the most experienced business analyst will find something new! There are requirements classifications, requirements modeling concepts, requirements attributes, and requirements states. You will not be able to pass your exam without an in-depth understanding of requirements and their characteristics as outlined in the *BABOK® Guide*.

The Requirements Theme starts with the business need, which is considered a high-level, stated, business requirement. This need is used to elicit more detailed requirements that are later prioritized, organized, and modeled. They are also verified and validated, and the feedback from these review processes may necessitate more requirements analysis. The lines between the knowledge areas do not have arrowheads because these tasks are often performed concurrently, not sequentially. For example, the business need may be elicited from a stakeholder, so the tasks Define Business Need (5.1) and the Elicitation knowledge area tasks are performed concurrently.

The double-headed arrow inside Requirements Analysis shows the iterative nature of the requirements development. As requirements are verified and validated, they are often reprioritized and reorganized, and models are adjusted. Actually, requirements work is happening in almost all of the knowledge areas at once! As you will see, you may be eliciting, analyzing, and allocating all at the same time!

In Requirements Management and Communication, requirements are traced, packaged, and communicated for approval. The task of Manage Solution Scope and Requirements is where the Requirements Theme and the Solution Theme converge. You perform this task whenever you make sure requirements are within scope and get them approved by the appropriate stakeholders. When the solution design is selected, requirements are allocated to solution components to make sure you didn't miss anything. Requirements are inputs to all of the Solution Assessment and Validation tasks.

The Solution Theme

The solution is the product, service, or change you are making to address the business need. It is important to understand that a solution may be a combination of software, hardware, process changes, policy changes, and/or personnel changes needed to satisfy the business need. The Solution Theme starts with the solution approach and scope, which are defined in Enterprise Analysis, either before or at the beginning of your project or initiative. The solution scope is managed in Requirements Management and Communication. In Solution Assessment and Validation, proposed solutions are assessed and a design is selected. The solution may be built or purchased. Clearly, the Solution Theme is closely tied to the Requirements Theme. The solution we build is based on the requirements, so you will see a dotted line linking the two themes in Requirements Management and Communication. The solution scope is managed as requirements are developed and the solution is built. All of your business analysis work depends on a clear definition of, and adherence to, the solution scope. Once the solution is completed, it is validated against the original business need and evaluated for its performance.

There Is No Sequence!

The *BABOK® Guide* does not prescribe a business analysis methodology or approach. The order of the knowledge areas does not indicate a sequence of work. It is important to understand that business analysis work is *not sequential*. The tasks within each knowledge area are not always done sequentially (many of them are performed concurrently), and the knowledge areas themselves often overlap. It will be useful for you to think of the knowledge areas and tasks as being *dependent* on each other rather than having to be performed in a particular order.

Task Dependencies

There is a subtle difference between the terms *dependent* and *sequential*. A task is dependent on another task when the output of the first task is needed as input to the other task. Every task produces some output; I will call it a business analysis work product. (If a task didn't produce anything, why would we do it?) Every task also uses some input; this is the material that we need to perform the task. Often, the output of one task is an input to another. But the output may not immediately be used by another task; it may sit in a holding place until it is needed. So the tasks don't need to be performed one immediately after another. (If you understand the concepts of inputs and outputs, you won't have any trouble learning the data flow diagramming technique (9.6)!)

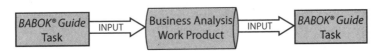

Understanding that business analysis work is not sequential is one of the most important concepts you'll need to know in order to pass the exam. A task can be performed at any time, as long as the inputs it needs are available.

Key Terms

Project vs. Non-Project Work

Business analysis work can be done as part of a project or as part of ongoing business operations. There are several different types of projects mentioned in the *BABOK® Guide* including new software development, upgrading of existing technology, changes to a business processes, and the purchase, customization, and implementation of a software or hardware application. Business analysis work done outside of projects includes customer service, help desk support, and consulting. Sometimes instead of using the word project, I will refer to your business analysis work as an *assignment* or *initiative*. Get comfortable answering questions about work performed both inside and outside of a project.

Solution, Product, Project—What's the Difference?

The words *project*, *product*, and *solution* are critical to your ability to answer exam questions correctly.

Project   A project is a temporary endeavor with a distinct beginning and end that is initiated to produce a product, service, or other solution.

If you have studied for the PMI® certification exam, be careful with your definition of a project. The PMP® exam assumes projects are very large initiatives. To business analysts, a project could be very small or very large. For example if a software user asks for a new report, it could be considered a project. A project may be completed by one person, the business analyst also acting as the project manager, designer, implementer, and tester.

Solution/Product   In the *BABOK® Guide*, the word *solution* is used to represent the result of a project. What are we building? A solution. The *PMBOK® Guide* calls this a *product*. The word solution was chosen by IIBA because it is broader than product. When people see the word product, they usually imagine a thing (e.g., a widget, a building, a software program, a mobile device), but as you have read in the description of the Solution Theme, many business solutions include process changes, personnel changes, or organization changes rather than just products or services. Remember that a *solution* can include any of these.

Think about solving a problem your family is having, maybe getting the kids to school on time. The solution may require a process change (going to bed earlier), a hardware change (setting the alarm clock to ring earlier), and a personnel change (Dad makes breakfast instead of Mom). Spend some time thinking about this word *solution* and getting a good example in your mind as you read this book. Many of the questions/answers on your exam will include the word solution. The word solution is used almost 900 times in the *BABOK® Guide*!

What is a Model?

A model is a collection of artifacts that together define a business domain or solution. It is made up of diagrams, tables, and descriptions to give a more complete view of a set of requirements. A model might include the deliverables from several techniques.

The concept of a model is important for business analysis professionals to understand. A simple analogy is a model car or a model of a new building. It is a small rendition of the proposed product that can be examined and evaluated by stakeholders. In some cases it may even be able to be tested—a model car with moving wheels, for example. Now imagine the model car being shown as a computer graphic in computer-aided design (CAD) or computer-aided manufacturing software (CAM) in three dimensions so it can be rotated and tested virtually. CAD/CAM software can simulate wind passing over the car and determine its impact on the energy use of the car.

Now try to imagine a model of a business process or service. We can build a model of the process or service by using diagrams and descriptions from different perspectives. These diagrams and descriptions viewed together make up a model. For example, a business process may be diagrammed in swimlane workflow diagrams supported by a glossary that defines the terms on the diagrams and the business rules that guide the process.

Workforce Tracking Project Business Rules		
Rule Number	**Rule**	**Rule Type**
BR14	An employee must declare a primary country of residence for payroll tax deduction processing.	Mandatory
BR27	Every worker must provide their legal name, primary residence address, government tax identification number, and primary citizenship.	Mandatory
BR28	All country specific tax withholding laws will be obeyed unless exceptions have been legally approved.	Guideline
BR34	Each employee is assigned an employee number for tracking within the organization. This number will be assigned sequentially by the HR system at the time of employment.	Automated

Workforce Tracking Project Glossary	
Term	**Definition**
Worker	A person who is working on any project for the benefit of our company regardless of their employment status.
Consultant	A person who is employed by an outside company and is assigned to review our company's processes and recommend improvements. A consultant usually does not perform day-to-day business operational work.
Contractor	A person who is employed by an outside company and is assigned to work on one or more of our projects as a part or full time team member. A contractor is expected to follow company standards and procedures while performing his or her assignments.
Employee	A person who is employed by our company and is paid a salary or hourly wage according to the laws of his or her country of residence.
Worker	A person who is working on any project for the benefit of our company regardless of his or her employment status.

A Business Model

System Does Not Equal Software!

Another important term in business analysis is *system*. If you have an IT/software background you may need to change your internal definition of this word. System is not the same as *software*. A system is an interrelated group of things forming a complex whole.

IT people often use this word as synonymous with the word "software." IT departments in the 1980's and 90's were often named "Systems Development" or "IT Systems." Software applications are still commonly referred to as "the payroll system" or "the SAP® system." If you have been using the word system to mean software, you need to adjust your thinking. When you hear "the payroll system," you should think of the software, the hardware, the users, the procedures, the policies, the management and all of the other things that make up payroll. The *system* includes all aspects of the payroll process. (If you don't have an IT bias, you are probably thinking, "Oh, this is one of the reasons I have trouble communicating with IT people! They use the word system differently!")

Another important thing to remember as you are studying for your exam is that business analysis is not only for software development projects. Anyone who helps an organization change is performing business analysis work. (If your background is in IT, be sure to widen your perspective and don't think of every business solution as being software.)

Business Analysis Stakeholders

Business analysis work involves interactions with people at all levels of operations and management, in every department of your organization, and in various outside organizations. To list all of the potential stakeholders for business analysis would be impossible. Instead we use generic stakeholder descriptions to represent all of the potential stakeholders.

APPLY YOUR KNOWLEDGE   There are ten categories of stakeholders (in addition to the business analyst) used in the *BABOK® Guide*. Most of these categories include stakeholders with whom you have worked. For the exam, you must understand the role of each stakeholder category and how they would be involved in each business analysis task. As you think about each type of stakeholder, write down the name of someone with whom you have worked who functioned in this role. Thinking about real people will help you visualize each role as you learn the best practices for interactions with them.

Stakeholder	Description	Person With Whom You Have Worked
Customer	Usually the ultimate consumer of your company's products and services	
Domain SME (subject matter expert)	Someone who understands the business area you are studying	
End User	Someone who will directly use the solution you recommend	
Implementation SME	Someone who helps to design and build the solution	
Operational Support	Someone who will maintain and support the solution after it has been implemented within the business	
Project Manager	Someone who manages projects	
Regulator	Usually someone from outside the organization who works for a regulatory agency, ensuring your solution complies with applicable regulations	
Sponsor	The person within your organization who authorizes and/or funds the work you are performing	
Supplier	Usually an outside organization that provides materials, services, or solutions to your organization	
Tester	Someone who designs and executes quality tests on the solution before it is implemented within the business	

Were you able to fill in a name for each role? If not, imagine a person who would perform this function and think about how you might interact with him or her. Or talk with other business analysts who have this experience to learn from them.

Project Teams

As you read this book, you will see many references to these generic stakeholder roles explaining how you, as a business analyst, should interact with each. Generally speaking there are stakeholders who are *assigned to your project team* and stakeholders who are *outside the team or organization*. The stakeholders usually *outside* the organization (or department) are customers, suppliers, and regulators. When I refer to the project team, I am referring to the roles of sponsor, project manager, domain SME, end user (usually a representative of each end user group), implementation SME, and testers. Operational support people may be initially assigned to the project or brought in after the solution has been built to help with transition requirements.

Stakeholders Usually Outside the Organization or Your Project Team	Stakeholders Usually Part of the Project Team
Customer	Project Manager
Supplier	Sponsor
Regulator	Domain SME (and/or End User representatives)
	Implementation SME
	Tester
	Operational Support
	Business Analyst

Implementation SMEs

Implementation SMEs are responsible for designing and implementing solutions. A few examples are listed in the *BABOK® Guide*, but there are many other potential roles depending on the type of solution involved. For example, if your solution includes a new office building, implementation SMEs would include plumbers, electricians, architects, and interior designers.

 Review the Implementation Subject Matter Expert (SME) section of the *BABOK® Guide* Introduction Chapter (1.5.6.5)

Departments, Divisions, Domains

The use of terminology about groups of stakeholders can be tricky. You must be comfortable with terms like *department*, *division*, and *operating unit* as formal groups in an organization, even if your company doesn't use these names. Another term you will frequently see is *domain*. A domain is a field or sphere of activity. When used in business analysis, it usually means an area of the business which is being studied or analyzed. A business domain may not align exactly with a formal organization unit like a department or a division. A business domain encompasses all of the parts of the business that are involved with the business need you are trying to address, or the solution you are designing. For example, a business problem identified through a customer complaint might involve some of the people and processes in the customer service department and some of the people and processes in the accounting department. The business domain in this example is a *conceptual boundary* of the people and processes involved with the problem. The word *context* is used in almost the same way as domain. Context describes the whole situation or environment relevant to the business need.

A couple of other groups you should know are the PMO (Project Management Office) and BACoE (Business Analysis Center of Excellence).

PMO

A project management office is a business unit expressly created to support individuals performing project management. This department manages organizational process assets related to project management like templates, guidelines, and project management tools, and encourages the sharing of lessons learned.

BACoE

A business analysis center of excellence is a business unit expressly created to support individuals performing business analysis work. This department manages business analysis assets like templates, requirements guidelines, requirements management tools, and encourages the sharing of lessons learned.

Plan-Driven and Change-Driven Approaches

There are two general approaches to business analysis work. Plan-driven approaches (traditional waterfall-type methodologies) expect business analysis work to be more structured and well-documented. Change-driven approaches (like agile and Scrum) focus less on formal techniques and documents and more on collaborative communications and rapid solution development. As you prepare for your exam, consider how you would perform each knowledge area task within these different environments. The tasks of the *BABOK® Guide* are designed to be useful in any environment, on any type of project, using any type of approach. Don't get locked into thinking they only work in one way. Business analysts must be flexible enough to work in any methodology with any stakeholder.

When the *BABOK® Guide* was originally drafted, agile was still a description of quick and nimble movements usually describing animals like cheetahs! From the time of the first version of the *BABOK® Guide* until the second, *agile* became known as a successful software development approach, seeming to reject many of the structured business analysis best practices. To respond to this new approach, all of the tasks in the *BABOK® Guide* were revised to include descriptions of how they could be used in any development environment. Critical thinking and analyzing are core to the success of any business solution, regardless of the methodology or approach being used. The terms plan-driven and change-driven approaches were added to the *BABOK® Guide* in Version 2.0 to acknowledge the different environments in which business analysts are expected to perform.

 Review the definitions of plan-driven and change-driven approaches in task 2.1, element 2.1.4 of the *BABOK® Guide*. These concepts are referred to throughout business analysis work and are foundational concepts you need to learn before you begin to study specific tasks.

Approach

The word approach is used in two important ways in business analysis. There are the business analysis approaches (e.g., plan-driven and change-driven), and there is a solution approach. The word approach is used to acknowledge the fact that we often make decisions in business analysis at a high level first and then progressively elaborate to more detail. *Levels of abstraction* is another phrase you will learn which describes this same concept. As we get more information through detailed elicitation, we can refine our ideas, strategies, plans, solution designs, and transition plans. When you see the word approach in an exam question, it is referring to a high-level decision point that will be further refined.

Requirements

One of the most important concepts of business analysis is requirements. Requirements are things that are wanted or needed by stakeholders to solve a problem or achieve an objective. This is a simple definition for a very complex topic. Almost every task in business analysis involves requirements.

When you are studying for your exam, you must broaden your definition of requirements to include different types, different formats, different levels of detail, and different states. This is often the toughest part of the *BABOK® Guide* for first time readers and another of those differences between project management and business analysis! The words features, functions, capabilities, models, and requests are all included in our definition of requirements.

Requirements are much more numerous, complex, difficult to communicate, and challenging to manage than people realize. Many people think of business analysts as requirements experts. Requirements are often separated into classifications to make them easier to create, review, and manage. The *BABOK® Guide* defines six classifications.

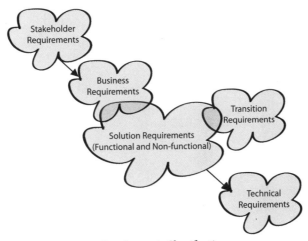

Requirements Classifications

A seventh classification, technical requirements, is not defined, but implied. Technical requirements are not the responsibility of business analysis professionals. However, they are developed from business analysis work.

Note about Classifications   These requirements classifications are rarely used as inputs and outputs to tasks. This is because most business analysis work can be performed on any type of requirement. For example, Prioritize Requirements (task 6.1) can be used to prioritize any of the requirements classifications.

 Business process management professionals do not use the word requirements. If BPM is your experience, you need to learn how the word requirements is used (it basically means *business needs* to BPM professionals) and includes both as-is and to-be business processes.

Stakeholder Requirements

Generally business analysis work starts with a stakeholder request, need, idea, or "requirement." Work may also be initiated by a government regulation change or an external requirement. Stakeholder requirements may be thought of as raw or unrefined. They may be stated by an individual or a representative of a stakeholder group. They may be in conflict with other stakeholder requirements. Stakeholder requirements will be analyzed and refined into business, solution, and transition requirements. Stakeholder requirements are described in the *BABOK® Guide* as a bridge between business and solution requirements, but in reality they are often identified first or in conjunction with business and solution requirements.

Business Requirements

The three requirements types in the center of the diagram are the ones typically managed by business analysts: business, solution, and transition requirements.

Business requirements are descriptions of the business problem, opportunity, process, information, organization, rules, and details from a business perspective. They should be independent of technical descriptions. Business requirements focus on understanding the core business and include business models. The *BABOK® Guide* defines these as high-level requirements that are developed in Enterprise Analysis. The important thing to remember here is that business requirements are focused on the business objectives, and are independent of a particular user or department.

Solution Requirements

Solution requirements (functional and non-functional) describe the solution to be built. They include diagrams, blueprints, models, and descriptions of the functions of the solution. A solution may be a product, a software system, a hardware system, a new procedure, or any combination of these. Solution requirements are described by two sub-types: functional and non-functional requirements. Functional requirements describe the behaviors and functions of the solution. Non-functional requirements describe the quality-of-service characteristics of the solution, such as its required level of performance, its portability, its security, etc.

Transition Requirements

Transition requirements describe what needs to happen before the business can implement the solution. These may include employee training needs, procedure changes, rollout plans, conversion rules, and communication plans. As a knowledgeable business analyst, you are one of the best resources to help the organization make a smooth transition to the new solution, and these requirements assist that work.

Technical Requirements

The technical requirements are usually the last step, and are developed by technical architects, leads, or developers.

Requirements States

The *BABOK® Guide* uses a square bracket after the word requirements to show the *state* of the requirements. For example, an output of Document Elicitation Results (task 3.3) is unconfirmed requirements shown as:
- Requirements [Unconfirmed]

Be sure you think about each state when you see it, because the state gives you information about the requirements. For example, the output of Confirm Elicitation Results (task 3.4) is:
- Requirements [Confirmed]

Do you understand the difference between an unconfirmed and confirmed requirement? Be sure you understand all of the requirements *states*. Note: The *BABOK® Guide* also defines states for the solution and stakeholder concerns. Of course, we will discuss all of this in much more detail later in the book!

Requirements Management Tools

Requirements management tools are software packages designed to help you manage requirements. They are sophisticated support tools for business analysis that allow you to describe requirements and connect requirements to each other. The packages provide a repository or database for storing requirements so you can easily refer back to them as you need to. Most packages allow for reports to be generated for requirements reviews. Unfortunately, many business analysts don't have access to a requirements management tool because the tools are expensive and many companies have not invested in this technology. For the exam, it will be important for you to know that such tools exist and that some business analysts use them to store and update requirements.

Prioritization

In business analysis work, prioritizing requirements is as important as prioritizing your time. Priorities are set by agreement of the by domain SMEs, implementation SMEs, and the sponsor. Prioritizing requirements is a complex process because many factors, such as the business need, urgency, implementation constraints, costs, and dependencies are involved. During business analysis planning, you, the project manager, and possibly the sponsor will discuss how best to facilitate requirements prioritization. This decision process will become part of the business analysis plans. You will follow these plans while performing Requirements Analysis, Requirements Management and Communication, and Solution Assessment and Validation. The factors that drive the prioritization sometimes change and priorities may need to be adjusted. It is your responsibility to notify the team if a new requirement or a change in the business impacts prioritization decisions, and then help the team reprioritize based on the new information.

It Depends!

One of the most interesting aspects of business analysis is the subtle ambiguity of the work. There are as many different ways to analyze as there are human beings. Each person approaches analysis in a slightly different way. Analysis techniques help you look at problems and ideas in different ways. Even when using a well-defined, structured technique, two analysts may come up with different answers. The steps to perform analysis are different for different projects and different situations. One of the most common answers you will hear when you ask a question about business analysis is, *"It depends!"* For example, if I ask my mentor, "Should I use the data modeling technique on my current project?" My mentor may answer, "Well, it depends." And then he will ask me a series of questions about the project, my knowledge, my stakeholders, etc., which will help him make a judgment about whether data modeling would be a worthwhile technique in this situation. Judgments are a huge part of excellent business analysis. If you are not comfortable with ambiguity and judgment calls, you may struggle with much of the business analysis body of knowledge. But if you love complexity and problem solving and thinking about things in new ways, you will learn to love the phrase *"It depends,"* and hear yourself using it frequently!

Study References

The next four pages are references to help you as you read this book and prepare for your exam. The first is the Tasks/Techniques Reference sheet, showing where each technique is used. The highlighted cell indicates the knowledge area task in which I will discuss the technique in detail.

The Business Analysis Terms Reference Sheet includes lists of terms, acronyms, types, and states you will be learning. Some of these lists may become part of your download sheet.

TECHNIQUES	Acceptance & Evaluation Criteria Definition	Benchmarking	Brainstorming	Business Rules Analysis	Data Dictionary & Glossary	Data Flow Diagrams	Data Modeling	Decision Analysis	Document Analysis	Estimation	Focus Groups	Functional Decomposition	Interface Analysis	Interviews	Lessons Learned Process	Metrics & Key Performance Indicators	Non-Functional Requirements Analysis
BA Planning & Monitoring																	
Plan Business Analysis Approach								X									
Conduct Stakeholder Analysis	X		X											X			
Plan Business Analysis Activities										X		X					
Plan Business Analysis Communications																	
Plan Requirements Management Process								X									
Manage Business Analysis Performance														X	X	X	
Enterprise Analysis																	
Define Business Need		X	X	X							X	X					
Assess Capability Gaps									X								
Determine Solution Approach		X	X					X		X							
Define Solution Scope												X	X				
Define Business Case								X		X						X	
Elicitation																	
Prepare for Elicitation			X						X		X		X	X			
Conduct Elicitation			X		X				X		X		X	X			
Document Elicitation Results			X						X		X		X	X			
Confirm Elicitation Results														X			
Requirements Analysis																	
Prioritize Requirements								X									
Organize Requirements				X		X	X					X					
Specify & Model Requirements	X			X	X	X	X						X	X		X	X
Determine Assumptions & Constraints																	
Verify Requirements	X																
Validate Requirements	X															X	
Solution Assessment and Validation																	
Assess Proposed Solution	X							X									
Allocate Requirements	X		X					X				X					
Assess Organizational Readiness	X					X					X			X			
Define Transition Requirements				X		X	X										
Validate Solution	X																
Evaluate Solution Performance								X			X						
Requirements Management & Communication																	
Manage Solution Scope and Requirements																	
Manage Requirements Traceability																	
Maintain Requirements for Re-use																	
Prepare Requirements Package																	
Communicate Requirements																	

TECHNIQUES	Observation	Organization Modeling	Problem Tracking	Process Modeling	Prototyping	Requirements Workshops	Risk Analysis	Root Cause Analysis	Scenarios & Use Cases (9.26)	Scope Modeling	Sequence Diagrams	State Diagrams	Structured Workthroughs	Survey/Questionnaire	SWOT Analysis	User Stories	Vendor Assessment
BA Planning & Monitoring																	
Plan Business Analysis Approach				X									X				
Conduct Stakeholder Analysis		X		X		X	X		X	X				X			
Plan Business Analysis Activities							X										
Plan Business Analysis Communications														X			
Plan Requirements Management Process			X				X										
Manage Business Analysis Performance		X	X					X						X			
Enterprise Analysis																	
Define Business Need								X									
Assess Capability Gaps															X		
Determine Solution Approach															X		
Define Solution Scope										X						X	
Define Business Case							X								X		X
Elicitation																	
Prepare for Elicitation	X					X	X						X				
Conduct Elicitation	X					X	X						X				
Document Elicitation Results	X		X			X	X						X				
Confirm Elicitation Results	X																
Requirements Analysis																	
Prioritize Requirements							X										
Organize Requirements		X		X					X	X						X	
Specify & Model Requirements		X		X	X				X		X	X				X	
Determine Assumptions & Constraints			X				X										
Verify Requirements			X										X				
Validate Requirements						X	X						X				
Solution Assessment and Validation																	
Assess Proposed Solution																	X
Allocate Requirements				X					X								
Assess Organizational Readiness			X	X	X		X							X	X		
Define Transition Requirements			X	X													
Validate Solution			X					X									
Evaluate Solution Performance	X													X			
Requirements Management & Communication																	
Manage Solution Scope and Requirements			X														
Manage Requirements Traceability																	
Maintain Requirements for Re-use																	
Prepare Requirements Package																	X
Communicate Requirements						X							X				

Business Analysis Terms Reference Sheet

Business Analysis Approaches
Plan-driven
Change-driven
Lean
Six Sigma®

Modeling Concepts
User classes, profiles, roles (parties)
Concepts and relationships (data)
Events
Processes
Rules

MoSCoW Analysis
Must
Should
Could
Won't

Prioritization Criteria
Business value (cost-benefit)
Business or technical risk
Implementation difficulty
Likelihood of success
Stakeholder agreement
Regulatory or policy compliance
Relationships between requirements
Urgency

RACI
Responsible
Accountable
Consulted
Informed

Requirements Attributes
Absolute reference
Author
Complexity
Ownership
Priority
Risks
Source
Stability
Status
Urgency

Requirements Classifications
Business
Stakeholder
Solution
    Functional
    Non-functional
Transition

Requirements Quality Characteristics
Cohesive
Complete
Consistent
Correct
Feasible
Modifiable
Unambiguous
Testable

Requirements States
[Communicated]
[Confirmed]
[Maintained]
[Modeled]
[Ongoing]
[Prioritized]
[Reusable]
[Satisfied]
[Stated]
[Specified]
[Unconfirmed]
[Verified]
[Validated]

Risk Responses
Accept
Transfer
Avoid
Mitigate
Share
Enhance
Exploit

Risk Tolerances
Risk averse
Neutral
Risk seeking

Scope
Domain scope
Solution scope
Project scope
Scope of business analysis work

SMART
Specific
Measurable
Achievable
Relevant
Time-bounded

Solution States
[Constructed]
[Deployed]
[Designed]

Stakeholders

Business Analyst
Customer
Domain SME
End User
Implementation SME
  Developers/software engineers
  Organizational change management
  professionals
  System architects
  Trainers
  Usability professionals
Operational Support
Project Manager
Supplier
Tester
Regulator
Sponsor

Underlying Competencies

Analytical Thinking and Problem Solving
Behavioral Characteristics
Communication Skills
Interaction Skills
Software Applications

Business Analysis Planning

Stakeholder List, Roles, Responsibilities
  Business Analysis Plan
  Deliverables (work packages)
  Activities with estimates
  BA Communication Plan
  Communication frequency
  Communication formality
  Requirements Management Plan
  Prioritization process
  Change management process
  Traceability
  Requirements attributes
  Organization process assets
  Requirements repository

CHAPTER 3

Enterprise Analysis

Aligned with the *BABOK® Guide* Chapter Five

Enterprise Analysis describes the work necessary to define a business need, decide on an approach to address that need, and determine if the organization should invest in the proposed change. The term *enterprise analysis* is relatively new, and some business analysts don't realize they have experience doing it. This is the knowledge area that most concerns people preparing to take the CBAP® or the CCBA® exam. My goal is to alleviate your fear of this knowledge area and help you discover you probably have more experience with this type of work than you think. When you realize you have done the tasks in this knowledge area many times, you will be more prepared to answer the exam questions. Expect to see approximately 23 exam questions on this knowledge area.

Let's start by considering the words *enterprise* and *analysis*. You perform analysis all the time, both at work and in your personal life. *Analysis* means to break a whole into its parts to study and understand it.

QUICK TEST

- Business need
- Business case
- Metrics
- Cost-benefit analysis
- Benchmarking
- Decision analysis
- Goals
- SMART objectives
- Desired outcome
- Organizational process assets
- Assumptions and constraints
- Financial analysis
- Key performance indicator
- Solution approach
- Domain scope
- Solution scope
- Project scope
- Context diagram
- Interface

- External agent
- Event
- Capability
- Feature
- Enterprise architecture
- Business risk
- Project risk
- SWOT analysis
- Risk tolerance
  - Risk aversion
  - Neutrality
  - Risk seeking
- Risk responses
  - Accept
  - Transfer
  - Avoid
  - Mitigate
  - Share
  - Enhance
  - Exploit

Now think about the word *enterprise*. An enterprise is a bold, difficult undertaking, or an important undertaking for a business venture or company. Someone who is *enterprising* is said to be full of energy and initiative, willing to undertake new projects.

So, Enterprise Analysis is the breaking apart of an enterprise. This includes looking at the people, processes, and technology aspects of the enterprise to better understand it and to recommend changes and improvements. If you have ever owned a business (even if it was just a lemonade stand) you have performed enterprise analysis. In a large organization, enterprise analysis can be performed at the division, operating unit, or department level. Enterprise analysis work in a large company often takes place in meetings where people discuss problems and organizational goals, looking for ways to improve the business. For most organizations, there are many more business needs than resources to satisfy them, so analyzing and prioritizing potential projects are important. Tasks in the Enterprise Analysis knowledge area describe the work required to understand each business need, analyze potential solutions, and determine priority of the need based on cost-benefit analysis. This allows the organization to use its limited resources on the most valuable projects.

The ultimate goal of business analysis is to satisfy a business need, solve a problem, or take advantage of an opportunity with a *solution*. A solution is anything that satisfies the business need. It might include new or updated software, new or updated hardware, a business process or procedural change, an organization or personnel change, or the purchase of a product or service to improve the business efficiency. In Enterprise Analysis, you gain understanding of the needs of the business, find a viable solution, and help the business decide if it should allocate resources to the creation of the solution.

Business Analysts Help Define and Select Projects

To help an organization select the projects with the most potential value, business analysts must understand the business: its risks, processes, problems, opportunities, goals and objectives, as well as the competitive landscape. Most business people recognize their risks and their challenges, but they may not know how to mitigate the risks or solve the problems. Learning about the business gives you the opportunity to understand how work is currently being done and to consider how processes could be improved. You also learn about the organization's risks and problems and begin to identify areas where a solution should be designed. You help the business determine which are the biggest risks and biggest problems, so solutions can be prioritized. Assessing needs involves measuring current, or as-is, processes and risks. And it involves looking for opportunities to better utilize organizational assets and resources.

The easiest way to describe Enterprise Analysis is to look at the typical organization and what it does. First, there are well-defined operating units that support the ongoing operations. Every organization makes or provides some type of product or service, so it has a production, manufacturing, operations, or servicing group. Every organization also has some type of sales or marketing department to make customers aware of their product or service. Finally, they all have financial operations and a human resource area. This is obviously an oversimplification of an organization, but it is enough detail for this discussion. Each organizational unit is managed by a line manager.

© 2012 RMC Publications, Inc • 952.846.4484 • info@rmcproject.com • www.rmcproject.com

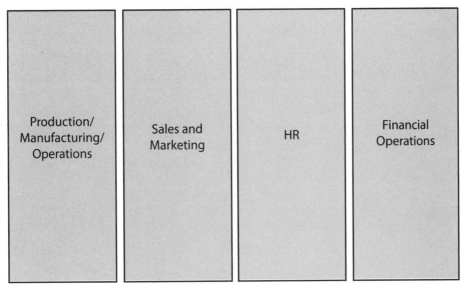

Operations within a Typical Enterprise

On top of the day-to-day, month-to-month, and year-to-year ongoing operations of an organization, there are projects. Each project has a distinct beginning and end and is intended to develop a new product or service, or change the way the organization conducts its business. These projects are initiated to improve the ongoing business. They are run by project managers and usually have a team of people assigned to execute the project. Projects may involve one or more organizational units. For example, a Human Resources (HR) project may focus solely on HR functions, while an enterprise resource planning (ERP) project spans many departments.

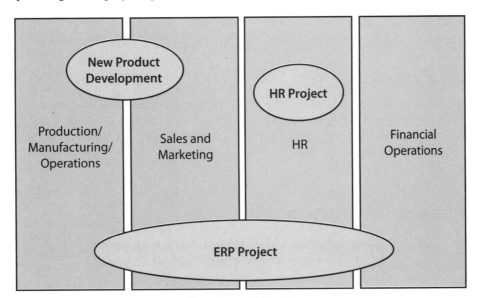

Operations with Projects

Finally, Enterprise Analysis is high-level analysis that requires the analyst to consider not just an individual project, but how projects and ongoing operations fit together. Enterprise analysis can be performed on one or many operational areas. Strategic planning is considered enterprise analysis work because it looks at the organization from a high level and sets goals for work to be done.

Architecture planning is also considered enterprise analysis because it looks at the organization as a whole and plans how the organization will work as a cohesive system.

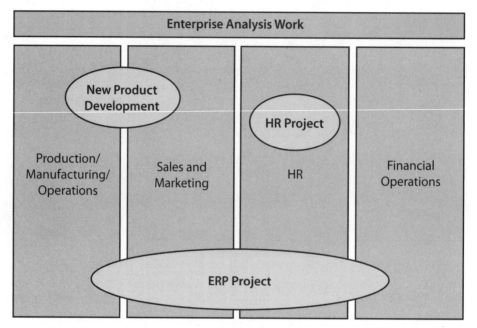

Enterprise Analysis

As you can see, Enterprise Analysis requires a business analyst to understand the organization from many different levels. In the *BABOK® Guide,* you will see the phrase *levels of abstraction,* which acknowledges that sometimes we look at parts of the business from a very high level (10,000 foot view), sometimes we look at very low-level, detailed areas, and most of the time we are somewhere in between. Business analysts must be able to focus on whatever level of detail is necessary for their current assignment.

The tasks of Enterprise Analysis may not be clearly defined or assigned within your organization, but they encompass very important work. Most top-level corporate officers are constantly looking at the enterprise from a high level and assessing how all of the pieces fit together. Business analysis professionals have the skills and knowledge to add value to this work even if they are not officially assigned to it.

Enterprise Analysis in Action

I have started and managed two small businesses, so I have had to make thousands of decisions related to enterprise analysis over the course of 18 years. One decision, common to almost every organization, was how to collect and manage customer information.

As a start-up business, we couldn't afford many software applications, just basic office automation packages. As we began to advertise, market, and sell our product, we began collecting information on potential customers. This information is very important to any company's success and must be carefully maintained. The question of how to manage this data is one of the first issues to arise in a start-up organization, and it is one that needs to be revisited as the organization grows.

When my organization had only 5 or 10 potential customers, it was easy to keep track of their names, phone numbers, and e-mail addresses, along with some personal information such as where they like to vacation. As the number of potential customers grew from 40 to 50 to 100, managing this data became more difficult. We knew about software applications called customer relationship management (CRM) systems that could help capture this data and allow reporting. Did we need one?

Whether a change like this is necessary depends on many factors. Does the enterprise have enough resources (money and time) to acquire such a package? How much time is being consumed managing this data without a package? Is it taking time away from more important tasks—like delivering our products? What features do we really need? What features will be useful in the future? How soon will we need them? This analysis relies on the organization having a long term vision, a strategic plan, and realistic projections for expected sales and expenses.

Once we determined that our organization needed a system to help manage the data, we next faced decisions about which package was right for our business. There are hundreds of CRM packages, from the very simple and inexpensive to the very large and costly. We knew we didn't need the biggest ones, but would the smallest solution work, and if so, for how long? Assessing the features needed in the present and in the coming months and years involves thinking ahead about future changes as the company grows.

Our existing architecture also influenced our decision about which packages to consider. We didn't even consider packages that used a different operating system than what we were using. Of course, we could have decided to change our hardware platform, but that would have been an even more costly and disruptive choice. We knew multiple users needed to access the customer information, and we had to estimate how many more users might need such access in the future. We also had to consider how we would get our current customer information into the new system. Would it be time-consuming to manually load the data, or was some type of conversion software available? We had to think about other functions that used customer data, such as billing. How would we make sure the customer data was consistent and correct across all functions?

We decided not to include billing functions in our CRM system, as the billing system we had in place was working well. We performed interface analysis to consider how this new system would work with our other procedures (even though our interfaces were initially all manual). We decided we wanted a solution that would work for at least three years. We then wrote down our requirements for the system, to clarify them and to make sure everyone was in agreement. Finally, we built a business case to present to our investors. We needed to convince them that purchasing this software would pay off for the organization over time. This involved researching costs, estimating conversion time, and estimating the benefits.

A CRM package was selected and implemented relatively quickly. It met our needs extremely well. Over the years, as we continued to grow, we experienced the need to reexamine the CRM situation several times. Each time, the analysis was different because of the current size of the company, the architecture, our customers' needs, and so forth. Each time it got a little easier, because we had experience and knowledge from past analysis, but each time the needs were reconsidered in light of the current environment and decisions were based on current metrics. Enterprise Analysis is an ongoing activity, ensuring the organization is always addressing current needs and opportunities.

EXERCISE   There are five tasks in the Enterprise Analysis knowledge area: Define Business Need, Assess Capability Gaps, Determine Solution Approach, Define Solution Scope, and Define Business Case. Each task logically leads to the next, and the inputs and outputs reflect this progression. Can you identify the five tasks in the previous story?

Enterprise Analysis Knowledge Area Task	Work Performed in the Story
Define Business Need	
Assess Capability Gaps	
Determine Solution Approach	
Define Solution Scope	
Define Business Case	

ANSWER

Enterprise Analysis Knowledge Area Task	Work Performed in the Story
Define Business Need	Recognized that customer data was growing and needed to be managed
Assess Capability Gaps	Considered the current architecture, number of users, and the expected growth of company and customers; determined what type of data was important to maintain
Determine Solution Approach	Decided to purchase a CRM package
Define Solution Scope	Decided to purchase a mid-size CRM package that did not include billing functions
Define Business Case	Researched costs, conversion times, and estimated benefits; presented data to investors

Barb's BA Themes

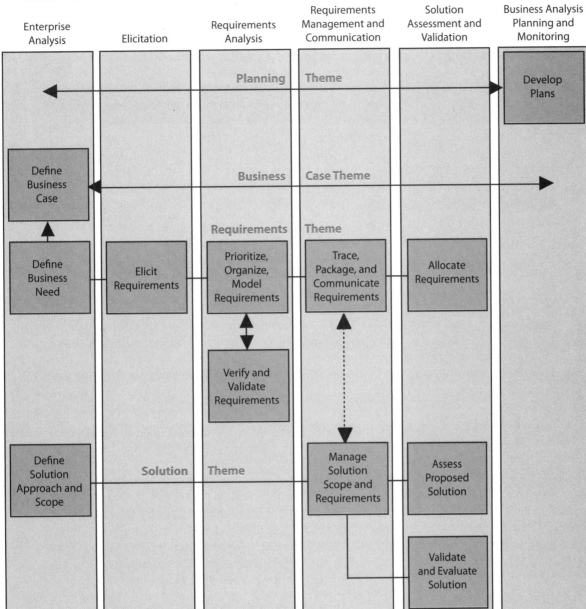

Enterprise Analysis provides the context and objectives for business analysis work. It is involved in all four of the business analysis themes. The Business Case Theme spans all of the knowledge areas because the business case (and business need) defined in Enterprise Analysis are used in every other part of business analysis work. Enterprise Analysis work may be done before a project is initiated, to help the sponsor decide if a project should be funded. Sometimes a project is initiated without much analysis, and Enterprise Analysis tasks are performed as the first step to clarify the objectives and scope and thereby assist with planning.

The Planning Theme intersects with Enterprise Analysis because it is difficult to plan if you don't know what you are planning for. Most business analysts perform planning and Enterprise Analysis concurrently, refining plans as the solution scope is more clearly understood. Enterprise Analysis is also performed as an ongoing strategic planning activity. Businesses are always identifying needs and determining where they fit in the current strategic plans.

In the Requirements Theme, the business need is considered to be the first requirement. It is usually a high-level, stated business requirement and is used to elicit all of the other requirements. Every excellent requirement can be traced back to the original business need.

In the Solution Theme, the solution approach and scope are defined in Enterprise Analysis as the starting point of solution design. They are usually stated in business terms and describe what the solution will do for the business, rather than how the solution will be built.

Things to Know about Enterprise Analysis for the Exam

- An enterprise can be an entire organization (large or small) or a part of an organization (division, department, or operating unit).
- The exam assumes that business analysts make high-level recommendations on project selection. Even if you haven't done this, answer questions from this perspective.
- The word *scope* is used in the *BABOK® Guide* more than 200 times! Make sure you have a clear understanding of its usage as a noun and a verb. Also make sure you know the different types of scope: domain scope, solution scope, project scope, and the scope of business analysis work.
- Make sure you understand the difference between business risks and project risks. These two types are not defined in the *BABOK® Guide*, but understanding the difference will help you answer questions about risk. Managing business risks is as important for successful business analysis as managing project risks is for successful project management.
- The important things to know for the exam are 1) why each task is performed and 2) how it is best accomplished.

Introduction to the Tasks of Enterprise Analysis

Business analysts are constantly performing enterprise analysis. While you are analyzing requirements on one project, your stakeholder may tell you about another business problem and you may begin to think about how you might solve it.

When first learning about the Enterprise Analysis knowledge area, many people say, "My company doesn't do these tasks." I would argue, however, that every organization performs these tasks! They may not be performed formally, and the work may not be referred to in these terms, but every organization identifies needs and gaps, decides on a solution approach and scope, and develops a business case to justify expenditures (even if the justification is not written down).

Enterprise analysis work may be performed by a steering committee or strategic planning group. It may also be performed by a project sponsor before a project is initiated. In either case, a business analyst's skills enhance strategic decision making. Unfortunately, not all organizations appreciate the value a business analyst can add at this stage of the project, and may attempt to do the analysis without the involvement of a business analyst.

If you are not included in this initial analysis work, be sure you understand the business case for the project when you are assigned to it and ask questions to clarify the scope of your work. It is your responsibility to ask questions of the steering committee, sponsor, project manager, and key stakeholders, and to perform additional analysis to clarify the organization's plans and priorities. You may find the enterprise analysis work was not done as thoroughly as needed and that you can add value to the project by performing a more complete analysis before the detailed project work gets underway.

The tasks of Enterprise Analysis are sequential. Make sure you know the order of the tasks as shown in the following graphic. (Unfortunately, the other knowledge areas aren't so straightforward!)

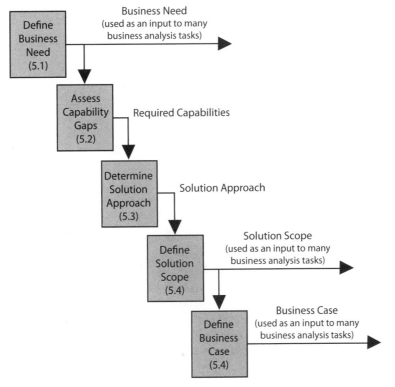

Enterprise Analysis Tasks and Outputs

———— **ENTERPRISE ANALYSIS TASKS** ————

Define Business Need (5.1)

Defining the business need is the first task in Enterprise Analysis. In fact, it is generally the first task of all of business analysis! Rarely does any work get started if there is no business need. If your organization was humming along with no problems, no concerns, and no desire to grow or change, what business analysis work would you do? Fortunately for us, organizations are always changing and uncovering new needs. Businesses are always looking for ways to improve performance, increase revenue, decrease costs, and capitalize on opportunities. These *business needs* drive the work of business analysis.

Think of a business need as a seed that may germinate into a project. In this first task of Enterprise Analysis, the seed is "planted," and then nurtured through the tasks of Assess Capability Gaps, Determine Solution Approach, Define Solution Scope, and Define Business Case. If the seed "sprouts," it becomes a project!

Define Business Need		
Inputs	**Techniques**	**Outputs**
Business Goals and Objectives	Benchmarking (9.2)	Business Need (5.1)
Requirements [Stated] (3.3)	Brainstorming (9.3)	
	Business Rules Analysis (9.4)	
	Focus Groups (9.11)	
	Functional Decomposition (9.12)	
	Root Cause Analysis (9.25)	

BA's Responsibilities in Defining the Business Need

- Work with the customer, end users, and domain subject matter experts (SMEs) to obtain their input regarding the current business need
- Review existing requirements or requests to learn about the need
- Ensure support of the sponsor in the effort to address the business need
- Clarify the specific objectives of the business domain SMEs

What Do You Need to Successfully Define the Business Need?

Business goals and objectives may be developed through formal or informal strategic planning at any level of the organization. As defined by the *BABOK® Guide*, goals are generally high-level, long term desired outcomes for the organization, while objectives are more specific and concrete. These goals and objectives generally come from outside the business analysis discipline. The stated requirements represent items the stakeholders *say* they want. These requirements are elicited during Enterprise Analysis (using tasks from our next chapter, Elicitation).

Goals and Objectives

Goals and objectives are inputs to defining the business need. However, they are often poorly defined or unspecific when first communicated. The business analyst is instrumental in the process of refining them into SMART objectives.

SMART Objectives   Determining specific, measurable, achievable, relevant, and time-bounded (SMART) objectives requires the collaboration of the project sponsor, the project manager, the business analyst, and the solution architect. All of these parties must agree if the project is to be successful. Getting this agreement is not easy, and can best be facilitated by collaboratively working on root cause analysis, brainstorming solution ideas, and developing a business case.

SMART Objectives
S—Specific
M—Measurable
A—Achievable
R—Relevant
T—Time-bounded

> **Example of a Smart Objective** Decrease legal costs of the Human Resources department by 25 percent within two years by providing a more consistent level of benefits and performance reviews to all workers.

Notice the objective is specific (decrease HR legal costs), measurable (by 25 percent), and time-bounded (within two years). We can't tell by reading this objective if it is achievable (realistic) or relevant (important for the organization to do now), but those are also critical characteristics.

 The acronym SMART has been used for many years. You may have seen other words used in the acronym, but for the exam, be sure to know the terms used in the *BABOK® Guide*.

APPLY YOUR KNOWLEDGE   Think about your current project. What are the objectives? Are they SMART? List one objective for a current or past project. Then answer the questions about your objective.

Objective	
Is this objective **specific**?	Y or N
Is this objective **measurable**? How will you measure it?	Y or N
Is this objective **achievable**? (Is it realistic?)	Y or N
Is this objective **relevant**? (Is it important for the organization to do now?)	Y or N
Is this objective **time-bounded**? When will the benefits be realized? (Within a month? Within a year? Other?)	Y or N
How would you improve the objective to make it SMART?	

Unfortunately, many projects do not have SMART objectives. An excellent business analyst asks questions to help the team develop them. Examples of good questions include: What would the sponsor and/or key stakeholders like to accomplish? What is the core problem?

You might be surprised to find your stakeholders haven't thought about such questions as specifically as they should have. You are already adding value to the project by helping the stakeholders think about what they are asking for and why they are asking! SMART objectives are important because they become success criteria. After the project is complete, it will be easy to determine whether the objectives were met if they were SMART objectives.

 Objectives are often confused with requirements. Objectives don't describe the needs or requests for the solution as requirements do. If your objectives are describing functions or features, they are not objectives.

EXERCISE Review each objective and determine which SMART characteristic is missing. (You can assume the objectives are all relevant and achievable.)

Objective	Missing Characteristic (S-Specific, M-Measurable, or T-Time-bounded)
Cut HR expenses by 5 percent.	
Decrease the new worker on-boarding process within 18 months.	
Improve the response times of HR to employee requests.	
Increase employee satisfaction with the HR department within two years.	

ANSWER

Objective	Missing Characteristic (S-Specific, M-Measurable, or T-Time-bounded)
Cut HR expenses by 5 percent.	(T) In what timeframe?
Decrease the new worker on-boarding process within 18 months.	(M) How much of a decrease is expected?
Improve the response times of HR to employee requests.	(M, T) Improve by how much? What is the expected timeframe?
Increase employee satisfaction with the HR department within two years.	(M) How will satisfaction be measured? How much of an increase is expected?

Defining the Business Need

When a business problem or opportunity is identified, it should be analyzed. The idea or need must be fully understood before detailed work can begin. To define the problem or opportunity as a business need, elicit information and ask questions to gain clarity. Facilitate discussions to bring stakeholders to a common understanding of the need. The Define Business Need task may begin when:

- A stakeholder makes a formal request for a change (e.g., project charter, change request form)
- A stakeholder makes an informal request (in conversation with a business analyst, he or she mentions a problem or opportunity)
- A business analyst identifies a need while learning about the business (e.g., during observation or interviews)
- The organization's strategic plan includes a new initiative

- A customer makes a request or complaint
- An outside organization generates a regulatory change, competitive change, or market change

When a business stakeholder requests a change, he or she often asks for a very specific solution, such as, "Install a new payroll system" or "Develop a forecast report." Sometimes the request has been generated by a problem. It is the business analyst's responsibility to find the root cause of the identified problem and then determine whether the requested solution addresses that root cause.

Defining a business need does not always lead to the creation of a new project. Your analysis may reveal that the problem or opportunity is not as significant as originally presented. Simply clarifying a request may save your organization the time and cost of pursuing a project.

Here is an example. The neighbor of a VP asked him why his company didn't make XYZ widget, and the VP thought it sounded like a great idea! When he arrived at the office the next morning, he asked his assistant to get right on it. The assistant wisely contacted a business analyst, who began defining the need. The business analyst asked the VP about his reasons for making the request and researched the product to find out about the competition. Which companies already offered this product? How much did they charge? What were their costs? Where did they get the raw materials? Who were their customers? She also tried to find out about the volume of sales and profit margins and assessed her company's internal resources to determine if the skills and facilities were readily available to produce this product. She concluded that the resources required to produce this product were not available in the organization and would be expensive to obtain. She wrote an executive summary of her findings and scheduled a meeting with the VP. She presented her findings in a factual, objective way. After hearing and evaluating her research, the VP decided not to go forward with the new product idea.

Techniques to Define the Business Need

Benchmarking (9.2)

One way to identify and define a business need is to look at the competition. Benchmarking involves research and analysis of competitive organizations and products. It focuses on measuring an organization's performance compared to other organizations in the same industry. Benchmarking results in an evaluation of best practices and ideas for product and service changes. It is frequently used in strategic planning to set the organization's direction for change. There are limitations to this technique, however. Benchmarking can be very time-consuming and costly. It also may inhibit the team's creativity, because rather than developing new, innovative ideas, the team studies solutions that have been used elsewhere, and may be tempted to simply copy the ideas of others.

Brainstorming (9.3)

The brainstorming technique is often used to creatively generate ideas for solutions to the business need. Brainstorming is a great way to encourage people to voice ideas that they may normally be reluctant to mention. Participants are initially encouraged to generate a large volume of ideas. Since ideas are not evaluated right away, stakeholders are more willing to suggest solutions that are unusual or "out of the box." (See the Elicitation chapter, page 109, for a discussion on how to conduct a brainstorming session.)

Business Rules Analysis (9.4)

A business rule is a policy, guideline, or constraint that dictates the work of the business. The business rules analysis technique is useful for reviewing high-level policies and guidelines for their relationship to the business need. During Enterprise Analysis, business rules may be changed as a result of defining the business need or as the strategic plans of the organization evolve. A project may be initiated to implement these changes throughout the organization. (See the Specify and Model Requirements task in the Requirements Analysis chapter, page 180, for a detailed discussion of the business rules analysis technique.)

Focus Groups (9.11)

A focus group is a structured elicitation session aimed at gathering information about customer preferences. Developed by marketers who want to have their customers' perspectives on new product ideas before a product is released, the purpose of a focus group is to get very specific feedback on a new product or service. Sometimes problems and opportunities are identified by outside customers during a focus group. These problems and opportunities should be analyzed to determine if an additional business need exists. See the Elicitation chapter, page 115, for a more detailed discussion of the focus group technique.

Functional Decomposition (9.12)

Functional decomposition is a fundamental and powerful analysis technique, useful for many tasks in business analysis. To decompose is *to break up or separate into basic components*. So you can think of functional decomposition as functional analysis, or the breaking apart of functions. It can help to define the business need by breaking down large, complex needs into smaller, more manageable pieces. A decomposition diagram shows this breakdown or separation in an easy-to-understand format. Notice it does not show or imply any sequence.

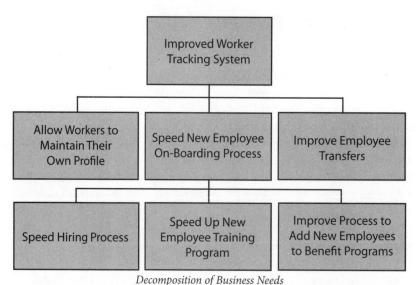

Decomposition of Business Needs

Functional decomposition can be performed at any level of detail. During Enterprise Analysis, this technique is typically used at a high level to help define the business functions and needs.

TRICKS OF THE TRADE® The decomposition diagram can be used for organization charts, processes, goals, strategic planning, and later in the project, to assist with detailed system design. You will see this technique referenced in many of the knowledge areas. Be sure you are comfortable with the act of *decomposing* or breaking something into its parts.

Root Cause Analysis (9.25)

Root cause analysis is used to determine the true nature of the business need before the team decides on the solution. This is an important responsibility of the business analyst because, in many organizations, people tend to jump to solution design before thoroughly analyzing the problem and desired outcomes.

Here is an example. Employees are unhappy with service received from their Human Resources department. It is easy to come up with lots of possible causes, but analysis is required to be sure the true root cause has been discovered. The team should brainstorm about possible causes, rather than addressing the first one someone mentions.

Possible causes include:
- Employees in HR are lazy.
- Employees' expectations for HR are too high.
- HR processes are inefficient.
- HR employees are not trained properly.
- The HR system is antiquated.

Can you think of any more possible causes? As we look at each possible cause, it becomes obvious that the solution will be different depending on which cause we choose to address. Addressing the wrong cause may not solve the real problem.

 An experienced business analyst will perform root cause analysis on every project, even when the sponsor, project manager, and other members of the team have already decided on a solution. When you think the solution will not address the root cause, you must notify your project manager and sponsor immediately.

Fishbone Diagram   A fishbone diagram, also referred to as an Ishikawa, or cause and effect, diagram, is sometimes used to assist with root cause analysis. Consider this question: Is it better to fix a defect or get to the root cause of the defect? The answer is that you should do both. A fishbone diagram can help you. The following diagram shows the defect of "system will not install" on the right and then lists the potential causes, such as hardware issues, software issues, etc. Various subcauses of each potential cause are also listed in an effort to find the root cause of the defect.

Fishbone diagrams look backward at what may have contributed to quality problems on the project. A fishbone diagram:
- Is a creative way to look at the causes of a problem
- Helps stimulate thinking, organize thoughts, and generate discussion
- Can be used to explore the factors that will result in a desired future outcome or solution

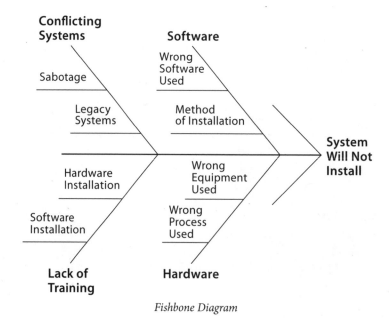

Fishbone Diagram

Five Whys   Another approach to finding the root cause of a problem is asking the Five Whys. Asking "why" more than once usually leads to deeper answers. When people are encouraged to think at a deeper level, they often discover they know more about a problem than they originally realized.

Consider this example: **Why** are employees unhappy with HR? Service is slow. **Why?** HR personnel are overworked. **Why?** There are not enough people working in HR. **Why?** The number of employees in the company has increased, and the complexity of the global workforce has increased without a corresponding increase in the HR staff. **Why?** Organizational growth around the world was unexpected! (Note that the root cause may be a positive factor or a negative factor.)

TRICKS OF THE TRADE® The "why" question is extremely valuable, but you need to be careful about how you use it. Simply asking why over and over again can become very annoying to a stakeholder. You must be aware of your tone of voice. If your tone sounds like you are challenging the person's judgment, he or she will become defensive and the interview will be a waste of time. When using this technique, it is essential to communicate an attitude of curiosity, not criticism.

EXERCISE   Which technique would you use to define a business need in the following situations?

Situation	Technique
Competition is threatening or beating us in a particular product or market	
We need innovative, creative ideas to solve a problem	
Business rules are constraining work and should be reviewed for changes; regulatory rules have changed	

Situation	Technique
Customer complaints or a drop in sales highlight a problem; the organization seeks to identify the problem and possible solutions	
A complex problem needs to be broken down and studied at a lower level or in smaller pieces	
A problem has been identified, but the cause of the problem is unclear	

ANSWER

Situation	Technique
Competition is threatening or beating us in a particular product or market	Benchmarking
We need innovative, creative ideas to solve a problem	Brainstorming
Business rules are constraining work and should be reviewed for changes; regulatory rules have changed	Business Rules Analysis
Customer complaints or a drop in sales highlight a problem; the organization seeks to identify the problem and possible solutions	Focus Groups
A complex problem needs to be broken down and studied at a lower level or in smaller pieces	Functional Decomposition
A problem has been identified, but the cause of the problem is unclear	Root Cause Analysis

Summary

The business need is a refined description of the business problem or opportunity. It is usually a high-level description of the desired outcome and is used throughout business analysis work. The business need is an input to tasks in every other knowledge area of the *BABOK® Guide*! Although your organization may not formally document the business need, that need still drives all business analysis work.

Assess Capability Gaps (5.2)

When a business need has been identified and defined, it is useful to assess the holes or *gaps* between current capabilities and the desired outcomes. Think of this task as your stakeholders saying, "We wish we could do…..in our system." These capability gaps will help to define the solution needed.

Assess Capability Gaps		
Inputs	**Techniques**	**Outputs**
Business Need (5.1)	Document Analysis (9.9)	Required Capabilities (5.2)
Enterprise Architecture	SWOT Analysis (9.32)	
Solution Performance Assessment (7.6)		

BA's Responsibilities in Assessing Capability Gaps

- Learn about current capabilities (enterprise architecture) from both a business and technical perspective
- Obtain input from the customers, suppliers, SMEs, and the sponsor regarding existing gaps in capabilities, and the potential impact of addressing those gaps
- Review current system performance and defect reports to identify gaps

What Do You Need to Successfully Assess Capability Gaps?

The business need comes from the previous task, Define Business Need. Current capabilities are compared to the defined business need to identify gaps. Enterprise architecture is developed outside of the business analysis discipline and is used to help understand current capabilities. Solution performance assessment means looking at the as-is system (a solution that has been built and implemented), and determining how well it meets the current needs of the business.

Enterprise Architecture

Architecture is a great word that is now being used in business. Just as traditional architects draw diagrams and plans showing how a structure will be built, enterprise architects draw diagrams and plans showing how the organization operates. And just as maintenance and repair workers use blueprints on an on-going basis to maintain a building, business analysts can use the enterprise architecture documents to assess and maintain the organization's systems.

Enterprise architecture refers to the roadmap, plan, or design of the organization with respect to products, services, infrastructure, IT systems, and personnel. Business analysts need to be aware of the current enterprise architecture and strategic plan to make sure new solutions being considered fit into that architecture. The larger the organization, the more important this becomes. The purpose of enterprise architecture is to link and transform business and IT in order to create greater business value.

An enterprise architecture describes the structure of the enterprise in terms of its components:
- Enterprise goals
- Roles
- Organization structures
- Organization behaviors (processes)
- Business information (data)
- Software applications
- Hardware, networks, communications systems

Within enterprise architecture there are several other architectures your organization may use:
- Business architecture
- Organization architecture
- Information architecture
- Applications or systems architecture
- Security architecture

It is helpful to realize that every organization has enterprise architecture, even if they don't know it! The enterprise architecture may or may not be documented, discussed, and supported in a formal way, but every organization has structure, policies, direction, etc.

Enterprise architecture is still a very new discipline, so there is not yet an agreed-upon standard definition. Some people use the terms business architecture and enterprise architecture interchangeably, but the *BABOK® Guide* defines business architecture as a subset of enterprise architecture.

Zachman Framework for Enterprise Architecture   In the 1980s, John Zachman created a framework to define the architecture of an enterprise. This framework has been expanded, and is still used today. A simplified version of it includes:
- Who (Roles and responsibilities)
- What (Inventory and information)
- When (Timing)
- Where (Distribution, location)
- Why (Motivation)
- How (Process)

Finding the answers to these questions provides a way to understand the architecture of an enterprise.

Learning the As-Is Capabilities

An excellent business analyst must develop an understanding of each business domain at a high level and at a detailed level when assigned to a specific project. To learn the business requires much more than an hour or two overview provided by an operations manager. You need to spend time in the business area, watching or doing the work of several different employee positions. (In the next chapter, Elicitation, we'll talk about the observation technique.) You need to be intimately familiar with how the organization makes money and who the customers are. You need to understand the pain points and most critical areas. You also need to understand the enterprise architecture before you will be able to identify capability gaps.

Learning a complex business takes time and ideally is done *before* you are assigned to a particular project. This is why Enterprise Analysis knowledge area tasks are better performed outside of project work.

 Does your organization give you time to learn the business before starting a project? If not, discuss the value of this approach with your managers and the business stakeholders. Know that going into a project with a clear understanding of the business allows the project to move along more quickly and the business analyst to add value to the project sooner.

Gap Analysis   To assess capability gaps, you must first know what the current capabilities are and then compare them to the desired new capabilities. Business analysts discover as-is capabilities while they help define future capabilities. Learning about current and desired capabilities is done through elicitation and analysis. Desired future capabilities are referred to as gaps.

A Simple Gap Analysis		
HR Functions	**Current System Capabilities**	**New Capabilities**
Ability to accept applications from candidates via Internet	None	We need this ability **This is a GAP**
Ability to process payroll for workers in different countries	This is partially automated but requires lots of manual processes	We would like this to be totally automated ** This is a GAP**
Ability to remotely administer annual performance reviews	Already exists	

The result of a gap analysis is a list of new capabilities desired, along with identification of needed updates to existing capabilities. This list helps to frame the solution size and scope.

Gap analysis can be performed at any level of the organization or system. It can be focused on particular types of capabilities or features. For example, gap analysis could be performed to:

- Compare the features of a vendor software package with your organization's business processes
- Assess the company's business processes against the acquired company's analogous processes (for a corporate acquisition)
- Compare as-is processes with desired to-be processes
- Compare current database fields with those provided by a software package

Gap analysis is not listed as a technique in the *BABOK® Guide*, but is implied in this task. Don't be surprised to a see a question about it on your exam.

Techniques to Assess Capability Gaps

Document Analysis (9.9)

The document analysis technique is frequently used to learn about business practices, research current capabilities, and find gaps. Documents from which you can learn about current capabilities include software manuals, vendor marketing materials, and as-is business models. These sources will help you get started learning about the business, but the information should be confirmed in follow-up discussions with the domain stakeholders, as they may be out-of-date or contain inaccurate information. We will talk more about document analysis in the Elicitation chapter.

SWOT Analysis (9.32)

A great technique for use in competitive analysis and new development projects, SWOT analysis can help to identify capability gaps. The technique allows the team to identify the strengths, weaknesses, threats, and opportunities for the entire enterprise, or within a specific division or department.

A grid similar to the one shown next is typically used to conduct a group session. Participants generally include people from management, marketing, and sales, with a facilitator who may be a business analyst.

Strengths and weaknesses are listed on the left. Across the top are opportunities and threats, and the grid shows how the factors intersect.

The next step is to consider the intersections:

- How could opportunities be exploited by the strengths?
- How could threats be combated by the strengths?
- How could weaknesses be eliminated or mitigated to benefit from opportunities?
- How could risks be minimized where threats intersect with weaknesses?

This is a great way for a team to brainstorm about various situations and product ideas. Thinking about your organization's strengths with respect to the opportunities in the industry facilitates brainstorming about possible new products and services. Examining internal weaknesses against threats highlights where the organization is most vulnerable and allows the team to consider how to address these high-risk areas.

	Opportunities • We can consider candidates from anywhere in the world • Current employees recommend us • Growth allows us to increase employee base	**Threats** • Competitors try to steal workers • Clients try to steal workers • Finding high-quality directors to supervise
Strengths • Low turnover rate • Highly skilled workforce • Locations around the world	• Recruit globally • Increase client fees to reflect high- quality workers	• Retain employees by frequent review cycles to discuss job satisfaction • Increase client fees to reflect high quality workers
Weaknesses • Worker stress created by high-visibility projects • Need to hire specific skills for specific projects	• Reduce stress by improving client management • Keep a database of candidates and skills	• Monitor assignments to take advantage of employee skil sets • Improve matching of employees to projects

SWOT Analysis

APPLY YOUR KNOWLEDGE Perform a SWOT analysis for your organization.

SWOT Analysis for _____ Organization

	Opportunities 1. 2. 3.	Threats 1. 2. 3.
Strengths 1. 2. 3.	Strength-Opportunity Strategies 1. 2.	Strength-Threat Strategies 1. 2.
Weaknesses 1. 2. 3.	Weakness-Opportunity Strategies 1. 2.	Weakness-Threat Strategies 1. 2.

Did this activity highlight any capability gaps you had not thought about before?

Summary

The result of the Assess Capability Gaps task is a specific list of the capabilities (e.g., features, functions, high-level requirements) needed to address the business need. You will discover these gaps in various ways: a stakeholder will tell you about them as you analyze the as-is business, problem tracking reports list problems with the existing capabilities, and you will find more by performing gap analysis. You may concurrently perform some of the tasks in the Requirements Analysis knowledge area, like Specify and Model Requirements, to help you identify and articulate gaps. Your responsibility is to find all of the gaps, referred to as *required capabilities,* so they can be used to determine a solution approach and scope (the next two tasks). Prioritization and approvals are not required at this point. You are just developing a list of things the stakeholders want and need. These capabilities will be turned into requirements as you move forward.

Determine Solution Approach (5.3)

The *solution approach* is the general direction or description of the solution. This is where the team begins to figure out how to address the business need and the gaps (the *required capabilities* from the previous task) with the most viable solution. The specifics of the solution will be defined further in the next task: Define Solution Scope.

Determine Solution Approach		
Inputs	**Techniques**	**Outputs**
Business Need (5.1)	Benchmarking (9.2)	Solution Approach (5.3)
Required Capabilities (5.2)	Brainstorming (9.3)	
Organizational Process Assets	Decision Analysis (9.8)	
	Estimation (9.10)	
	Feasibility Analysis	
	SWOT Analysis (9.32)	

BA's Responsibilities in Determining the Solution Approach
- Work with stakeholders to identify possible solutions and assess their feasibility
- Facilitate ranking or other comparative evaluation of solution options
- Gain approval of the sponsor for proposed solution approach

What Do You Need to Successfully Determine the Solution Approach?
The outputs of the previous Enterprise Analysis tasks (business need and required capabilities) are inputs to this task. Organizational process assets, or OPAs (things like approved methodologies and processes) are used to develop a solution approach that complies with organizational standards.

The Solution Theme
The idea of a solution that satisfies a business need is an important concept in business analysis. The solution is our target as we attempt to solve the business problem by making a change to the business. The solution may include a procedural change, a technology change, or a personnel change. Tasks that specifically deal with the solution span three different knowledge areas. You may find it helpful to think of the progression of these tasks as the life cycle of the solution. The solution is "born" in Enterprise

Analysis, managed in Requirements Management and Communication, and assessed and evaluated in Solution Assessment and Validation (and it eventually "dies" here when it is replaced or removed).

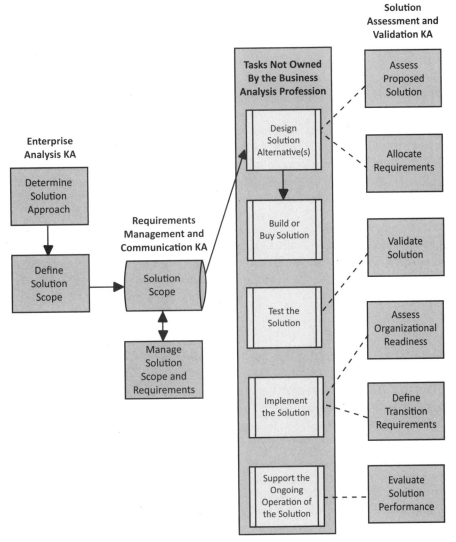

The Solution Theme

There are two tasks in Enterprise Analysis that refer to solution: Determine Solution Approach and Define Solution Scope. These tasks may be performed before a project starts or at the beginning of a project. They define the type of solution desired and set the boundaries for the solution. It is important to note that the solution approach and scope are defined, but *not formally approved*, during Enterprise Analysis. Approval and signoff take place in the Manage Solution Scope and Requirements task of Requirements Management and Communication. As you will learn, the Manage Solution Scope and Requirements task is "command central" for business analysis work. It is the ongoing work of making sure all the requirements are within the approved scope and finding potential scope changes as work progresses.

Once the scope is approved, the solution scope is used by implementation SMEs to design, build, and implement the solution. Business analysts work with implementation stakeholders to make sure the solution is the best choice for the business, meets the business need, and is implemented smoothly. They also work with testers to confirm the solution works as intended.

The Solution Approach

The solution approach is a high-level description or picture of the solution idea used to help the stakeholders envision the change. It describes the general direction of the solution. Think of the Determine Solution Approach task as your early discussions about how best to solve a particular problem. This task should involve lots of stakeholders because you are trying to collect and evaluate lots of ideas. Your role in this work is to help the group consider as many options as possible and keep the group focused on the business need and required capabilities. You will also help by identifying assumptions and constraints that may rule out some ideas. If there is more than one viable solution approach, you will help the group to determine the criteria for choosing a particular option, and rank the alternatives. You and the stakeholders will also consider the feasibility of each alternative and make a selection of the best possible approach given all of the constraints. Be sure you understand that the solution approach is less specific than the solution scope, which is defined in the next task.

 The Determine Solution Approach task sounds very similar to the task Assess Proposed Solution in the Solution Assessment and Validation knowledge area. The difference is in the level of detail. In Enterprise Analysis, we are looking at a high-level view of business needs and capabilities (business requirements). In Solution Assessment and Validation, we are looking at the detailed options for a solution (stakeholder and solution requirements).

Techniques to Determine the Solution Approach

Benchmarking (9.2), Brainstorming (9.3), and SWOT Analysis (9.32)

The benchmarking, brainstorming, and SWOT analysis techniques, introduced earlier in this chapter, are often used to creatively generate ideas for a solution approach.

Decision Analysis (9.8)

The decision analysis technique helps the group choose the best alternative, based on known financial constraints. Considering the financial implications of the solution approach might help to rank the alternatives. We'll talk more about the decision analysis technique later in this chapter when we are defining the business case.

Estimation (9.10)

The estimation technique is used to get a general idea of the time and cost to implement each alternative. Estimates are used to assess feasibility and decide whether each alternative should even be considered in the ranking. For example, if one solution alternative is to purchase an ERP vendor package, but the organization's budget is less than the least expensive package available, that idea would be thrown out without spending any time analyzing it. At this point, estimates are very high-level. These estimates will be refined after the solution scope is defined and will be included in the business case.

Feasibility Analysis

A feasibility analysis is a way to assess options. We look at each option from different perspectives such as technological, operational, schedule, and financial, and decide if it is possible given our environment and constraints. The more costly the potential solution, the more time should be spent on performing feasibility analysis. The business analyst works with the other stakeholders to determine the feasibility of each solution option.

Summary

The Determine Solution Approach task is a precursor to actually defining the scope of the solution. For many business problems, you will determine the solution approach and define the solution scope at the same time. These tasks are separate because when addressing larger business needs, the analyst should make sure the team considers several ideas and carefully chooses an approach that best meets the needs within the constraints of the organization. The solution approach is still rather high-level. The details will be filled in as part of the next task. This task is most important when you are working on a business need with many stakeholder opinions; your job is to get them to come to a general agreement about the solution direction.

Define Solution Scope (5.4)

Now we decide what will be included in the solution. The purpose of the Define Solution Scope task is to describe the boundaries or scope of the solution, as well as the capabilities to be provided by the solution. The scope is refined from the solution approach determined in the last task. Its description is written and/or diagrammed in business terminology understandable to domain SMEs.

Define Solution Scope		
Inputs	**Techniques**	**Outputs**
Business Need (5.1)	Functional Decomposition (9.12)	Solution Scope (5.4)
Required Capabilities (5.2)	Interface Analysis (9.13)	
Solution Approach (5.3)	Scope Modeling (9.27)	
Assumptions and Constraints (6.4)	User Stories (9.33)	

BA's Responsibilities in Defining Solution Scope
- Work with domain SMEs to make sure the solution scope includes the required capabilities
- Create a more detailed definition of the solution scope (major features and functions) – and identify what is NOT included in the solution scope
- Work with the project manager and other stakeholders to consider the approach to implementation; will the solution be developed and implemented in phases or all at once?

What Do You Need to Successfully Define Solution Scope?
To develop a well-defined solution, we start with the solution approach, along with the business need and required capabilities or gaps (from the previous tasks), and our assumptions and constraints. Assumptions are things that are assumed (but not proven) to be true. Constraints are limitations imposed on the solution. There is an entire task in the Requirements Analysis knowledge area called Define Assumptions and Constraints (discussed on page 210). This is an example of the non-sequential nature of the *BABOK® Guide* that I warned you about! Just because two tasks are in different knowledge areas doesn't mean we can't do them concurrently. Assumptions and constraints are actually identified throughout all of our work and as such can be defined at any time. The task is executed concurrently

with many other business analysis tasks. Whenever you learn about an assumption or constraint, you should make a note of it and make sure it is incorporated into your solution.

What Is Scope?

If you look up the word *scope* in an English dictionary you will find something like: the extent of the mind's grasp, or the range of understanding or action. Scope can also describe an instrument for seeing more clearly, like a microscope or telescope. It is easy to visualize the scope of a geographic territory or physical object. When looking through a microscope at a drop of blood, I can see cells, which have very clear boundaries. When I am looking at a map of the United States, I can see the lines around a state, like Georgia or New York. If I was working on a project, it would be easy to say, "I will only make changes within the scope of Georgia."

In business, we use the word scope to mean boundaries. What is the area or part of the business we are going to analyze? If we decide to include only one particular department in our scope, the boundaries may be quite clear. We know the people who work in the department and we know what processes they perform. But few business needs impact only one department. Most solutions we design impact pieces or sections of several departments. You will see the word *domain* used instead of department or division when the area of the project doesn't fit neatly into formal organizational units. It becomes challenging to define the scope when it includes people and processes from several departments (and maybe people outside the organization). It becomes much less clear what is inside and outside of scope.

It is no wonder that understanding scope is challenging. For business analysts to clearly define it can be difficult, but we must try. One of the most common problems with business projects is scope creep. When the stakeholders don't all have the same picture of the scope, they each include things that are important to them and the scope grows. As the scope grows, project timelines are compromised and the project is at risk. This is a critical topic for both project managers and business analysts.

Which Scope?

There are many different areas that can be scoped. Since the word scope can be used in so many different ways, business analysts strive to be more specific by naming the area being scoped. For example, a business domain, or domain scope, is any area of the business that is being studied. Review the scopes mentioned in the *BABOK® Guide* and shown in the following graphic. The *Guide* defines them as subsets of each other. Notice the term *solution scope* is synonymous with *product scope*.

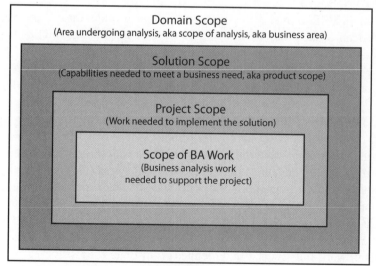

Names of Scope

I might be studying all of the processes in the company that deal with customers, my *domain scope*. The solution we decide on is a customer relationship management (CRM) system, my *solution scope*. A project will be initiated and a project manager assigned to select, purchase, customize, and implement a commercial CRM package. This is the *project scope*. As the business analyst on the project, I will perform process modeling of the current processes and gap analysis against the selected package to determine what customization is needed. I will also develop data conversion requirements and transition requirements to ensure a smooth implementation of the solution. This is the *scope of my business analysis work*, which is defined in the Business Analysis Planning and Monitoring chapter. (I know I haven't yet defined process modeling or data conversion. Don't worry, we'll get to them in the coming chapter!)

 The word scope is used in business analysis as both a noun and a verb. When used as a noun, think of it as a boundary or fence delineating a particular area. "That functionality is not inside our solution *scope*." As a verb, it is an action to create a boundary. "Let's *scope* the project to see how long it would take." Be sure to read exam questions about scope very carefully.

Because scope creep is so expensive and wasteful of resources, business analysis is very focused on helping organizations clarify solution boundaries and stay within them. Project managers are very good at defining project scope and keeping their team focused on the agreed-upon scope. As a business analyst, you are responsible for defining the solution scope (or product scope, as it is called by most project managers) and making sure the requirements are inside that scope. Requirements can be complex and not discrete, so they are difficult to contain. Rounding up and fencing in requirements can be like herding wild animals and domesticating them!

Summary of Scope Usage in Business Analysis			
Type of Scope	**Description**	**Also Known As**	**Referenced in Which Chapters of This Book**
Domain Scope	Area undergoing analysis	• Scope of analysis • Business domain • Business area	• Introduction • Enterprise Analysis
Solution Scope	Capabilities needed to meet a business need	• Product scope (in *PMBOK® Guide*) • Requirements scope	• Introduction • Enterprise Analysis • Requirements Analysis • Solution Assessment and Validation
Project Scope	Work needed to implement the solution		• Introduction • Enterprise Analysis
Business Analysis Work Scope	Business analysis work needed to support the project		• Business Analysis Planning and Monitoring

How Do We Define Solution Scope?

To define the solution scope, the business analyst must develop and communicate a clear understanding of what will be included in the solution. This includes business processes, functions, features, interfaces, and dependencies. It also should include the implementation approach, if possible. Will the solution be built in phases? Will some solution components be purchased? How will the team develop the solution?

Techniques to Define Solution Scope

There are many techniques for defining and representing the solution scope. Visual or graphic presentations of the scope can improve communications and facilitate approval by stakeholders.

Functional Decomposition (9.12)
A decomposition or breakdown of business processes can be used to show which business processes are inside the scope of the solution.

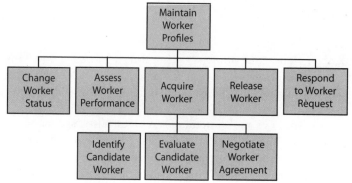

Decomposition Diagram of Solution Scope

The Context Diagram: Scope Modeling (9.27) and Interface Analysis (9.13) Combined!
Scope modeling is a generic name for analyzing and defining the domain or solution scope. There are several diagrams that can be used for scope modeling; the context diagram is highlighted in the *BABOK® Guide.*

Interface analysis is a generic name for identifying and describing the systems or organizations that interact with a particular scope. Coincidentally, interfaces are also shown on a context diagram, making it a very popular tool for scope definition!

A context level data flow diagram, or simply a context diagram, is frequently used for defining and presenting scope because it shows the boundaries of the domain or solution by highlighting its interfaces. Many people even refer to it as "The Scope Diagram." It utilizes the techniques of scope modeling and interface analysis.

A context diagram shows the domain or solution in the center with the interfacing organizations and systems around the outside. This is a very popular technique for illustrating the scope because of its simplicity. Without any training or special knowledge, stakeholders can review the diagram and get a good sense of the scope of the domain or solution. It is a good tool to use when communicating with stakeholders who do not have business analysis training.

But don't let its simplicity deceive you! For an analyst, this is a powerful tool, and it is not simple to create. To determine which parties are inside and outside the scope of the solution, you must seek answers to many questions. Part of your job is to help the sponsor and key stakeholders understand the complexity and size of the solution. In order to develop this diagram, you may ask questions your stakeholders haven't thought about, and to which they don't have an immediate answer! Keep in mind this is a scoping tool. We are not yet doing detailed requirements gathering, so we are going to stay at a high level.

A diagram or modeling technique can often be used for multiple purposes. The context diagram can be used to show a domain scope (the scope of the analysis or area of study) or can be used to show a solution scope (a more technical use of the diagram).

In the following example, the solution is named Worker Equipment Tracking. The boxes show there are five parties outside the scope that interact with the solution.

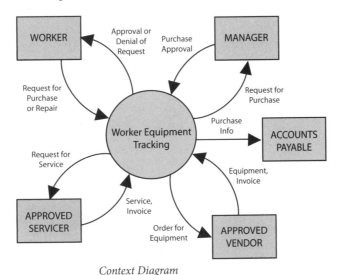

Context Diagram

Externals The boxes on the outside of the circle are called *external agents*, *external entities* (the *BABOK® Guide* term), or just *externals*. These are very important components of the diagram because they show the parties involved with the solution. The data flow arrows going to and from externals represent *interfaces*.

Remember, *external* means outside the scope or boundaries of the solution. The project team does not have authority to change the way externals perform work, but the ultimate solution may change the way the interface is handled. Every domain or solution scope has at least one external.

Examples of Externals

- Organizations outside the company
- Vendors or suppliers
- Government agencies
- Regulatory boards
- Business partners
- Departments inside the company, outside the project
- Systems within or outside the company

TRICKS OF THE TRADE® When using a context diagram, the terms systems, organizations, parties, and externals are used interchangeably.

You probably already understand the importance of finding all of the stakeholders who impact or will be impacted by the solution. (We'll talk more about this in the Conduct Stakeholder Analysis task in the Business Analysis Planning and Monitoring chapter.) Scope modeling helps to find stakeholders, because there will be stakeholders associated with each interface.

 There is a component of scoping not shown on the diagram: events. An event is something that occurs outside the scope, but causes a reaction or response inside the scope. For example, when a worker requests a new PC, the Worker Equipment Tracking solution must respond and either order the PC or deny the request. Events are initiated by external agents or by the passing of time, known as *temporal events*. ("Once a year we review the contracts with our approved vendors.") Events are also used in the Requirements Analysis knowledge area.

Interfaces   The final component of the diagram is the data flow arrows. These arrows may be named on the diagram or the details may be contained in a supporting document. Each arrow flows in only one direction and simply shows that information or data moves between the external and the solution.

Because each arrow shows that information must move between the external and the solution, it represents an interface. Interfaces may be manual (e.g., phone call), user interface (e.g., entry screen), an automated process (e.g., a file transmission), or a combination of these approaches. In this example, the Worker will enter his or her equipment request on a web page (user interface) and the request will automatically be sent to his or her manager for approval (via an e-mail message). Interfaces will be discussed in more detail in the next chapter, Elicitation.

Most analysts present the context diagram with supporting documents, including the stakeholder list, a business process decomposition diagram, and assumptions and constraints, to completely define the scope.

EXERCISE   Another business need in our Workforce Tracking area is a better solution for maintaining worker information. Review the case study description below. Decide on a project name, and then fill in the external agents and data flows for the case study.

Problem Statement
We need a solution to keep worker information up-to-date. With so many people working in so many different locations, it is difficult to add new workers and maintain worker profiles. We must make sure the workers' paychecks are deposited correctly and benefits information is current.

Specific Features Needed
- Allow candidate workers to apply for a position online from anywhere in the world.
- Allow workers to change their phone number, mailing address, bank account number for direct deposits, and tax information online from anywhere in the world.
- When worker information is added or changed, it should automatically be sent to all of the involved parties (government taxing authority, benefit providers, payroll system) to be updated. The worker should only have to make the change once and should be notified when the change has been completed.

© 2012 RMC Publications, Inc • 952.846.4484 • info@rmcproject.com • www.rmcproject.com

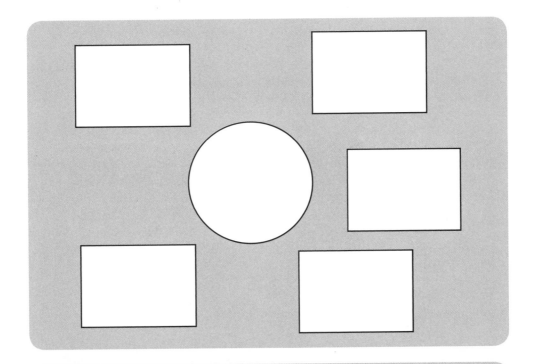

ANSWER

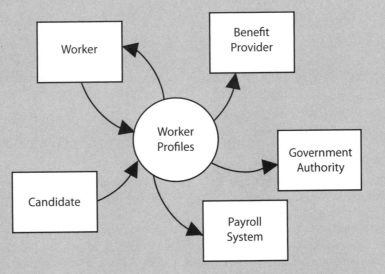

The project was named Worker Profiles, since its focus is the collection and maintenance of worker information. The solution receives information from workers and candidates. It sends information to benefit providers, government authorities, the payroll system, and back to the worker. This simple diagram conveys the boundaries of the solution.

You may have had some questions about the external agent "Worker." Should this be called employee or worker? What are the differences between these two terms? Business analysts should always maintain a glossary of terms to support their analysis work. Your glossary should include a definition to clarify this point. Clear glossary definitions are essential when using simple diagrams like the context diagram. In this case, a worker may be a consultant, contractor, or employee. Since we need to track all of their phone numbers and mailing addresses, the more generic term of worker is appropriate. The data dictionary and glossary technique (9.5) addresses these definitions. We'll further discuss the technique in the Elicitation and Requirements Analysis knowledge areas.

When you perform detailed requirements analysis, you will also break out the different types of end users who will use your solution. Be careful not to get too detailed when you are defining the scope. In this task, you will notice there is no mention of eliciting or analyzing requirements. Those details will come after we have a clear scope definition in the next knowledge areas.

Why aren't there any incoming data flows from the government authority, payroll system, or benefit provider? The Special Features Needed section of the exercise description doesn't indicate any data will be flowing back from these externals, so there are no incoming data flows. This is an important distinction. We are not saying the benefit provider never sends any data to the company, but those data inflows are *out of the scope* of this solution.

Imagine a scenario in which a benefit provider may change the benefits or fees when a worker moves to a different city, state, or country. In this situation, the benefit provider may send information back to the worker profile system. This information then needs to be processed and sent to the worker. If the team decides this process is within scope of the solution, another arrow will need to be added to the diagram.

Did you add HR as an external agent? Since HR is the department responsible for managing worker profiles, it is not *external* to the project. It is within the scope of the project. Your solution may include changes to the way the HR department operates.

The Use Case Diagram—Another Way to Combine Scope Modeling (9.27) and Interface Analysis (9.13)

Another graphic technique for showing solution scope is the use case diagram. When the solution includes a software component, the use case diagram is a very effective technique.

A use case diagram shows the software with actors (users) and the functions to be included in the software (called use cases). This diagram, like the context diagram, shows boundaries. The center rectangle is the automation boundary. The diagram also shows how users will interact with the system. This is a popular technique because the resulting diagram is easy for business stakeholders to review. Use case diagrams are part of a technique called Scenarios and Use Cases (9.26), which we'll discuss in more detail in the Requirements Analysis chapter.

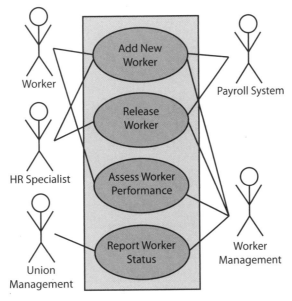

Use Case Diagram

User Stories (9.33)

Another popular way to elicit, analyze, and document solution scope is through user stories. User stories are employed in change-driven software development approaches (like agile) to capture short descriptions of features or functions the software should perform. Business stakeholders describe a specific scenario on a three-by-five-inch index card and make notes on the back of the card about how the scenario will be tested. This card gives the developer an idea of the feature needed, and the team estimates how long it will take to develop the feature. Each card is tracked as it is developed; reviewed by the user; tested; and completed.

Know the three Cs of user stories:

- **Card**: A card is used because it forces a short, informal description.
- **Conversation**: The card is a reminder to have a conversation with the stakeholder(s) when the team is ready to build. The user story itself will not contain enough detail for the project team to build the solution.
- **Confirmation**: The acceptance criteria on the back of the card will confirm the feature has been built properly.

#0023 Employee Login	Estimate	5
As an employee, I want to login to change my profile		
Require username + password		

User Story Card

When this technique is used to define the solution scope, a few high-level stories are created to get agreement on the functionality to be included in the solution.

Additional Techniques to Define Solution Scope

Next, we will look at other commonly used techniques for defining solution scope that are not included in the *BABOK® Guide*. Since the exam can include questions about techniques described in resources from the *BABOK® Guide's* bibliography, you should be aware of these also.

In- and Out-of-Scope Table   An in- and out-of-scope table is a simple way to document features, functions, or capabilities that fall inside or outside of the scope of your solution. This is a great facilitation tool for workshops and meetings. The group discusses whether each item should be included in the scope of the solution or not. Decisions are not always made immediately, so this table can also be used to track the outstanding items.

In- and Out-of-Scope Table			
Feature	**In**	**Out**	**Notes**
Allow HR department to keep track of home office equipment		X	Not a high priority right now
Allow employees to report to more than one manager	X		
Allow workers to report work by hour, day, or project assignment			Undecided; let's get an estimate from IT on the cost of this functionality
Allow workers to change their own phone number, e-mail address, or mailing address on the website	X		
Standardize new employee on-boarding process for all business units	X		
Allow conversion of employee to contractor, or contractor to employee		X	We'll do this in the next release

Product Backlog   When using a change-driven software development approach, another common scoping tool is the product backlog. The product backlog is a list of outstanding capabilities or features desired by stakeholders. This list is used by many software development organizations in agile development approaches. It allows users to provide their "laundry list" or wish list of wants and then prioritize the wants based on costs and benefits. This is often a good way to begin the work of achieving stakeholder agreement on the most important priorities.

Product Backlog					
ID	**Feature**	**Requested by**	**Priority**	**Estimated Cost**	**Sprint or Iteration**
F1	Allow HR department to keep track of home office equipment	B. Smith	3	Low	2
F2	Allow employee to report to more than one manager	S. Dinkins	6	High	3
F3	Allow worker to report work by hour, day, or project assignment	B. Smith	5	Med	3
F4	Allow worker to change phone number, e-mail address, or mailing address	B. Smith	4	Low	2

Product Backlog					
ID	Feature	Requested by	Priority	Estimated Cost	Sprint or Iteration
F5	Standardize new employee on-boarding process for all business units	R. Hughes	1	High	1
F6	Allow conversion of employee to contractor, or contractor to employee	B. Smith	2	Med	1

APPLY YOUR KNOWLEDGE   How have you defined the scope of your work? Have you used any of the techniques described in the Define Solution Scope task? If not, try using one now.

Summary

Defining the solution scope is one of the most important tasks of business analysis. If we don't have clear boundaries for the area we are going to be studying (domain) or the solution to be designed, we are likely to ask questions that cover a broader area than necessary and spend more time in analysis than we should. Many project managers are frustrated by business analysts who lose focus on the problem at hand and begin to elicit more requirements than were originally anticipated. Without clear agreement on what is in and what is out of scope, you won't know when to stop eliciting requirements and you won't know when you have complete requirements.

Define Business Case (5.5)

A business case is the justification for a project or initiative. Most organizations require a strong business case to fund a project, since there are so many competing needs for available resources. Defining a business case requires sophisticated analysis and evaluation. It will help the organization decide whether or not to move forward with creating the solution.

This final task in Enterprise Analysis helps the organization decide if a project should be initiated. The business case should be defined *before* the project starts, but *after* the solution scope is defined, so the business case can be as accurate as possible. It is difficult to build a strong business case to justify a project if you don't have a clear idea of what the solution will include.

Define Business Case		
Inputs	Techniques	Outputs
Business Need (5.1)	Decision Analysis (9.8)	Business Case (5.5)
Solution Scope (5.4)	Estimation (9.10)	
Stakeholder Concerns (3.3)	Metrics and Key Performance Indicators (9.16)	
Assumptions and Constraints (6.4)	Risk Analysis (9.24)	
	SWOT Analysis (9.32)	
	Vendor Assessment (9.34)	

BA's Responsibilities in Defining the Business Case

- Compile tangible and intangible costs and benefits of the solution
- Compare cost and benefit data related to the solution scope to assess the net business value expected
- Present and obtain approval of the business case from the sponsor

What Do You Need to Successfully Define the Business Case?

In addition to understanding the business need and solution scope, to build a business case we need assumptions and constraints, along with stakeholder concerns. Many business decisions are based strictly on financial analysis, but many are also influenced by intangible considerations. Stakeholder concerns may fall into this category. It is important for you to listen to your stakeholders' concerns and take them into consideration in your recommendations. Stakeholder concerns are usually identified when you are talking with stakeholders, eliciting information like costs, benefits, or requirements. (If you are *concerned* about where they came from—a little business analysis humor—they are an output of two tasks in the Elicitation knowledge area: Document Elicitation Results and Confirm Elicitation Results.)

What is a Business Case?

A business case may be a very simple financial justification (if we fix this problem for $10,000, we will save $25,000 every year) or it may be a very complex decision with lots of intangible benefits and costs (if we decrease our greenhouse emissions, we will improve the environment, make the planet more sustainable, and increase our esteem in the community). With limited resources, we must help our organizations make good decisions about which projects to fund. A strong business case is key to making these decisions.

A business case may include several sections. It can be documented and presented formally (in a written document) or informally (in a conversation in a hallway). The level of formality depends on the size and significance of the recommendation, and the preferences of the decision makers.

Table of Contents for a Formal Business Case

I. Introduction and Recommendation Overview

II. Current Environment and Problem

    a) As-Is Workflow Diagrams

    b) Description of the Problem

III. Detailed Description of the Proposal

    a) To-Be Workflow Diagrams

    b) Description of Proposed Development Plan

    c) Description of Proposed Implementation Plan

IV. Cost-Benefit Analysis Tables

    a) Tangible Costs and Benefits with ROI and Payback Period

    b) Intangible Costs and Benefits

V. Risk Assessment

VI. Summary

Costs and Benefits Included in a Business Case   Know the definitions of the following terms, and be able to identify examples of each.

Tangible Costs can be measured and are often the most accurate part of the cost-benefit analysis. If the proposed solution is well-defined and understood, cost estimates should be very accurate and reliable. It is important to separate these costs into at least two categories: one-time costs and ongoing costs.

> **Example: Tangible Costs**
> - Software development time for the Workforce Tracking System is estimated at $40,000
> - Training HR personnel on the new system will cost $10,000 during the implementation and then $500 for each new HR employee on an ongoing basis

Intangible Costs are difficult, if not impossible, to measure, but they are no less important to the organization. Be sure you think about how they might be measured before categorizing them as intangible.

> **Example: Intangible Costs**
> - Dissatisfied employees
> - Negative reputation known to potential job candidates

Tangible Benefits are benefits that are measurable and to which monetary value can be assigned. Financial benefits are calculated based on factors such as decreased costs of materials or services, increased revenue, decreased borrowing costs, and increased productivity.

> **Example: Tangible Benefits**
> - HR personnel will spend four fewer hours processing each new employee, saving $400 per employee
> - New employees will become productive faster, resulting in an estimated savings of $2,000 per employee

Intangible Benefits are also difficult, if not impossible, to measure and quantify. The classic example of an intangible benefit is the "goodwill" a company receives from participating in a community service project. Before you categorize a benefit as intangible, be sure it truly can't be measured. Think creatively about how you might be able to quantify the benefit, and then decide if the information you could gather is worth the time required to gather it. For example, increased quality of customer service could be measured by customer surveys, but surveys would take time and money. How important are the measurements to the project and your organization?

> **Example: Intangible Benefits**
> - Employee on-boarding will be less stressful for new employees
> - The organization will be perceived as innovative by employees and candidates

Simple Business Case for Proposed Worker Tracking Website
Benefits or Advantages
Decrease tax penalties caused by incorrect reporting—estimated savings $400,000 per year
Better utilization of existing office space and better planning for future needs —estimated savings $20,000 per year
Faster on-boarding of new workers
Easier relocation or reassignment of employees
Costs or Disadvantages
Survey of existing employees to prioritize changes—estimated cost $10,000
Software design and development time for new application—estimated cost $350,000
Communication/marketing activities to roll out new system—estimated cost $5,000

Cost-benefit analysis can be very simple, as shown in this example, or very detailed, with numerous charts and calculations. The level of detail will be decided by your sponsor and by the cost of the recommendation. The more detail and accuracy desired, the more time will be needed to collect facts and make realistic estimates. The more expensive the solution, the more formal the business case should be.

APPLY YOUR KNOWLEDGE   Using the following worksheet, build a business case to convince yourself to buy a new car. Think about the tangible and intangible costs and benefits of this change.

Worksheet: Should I Buy a New Car?		
	Benefits	**Costs**
Tangible	Short term Long term	Short term Long term
Intangible	Short term Long term	Short term Long term

What did you decide?

SAMPLE ANSWER

Worksheet: Should I Buy a New Car?		
	Benefits	**Costs**
Tangible	**Short term** • No maintenance costs • Sale of old car • Lower fuel costs **Long term** • Lower maintenance costs	**Short term** • Purchase price! • Higher insurance premiums • Higher license fees **Long term**
Intangible	**Short term** • FUN to have a new car!! • Less concern about breakdowns **Long term** • Better for the environment	**Short term** • Will I feel bad about spending the money or being in debt? **Long term** • Will I get tired of it after a few months? • Worry about the new car getting hit

Techniques to Define the Business Case

Decision Analysis (9.8)

The decision analysis technique primarily focuses on financial analysis. A senior business analyst needs to understand some basic financial analysis terms and formulas to make effective and responsible solution recommendations. You don't have to be an expert, but you need to understand the purpose of each type of financial analysis and be able to collaborate with financial professionals who will provide the detailed calculations.

 When you see the term decision analysis, think "Money." This technique focuses on financial considerations in making decisions. You will not be asked to perform any calculations on the exam.

 Financial Analysis Terms to Know for the Exam   The business case may be evaluated using common financial performance predictors:

Return on Investment (ROI) attempts to measure the profitability of an investment by calculating the amount of benefits received in relation to the amount of cost (investment). The higher the ROI, the better.

Discounted Cash Flow is used to estimate the attractiveness of an investment by predicting how much money will be received in the future and discounting it to its current value.

Net Present Value (NPV) is the present value of the total benefits (income or revenue) minus the costs over many time periods. Calculating the NPV of each possible project provides a means for the organization to compare many projects and select the best project to initiate. Generally, if the NPV is positive, the investment is a good choice unless an even better investment opportunity exists. The project with the greatest NPV is typically selected.

Internal Rate of Return (IRR)   You put money in a bank account and expect to get a return of X percent. You can think of a project in the same way, in that you expect a return of X percent. If a company has more than one project in which to invest, the company may compare the expected returns of the different projects and select the project with the highest expected return.

Payback Period refers to the length of time it takes for the organization to recover its investment in the project before it starts receiving net benefits.

Estimation (9.10)

To accurately assess a potential solution, we must be able to predict what it will cost to design, develop, implement, and operate. Estimation is used to predict these costs. The best information upon which to base an estimate is actual cost reports from past similar projects. You will need to compile estimates from the implementation SMEs for each component of the solution. You will predict benefits by working with the domain SMEs and estimating the value they will receive from the solution. In the Business Analysis Planning and Monitoring chapter, we will look at the types of estimation methods you'll need to know.

Metrics and Key Performance Indicators (9.16)

Metrics and key performance indicators are quantifiable measurements used to assess performance. A key performance indicator (KPI) is an agreed-upon measure that tracks progress toward a strategic goal of the organization. They are used to calculate costs and benefits for the business case.

One of the best ways to justify a proposed solution is to gather metrics of the current system ("It takes us an average of 12 minutes to record each purchase request") and estimate the performance of the proposed solution. ("We estimate the proposed solution will shorten this time to 6 minutes.") When the estimated savings is multiplied by the number of times the process is performed, a solid justification appears. ("We record about 400 requests per day, so by saving 6 minutes per request, we will save 40 person-hours per day!") Look for as-is metrics when learning about business processes. Capture any information you can about current times and costs. Ask for counts, measure with a stopwatch, analyze existing data sources; find these metrics in any places you can. They may not be easily found, but they are very valuable. Use these measurements in your business case to estimate the degree of improvement the proposed solution will generate.

You have already identified SMART objectives in your definition of the business need. They include specific improvements like decrease costs, increase revenue, increase throughput, etc. These items can be measured before and after the solution is implemented to Evaluate Solution Performance (a task in Solution Assessment and Validation). Business analysts always use measurements to assess, evaluate, and justify.

Risk Analysis (9.24)

In addition to numerical considerations, the business case should also include risk assessment. A risk is an uncertain occurrence that could impact the organization's ability to achieve an objective. There are two types of risk you should think about: business risks and project risks.

Business Risks   Threats or opportunities that may affect the *ongoing* operations of the business. A business risk might impact the business's ability to achieve its business objectives.

> **Example Threat:** The outside vendor that processes payroll transactions may have a system failure.
> **Example Opportunity:** A new product offering may exceed sales expectations, resulting in a backlog.

Project Risks   Threats or opportunities that may affect the project. A project risk might impact the project team's ability to finish the project within its budget, time, and quality objectives.

> **Example Threat:** Equipment needed to complete the project will be delivered late.
> **Example Opportunity:** An existing software component can be reused, eliminating the need for writing new software.

Business risks are managed on an ongoing basis in the business domain. When you are learning about the business, you will learn about its risks and current approaches to managing those risks. Project managers also identify, analyze, and manage risk, so you need to work closely with your project manager in this area. Project risks are primarily the responsibility of the project manager. Most project risks are identified during project initiating and planning. However, business and project risks are identified and managed throughout the life of the project.

Risk analysis is an important technique for business analysts to learn, and can be performed on project risks or business risks. Risk analysis includes identifying the risks, assessing their probability and impact, and determining how they will be handled. You will see this technique used throughout business analysis work; the word "risk" is used hundreds of times in business analysis references. Risks should be identified early and constantly during your work. Whenever a risk is identified, you and your team should consider its likelihood and potential impact. Risks can be positive or negative, but of course the negative ones are usually given more attention because we don't want bad things to happen.

Sample Risk Management Plan			
Risk	**Likelihood**	**Impact**	**Contingency**
Sponsor is reassigned	Low	High	Keep other potential sponsors informed about project progress
Outside vendor has payroll system failure	Low	High	Have a backup procedure for processing payroll in-house
New software will be delivered late	Medium	High	Stay in close contact with software vendor Schedule developers to work on interfaces while waiting for software

Be sure to know the risk tolerance terms along with the risk response options because these terms are frequently used by project managers and business managers.

Risk Tolerances
- Risk Averse
- Neutral
- Risk seeking

Risk Responses
- Accept
- Transfer
- Avoid
- Mitigate
- Share
- Enhance
- Exploit

 Read the *BABOK® Guide* description of the risk analysis technique (9.24) now if you are not familiar with risk tolerances and responses.

SWOT Analysis (9.32)

The SWOT analysis technique (discussed earlier) can be useful to identify risks in the business case when the solution impacts the organization's competitive environment.

Vendor Assessment Technique (9.34)

When the solution approach involves purchasing a product or service from an outside vendor, the vendor assessment technique is required to develop a business case. Before recommending a particular vendor or supplier, the organization should assess the product, reputation, and stability of the vendor. Purchasing a product or service involves some upfront costs and may also involve ongoing maintenance costs. You should make sure the costs have been formally documented by the vendor in their response to a request for proposal. Outsourcing decisions are sometimes made before a project is approved and sometimes as part of the project work. Getting an accurate estimate of the time and costs of a vendor solution contributes to a well-informed decision about whether or not to proceed.

The Prepare Requirements Package task in the Requirements Management and Communication chapter, page 257, includes more information about creating an RFP and other documents to help with your vendor assessment.

Summary

The business case allows the sponsor and other domain SMEs to make a well-informed decision about going forward with the proposed solution. Once the business case is approved and a project is initiated, the business case is used by the project manager as an input to the project charter. The business case will be used throughout the project to prioritize requirements and support decisions. You will see it as an input to tasks in Elicitation, Requirements Management and Communication, and Solution Assessment and Validation.

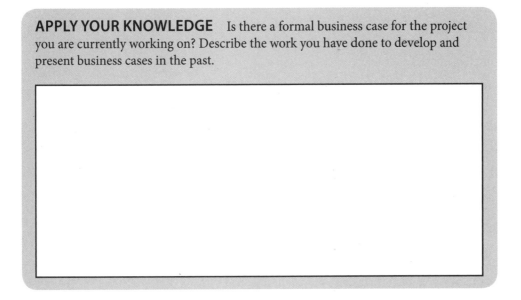

APPLY YOUR KNOWLEDGE   Is there a formal business case for the project you are currently working on? Describe the work you have done to develop and present business cases in the past.

SUMMARY OF ENTERPRISE ANALYSIS

Enterprise analysis describes important business analysis work that is used in everything else we do. We frequently refer back to the original business need and the business case as we are doing detailed requirements work and validating the solution. Having this solid foundation for analysis work will help you minimize scope creep and keep the team focused on the most important requirements. Helping your sponsor and other stakeholders carefully consider their requests before diving into detailed analysis and design prevents the organization from wasting precious resources and makes sure that you work on the most important solutions for the organization.

 Before taking the practice exam, I recommend that you read the Enterprise Analysis chapter of the *BABOK® Guide* (Chapter 5), and the descriptions of these key techniques of this knowledge area (in Chapter 9 of the *BABOK® Guide*):

- Benchmarking (9.2)
- Functional Decomposition (9.12)
- Root Cause Analysis (9.25)
- SWOT Analysis (9.32)
- Scope Modeling (9.27)
- Decision Analysis (9.8)
- Metrics and Key Performance Indicators (9.16)
- Risk Analysis (9.24)

Practice Exam

1. What is a SMART objective?

   A. Specific, measurable, achievable, relevant, time-bounded
   B. Satisfactory, measurable, accurate, routine, time-bounded
   C. Specific, monetary, accurate, routine, time-framed
   D. Supportive, monetary, achievable, realistic, textual

2. A context diagram shows:

   A. That the solution is simple.
   B. That work flows in a business area.
   C. That business rules are tied to business processes.
   D. That the solution interacts with other parties, organizations or systems.

3. Solution scope differs from project scope in that:

   A. The solution scope describes the result of the project work.
   B. A solution includes the project schedule and budget.
   C. They are actually two names for the same thing.
   D. The project scope is most important to the business analyst, while the solution scope is needed by the project manager.

4. Business analysis professionals spend their time:

   A. On projects, working for a project manager.
   B. Outside of projects, working in parallel with project managers.
   C. Assigned to projects while also supporting other initiatives.
   D. Only at the beginning of projects building business cases, charters and collecting requirements.

5. A roadmap or plan for how the organization structures business processes, business rules, application software, hardware, and organization resources is called the:

   A. Enterprise architecture.
   B. Data model.
   C. Context diagram.
   D. Decision model.

6. Enterprise analysis refers to:

   A. The work done from an overall organization perspective to achieve goals.
   B. The work done on software applications that are used by the entire enterprise (e.g., ERP, CRM).
   C. The purpose of the project management office (PMO) or business analysis center of excellence (BACoE).
   D. Developing the enterprise architecture.

7. A context diagram is considered which type of requirement?

   A. Transition or stakeholder
   B. Stakeholder or business
   C. Functional or non-functional
   D. Business or functional

8. SWOT stands for:

   A. Strengths, weaknesses, opportunities, and threats.
   B. Strengths, weaknesses, options, and timeframe.
   C. Strategic, workflow, operations, tactical.
   D. Stakeholder, workflow, operations, timing.

9. Which of the following is a SMART objective?

   A. Create a legal opinion database to decrease research time and cost.
   B. Decrease legal costs by 25 percent within two years.
   C. Cut legal costs by shortening research time.
   D. Streamline research by providing better data access within two years.

10. When considering the best solution for a business problem it is necessary to:

   A. Use feasibility analysis.
   B. Use observation.
   C. Use a focus group.
   D. Use benchmarking.

11. A business need:

   A. Is something a particular stakeholder wants.
   B. Is a capability the current system does not provide.
   C. Defines the problem to be solved.
   D. Describes the solution approach.

12. The difference between goals and objectives is:

   A. Goals are longer term, ongoing business desires.
   B. Objectives are longer term, ongoing business desires.
   C. Goals are more descriptive and specific.
   D. Objectives are analyzed and converted into goals.

13. Another name for a business problem or opportunity is:

   A. Goal.
   B. Objective.
   C. Desired outcome.
   D. Business need.

14. Once a business need has been identified, what should the business analyst do NEXT?

    A. Assess capability gaps.
    B. Determine the solution approach.
    C. Define the business case.
    D. Define the solution scope.

15. If the best solution to a business need appears to involve hiring more employees, the business analyst should:

    A. Allow the business stakeholders to figure out the solution themselves.
    B. Present this suggestion and help stakeholders to evaluate it against others.
    C. Contact Human Resources to start identifying candidates.
    D. Report to the sponsor and project manager that no business analysis work is needed here.

16. The boundaries of the requirements, along with outside parties, systems, and organizations describe the:

    A. Project scope.
    B. Solution scope.
    C. Transition scope.
    D. Business case scope.

17. What is needed to define a business case?

    A. Solution scope, business need, assumptions and constraints
    B. Solution scope, requirements, assumptions and constraints
    C. The business analysis plan, business need, assumptions and constraints
    D. The business analysis plan, solution scope, requirements

18. Important techniques used when defining a business case include:

    A. Estimation, decision analysis, and risk analysis.
    B. Data modeling, process modeling, and business rules analysis.
    C. Data modeling, estimation, and risk analysis.
    D. Decision analysis, process modeling, and risk analysis.

19. The solution scope is needed to:

    A. Define the Business Need.
    B. Assess Capability Gaps.
    C. Define the Business Case.
    D. Determine Solution Approach.

20. All of the following are valid solution approaches to addressing a business need EXCEPT:

    A. Purchase or lease hardware or software.
    B. Change business processes or procedures.
    C. Design or develop custom software.
    D. Assess capability gaps.

21. Functional decomposition is used to:

    A. Define the business need based on competitive analysis.
    B. Define the boundaries of the solution.
    C. Provide key measurements for the business case estimates.
    D. Break down business needs into sub-needs.

22. The fishbone diagram is used with:

    A. Root cause analysis.
    B. Risk analysis.
    C. Decision analysis.
    D. SWOT analysis.

Answers

1. **Answer** A

   Explanation According to the *BABOK® Guide*, the acronym SMART stands for specific, measurable, achievable, relevant, and time-bounded.

2. **Answer** D

   Explanation Just because the diagram is simple, doesn't mean the solution is! The arrows on a context diagram represent data flows, not workflows. Business rules are not shown on a context diagram. A context diagram shows the boundaries of the domain or solution by highlighting its interfaces with other parties, organizations, or systems.

3. **Answer** A

   Explanation The project scope describes how the work will get done, and is the responsibility of the project manager. The solution, or product, scope describes the solution or product that will be built by the project. The solution scope is the responsibility of the business analyst.

4. **Answer** C

   Explanation Business analysts typically work on projects and non-project work. When working on a project, the business analyst reports to the project manager, just like other project team members. When working outside a project, the business analyst reports to his or her manager, who may be in the business domain.

5. **Answer** A

   Explanation A data model is focused on data and business rules, not processes. A context diagram shows boundaries, and a decision model includes business rules. The enterprise architecture is a description of how the enterprise is organized, and how it functions and plans for future changes.

6. **Answer** A

   Explanation Individuals within the PMO or BACoE may perform enterprise analysis, but it is not the purpose of these groups. Enterprise analysis ensures all solutions support the strategic plans of the organization, but typically does not involve creating these high-level plans. A business analyst should be able to consider a specific solution design within the context of the enterprise to make sure the solution aligns with the organization's goals.

7. **Answer** D

   Explanation Transition requirements describe how to implement or roll out the solution. Stakeholder requirements are requests for features or capabilities, and few stakeholders would use a context diagram to make a request! Non-functional requirements are constraints or quality-of-service requirements like performance, security, etc., and are generally documented in text. A context diagram can be used to show the scope of a business domain, making it part of the business requirements. Or it can be used to show the solution scope, making it part of the functional requirements.

8. **Answer** A

   Explanation SWOT analysis considers the organizational strengths and weaknesses against market (outside) opportunities and threats.

© 2012 RMC Publications, Inc • 952.846.4484 • info@rmcproject.com • www.rmcproject.com

9. **Answer   B**
Explanation   The M in the acronym SMART stands for measurable. The only objective presented that can be completely measured is to decrease legal costs by 25 percent within two years.

10. **Answer   A**
Explanation   Feasibility analysis is used to consider alternative solution approaches and select the best one. The other choices are techniques that may support the feasibility analysis.

11. **Answer   C**
Explanation   Something a stakeholder wants is a stakeholder requirement. A capability not provided by the current system is a capability gap. The solution approach can't be determined until the business need is defined. It describes how the business need will be addressed. A business need is a problem or opportunity identified by the business.

12. **Answer   A**
Explanation   Goals are generally high-level, long term desired outcomes for the organization, while objectives are more specific and concrete.

13. **Answer   D**
Explanation   All of these terms have very subtle differences in the *BABOK® Guide*. A goal is a long term desired outcome or end state. An objective is a specific, measurable (SMART) observable outcome. A business need is a problem or opportunity. Projects are usually initiated to address a business need and have specific objectives that serve as success criteria for the project.

14. **Answer   A**
Explanation   The tasks in the Enterprise Analysis knowledge area have a specific order. Have you learned it yet? Assessing capability gaps comes after defining the business need.

15. **Answer   B**
Explanation   Identifying the need for more employees is a valid solution alternative that a business analyst should present for consideration. He or she should not decide it is the best solution without working with the domain stakeholders to objectively evaluate the idea and compare it to others. This type of solution involves business analysis work because the new employees will need training and procedures for their work (transition requirements).

16. **Answer   B**
Explanation   The project scope describes how the work will be done and includes the project management plans. Transition scope and business case scope are made-up terms. Yes, you may see made-up terms on your real exam as well! The solution, or product, scope describes the product that will be the result of the project. It is important in business analysis work to clearly define the solution scope at the beginning of the project.

17. **Answer   A**
Explanation   The solution scope is needed so you can create a high-level estimate of the costs to produce it, and the benefits to be gained. Business need describes the problem to be solved and the objectives. Assumptions and constraints are the limitations on the product. You don't have requirements yet and you can't develop the business analysis plan until you have a business case.

18. **Answer**   A

    Explanation   Estimation is needed to determine the costs and benefits, decision analysis is financial analysis like return on investment and payback period, and risk analysis allows the team to assess the risk of the solution approach. Data modeling, process modeling, and business rules analysis will be used to analyze requirements after the business case is approved.

19. **Answer**   C

    Explanation   Defining the business need, assessing capability gaps, and determining the solution approach all happen before the solution scope is defined. The solution scope is used to define the business case.

20. **Answer**   D

    Explanation   Capability gaps should be assessed before the solution approach is determined. It is a task to help find an appropriate and valid solution to the business need; it is not a solution itself. Assessing capability gaps is done after the business need has been defined.

21. **Answer**   D

    Explanation   Competitive analysis uses the benchmarking technique. Defining boundaries uses the scope modeling technique. Key measurements are defined in the metrics and key performance indicators technique. The functional decomposition technique is used to break something down or analyze it. Business needs can be decomposed into more detailed needs, as can processes, goals, or any other business component.

22. **Answer**   A

    Explanation   A fishbone diagram shows causes and effects of problems and as such is used with root cause analysis.

CHAPTER 4

Elicitation

Aligned with the *BABOK® Guide* Chapter Three

Elicitation is a communication technique used to discover information. The Elicitation knowledge area has four simple tasks: prepare, conduct, document, and confirm. The complexity in each of these tasks comes in the variety of techniques available to perform elicitation. Elicitation means to *draw forth* or *bring forward*. It is one of the most important words in business analysis. Business analysts are constantly eliciting, or bringing forward, information. We do this in almost every interaction we have. Because you likely have lots of experience eliciting information, you may find this to be the easiest knowledge area on the exam. Approximately 21 of the exam questions are focused on this knowledge area and its techniques.

Elicitation is the perfect word to describe the activity of

QUICK TEST

- Structured and unstructured interviews
- Focus groups
  - Homogeneous
  - Heterogeneous
  - Themes
- Facilitation
- Brainstorming
- Requirements workshops
- Data dictionary
- Document analysis
- Problem tracking
- Consensus
- JAD
- Elicitation event
- Survey or questionnaire
- Prototyping
  - Storyboard
  - Mockup
  - Horizontal
  - Vertical
  - Low-fidelity
  - Throw-away
  - Evolutionary
  - Simulation
- Interface analysis
- Active and passive observation
- Open-ended questions
- Closed-ended questions
- Deliverable
- Artifact
- Organizational process assets

determining a stakeholder's true requirement or need. Instead of complaining that the stakeholders don't know what they want, the excellent business analyst "draws out" or "causes the stakeholders to reveal" their true need. Elicitation is required because, even though stakeholders know they have a problem, they may not always know the root cause of the problem or the best solution. The job of a business analyst is to ask good questions, listen carefully, and investigate to find the best solution to the problem.

Understanding the definition of the word elicitation makes verbs such as gather, collect, and record, which are frequently used when discussing requirements, sound rather passive. Those words do not accurately reflect the complexity of the communications necessary to help stakeholders reveal their requirements.

Elicitation in Action

Imagine you are assigned to help your manager hire a new employee for your organization. Several qualified candidates have applied for the position and the Human Resources department has scheduled interviews. Before each interview, you review the candidate's résumé and compare his or her skills to the job description. You draft some questions to ask and proceed to the interview. During the interview, you introduce yourself, ask your questions, and listen carefully to the candidate's answers. You also observe the candidate's body language and ask additional questions as new topics arise. You pay attention to what kinds of questions the candidate asks you. After the interview, you make notes about your impressions and consider whether or not you would recommend making a job offer. Finally, you talk with your manager to compare notes and come to a consensus about the candidate.

You have just participated in an elicitation activity! If you have been involved in any type of interviewing situation, you have experience with elicitation that will help you understand and correctly answer exam questions on this knowledge area.

EXERCISE   There are four tasks in the Elicitation knowledge area: Prepare for Elicitation, Conduct Elicitation Activity, Document Elicitation Results, and Confirm Elicitation Results. The tasks are sequential and sometimes performed concurrently. Can you identify the four tasks in the previous story?

Elicitation Knowledge Area Task	Work Performed in the Story
Prepare for Elicitation	
Conduct Elicitation Activity	
Document Elicitation Results	
Confirm Elicitation Results	

ANSWER

Elicitation Knowledge Area Task	Work Performed in the Story
Prepare for Elicitation	Reviewed résumé, reviewed job description, compared résumé to job description, drafted questions
Conduct Elicitation Activity	Made introductions, conducted interview, asked questions, listened to and recorded answers, watched body language, asked follow-up questions
Document Elicitation Results	Made notes of impressions
Confirm Elicitation Results	Considered whether or not to recommend making a job offer, met with manager to discuss candidate and come to a consensus

Barb's BA Themes

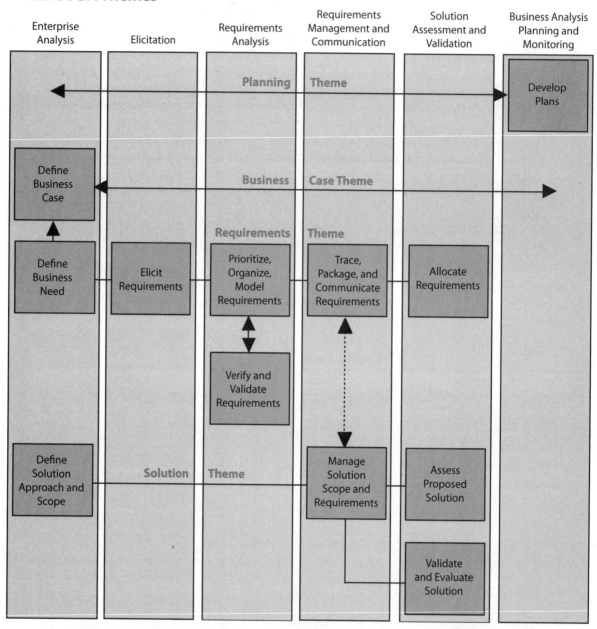

The Elicitation knowledge area is involved in all of the business analysis themes. Elicitation can be used in the Planning Theme to gather information about stakeholder communication preferences and about the team's development approach (change-driven vs. plan-driven). The business analysis communication plan describes how communications will be conducted and specifies which elicitation techniques will be used. Elicitation is used to elicit details about the business case in the Business Case Theme, elicit requirements in the Requirements Theme, and elicit solution ideas in the Solution Theme.

Things to Know about Elicitation for the Exam

- This is one of the two business analysis knowledge areas where sequence is important. (Hopefully you still remember the other one!) To effectively elicit information, you must perform the four tasks in order.
- Elicitation is not always a formal process. You could complete all four of these steps in one interaction—for example, in a brief hallway conversation.
- Not all elicitation work involves stakeholders directly. Techniques like document analysis and interface analysis allow you to elicit information from other sources. Elicitation activities that involve stakeholders are referred to as elicitation *events*.
- The four tasks in this knowledge area are performed a little differently depending on which technique is used. For example, preparing for a requirements workshop is more involved than preparing for a brainstorming session. Be sure to understand the differences between the techniques.
- Elicitation can be used anywhere, and at any time in business analysis work. It is usually performed in conjunction with tasks in the other knowledge areas. For example, when you are defining the solution scope, you are probably using elicitation.

Elicitation activities are planned in Business Analysis Planning and Monitoring. All work in this knowledge area assumes you have a plan and you are following it!

Introduction to the Tasks of Elicitation

The tasks of Elicitation are straightforward and logical. This chapter includes a brief description of each task, but includes more detail on the techniques. In the other chapters of this book, I discuss the relevant techniques within each task. However, in this chapter, many of the techniques are used in more than one of the tasks. Therefore, at the end of this chapter I have included a Techniques section that discusses each technique and how it applies to each Elicitation task. Spend most of your study time on the techniques in this knowledge area. Most of the exam questions on Elicitation will test your knowledge of techniques and how they are used in the tasks.

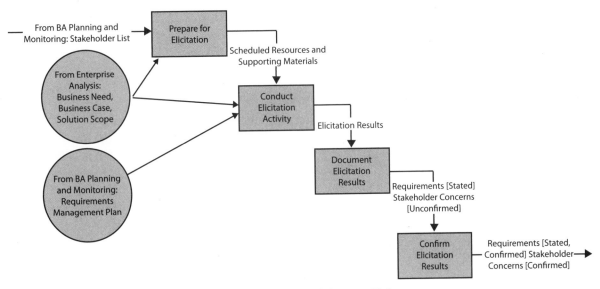

Inputs to and Outputs of Elicitation Tasks

Prepare for Elicitation (3.1)

Preparing for elicitation is as important as the elicitation event or activity itself. A well-prepared business analyst thinks in advance about the who, what, when, where, why, and how of the elicitation, thereby making the best use of time and corporate resources. This task is much more detailed than the elicitation planning done in the Business Analysis Planning and Monitoring knowledge area (the last knowledge area chapter in this book). In Planning, we decide which type of elicitation technique to use; here we *prepare for a specific event*. Preparing for elicitation includes the work of formulating your questions, setting up the facilities, and collecting the necessary materials.

Prepare for Elicitation		
Inputs	**Techniques**	**Outputs**
Business Need (5.1)	Brainstorming (9.3)	Scheduled Resources (3.1)
Solution Scope (5.4)	Document Analysis (9.9)	Supporting Materials (3.1)
Business Case (5.5)	Focus Groups (9.11)	
Stakeholder List, Roles, and Responsibilities (2.2)	Interface Analysis (9.13)	
	Interviews (9.14)	
	Observation (9.18)	
	Prototyping (9.22)	
	Requirements Workshops (9.23)	
	Survey/Questionnaire (9.31)	

BA's Responsibilities in Preparing for Elicitation

- Refer to the business analysis communication plan to determine the purpose of the elicitation and its expected results
- Decide how the elicitation will take place (time, date, location, people or type of research)
- Make necessary arrangements for the elicitation
- Prepare agenda, questions, and facilitation tools needed for each elicitation
- Prepare stakeholders for the elicitation (when appropriate)

What Do You Need to Successfully Prepare for Elicitation?

Much of the groundwork for Elicitation was completed in Enterprise Analysis. In Enterprise Analysis, the business need, business case, and solution scope were determined. Why are these inputs important? The business need (problem or opportunity the business is trying to address) must be understood before you can prepare for elicitation. The business case justifies the project and provides details about the anticipated costs and benefits of the work. Being aware of the business need and business case helps you know what types of questions to ask during elicitation. The solution scope defines the boundaries of your analysis work. The stakeholder list is created in Business Analysis Planning and Monitoring. This input should be obvious; you can't elicit from stakeholders if you don't know who the stakeholders are! The stakeholder analysis performed in Planning gives you information to prepare for a specific elicitation activity.

Notice that several of the inputs to this task are outputs of Enterprise Analysis. But couldn't you use elicitation to develop these deliverables? Yes! For example, you could interview a sponsor to define the business need, and you could conduct a requirements workshop to get agreement about the solution scope. You need at least a general idea of the business need and business case to get started; elicitation will probably be used to refine them.

Be Prepared!   Preparing for elicitation involves collecting documents you need to study, or creating an agenda for the elicitation event, reserving a meeting room or setting up access to collaboration tools, and communicating with stakeholders about the elicitation event.

Having clear, well-documented boundaries helps keep you and your stakeholders on topic. Many business analysts bring their scope diagram to elicitation events to remind the group to stay within the solution scope.

 It is easy to confuse the Prepare for Elicitation task with the tasks in the Business Analysis Planning and Monitoring knowledge area. The decisions on which elicitation techniques to use and which stakeholders to involve should have been made in Planning. The Elicitation knowledge area is dedicated to executing according to the plan. Exam questions about identifying stakeholders and choosing an elicitation technique relate to Business Analysis Planning and Monitoring knowledge area tasks. Questions about specific elicitation activities are generally referring to the Elicitation knowledge area.

EXERCISE   Imagine one morning your manager assigns you to a new project. He tells you he has scheduled an interview for you with the sponsor that afternoon. What will you do for the next few hours to prepare?

ANSWER

- Find out if a location for the interview has been reserved.
- Review the business analysis plans, which include information about the sponsor and the project. Is there a charter, business case, initial scope statement—anything that can help you understand the problem? Who is the sponsor? What are his or her title, department, reporting lines (above and below), number of years with the company? What is the business domain for the project? Does it involve Accounting? Marketing? Operations? What is the current business environment? Which locations will be involved on the project? What software applications are currently being used? How many employees are involved?
- As you review available information, develop a list of questions and prioritize those questions.
- Arrive at the meeting early, introduce yourself, and express enthusiasm for learning about the project.

Summary

Preparing for elicitation doesn't need to take a lot of time, but it must be done. The outputs of this task are your materials (e.g., questions, documents, flip charts) for elicitation events, and scheduled resources (your stakeholders). This means you have set up the meeting time, you have a place to meet, an agenda, and you are ready to go.

Conduct Elicitation Activity (3.2)

Conducting the elicitation means obtaining the information you are looking for. It may require you to read, research, listen, watch, talk, present, or to actually engage in the work of the business to gain a detailed understanding of the information needed.

You will frequently hear people use the words facilitate and facilitation when talking about business analysis. To facilitate means to *make easier*. And, as you recall, to elicit means to *bring forth* or *reveal*. During elicitation, we want to make the *revealing* of information *easier*. Think of a time when you heard two people talking but not understanding each other. If you joined the conversation to clarify and speed their understanding, you acted as a facilitator.

Conduct Elicitation Activity		
Inputs	**Techniques**	**Outputs**
Business Need (5.1)	Brainstorming (9.3)	Elicitation Results (3.2)
Solution Scope (5.4)	Data Dictionary and Glossary (9.5)	
Business Case (5.5)	Document Analysis (9.9)	
Requirements Management Plan (2.5)	Focus Groups (9.11)	
Scheduled Resources (3.1)	Interface Analysis (9.13)	

Conduct Elicitation Activity		
Inputs	**Techniques**	**Outputs**
Supporting Materials (3.1)	Interviews (9.14)	
Organizational Process Assets	Observation (9.18)	
	Prototyping (9.22)	
	Requirements Workshops (9.23)	
	Survey/Questionnaire (9.31)	

BA's Responsibilities in Conducting an Elicitation Activity

- Perform research to find the answers to your questions
- Meet with the stakeholders to obtain the information needed (for elicitation techniques that directly involve stakeholders)
- Listen to stakeholders intently, both their words and their nonverbal communications
- Search for important words and concepts in the information you are provided and connect or *trace* the links between the concepts

What Do You Need to Successfully Conduct an Elicitation Activity?

Conducting elicitation relies on the inputs of the business need, business case, and solution scope to keep the elicitation focused. Additionally, the requirements management plan, created in the Business Analysis Planning and Monitoring knowledge area, specifies where requirements will be stored and what characteristics or *attributes* (discussed in this task) should be collected for each requirement. As your stakeholders tell you what they want, you will have a place to store the information.

The resources and materials you prepared in the previous task are used as inputs for this task. Historical information recorded from elicitation activities on previous, similar projects (part of organizational process assets) will help make your elicitation more effective. OPAs may include templates for surveys or questionnaires, or lessons learned from elicitation activities. For example: A project team gave workshop participants a 20 minute break halfway through the workshop so they could check their messages and get snacks. Participants didn't feel rushed and came back to the session on time.

Collecting Information During Elicitation

During the elicitation event or activity, you may be reading, observing, or listening, while learning lots of information about the business capabilities and requirements. It is important to collect this information as efficiently as possible. There are many ways to take notes during elicitation activities. Find the approach that works best for you by trying different techniques. Continuing to practice a technique will make it easier. Your note taking approach must be quick enough to allow the stakeholder(s) to talk at their own pace.

Note Taking Using Requirements Templates   One way to take notes is to use a template for categorizing requirements as you record them. Since most stakeholders will talk about different types of requirements in the same sentence or paragraph, you need to be able to hear the difference. A simple note taking template helps to minimize missed requirements.

Requirements For Project XYZ	
Business Requirements	
Stakeholder Requests and Requirements	
Functional Requirements	
Non-functional Requirements	
Transition Requirements	

Note Taking Using Diagrams   Many business analysts take notes by drawing a diagram of the business process as the user describes it. This may be a workflow or simple flowchart (diagram without swimlanes). Since many people communicate in a sequential order, drawing a simple diagram showing the steps of a process is often useful. Arrows show direction and decision boxes show different paths. Workflow diagrams, like the one below, will be discussed in the Requirements Analysis chapter.

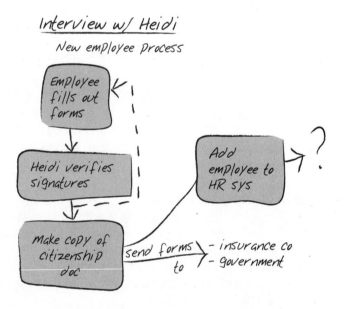

Note Taking Using Mind Maps   A mind map is a free-flowing, yet organized, way to capture notes. The elicitation topic goes in the center and main points are added on long lines radiating out from the center. Subtopics are added on shorter lines branching off of the related main point. This technique is effective because it works in the same way as the human brain. The brain connects every new thought to an existing one. If we can't find a connection between a new thought and an existing one, we have a hard time remembering or learning new information.

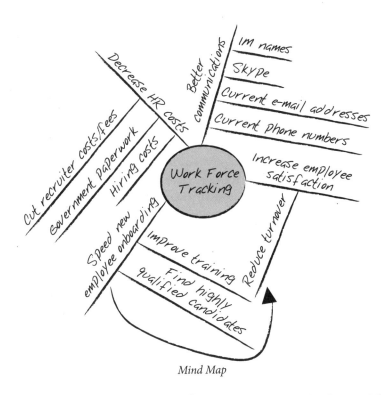

Mind Map

Note Taking Using Audio or Video Recording   Both audio and video recordings are becoming much easier and less expensive to use, so consider them as a note taking alternative. You must get permission from anyone you will be recording and from their management. Explain why you want the recording and how you plan to dispose of it. Determine the level of quality needed. If you are simply going to listen to the interview a second time to validate your notes, you probably don't need a high-quality microphone. If you are going to show a video observation to your team, make sure the sound quality and lighting will support it.

 It sounds easier to record an interview or requirements workshop than to take notes, but keep in mind that listening to the recording takes as long as the event itself, so recording may not be the best use of your time.

Active Listening   During elicitation events, your most important activity will be listening. Much of a message comes across in body language and tone of voice, in addition to what is communicated through words! Therefore, you must learn to "listen" with your eyes, your ears, and your brain, paying attention to all components of the communication. Sometimes the nonverbal message will contradict the words, or strong emotions may prevent a stakeholder from giving you a clear picture of the problem.

Active listening is physically demanding. Studies have shown your temperature, blood pressure, and heart rate all rise when you are actively engaged in listening. Understanding the message can be difficult when the speaker's body language and tone of voice don't match his or her words. Listening involves identifying conflicting inputs and politely asking for clarification. The better your relationship with the stakeholder, the easier the communication will be. *Paraphrasing* involves communicating back to the stakeholder your understanding of the information. This is another important component of listening. A good listener maintains an attitude of curiosity, using eye contact and body language to show interest and confirming understanding as the conversation progresses.

Imagine a human resources administrator telling you his procedure for handling an employee benefit change. He may read the documented procedure to you, but you can tell from his tone and body language that he doesn't follow the procedure. You want to find out why. The procedure may be overly complex or outdated, and he may be reluctant to be honest for fear of being reprimanded for not following procedures. You need to pick up on the nonverbal cues and follow up with questions to show you are not judging him, but rather questioning the procedure. If the procedure is broken, you want to know how best to fix it. This is where the stakeholder's trust in you is important. If he trusts you, the administrator will reveal the truth and help you find the root cause of the business problem. This is *active* listening.

Requirements Tracing

"Tracing" a requirement means linking it or connecting it to other requirements and solution components. Tracing is important because it helps the business analyst make sure nothing is missed and to confirm that requirements are necessary and within scope. During an elicitation activity, think of tracing as a way of making sure you ask questions that help you understand how all the pieces fit together. During an interview, if a stakeholder mentions a piece of information, like "I consider the candidate's educational background when I make a job offer," your job as the analyst is to "trace" the requirement (educational background) to other requirements. You do this by asking follow-up questions such as, "Why is educational background important? What educational background do you hire? What if a candidate has two different degrees? Do all of the hiring managers use this criterion, or only you? Is this a necessary requirement?" And most importantly, "Is this within scope?" Following a requirement to all of its related requirements and components is tracing.

Tracing requirements is also an important part of research techniques including document analysis and interface analysis. We'll talk more about requirements tracing in the Requirements Management and Communication chapter.

Capture Requirements Attributes

Requirements attributes are details or characteristics of requirements that are important to capture during elicitation. Your requirements management plan lists the attributes to be captured (like the complexity and priority of each requirement). During the elicitation activity, look for these characteristics to make sure you have thoroughly gathered all of the important details. We will look at requirements attributes in the Business Analysis Planning and Monitoring chapter.

Gather Metrics

In addition to recording the information you elicit, you should also record time spent on elicitation activities, and the resources involved. It is always a good practice to track the amount of time spent performing each task. A record of the actual time spent on each business analysis activity, and a list of the participants involved provide information for ongoing monitoring of business analysis performance and for lessons learned, which will improve your time estimates on future projects.

> **Examples of Requirements Attributes**
>
> - Absolute reference
> - Author of the requirement
> - Complexity
> - Ownership
> - Priority
> - Risks
> - Source of the requirement
> - Stability
> - Status
> - Urgency

Summary

Conducting an effective elicitation activity requires a note taking strategy and strong communication skills, along with time management, critical thinking skills, and the ability to focus on details. The only outputs of the Conduct Elicitation Activity task are elicitation results (your notes, in whatever format you captured them). These results move directly to the next task of this knowledge area, Document Elicitation Results.

Document Elicitation Results (3.3)

It is your responsibility as a business analyst to document what was learned during elicitation. There are many reasons for documenting the elicitation results:

- To record the results for future reference by yourself or others. You may have taken really good notes, but could someone else review them? Probably not. They need to be reviewed and organized.
- To highlight areas that are still unclear or were missed during the elicitation.
- To help confirm the elicitation results (the next task of this knowledge area).

Document Elicitation Results		
Inputs	**Techniques**	**Outputs**
Elicitation Results (3.2)	Brainstorming (9.3)	Requirements [Stated] (3.3)
	Document Analysis (9.9)	Stakeholder Concerns [Unconfirmed] (3.3)
	Focus Groups (9.11)	
	Interface Analysis (9.13)	
	Interviews (9.14)	
	Observation (9.18)	
	Problem Tracking (9.20)	
	Prototyping (9.22)	
	Requirements Workshops (9.23)	
	Survey/Questionnaire (9.31)	

BA's Responsibilities in Documenting Elicitation Results

- Capture and organize the results of the elicitation activity
- Review and analyze the results to develop follow-up questions
- Identify and track requirements conflicts as they are discovered
- Turn elicitation results into stated requirements
- Prepare to present the stated requirements to stakeholders for confirmation

What Do You Need to Successfully Document Elicitation Results?

This task has only one input, your results from the elicitation activity. These might be handwritten notes, flip charts from a workshop, or simply your recollections.

Document?

Document Elicitation Results is singled out as a separate task in the *BABOK® Guide* because often your notes and recollections are not reliable or useful to anyone other than you! Taking accurate notes during elicitation allows you to review and analyze information after you complete the interview or other activity. As you are reviewing your notes for completeness and clarity, you will find areas that require follow-up questions. You may find conflicting notes indicating inconsistent requirements. When you compare these notes to notes from other elicitation activities, you may find differing answers to the same questions, because stakeholders do things differently and see things from unique perspectives. Analysis of these differences will lead to additional questions. You may find yourself scheduling another elicitation event to follow up on these items. (Remember to prepare for the new event first!)

Please focus on the use of the word *document* in this task. Document is used as a verb, not a noun. Let me explain why this is important. A verb describes an action or activity. "To document" is to make a record of or make a note of. This task does not require you to create a formal document (noun). Don't make the mistake of assuming that a formal document must be produced for the elicitation to be considered successful or complete. Making notes on a whiteboard, flip chart, or napkin all constitute documenting (verb) and qualify as valid ways to record what happened during the elicitation activity. This will be very important when answering exam questions referring to a change-driven software development approach! Some change-driven teams shudder at the term document, because they assume it implies a formal, edited, published deliverable.

In prototyping, the results of the elicitation may be "documented" in working software that your software developer builds after listening to you or your stakeholder describe what is wanted. With the increasing use of change-driven approaches like agile, formal requirements documents are less common. Your business analysis plans will specify how you will document the requirements.

When documents are produced, they are often referred to as deliverables or *artifacts*. Deliverables or artifacts are any product created to communicate business analysis work. Examples include a list of features, a workflow diagram, a requirements package, or meeting minutes.

APPLY YOUR KNOWLEDGE   Which of the following methods have you used to document, present, or confirm requirements?

Requirements Documentation Method	✓
Verbal/conversations	
Structured sentences like "The system shall …"	
Tables or spreadsheets	
Bulleted lists	
Formal requirements packages	
Documents created in office automation software (word processing, spreadsheets, etc.)	
Diagrams	
Requirements management tool	

All of these are valid ways to document elicitation results.

The elicitation results will be captured in different formats and at different levels of formality depending on the content of the conversation, type of project, complexity of the problem/solution, and communication preferences of the stakeholders. It is important that there is some written record of the requirements agreement because in the complexity of our environments, it is easy to forget details agreed upon in discussion. Relying on memory is risky. In addition, verbal communication is often less specific than written, and seeing something in writing makes it more "real" and often reveals different interpretations of the same item.

Summary

Did you notice the input to this task is elicitation results and one of the outputs is requirements? This is an important transformation in business analysis. We have turned *elicitation results* into *requirements*! At this point, they are only *stated* requirements, which means they have not yet been confirmed or approved. You have discovered and recorded them and they will be used in your subsequent analysis work.

Stakeholder concerns are another important output of elicitation. While you are learning about the business and its problems, and discussing possible solutions, you may learn about stakeholder concerns. The more a stakeholder trusts you, the more concerns you will hear. It is important to listen to and note these concerns. These concerns are considered and addressed in Enterprise Analysis, Requirements Analysis, and Solution Assessment and Validation. These outputs also go directly into the next task, Confirm Elicitation Results.

Confirm Elicitation Results (3.4)

Eliciting requirements is an important aspect of understanding user needs, but just as important is confirming your conclusions. Discussing requirements brings up lots of issues, problems, concerns, and ideas. While you are communicating with a stakeholder, the two of you are analyzing as you are talking, listening to each other's questions and answers, and building on each other's thoughts. A meaningful discussion about a business problem and possible solutions is a key part of the analysis process. After a discussion like this, it is important to make notes about the discussion and present your conclusions back to the stakeholder for feedback, corrections, and ultimately confirmation.

Confirm Elicitation Results		
Inputs	**Techniques**	**Outputs**
Requirements [Stated, Unconfirmed] (3.3)	Interviews (9.14)	Requirements [Stated and Confirmed] (3.4)
Stakeholder Concerns [Unconfirmed] (3.3)	Observation (9.18)	Stakeholder Concerns [Confirmed] (3.4)

BA's Responsibilities in Confirming Elicitation Results
- Present requirements and concerns to stakeholders for confirmation
- Make adjustments as necessary
- Get approval of your understanding of the requirements and stakeholder concerns

What Do You Need to Successfully Confirm Elicitation Results?
The inputs to this task are unconfirmed, stated requirements and unconfirmed stakeholder concerns, (the outputs of Document Elicitation Results). These requirements and concerns are presented to the stakeholder(s) for confirmation in this task. Notice the outputs of this task are *confirmed* requirements and *confirmed* stakeholder concerns. The inputs are the same as the outputs, except they have progressed to a different *state*, from *unconfirmed* to *confirmed*.

 I recommend you present elicitation results the next day or even the next week after the elicitation event. When stakeholders return to their business and working environment, they will think about what was discussed in your elicitation event. They may think of other relevant information they forgot to tell you. By allowing time to pass before presenting the results, you will give the stakeholders a chance to correct and refine the information they shared with you. The elicitation results will therefore be more accurate.

How Do You Confirm Results?

You may use rough notes to confirm understanding with your stakeholders, or you may prepare a formal document or package. (We'll look at requirements packages in the Requirements Management and Communication chapter.) Confirmation ensures you correctly understood the requirements provided during the elicitation. Even if you use a technique that doesn't involve stakeholders, like document analysis or interface analysis, you always need to confirm your understanding with your stakeholders.

The formality of the presentation and the format of written documentation will be different for each situation. In traditional software development waterfall methodologies, requirements are documented in very formal packages with executive summaries and long textual descriptions. In change-driven approaches like agile or Scrum, requirements are discussed with the team, summarized in a backlog list or in a user story, and built quickly for review. In architecture and engineering projects, requirements are presented in blueprints, pictures, models, and other graphic formats. For a business process change, the new procedure might be shown in a workflow diagram or a set of sequentially numbered steps. All of these approaches are valid ways to present your findings and get confirmation.

Summary

When this task is complete, the requirements and stakeholder concerns are confirmed as stated. This doesn't mean the requirements are approved, it only means that we accurately heard what our stakeholders told us. Now that we know what the stakeholders have asked for, we can use these stated requirements to perform requirements analysis: prioritizing, specifying, modeling, and getting approval of requirements, and thinking about solution alternatives to satisfy the business need. These requirements are used in every other knowledge area!

———— ELICITATION KNOWLEDGE AREA TECHNIQUES ————

Each technique referenced in the Elicitation knowledge area has unique characteristics that support effective communications. Different situations call for different techniques. Sometimes you may use more than one technique to address the same problem—you may find that each technique will help to expose new information. Most techniques describe how to conduct and document elicitation activities. A couple of the techniques are used to confirm results. Be sure you can define and describe each technique.

Elicitation Knowledge Area Techniques										
	Brainstorming	Data Dictionary and Glossary	Document Analysis	Focus Groups	Interface Analysis	Interviews	Observation	Problem Tracking	Prototyping	Requirements Workshops	Survey/ Questionnaire
Prepare for Elicitation	X		X	X	X	X	X		X	X	X
Conduct Elicitation Activity	X	X	X	X	X	X	X		X	X	X
Document Elicitation Results	X		X	X	X	X	X	X	X	X	X
Confirm Elicitation Results						X	X				

Notice only two techniques can be used to confirm elicitation results (interviews and observation). This can be confusing because no matter what technique you use to elicit, all elicitation results must be confirmed. Watch for this as you learn about each technique.

Brainstorming (9.3)

Brainstorming is a great way to encourage people to think creatively and to generate new ideas. This activity requires only a group of people, a topic, and a timing device. To facilitate a brainstorming session, give the group a limited amount of time, maybe two to three minutes, to generate as many ideas as possible around a topic. Do not allow any evaluation or discussion of the ideas. The time limit puts participants under a little pressure and forces them to voice ideas before their brain has time to evaluate them and rule them out. Many of the ideas generated during brainstorming may be silly, not feasible, or too costly, but sometimes a unique, creative idea comes out and your organization benefits from a truly innovative change. Brainstorming is particularly useful when a team is having trouble generating ideas. Once a group has generated a list of ideas, they typically consider each idea and narrow down the list to the ones that seem to have the most potential and should be pursued.

Brainstorming can be done in person, virtually via chat, or even via e-mail. Brainstorming virtually may be more effective than in person because people may feel more comfortable submitting ideas anonymously rather than stating them in the group.

APPLY YOUR KNOWLEDGE   Set a timer for two minutes and write down as many ideas as you can for the following question. Force yourself to keep writing for the entire two minutes.

What can I do to make sure I pass the CBAP® or CCBA® exam on my first try?

You probably came up with at least one outlandish idea. You also probably came up with several reasonable ideas. Imagine if five other people were also thinking about the same question. One of you is bound to come up with an outstanding idea.

EXERCISE Think about how you would elicit using brainstorming.

Elicitation Knowledge Area Task	Specific Work When Using Brainstorming
Prepare for Elicitation	
Conduct Elicitation Activity	
Document Elicitation Results	
Confirm Elicitation Results	

ANSWER

Elicitation Knowledge Area Task	Specific Work When Using Brainstorming
Prepare for Elicitation	• Frame the topic as a simple question. • Select and invite appropriate participants. • Determine how ideas will be recorded (as fast as possible; do not let recording slow the process). • Determine how you will evaluate ideas after the list of responses is developed. • Have a timing device.
Conduct Elicitation Activity	• Explain brainstorming rules to the group. • Make sure participants are alert and ready to begin. • Start the timer. • Collect ideas without comment or discussion. • Use your evaluation method to narrow down the list or select one idea, if appropriate.
Document Elicitation Results	• Keep the initial list of ideas, or just the narrowed down list. • Document the final result and the rationale (this can often be done during the session). • Distribute the final list of ideas, if appropriate.
Confirm Elicitation Results	• Brainstorming cannot be used to confirm elicitation results, but the results of your brainstorming session must be confirmed! Confirm results with involved stakeholders using an *interview*.

APPLY YOUR KNOWLEDGE   If you have never participated in a brainstorming session, conduct one. Ask your family or friends to spend a few minutes with you, allowing you to practice the technique. Give the group a fun problem to solve (e.g., where should I go on vacation?) and watch the great ideas develop!

Data Dictionary and Glossary (9.5)

It would be difficult to conduct a meaningful elicitation activity without a shared language. Having agreed-upon terms with common definitions is a basic need for all elicitation. A glossary of terms and definitions is an important component of requirements. Most business analysts start with existing terms and their definitions from other projects. During every elicitation activity, you should confirm key terms are included in your list and make a note of any terms that are used inconsistently from one source to another. A data dictionary is a more detailed list of data elements with definitions along with data characteristics. We'll look at an example of a data dictionary in the Requirements Analysis chapter. With respect to elicitation, the definitions and consistent use of terms are keys to success.

Document Analysis (9.9)

Most organizations and industries have hundreds, if not thousands, of documents explaining what they do and why they do it. This rich resource is one you can access and learn from without using the time of any stakeholders. Reviewing documentation is a great way to become familiar with a company, industry, or business domain when beginning a new assignment. It also can be a good way to learn about software applications. An experienced business analyst knows how to find the information needed and how to critique the quality of the information. Be aware that some documents may be out-of-date, or may not reflect the true workflow. Document analysis is eliciting information from documents.

 If documents are out-of-date, is it worth your time to review them? Often the answer is yes. Some documents can be a good introduction to a topic and a source of questions for your elicitation events, even if they seem dated. Your first questions might be "Is this procedure up-to-date? If not, what do you do differently from the procedure? Why?"

Document Examples

- Corporate annual report
- Regulations
- Operating procedures
- Vendor software application brochures and manuals
- Employee procedure manuals
- Existing requirements documents
- Industry publications

APPLY YOUR KNOWLEDGE There are many requirements in existing documentation. Data elements, business processes, and business rules are embedded in descriptions of work and software. What documents have you used to learn about a business domain?

Document	What Did You Learn?

EXERCISE Think about how you would use document analysis to elicit information.

Elicitation Knowledge Area Task	Specific Work When Using Document Analysis
Prepare for Elicitation	
Conduct Elicitation Activity	
Document Elicitation Results	
Confirm Elicitation Results	

ANSWER

Elicitation Knowledge Area Task	Specific Work When Using Document Analysis
Prepare For Elicitation	• Search for electronic or hard copy documents in your organization's offices. • Ask people about available documents. • Determine what you are looking for and how much time you have to spend in the search.
Conduct Elicitation Activity	• Determine the creation date, last update, and author of the document. • Review each document to get an overview of its contents. • Read the sections that will provide the information you need. • Make notes about your findings and make copies of important sections/pages.

Elicitation Knowledge Area Task	Specific Work When Using Document Analysis
Document Elicitation Results	• Create drafts of current business models from the documentation • Record business rules, data used, processes identified and parties involved.
Confirm Elicitation Results	Document analysis cannot be used to confirm elicitation results but the results of your document analysis must be confirmed! Confirm results with involved stakeholders using an *interview*, or using *observation* (when you have elicited information about a current process).

ACTIVITY What do you think are the advantages and disadvantages of document analysis?

Advantages	Disadvantages

SAMPLE ANSWER

Advantages	Disadvantages
Good place to start if you don't know much about the business	Documents may be out-of-date or inaccurate
Good way to double-check other information or requirements	Can be time-consuming
Takes advantage of information that has already been captured	Only useful for learning about current capabilities

Focus Groups (9.11)

For many years, marketing groups have been "eliciting requirements" without calling it that. Focus groups were developed by marketers who wanted to have their customers' perspectives on new product ideas before the product was released. The purpose of a focus group is to get very specific feedback on a new product or service, or to get more general information about where the market is heading and to generate new product ideas.

The selection of participants is usually random within a set of predefined characteristics (e.g., demographics, buying history). The more characteristics specified, the more *homogeneous* the group. A *heterogeneous* group is more random, leading to a broader range of opinions. Participants may not be told why they have been selected or the purpose of the focus group. They are usually offered an incentive to participate. They rarely receive any follow-up results or confirmation.

The preparation for a focus group involves selecting participants, designing questions and/or activities to generate discussion, and recording participant opinions. During the session, participants are encouraged to discuss their thoughts, preferences, and perceptions. The person who runs the focus group is referred to as the moderator. Focus groups are usually limited to a small group (6-12) to allow for comfortable discussions.

The findings of a focus group may be referred to as *themes* or a report. They include conclusions and recommendations for the product or service discussed. Results will be reviewed with internal marketing stakeholders who represent the customers.

Have you ever attended or moderated a focus group? If you have, exam questions on this technique should be quite easy for you. Map your experience to the Elicitation knowledge area tasks. Even if you were just a participant, can you imagine how the facilitator prepared, elicited, and documented the results?

Let me share an experience with you.

Focus Groups in Action

An independent marketing research firm invited me to participate in a focus group on the car tire purchasing habits of women, offering $100 for three hours of my time! The focus group was held at a tire store. When I arrived, I was greeted by the moderator and her team. She had a camera set up to record the session. There were eight women in the group and we were seated in a circle in the center of the store. The moderator started by asking a series of questions, including: "How do you know when you need new tires for your car?" and "What brand do you usually buy?" After she posed each question, she allowed the group to talk freely, with participants discussing their answers and playing off of each other's experience. She did not lead the discussion or try to get everyone to participate. This was a warm-up period for us to get to know each other and share as we felt comfortable. After this warm-up, she asked us more specific questions ("Where did you buy your most recent set of tires?" and "How many did you buy at one time?") and went around the circle to get an answer from every participant. During the last part of the focus group, we were introduced to a tire store salesperson. We were asked to participate in a role play as a typical customer entering the store and being approached by the salesperson. He asked us if he could help us and proceeded to determine our needs and make the sale. Periodically during the role play, the moderator would ask the group to comment on how we felt the salesperson was doing. Did we want to be approached as soon as we entered the store, or did we want to look around first? Was he intimidating, or were we comfortable talking with him? At the end of the session, we were given sodas and snacks and we each received a brand new $100 bill. The salesperson and moderator thanked us for our time and we left promptly at the scheduled ending time.

 Review the *BABOK® Guide* discussion of the advantages and disadvantages of focus groups (9.11) now.

EXERCISE Think about how you could use a focus group to elicit requirements.

Elicitation Knowledge Area Task	Specific Work When Using a Focus Group
Prepare for Elicitation	
Conduct Elicitation Activity	
Document Elicitation Results	

ANSWER

Elicitation Knowledge Area Task	Specific Work When Using a Focus Group
Prepare for Elicitation	• Identify targeted participant characteristics (e.g., demographics, gender, buying history). • Determine number of participants, incentive (if any), date, and location. • Select/invite participants. • Obtain camera or other recording device. • Obtain incentives and refreshments if desired. • Develop an agenda with questions and/or activities.
Conduct Elicitation Activity	• Welcome participants and make them feel comfortable. • Start the recording device. • Follow the agenda as closely as possible. • Adjust or ask additional questions as appropriate. • Thank participants and provide the promised incentives.
Document Elicitation Results	• Record the session. • Have someone from the facilitation team take notes. • Review the recording for detailed analysis and conclusions.

Interface Analysis (9.13)

Interfaces are connections between people or systems. Interfaces can be manual (I give information to a co-worker over the phone) or automated (I e-mail information to my co-worker). Interface analysis is probably the most unusual elicitation technique, because it is both a discovery and analysis technique. We need to identify or discover all of the interfaces of the business domain with other people and systems, and we need to analyze each connection to determine if it needs to change and how best to change it.

In our Workforce Tracking case study, when the HR department sends payroll data to their outside payroll servicer for processing, there is an interface (probably an electronic file transfer). When an employee contacts HR to change his address or phone number, there is an interface. When a user enters a new employee into the HR system, he is using a *user interface*. Interfaces move information from one place to another.

Interface analysis involves two components:
• Identifying all of the interfaces for the solution
• Defining (or writing requirements for) each one

To determine which parties interface with the solution, the business analyst elicits information from the stakeholders. You should begin identifying interfaces early in the project, while scoping the solution, because the number and complexity of interfaces will impact the time estimate for completion of the analysis.

Types of Interfaces

User Interface   The most common interface is a user interface. Human beings (users) interface with a system (hardware or software) to accomplish work. For example:

* An HR adminstrator may log into a network to query an employee status.
* A system may generate a report of sales totals that is used by a worker to monitor inventory levels.

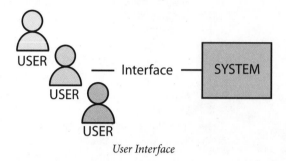

User Interface

System-to-System Interface   When two systems communicate directly, the interface is automated, or automatic. These can be hardware or software connections. Most websites that accept credit card payments have an automated interface with the credit card processing company. The website sends the credit card information along with the payment amount to the credit card processing system and the credit card processing system returns an acceptance or denial of the payment. The requirements for this type of interface are fairly technical, usually including things like the communications protocol, data transmission format, and data encryption algorithms.

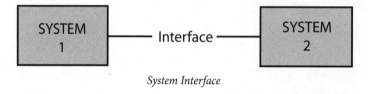

System Interface

Identifying Interfaces

Interfaces are often identified during initial solution scope meetings. Identifying and analyzing existing interfaces is a great way to understand the current business and technology. In addition, discussing future interfaces during solution scoping improves business analysis planning and estimating. Interfaces provide the information needed for a business area to do its work. Interfaces also send information from the business to outside parties who need the results.

Context Diagram   The context diagram we created to document the solution scope can be used to identify interfaces.

You'll remember from Enterprise Analysis that the domain or solution is in the center, and the interfacing organizations and systems are around the outside. The boxes on the outside of the circle are called external agents, external entities, or just externals. These boxes represent the parties involved with the solution that are *outside* the scope of the solution. Each data flow arrow shows that information must move between the external and the solution: an interface. Interfaces may be manual (e.g., phone call), user interface (e.g., entry screen), automated (e.g., file transmission), or a combination.

In the Worker Equipment Tracking example, there are five parties (organizations, people, or systems) that interface with the solution.

While this diagram helps to identify some of the interfaces, it does not show them all. Additional user interfaces must be identified and analyzed as well.

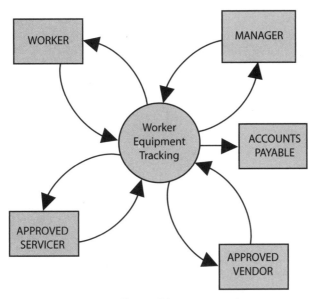

Context Diagram

Every solution has at least one external or, in other words, at least one interface. And every interface will probably involve at least one stakeholder, many of whom will be external to the organization. For example, if your solution will interface with a regulatory agency, you probably will have a contact person at that agency with whom you will communicate. Can you see that interface analysis is also a useful technique for identifying stakeholders?

Use Case Diagram   Another useful technique for interface analysis is the use case diagram. You will recall a discussion of this technique in the Enterprise Analysis chapter. The use case diagram shows a system boundary (typically software) along with the people or other systems (actors) with which it interacts or interfaces.

In a use case diagram, actors (organizations, people, and systems) are shown as stick figures, with association lines to each use case with which they participate. Use cases are functions that will be included in the software—the goals of the system. So each association line represents an interface.

To identify *user interfaces*, look for actors that represent people. These are end users of the software. Whenever there is an association line from an end user to the system, you need to define a user interface (screen or report layout) that will allow the user to access the system.

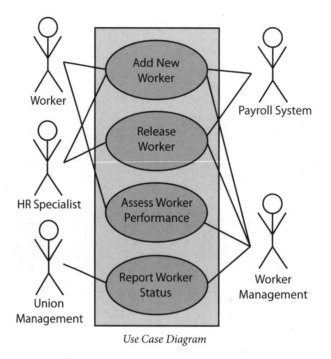

Use Case Diagram

Defining Interfaces

Each interface should be analyzed and defined as part of the solution requirements.

Type of Interfaces	How Are They Defined?
Human-to-Human, Manual Interfaces	These connections are usually defined in employee procedure manuals and department guidelines in the business. Business analysts often help write and update these documents as part of their transition requirements.
User Interfaces	Screen and report prototypes, along with use case descriptions, user stories, and scenarios, are used to define user interfaces. You will learn about the prototyping technique in this chapter and the other techniques in the Requirements Analysis chapter.
System-to-System Interfaces	When data is electronically sent, technical requirements describe how each piece of information will be transmitted. Data may require special formatting, consolidation, summarization, encryption, or translation. Business analysts often work with implementation SMEs to develop these requirements, making sure the business information is accurately sent and received by each interface. Many of the requirements techniques in Requirements Analysis are used to document interface requirements.

EXERCISE Think about how interface analysis could be used for elicitation.

Elicitation Knowledge Area Task	Specific Work When Using Interface Analysis
Prepare for Elicitation	
Conduct Elicitation Activity	
Document Elicitation Results	
Confirm Elicitation Results	

ANSWER

Elicitation Knowledge Area Task	Specific Work When Using Interface Analysis
Prepare for Elicitation	• Identify all existing interfaces with people, organizations, and systems. • Research details on how the existing interfaces work (manually, file transfer, online screens). • Consider new interfaces that may be needed for the solution.
Conduct Elicitation Activity	• Talk with software developers about current automated interfaces (file transfers, etc.) and learn as much as you can about how the technology works. • Review screens and reports and learn how stakeholders use them.

Elicitation Knowledge Area Task	Specific Work When Using Interface Analysis
Document Elicitation Results	• Create a list of interfaces, a context diagram, and/or a use case diagram showing interfaces. • Refer to existing documentation on current interfaces and include notes on how these might change. • Describe new interfaces with screen prototypes, data elements lists, or other detailed specifications.
Confirm Elicitation Results	Interface analysis cannot be used to confirm elicitation results, but the results of your interface analysis research must be confirmed. You will use interviewing and/or observation to confirm your understanding: • Review the list of interfaces with stakeholders • Review your understanding of the current interfaces • Confirm the specifications for new interfaces

Interviews (9.14)

Interviewing is probably the most commonly used elicitation technique for business analysis. Interviews can be *structured* or *unstructured*. They can be conducted with as few as two people (the interviewer and the interviewee) or as many as five or six interviewees. Interviews can last between a few minutes and two hours. They can cover one specific topic or a whole list of topics. As a business analyst, you should be comfortable designing, planning, scheduling, conducting, and reporting results of interviews. Let's look at some best practices.

Preparing for an Interview

Review the business analysis plan when preparing for an interview. On a large project, the plan may only include a high-level description of elicitation events. Some project plans may include detailed guidelines for conducting interviews and other elicitations. Before beginning an interview, be sure you have answered all of the following questions.

Who?   Whom will you interview? How many stakeholders will be in each interview? What position(s) do they hold in the organization? How involved are they on the project? What is their background? Stakeholder analysis is a key part of preparing for an interview. Ideally these details are available in your business analysis communication plan. The more you know about each stakeholder, the better you can prepare.

What?   What information do you expect to gain from the stakeholder? What is his or her area of expertise? What questions will you ask?

Where?   Where does the stakeholder work? Where will you conduct the interview? Selecting a place with limited interruptions will save time, but interviewing a stakeholder in his or her work environment will also give you valuable information.

When?   When will the interview be conducted? Always try to accommodate your stakeholder's schedule and preferences when scheduling an interview.

Why?   Why are you conducting this interview? Do you and your stakeholder understand why you are spending this time together?

How?   How will you conduct the interview? Will you conduct the interview in person? By phone? In writing? Virtually? Will you provide the interviewee with your questions in advance? How will you record the answers? How will you confirm your understanding? How will you follow up afterward?

Try to keep each interview focused on one or two major topics that can be discussed within a period of no more than two hours. Short, focused interviews will be more productive for you and your stakeholders, as these detailed conversations can be intense and tiring. After a couple of hours, the effectiveness will probably diminish. Schedule additional interviews if you need more time.

Know the Steps to Conducting an Interview
1. Prepare.
   - Develop questions *before* setting up the interview
   - Create an agenda
   - Schedule a beginning and ending time
   - Be well-rested and ready to *listen*
2. Conduct.
   - Adhere to your agenda and schedule
   - Begin by explaining the purpose of the interview
   - Take notes
   - Paraphrase information back to the interviewee
3. Close.
   - End with an explanation of the next steps and a thank you
4. Confirm.
   - Send elicitation results to interviewee for confirmation or meet for a second interview

To prepare your interview questions, use the Who, What, Where, When, Why, and How list to think about what requirements are relevant to the project. Consider when to ask open-ended questions versus closed-ended questions. Open-ended questions require the interviewee to explain a process or rationale, and encourage more discussion. For example, "How do you decide to approve an employee transfer request?" Open-ended questions are most often asked early in the project, when you are trying to learn as much as possible. Closed-ended questions require a yes or no answer. For example, "Do all new employees get a computer?" As you refine your understanding and work on solution design, closed-ended questions will be useful in getting specific solution and transition requirements. For example, "Do you want the website to send you an e-mail when an employee requests a transfer?"

APPLY YOUR KNOWLEDGE   What do you think are the advantages and disadvantages of an interview?

Advantages	Disadvantages

Review the *BABOK® Guide* description of the interviews technique (9.14) now to confirm your answers.

Follow Up After an Interview

To get the most value from an interview:
- Review notes immediately after the interview.
- Develop follow-up questions.
- Conduct a second interview or follow-up phone call.

 When you schedule an interview, schedule a second meeting with yourself immediately afterward while the discussion is still fresh in your mind. If you don't have an office with a door, reserve a conference room where you can work without distraction. Review your notes, filling in missing pieces from the conversation. Think about questions you forgot or didn't have enough time to ask. List your follow-up questions and determine how best to ask them (via e-mail, phone, or another interview).

EXERCISE   Think about how interviews are used to elicit.

Elicitation Knowledge Area Task	Specific Work When Using an Interview
Prepare for Elicitation	
Conduct Elicitation Activity	
Document Elicitation Results	
Confirm Elicitation Results	

ANSWER

Elicitation Knowledge Area Task	Specific Work When Using an Interview
Prepare for Elicitation	• Plan the logistics of the interview (time, date, place, communication media). • Schedule time with your interviewee(s). • Decide how you will take notes (e.g., shorthand, mind map, requirements template, audio recording). • Develop your list of questions and estimate time required for each answer.
Conduct Elicitation Activity	• Introduce yourself and explain the purpose of the project and the interview. • Ask your questions, one at a time, allowing time for the interviewee(s) to think about each answer and to explain fully. • Watch for nonverbal cues, listen to tone of voice, look for inconsistencies between words and body language. • Ask follow-up questions for answers that are unclear. • Paraphrase back to the interviewee(s) as you receive each answer. • Make notes. • Tell the interviewee(s) how you plan to confirm your understanding with them.
Document Elicitation Results	• Review notes taken during the session and transfer requirements to your requirements repository, document, or notes. • Develop follow-up questions.
Confirm Elicitation Results	• Provide notes, documents, diagrams, etc. to interviewee(s) for confirmation, or schedule a meeting to verbally confirm understanding. • Receive clarifications and confirmation.

Observation (9.18)

Observation is a great way to learn about business processes and get a feel for the work environment of your stakeholders. Observation usually requires you to travel to the stakeholders' workplace and watch as real work is being done. You may also be able to "watch" stakeholders use a software application by remotely logging onto their system and observing their desktops. The information gathered during observation is often referred to as the *as-is* model or *current state* of the business. Watching how work is performed can help you recommend changes and solution alternatives.

Several things are accomplished when you use observation for eliciting requirements. You see how work is actually done, rather than having someone tell you how it *should* be done. You see problems and exceptions as they arise during the work. You see how many different processes are going on at the same time and how many interruptions workers experience during the process. You may see how one worker performs the task differently than another.

Know the Rules to Follow When Using Observation

1. Speak to the business manager ahead of time to get approval for the observation, and get his or her recommendations about whom to observe, what to observe, and the best days/times.
2. Let everyone being observed know what you are doing and why. Make it clear you are studying the process, not evaluating their work performance.
3. Take notes, videotape (with permission), capture screen actions, record as much as possible.
4. Schedule time to return and confirm your models/documents/understanding and ask follow-up questions.
5. Thank the participants.

Variations of the Observation Technique

Passive or Invisible Observation Passive observation involves observing workers without having any conversation or interaction. Passive observation is the least disruptive to the business because you don't interrupt work. Unfortunately, you may miss details and, without being able to ask questions, have to observe for a longer period of time. Audio and video recordings are great ways to capture observations.

Active or Visible Observation Active observation involves asking questions or actually doing work alongside the stakeholders, and can be more effective for gathering detailed information. Working in the business environment allows you to not only learn how the work is done, but also to learn how the workers feel when doing it. This can help you design a solution that workers will adapt to easily. It also enhances relationships with business stakeholders.

EXERCISE Think about how observation is used to elicit.

Elicitation Knowledge Area Task	Specific Work When Using Observation
Prepare for Elicitation	
Conduct Elicitation Activity	

Elicitation Knowledge Area Task	Specific Work When Using Observation
Document Elicitation Results	
Confirm Elicitation Results	

ANSWER

Elicitation Knowledge Area Task	Specific Work When Using Observation
Prepare for Elicitation	• Determine the type of work you need to observe. • Talk to the business area manager(s) to explain your request, get permission, and determine whom you should observe. • Contact the workers to be observed to schedule a convenient observation time. • Make travel plans to get to the observation.
Conduct Elicitation Activity	• Introduce yourself to the workers being observed. • Explain your goal and your approach (active or passive). • Watch, listen, and record what you observe. • Ask questions (if you are performing an active observation). • Capture metrics (e.g., number of transactions performed, time required per transaction, number of interruptions, response time of software or hardware used). • Note exceptions, error handling, and variations from the typical business process.
Document Elicitation Results	• Capture as-is processes, data, and business rules. • Draw workflow diagrams where useful. • Compare observation notes to documented procedures, make notes about differences for follow-up elicitation.
Confirm Elicitation Results	• Schedule follow-up meetings with workers who were observed and their managers. • Ask follow-up questions. • Present notes, diagrams, and findings. • Get clarification and confirmation.

APPLY YOUR KNOWLEDGE   What do you think are the advantages and disadvantages of observation?

Advantages	Disadvantages

SAMPLE ANSWER

Advantages	Disadvantages
Good place to start if you don't know much about the business	Not good for intellectual, non-physical work that is difficult to observe (e.g., decision making)
Get a realistic picture of the business processes	Can be time-consuming
Shows the environment in which the stakeholders operate, including informal communications	Only useful for learning about current capabilities
	May be disruptive to workers
	You may not see all possible exceptions to the regular procedures

Problem Tracking (9.20)

The problem tracking technique is used to manage and resolve problems throughout business analysis. You'll see this technique used in many tasks. Problems identified and tracked in elicitation are usually conflicting requirements: one stakeholder wants a requirement that conflicts with the needs of another stakeholder. Keeping track of conflicting requirements as they are discovered is the responsibility of the business analyst. Most analysts use a problem tracking log or issue list for this purpose. As each issue is addressed, the resolution is documented in the issue log. Resolving a requirements issue may involve going back to your stakeholders to discuss the conflicting opinions.

Prototyping (9.22)

Prototyping is creating a picture or model of the final product so stakeholders can "see" what it will look like and possibly experience how it will work (a simulation). Are you surprised to see prototyping as an elicitation technique? This technique combines elicitation, requirements analysis, and solution design into one activity. Getting three things done at once makes this a popular technique. It is a powerful way to visualize solution ideas and confirm solution designs. A stakeholder may request a web page for customers to browse a product catalog, but when she sees a screen layout or *mockup*, she may not like the way the products look on the screen. Iteratively showing solution ideas and getting stakeholder feedback help stakeholders more accurately express their needs.

Types of Prototypes

Prototypes can be developed in many different ways. They can be simple, hand-drawn mockups or they can be sophisticated, realistic looking designs. Prototypes that are simple and easy-to-create are referred to as *low-fidelity*. They just give the users an idea of how the solution would look and are considered *throw-aways*. They might be hand-drawn or created with a simple drawing tool.

High-fidelity prototypes are built in the same environment as the final product would be built. If you were considering a new website, the prototype could be a set of sample web pages so users could see exactly what the final solution would look like. High-fidelity prototypes that have some working functionality are referred to as *simulations*, where users can actually test the solution. Sometimes the development of a prototype evolves into the working product. These prototypes are called *evolutionary* and are used in most change-driven software development approaches. A set of prototypes can be referred to as a model.

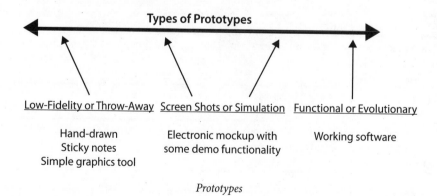

Prototypes

Another aspect of prototyping is the width and depth of the model. A *horizontal* prototype spans a wide range of the business solution. In the case of a new website, it might include high-level screen layouts for each of the major functions to be available on the website. A *vertical* prototype drills down into more detail on a particular function.

Prototypes for Workforce Tracking

Horizontal Prototyping →

	Add New Employee	Release Employee	Transfer Employee	Change Employee Profile	Order New Equipment
Vertical Prototyping ↓	Web page to allow data entry of employee profile	Web page to allow entry of reason for release	Web page to enter new manager and job description	Web page to allow changes to addresses and phone numbers	Web page to allow entry of request
	Web page to allow data entry of job description and department			Web page to allow changes to marital status and number of dependents	Web page to check status of order
	Web page to allow data entry of benefits information				

A *storyboard* is a series of screen layouts that show how the screens will relate to one another. Review the example of a storyboard. Imagine you are starting your own online business to sell cookies made with your grandma's secret recipe. You want to design a website to sell the cookies.

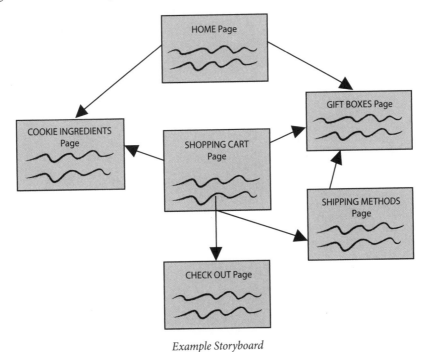

Example Storyboard

This is also an example of horizontal prototyping, because it covers a wide section of functionality without lots of details. It is low-fidelity, since it is a simple drawing without any realistic details.

A storyboard is also referred to as a dialog map, dialog hierarchy, or navigation flow.

Choose the Fastest, Lowest Cost Method of Communication to Effectively Present Your Prototype

Choosing a type of prototype requires you to think about the purpose of this activity. Low-fidelity, handwritten designs made with sticky notes and markers can often generate a meaningful conversation and result in an agreement about the solution direction. There are sophisticated tools that can be used to build online prototypes and simulations. Simulations allow the user to try out the application, navigating between screens and entering some data. A working prototype or simulation allows users to "test drive" the solution. These may be important for high-risk applications or very expensive development projects. Consider who will be building the solution. If your development team is offshore and/or outsourced, your prototype may be included as part of the contract requirements and, as such, should be well-reviewed and tested. If your team is working in an agile or change-driven environment, the developer may work with you, prototyping and building pieces of the potential solution as the requirements are presented. Be sure to discuss all of these options with your team and project manager to make sure you select the right approach. Also consider to whom you are presenting when determining the level of detail to use.

 High-fidelity, working prototypes can give stakeholders the false impression that the solution is done. Be sure to set user expectations about the timeframe for completion when designing prototypes.

EXERCISE Below is an example of a prototype for entering employee profile information. Answer the following questions about this example.

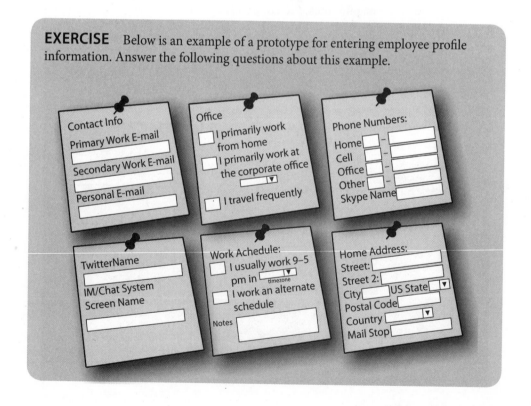

Would you categorize this as low- or high-fidelity?	
Would you consider this a throw-away?	
Is this vertical or horizontal?	

ANSWER

Would you categorize this as low- or high- fidelity?	Low-fidelity
Would you consider this a throw-away?	Yes
Is this vertical or horizontal?	Vertical, because it contains lots of details about one particular part of the solution

Building a prototype is an iterative process with users frequently changing their minds about where something should appear on a screen or how the columns should look on a report. Low-fidelity prototypes are easy to change and are therefore the most efficient approach to use in early prototyping meetings.

APPLY YOUR KNOWLEDGE   What do you think are the advantages and disadvantages of prototyping?

Advantages	Disadvantages

SAMPLE ANSWER

Advantages	Disadvantages
Low-fidelity prototypes are a quick, easy way for users to "see" the design ideas	High-fidelity prototypes can be expensive and time-consuming to build
Evolutionary prototyping can speed development time	Users may think the prototype is the working software and be disappointed when it cannot be rolled out immediately
Iterative nature of prototyping includes feedback from users early in the process	Users can get distracted by the visual design of the product and forget about important requirements

Understand the terms used to describe prototypes, and expect exam questions on these different types of prototypes.

Best Practices for Prototyping

Utilize Human Factors and Usability Experts if Available   Professionals who specialize in user interface design are referred to as usability engineers, human factors experts, or usability experts (UX) and they focus on creating easy-to-use solutions. These professionals are implementation SMEs who help with designing and building the solution. They are considered members of the business analysis discipline because they also elicit, analyze, and solve business problems. When your solution includes user interfaces, enlist the help of a usability expert if you can.

Know the Technical Limitations of the Solution   Be sure you understand the technical limitations of the environment so you can accurately set business stakeholder expectations. For example, if your technical environment doesn't support hover messages, be sure screen labels are very clear.

Utilize Screen Standards and Existing Applications to Ensure Consistency   When creating a prototype, be aware of the organization's screen standards as well as the other software applications the users will access. For example, if other systems have dropdown menus, use a similar format on new screens as well. Making applications consistent with each other increases worker productivity because it eases the cognitive load. This requires you to understand your users and their work. Hopefully you will have time to learn about the business before you start designing a solution (either as part of this project, or outside the project during Enterprise Analysis). The better you understand your user's environment and day-to-day work, the better you will be able to recommend a design that will support them.

Understand Your User Profiles   A user profile or user class is a description of a user or group of users. The profile might include characteristics such as educational background, experience, or industry knowledge. These descriptions of user groups or classes will help your team design a solution that supports good usability principles.

EXERCISE   You have been asked to elicit requirements for a smart phone application that allows employees to scan receipts and track their travel expenses. The developers of this application work in the same building as you do. What type of prototype would you use? Why?

Low- or high-fidelity?	
Horizontal or vertical?	
Throw-away or evolutionary?	

SAMPLE ANSWER   You could start by reviewing existing smart phone apps to get ideas. Then, because the developers are onsite, you could sketch out a few screens (low-fidelity prototypes) and have the developers review them for feasibility. It will probably be just as fast to have the developers build the software and make adjustments to it based on user feedback than to build a simulation.

Low- or high-fidelity?	Start with low-fidelity to quickly get agreement on the direction of the design.
Horizontal or vertical?	Since the application is fairly narrow and detailed (receipts and expenses), a vertical approach is best.
Throw-away or evolutionary?	Since developers are onsite, they could build working software, get user feedback and incorporate changes to produce the final product (evolutionary).

EXERCISE Think about how prototyping work fits into the tasks of Elicitation.

Elicitation Knowledge Area Task	Specific Work When Using Prototyping
Prepare for Elicitation	
Conduct Elicitation Activity	
Document Elicitation Results	
Confirm Elicitation Results	

ANSWER

Elicitation Knowledge Area Task	Specific Work When Using Prototyping
Prepare For Elicitation	• Review standards and existing applications. • Identify requirements specific to this function. (What data needs to be on the screen? What are the edits? Who will have access?) • Draft an initial design to initiate the conversation.
Conduct Elicitation Activity	• Review draft prototype and/or existing solutions with similar functionality. • Utilize a whiteboard or software prototyping tool to make changes and brainstorm ideas. • Refine the prototype through iterations. • Double-check prototype against known requirements. • Capture any additional requirements as they are discovered.
Document Elicitation Results	• "Clean up" the prototype developed during the session. • Have a technician build a simulation or working prototype if appropriate.
Confirm Elicitation Results	Prototyping cannot be used to confirm elicitation results, but your prototypes need to be confirmed! You must confirm the prototype meets the needs of the users and you will use the *interviewing* technique. • Present the prototype to the stakeholders and potential users for feedback. • Capture suggested changes. • Get approval for going forward.

An exam question states that you are working with stakeholders to design a data entry screen, and asks you to identify the elicitation technique you are using. Are you prototyping or performing interface analysis? You are expected to answer "prototyping" because it is considered an elicitation event with stakeholders actively involved. Interface analysis is a research-oriented elicitation activity.

Requirements Workshops (9.23)

A requirements workshop is a group discussion with key stakeholders who are impacted by the same requirements. This is also referred to as joint application design (JAD). Participants discuss their individual needs and preferences and then develop agreement about a shared need or solution. You may also see the acronym RAD (rapid application design), which describes a collaborative structured software design process that utilizes JAD sessions. It is considered by some to be the forerunner of the new agile change-driven approaches.

Requirements workshops include more stakeholders than an interview, usually 5-20 people. They become less effective as the number of participants increases.

Of the four elicitation tasks, Prepare for Elicitation is the most time-consuming part of a requirements workshop. A requirements workshop WILL NOT be successful if you do not prepare properly.

To be successful, a requirements workshop must:
- Be focused on a particular objective (e.g., scope the product, design a screen layout or report, redesign a business process)
- Be well-planned (including pre-workshop interviews, timed agenda, meeting room setup, and collaboration tools if virtual)
- Be run by an experienced facilitator (someone who knows how to manage group dynamics; this is often a business analyst)
- Be supported by a facilitation team (time keeper, gate keeper, recorder/scribe)
- Include the appropriate participants
- Produce an agreed-upon deliverable (e.g., as-is business model, data model, workflow diagram)

Group Decision Making

Often, a goal of the workshop is to reach a decision. The group might be trying to choose a proposed solution approach, decide which requirements are in scope, or agree on how a particular interface will work. During the workshop, the business analyst identifies conflicting viewpoints held by stakeholders and uses his or her facilitation skills to bring the group to a decision. There are a number of ways a group can come to a decision.

Consensus   Consensus means each party has an opportunity to influence the decision and each party agrees to or "buys into" the final decision. Everyone agrees on the decision because they have worked collaboratively and understand each other's needs. Reminding participants about the original business need and the objectives included in the business case will help the group come to consensus. This is the preferred decision-making approach.

Compromise   Compromise sounds good, but is different from consensus. Compromise means each side gives up something. This can lead to negative attitudes about the decision because none of the stakeholders really feel satisfied with the result.

Majority Rules   The decision preferred by a majority of the group is determined by a vote. This is the least desirable decision-making approach. When the majority of stakeholders agree on the solution design, but one or more minority stakeholders disagree, the minority may negatively impact the successful implementation of the decision. Even if just one person voted against the decision, he or she may consider himself the "loser" and maintain a negative attitude. This negative attitude may be shared with others in the organization, making the remainder of the project difficult.

Unanimity   Occasionally, all of the involved stakeholders will agree on a decision. Although this sounds like the best result, you must be careful to ask questions to ascertain if the decision has really been well thought-out. Sometimes stakeholders are very busy and don't take time to carefully consider the choices. Sometimes the stakeholders don't want to disagree with each other because they don't want to jeopardize existing relationships. It is your responsibility to be sure the importance of making the best decision is understood by stakeholders.

Autocratic Decision   Sometimes, when you can't get agreement no matter how hard you try, you and the project manager will ask the sponsor to make the call. This can set up a negative situation on the project, as team members may feel the sponsor is not close enough to the day-to-day operations of the business to understand the ramifications of his or her decision. As in the majority rules situation, any stakeholder who disagrees with the decision may become disengaged and spread negativity around the organization.

APPLY YOUR KNOWLEDGE   If you have not participated in a requirements workshop:

- Find out if other business analysts in your organization are skilled facilitators and ask to observe their sessions.
- Get instructor-led training or mentoring on facilitation skills—this must include time for you to practice facilitating and get feedback from the instructor.
- Read books and articles on managing group dynamics, specifically conflict, lack of participation, and interruptions.
- Volunteer to facilitate a meeting outside of work (e.g., an exam prep study session, a meeting of a charitable organization, or a PTA meeting).

EXERCISE   Think about how requirements workshops are used to elicit.

Elicitation Knowledge Area Task	Specific Work When Using a Requirements Workshop
Prepare for Elicitation	
Conduct Elicitation Activity	
Document Elicitation Results	
Confirm Elicitation Results	

ANSWER

Elicitation Knowledge Area Task	Specific Work When Using a Requirements Workshop
Prepare for Elicitation	• Determine the purpose and desired output of the workshop. • Select and invite the appropriate participants. • Create a facilitation team (recorder, scribe, facilitator, time keeper). • Pre-screen and possibly interview the participants. • Set up facilities for productive collaboration (e.g., tables in U shape, name tents). • Create a detailed agenda with planned timeframes. • Prepare tools for the session (modeling tools, flip charts, whiteboards, etc.).
Conduct Elicitation Activity	• Introduce the facilitation team, the format of the workshop and the ground rules. • Have participants introduce themselves and their roles in the workshop. • Follow the agenda. • Facilitate conflicts. • Handle difficult participants. • Wrap up on time.
Document Elicitation Results	• Meet with the facilitation team to compile notes and observations. • Create the deliverable as defined in Planning. • Develop a list of follow-up questions.
Confirm Elicitation Results	Requirements workshops cannot be used to confirm elicitation results, but the results of your workshop must be confirmed. Use interviews and/or observation to: • Ask follow-up questions as needed. • Present the deliverable to participants for clarification and confirmation.

 Expect a couple of situational questions about requirements workshops on the exam. You may be presented with a question that asks you how to handle a challenging participant or a conflict between two participants. Use your experience to choose the correct answer. Remember, collaboration and consensus are the goals. Reporting a stakeholder to his or her manager or making a decision for the group are not good business analysis practices.

TRICKS OF THE TRADE® Do not confuse focus groups and requirements workshops. They both involve a group of stakeholders talking about their requirements, but there are differences. Review the following table to help you understand the differences.

	Focus Group	Requirements Workshop
Leader	"Moderator" asks questions and records discussions	"Facilitator" asks questions, manages participation, builds consensus
Types of project	Usually used on marketing or product development projects	Any
Participants	Most often they are external customers, randomly chosen within a set of demographic characteristics Incentives are offered for participation	Stakeholders specifically selected and interviewed before the session to make sure they bring the needed knowledge Participants often take time away from their regular work to attend and may be formally assigned to the project
Results	Feedback, ideas	Specific requirements

Survey/Questionnaire (9.31)

Surveys and questionnaires are primarily used when there are too many stakeholders for the business analyst to interview individually. A series of written questions is presented to stakeholders for their feedback. Designing effective surveys or questionnaires requires careful wording of questions, usually closed-ended questions with multiple choice answers.

The preparation task is most important for this technique. You must think carefully about the desired results from the survey or questionnaire to make sure it is designed and administered correctly.

Know the Steps to Conducting a Survey or Questionnaire
1. Develop questions and write an introduction for the participants.
2. Determine who will receive the survey or questionnaire.
3. Determine how the survey or questionnaire will be administered.
4. Decide if an incentive will be offered.
5. Test the questions on a few sample participants.
6. Plan for tabulation and reporting of results.

Best Practices for Using a Survey or Questionnaire
- The fewer the questions, the higher the response rate. People are not likely to respond to a survey or questionnaire that takes them more than a few minutes to complete.
- Closed-ended questions elicit better responses and are easier to tabulate.
- Writing a clear, concise introduction to the survey or questionnaire is critical. You want to explain to participants why their feedback is important and how it will be used.
- Commit to anonymity of responses if there are politically sensitive topics.
- Administer the survey or questionnaire electronically if possible, with an automated tabulation feature to speed results. Make sure the technology is extremely easy-to-use and works in any environment.
- Set a short timeframe for responses.
- Test both the content of the questions and the technology on a few participants before releasing the survey or questionnaire to a large number of people.
- Response rates for surveys or questionnaires are historically very low. To increase the number of responses, offer an incentive (a special parking space or free lunch in the cafeteria, for example). Studies have shown that any incentive increases the likelihood of responses.
- Many participants will be interested in the results of the survey or questionnaire. Follow up with them with a thank you and a consolidated report of your findings.

If you prepare the survey or questionnaire well, the conducting and documenting tasks are easy. Confirmation is not normally done with each participant, but results are reported to key stakeholders and the sponsor.

EXERCISE How would surveys or questionnaires be used to elicit?

Elicitation Knowledge Area Task	Specific Work When Using a Survey or Questionnaire
Prepare for Elicitation	
Conduct Elicitation Activity	
Document Elicitation Results	

ANSWER

Elicitation Knowledge Area Task	Specific Work When Using a Survey or Questionnaire
Prepare for Elicitation	• Determine the purpose of the survey or questionnaire. • Develop questions, primarily closed-ended ones. • Determine who will receive the survey or questionnaire. • Decide if an incentive will be offered to • participants. • Test the questions on a few typical participants. • Revise as needed.
Conduct Elicitation Activity	• Deliver the survey or questionnaire to the selected group. • Clearly explain the purpose, time required to complete, incentive, and follow-up plans.
Document Elicitation Results	• Collect responses and compile results. • Calculate averages, highs and lows, or whatever metrics are useful. • Write a report for the sponsor and key stakeholders on the results, including the response rate. • Write a report for participants, if desired, on overall findings and next steps.

Reverse Engineering

Reverse engineering is a technique for eliciting current business capabilities supported in an existing software system. Reverse engineering involves examining existing computer programs to understand the processes of an existing software application. Sometimes this is the only way to really understand what a current application does, because often employees in the business area rely on the software but don't know the underlying business rules. Reverse engineering may be done manually by a technical software expert or by a software tool that tries to decipher the meaning behind the code. (Although this technique is not listed in the current version of the *BABOK® Guide*, it is commonly used. Don't be surprised if you see it in a question or distracting answer on the exam.)

Review of the Elicitation Techniques

Many of the elicitation techniques we have discussed are *event-based*. Elicitation events directly involve the appropriate stakeholders (sponsor, customer, end user, etc.) and require ground rules to conduct the event effectively.

EXERCISE Which of the following techniques are event-based?

Technique	✓
Brainstorming	
Data Dictionary and Glossary	
Document Analysis	
Focus Groups	
Interface Analysis	
Interviews	
Observation	
Problem Tracking	
Prototyping	
Requirements Workshops	
Survey or Questionnaire	

ANSWER

Technique	✓
Brainstorming	✓
Data dictionary and Glossary	
Document Analysis	
Focus Groups	✓
Interface Analysis	
Interviews	✓
Observation	✓
Problem Tracking	
Prototyping	✓
Requirements Workshops	✓
Survey or Questionnaire	

You may be asked to determine whether an elicitation technique is event-based on the exam.

EXERCISE Choose the appropriate elicitation technique for each situation described.

Situation	Technique
Your team needs innovative new ideas.	
One or two stakeholders have information about a specific topic.	
Stakeholders from different groups or departments share some data, processes, and applications, and will all be affected by a change to their systems.	
You are unfamiliar with the details of the business domain, but there is information available to you about the industry, competition, existing systems, procedures, regulations, and policies within the scope of the solution.	
Your company is going to change the packaging of its best-selling product and wants to make sure existing customers will still buy the product.	
You have a large group of stakeholders located in different cities and you want to learn their specific preferences about a new system.	
The solution scope for your project communicates with two other systems and your stakeholder would like the transfer of information between the systems to happen automatically.	
Your solution is a new website that will allow customers to order custom products, but the stakeholders don't have a vision of what they need.	

ANSWER

Situation	Technique
Your team needs innovative new ideas.	Brainstorming
One or two stakeholders have information about a specific topic.	Interviews
Stakeholders from different groups or departments share some data, processes, and applications, and will all be affected by a change to their systems.	Requirements Workshops
You are unfamiliar with the details of the business domain, but there is information available to you about the industry, competition, existing systems, procedures, regulations, and policies within the scope of the solution.	Document Analysis
Your company is going to change the packaging of its best-selling product and wants to make sure existing customers will still buy the product.	Focus Groups
You have a large group of stakeholders located in different cities and you want to learn their specific preferences about a new system.	Survey or Questionnaire
The solution scope for your project communicates with two other systems and your stakeholder would like the transfer of information between the systems to happen automatically.	Interface Analysis
Your solution is a new website that will allow customers to order custom products, but the stakeholders don't have a vision of what they need.	Prototyping

Make sure you understand why each of the answers above is correct!

EXERCISE Choose the stakeholder group size most appropriate for each technique.

Technique	Stakeholder Group Any None (0) Small (1-4) Medium (5-20) Large (20 or more)
Requirements Workshops	
Brainstorming	
Interviews	
Document Analysis	
Focus Groups	
Survey or Questionnaire	
Interface Analysis	
Prototyping	

ANSWER

Technique	Stakeholder Group (Small, Medium, Large, or None)
Requirements Workshops	Medium (As the group gets larger, it becomes more difficult to ensure participation)
Brainstorming	Any number
Interviews	Small
Document Analysis	None
Focus Groups	Medium (6-12 recommended)
Survey or Questionnaire	Large
Interface Analysis	None
Prototyping	Small to medium

SUMMARY OF ELICITATION

Elicitation is used extensively in business analysis work, providing us with information we need to understand business needs and capabilities, learn about stakeholder requests for changes, and discover the impacts of the solution on existing business systems. It is performed in conjunction with business analysis tasks throughout all of the knowledge areas. Many people believe that communication skills are the most important assets for successful business analysis. Elicitation is at the heart of this communication.

APPLY YOUR KNOWLEDGE   If you don't have experience with a particular technique, try it before you take the exam!

1. *Interview* a family member on the requirements for an addition to your home. Prepare your questions, conduct the interview, document the results, and meet again to confirm your understanding. You may want to sketch the new room to give your interviewee a visual confirmation.
2. Take a business person in your company to lunch and use the time to learn about that person's job. Ask if you can *observe* the person at work after lunch. Draw a workflow diagram for one of his or her processes and present it back for confirmation.
3. Redesign a website you access frequently to make it more user-friendly (build a *prototype*). Ask your friends for ideas and then incorporate those suggestions into another redesign. (You could send it to the company as a suggestion!)
4. Have a dinner party with 4 to 10 people and facilitate a discussion about how to solve a local or national community problem (e.g., traffic congestion, a dilapidated neighborhood, an overcrowded school). This is actually a *requirements workshop*!
5. Design a *questionnaire* for members of your place of worship or a charitable organization to find out what additional services they would like. Test it out on a few members to see if your questions are clear. Think about how many people you would send it to and how you would tabulate the results.

Before taking the practice exam, I recommend that you read the Elicitation chapter of the *BABOK® Guide* (Chapter 3), and the descriptions of the key techniques of this knowledge area (in Chapter 9 of the *BABOK® Guide*):

- Brainstorming (9.3)
- Document Analysis (9.9)
- Focus Groups (9.11)
- Interface Analysis (9.13)
- Interviews (9.14)
- Observation (9.18)
- Prototyping (9.22)
- Requirements Workshops (9.23)
- Survey/Questionnaire (9.31)

Practice Exam

1. Which elicitation technique would be MOST appropriate for a large stakeholder group?

   A. Survey or questionnaire
   B. Requirements workshop
   C. Focus group
   D. Interface analysis

2. Which elicitation technique requires you to prepare by developing questions tailored to a specific stakeholder and having an interactive conversation?

   A. Survey or questionnaire
   B. Requirements workshop
   C. Interview
   D. Observation

3. Which elicitation techniques are BEST at the beginning of a project or when learning about the business?

   A. Observation and interface analysis
   B. Interviews and requirements workshops
   C. Surveys and questionnaires
   D. Observation and document analysis

4. What is the BEST thing to do when you hear someone say, "The user doesn't know what she wants?"

   A. Learn about the business on your own and make recommendations to the user.
   B. Ask your project manager to have a different stakeholder assigned.
   C. Maintain an open mind and discuss the business objectives and possible solutions.
   D. Ask the user to let you know when she has decided on her requirements.

5. Interface analysis:

   A. Is a structured analytical technique for identifying the root cause of a problem.
   B. Refers to identification and design of outside connections required by the solution.
   C. Describes software components that can "plug and play" automatically.
   D. Describes how competitive forces in the industry impact each other.

6. During elicitation, the business analyst should be:

   A. Note taking, tracing, and capturing requirements attributes.
   B. Tracing, documenting, and capturing requirements attributes.
   C. Note taking, listening, and documenting.
   D. Note taking, assessing performance, and capturing requirements attributes.

7. When listening to a stakeholder describe a requirement, an excellent business analyst should FIRST:

   A. Agree with the stakeholder about the business need.
   B. Paraphrase the requirement back to the stakeholder to make sure he or she understood the stakeholder.
   C. Repeat the requirement in exactly the same words to make sure he or she heard it properly.
   D. Write down the requirement in detail in his or her notes.

8. The tasks in the Elicitation knowledge area should be performed in order. The correct order is:

   A. Prepare, conduct, document, confirm.
   B. Conduct, prepare, document confirm.
   C. Document, prepare, conduct, confirm.
   D. Prepare, document, conduct, confirm.

9. When selecting participants for a focus group, an advantage of a homogeneous group is:

   A. Participants come from diverse backgrounds.
   B. Participants will have diverse perspectives.
   C. Participants will be comfortable with each other and willing to share.
   D. Participants will be existing users of the product.

10. Which of the following is NOT an event-based elicitation technique?

    A. Interview
    B. Survey
    C. Requirements workshop
    D. Observation

11. In a passive observation, the business analyst:

    A. Asks questions about the process being observed.
    B. Participates in the work of the business.
    C. Makes notes as he or she watches.
    D. Stops the worker at each step during the process.

12. To facilitate a conversation is to:

    A. Direct the participants to a particular conclusion.
    B. Make the conversation easier.
    C. Gather information from every participant.
    D. Conduct a requirements workshop.

13. To conduct an effective brainstorming session, the facilitator must:

    A. Invite as many participants as possible.
    B. Give the participants a long time to think of ideas.
    C. Leave the topic very open-ended to encourage creativity.
    D. Clearly state the ground rules before starting.

© 2012 RMC Publications, Inc • 952.846.4484 • info@rmcproject.com • www.rmcproject.com

14. Which of the following describes how interviews and requirements workshops are used together in elicitation?

    A. The facilitator interviews each workshop participant before the workshop to better plan the agenda and prepare for group dynamics.
    B. The facilitator interviews each workshop participant after the workshop to gather his or her specific thoughts and requirements and finalize the requirements document.
    C. The facilitator prepares for the workshop just like he or she prepares for an interview, performing stakeholder analysis and developing a list of questions to ask.
    D. These two techniques are rarely used together.

15. Which group decision making result is considered the BEST?

    A. Consensus
    B. Majority rules
    C. Unanimous
    D. Sponsor decides

16. Elicitation:

    A. Is a complex word describing a complex set of tasks.
    B. Describes how business analysts make conversations between stakeholders easier.
    C. Means to draw forth or pull out.
    D. Reflects the fact that not all business analysis work is related to requirements.

17. Elicitation is used:

    A. To discover business requirements only.
    B. At the beginning of a project only.
    C. Throughout the project whenever requirements are unclear.
    D. Both inside and outside of project work.

18. Which of the following is an output of the Conduct Elicitation Activity task?

    A. Elicitation results
    B. Requirements package
    C. Business need
    D. Stakeholder list

19. The brainstorming technique cannot be used to confirm elicitation results because:

    A. It is not an elicitation technique.
    B. Confirmation is always done with a requirements package.
    C. Confirmation is simply a formality, so stakeholders don't want too much detail.
    D. It is an idea-generation technique.

20. A vertical prototype:

    A. Is created for a tall, narrow viewing screen.
    B. Includes a high-level screen shot (like a menu) and lower-level, more detailed screens (like an entry screen and confirmation screen).
    C. Is built with sticky notes on a flip chart and called vertical because most flip chart paper is tall and narrow.
    D. Is developed with a prototyping tool so the stakeholders can try out the screen electronically.

21. One of the BEST techniques to Confirm Elicitation Results is:

    A. Focus group.
    B. Brainstorming.
    C. Interview.
    D. Survey.

22. The main difference between a focus group and a requirements workshop is:

    A. Focus group participants are randomly chosen from a demographic profile.
    B. Requirements workshop participants are randomly chosen from a demographic profile.
    C. In a focus group, the participants are asked specific, pre-defined questions.
    D. In a focus group, the participants are encouraged to discuss their requirements.

23. The MOST important elements of the problem tracking technique are:

    A. Recording the problem and finding the root cause.
    B. Recording and solving the problem.
    C. Finding the cause of the problem and solving it.
    D. Prioritizing and assigning the problem for resolution.

24. Interface analysis is an elicitation technique because:

    A. It requires stakeholders to interface with each other.
    B. It is another name for prototyping.
    C. Identifying and understanding interfaces uncovers requirements.
    D. It actively involves key stakeholders.

25. To prepare for elicitation you need the:

    A. Business analysis plan, business analysis communication plan, and requirements management plan.
    B. Stakeholder list, business case, and scheduled resources.
    C. Business analysis plan, business need, and scheduled resources.
    D. Stakeholder list, business need, and the business analysis plan.

26. Elicitation results are:

    A. Requirements [confirmed].
    B. Requirements [stated].
    C. Requirements [approved].
    D. Requirements [prioritized].

© 2012 RMC Publications, Inc • 952.846.4484 • info@rmcproject.com • www.rmcproject.com

27. Techniques to confirm elicitation results are:

    A. Interviews and observation.
    B. Interviews and prototyping.
    C. Focus groups and observation.
    D. Observation and prototyping.

Answers

1. **Answer**   A
    Explanation   A requirements workshop is a group elicitation technique, but not appropriate for groups of more than 20, because it requires every attendee to participate. A focus group usually includes 6-12 people. Interface analysis is not a group elicitation technique. A survey or questionnaire is the most appropriate elicitation technique to use for a large stakeholder group.

2. **Answer**   C
    Explanation   An interview is an interaction conducted with a specific stakeholder. Questions must be developed ahead of the interview to make the best use of the stakeholder's time. As the stakeholder answers one question, the business analyst may adjust his or her next question to follow a line of discussion. The business analyst may also develop additional questions as the interview progresses to trace a particular requirement or to clarify an unclear description.

3. **Answer**   D
    Explanation   The best techniques to use when learning about a new business area are observation and document analysis. These are best because the business analyst can obtain a significant amount of information about the current business without taking the time of stakeholders. Observation allows the business analyst to learn the business and also see possible opportunities for process improvements. Document analysis involves reading and researching available information on current business practices (annual report, operating procedures, industry publications), application software packages (vendor manuals, user manuals, access to the system itself), and performing competitive analysis.

4. **Answer**   C
    Explanation   This statement is overused and misleading. A good business analyst will discuss the business needs and work with stakeholders to clarify requirements, and with the solution team to design an effective solution.

5. **Answer**   B
    Explanation   Interface analysis is used to identify people, organizations, and systems that have some connection to the solution being developed. These connections or interfaces must be analyzed and designed to allow the solution to be implemented into an ongoing business operation.

6. **Answer**   A
    Explanation   Documentation should not be done during elicitation, but afterward, if necessary. Performance assessment is not related to elicitation. Note taking is a critical part of elicitation. Tracing requirements should be done during the elicitation activity to follow linkages, and requirements attributes are characteristics of the requirements that should be captured.

7. **Answer**   B
    Explanation   Repeating back in the exact words does not demonstrate understanding. Agreeing with the stakeholder about the need is not necessary. If you disagree, you should ask follow-up questions to make sure the requirement is accurate and necessary. Although it is important to write down the requirement, the first and most important task is to paraphrase to make sure the requirement is understood.

8. **Answer** A

   Explanation This is one of the few places in the *BABOK® Guide* where tasks need to be performed in order. The order is pretty logical and should be easy to remember. The only tricky part here is that you may perform these tasks concurrently. For the purposes of the exam, think of them as separate tasks.

9. **Answer** C

   Explanation Diverse backgrounds and perspectives are advantages of selecting a heterogeneous group. Focus group participants are not necessarily users of a particular product. Most often, focus groups are built with homogeneous groups so the participants are comfortable talking together. They often come to agreement about ideas for future direction for the product or service being studied.

10. **Answer** B

    Explanation By definition, an event-based elicitation technique involves direct interaction with stakeholders, and requires ground rules. Of the choices offered, a survey is the only technique that does not fit the definition.

11. **Answer** C

    Explanation Asking questions, participating, and stopping the worker to make notes occur during active (or visible) observation. In a passive observation, also referred to as invisible observation, the analyst makes notes while watching the worker without conversation or interaction.

12. **Answer** B

    Explanation To facilitate means to make easier. Facilitation is used in requirements workshops, but it may also be used in any conversation. Facilitators should not direct the conversation. A business analyst facilitates a conversation or interview by making it easier for the stakeholder to describe his or her requirements.

13. **Answer** D

    Explanation A larger number of participants does not guarantee better ideas. A long time period stifles creativity and encourages too much evaluation of ideas rather than the generation of ideas. The topic should be specific so participants can easily contribute concise answers/possible solutions and ideas. Ground rules set the tone for the event, and should be communicated at the beginning of the session. Ground rules for brainstorming generally include the following:
    - Every idea is recorded.
    - No idea is "bad".
    - Ideas are not evaluated during the brainstorming.
    - Stick to a specific topic.
    - Set and adhere to a time limit.

14. **Answer** A

    Explanation Good preparation for a requirements workshop includes interviews with each participant before the agenda is finalized. These interviews may be brief phone calls or even e-mails to establish clarity on the participant's role in the workshop. They also give the facilitator information about potential conflicts that may arise during the workshop.

15. **Answer**   A

   Explanation   Unanimous decisions sound appealing, but if everyone simply agrees, there is a risk that other, potentially better options were not considered, or the group's decision was not properly evaluated. Majority rules always leaves out at least one stakeholder, who may feel like a "loser" and this emotion can be damaging to the team. If the sponsor makes the decision, there is a risk of the stakeholders not "buying in" to the decision, and not supporting it throughout the initiative. Consensus means every stakeholder has had a voice in the decision. His or her opinion has been heard and considered by the group and he or she can support the group's final decision.

16. **Answer**   C

   Explanation   Making conversations easier is *facilitation*. Elicitation means to draw forth. It is an active approach to learning the requirements of stakeholders.

17. **Answer**   D

   Explanation   Elicitation techniques can be used to learn any type of information at any point in a project or outside a project. For example, much enterprise analysis work, that is completed before a project is officially initiated, relies on elicitation.

18. **Answer**   A

   Explanation   The only output of an elicitation activity is the results. This seems almost too easy, but it is true. In the next elicitation task, Document Elicitation Results, the results are recorded. The business need is an input to Conduct Elicitation Activity, because you can't ask the right questions if you don't know what you are trying to accomplish.

19. **Answer**   D

   Explanation   Confirm Elicitation Results is an important elicitation task in which stakeholders review the business analyst's understanding of the requirements (either on paper or verbally) and make sure of clarity. There are only two techniques that can be used to confirm results: interviews and observation. Packaging requirements is optional. Brainstorming is idea generation.

20. **Answer**   B

   Explanation   Vertical refers to the depth of the prototype. You can think of this as "drilling down." The team creates a series of screen mockups showing how a user would progress through the application, performing more detailed work or reviewing more detailed information. The word horizontal is used to describe a prototype with a series of screen mockups that represent parallel business functions (such as adding a customer, changing a customer profile, deleting a customer) all at the same level of detail.

21. **Answer**   C

   Explanation   Focus groups are used to learn about customer preferences, surveys are used to collect information from large groups, and brainstorming is idea generation. An interview is useful in confirming elicitation results.

22. **Answer**   A

   Explanation   In both types of elicitation sessions, participants are asked specific, pre-defined questions and encouraged to discuss their requirements. (If discussion is not desired, don't hold a group elicitation session!) The main difference is the selection of the participants. Requirements workshops include stakeholders with specific expertise and knowledge who have been interviewed before the session to make sure their expertise is related to the workshop agenda.

23. **Answer**   C
    Explanation   Of course, solving the problem is the most important task, but finding the root cause is also critical, because it can help prevent similar problems in the future. Recording the problem and assigning it to someone for follow-up are necessary but not the most important elements of the technique.

24. **Answer**   C
    Explanation   Interface analysis is not the same as prototyping. Although it doesn't always actively involve stakeholders, identifying and understanding interfaces are a critical part of requirements elicitation. In many complex business areas, there are more requirements to support interfaces than solution requirements that define the core product being built!

25. **Answer**   D
    Explanation   The requirements management plan does not include elicitation activities. Scheduled resources are an output of Prepare for Elicitation. Although the business analysis plan is not listed as a specific input to the Prepare for Elicitation task, remember that all work is done according to the business analysis plan. You also need to know who the stakeholders are (stakeholder list) and what the stakeholders want (business need).

26. **Answer**   B
    Explanation   Requirements received during elicitation are raw or unrefined (stated). They have not yet been confirmed, approved, or prioritized. They will be confirmed, approved, and prioritized later in the project.

27. **Answer**   A
    Explanation   Prototypes can be shown to stakeholders to confirm elicitation results, but the discussion about the prototype is considered an interview. Focus groups are used to get outside customers' opinions about new product ideas. Interviewing is the most common technique to confirm results. We ask the stakeholder(s) who were involved in the elicitation activity if we got it right. Observation is also useful for confirming as-is requirements.

CHAPTER 5

Requirements Analysis

Aligned with the *BABOK® Guide* Chapter Six

All aspects of business analysis are important, but if you had to name the core of it all, this is it: Requirements Analysis. Analysis is a key skill for business analysts. Being analytical comes more naturally to some people than others, but everyone can learn to be more analytical. Analyzing involves breaking a problem or situation into components and looking at those individual components to truly understand them. Requirements Analysis describes the work necessary to break down and study requirements; modeling, organizing, prioritizing, verifying, and validating. It includes all of the modeling and diagramming techniques. Remember in the introduction I suggested you will probably need to broaden your understanding of requirements? The analysis tasks and techniques described in this chapter can be used on requirements of the current environment (as-is) or a future environment (to-be), of any type (business, stakeholder, solution, or transition requirements) and at any level of detail. As you learn about Requirements Analysis, think about the different ways analysis can be performed.

QUICK TEST

- Data model
- Cardinality
- Process model
- Business rule
- Structural vs. operational rules
- Phases or iterations
- Glossary
- Data dictionary
- Data flow diagrams
- Flowchart
- Swimlane
- Requirements modeling concepts
- Requirements classifications
- Workflow diagram
- Event
- Trigger
- Sequence diagrams
- State (machine) diagrams
- State (transition) diagrams
- MoSCoW analysis
- Verify
- Validate
- "All in" approach to prioritization
- "All out" approach to prioritization
- Levels of abstraction
- Entity relationship diagram (ERD)
- Entity
- Attribute
- Relationship
- Crow's foot
- Many-to-many relationship
- Non-functional requirements
- Business Process Modeling Notation (BPMN)
- American National Standards Institute (ANSI)
- Use case extends and includes
- Unified Modeling Language (UML)
- Object-Oriented (OO)
- Class diagram
- Requirements attributes
- Model

The tasks in this knowledge area are not necessarily performed in order. They are usually performed concurrently, and in parallel with tasks from several other knowledge areas. About 30 of your exam questions will come from the tasks and techniques in this knowledge area. Because there are so many techniques used only in this knowledge area, this is the longest chapter of this book.

Requirements Analysis in Action

I was a senior business analyst on a state government budgeting project. The scope of the solution was well-defined, as were the business case and stakeholder list. Several constraints had been identified during project initiating. Our system was to be built on a mainframe using the existing database management system and had to be completed by the end of the fiscal year.

The project manager and I reviewed the agency's requirements management standards, purchased a requirements management software tool, and hired two other business analysts to help with the requirements.

Our business analysis team created a high-level functional decomposition diagram to visualize the main processes of the budgeting group and get an initial understanding of our business domain. We defined key terms in a glossary. We divided up the functions, and each analyst developed requirements for his or her assigned area. We each created data flow diagrams with detailed links to our shared data model and wrote textual descriptions of the individual business processes we identified. We met together regularly to make sure our requirements were using consistent terminology and were not in conflict. As questions or issues came up, we logged them in our issues log. Each issue was assigned to one of us for resolution. We also met with our technical developers to discuss how each business process would best be implemented. We added new assumptions and constraints to the original list that was created at the beginning of the project, and frequently confirmed that we were still operating within the scope and its constraints. We worked with our business stakeholders to prioritize the requirements and determined which requirements we could implement within the time available. We conducted structured walkthroughs of each section of the requirements with the business stakeholders and then with the development SMEs to verify and validate them.

EXERCISE   There are six tasks in the Requirements Analysis knowledge area: Prioritize Requirements, Organize Requirements, Specify and Model Requirements, Define Assumptions and Constraints, Verify Requirements, and Validate Requirements. Can you identify the six tasks in the previous story?

Requirements Analysis Knowledge Area Task	Work Performed in the Story
Prioritize Requirements	
Organize Requirements	

Requirements Analysis Knowledge Area Task	Work Performed in the Story
Specify and Model Requirements	
Define Assumptions and Constraints	
Verify Requirements	
Validate Requirements	

ANSWER

Requirements Analysis Knowledge Area Task	Work Performed in the Story
Prioritize Requirements	Worked with the business stakeholders to prioritize requirements
Organize Requirements	Reviewed the agency's requirements standards, acquired a requirements management software tool
Specify and Model Requirements	Created a functional decomposition diagram, data flow diagrams, a data model, and glossary definitions
Define Assumptions and Constraints	Defined shared assumptions and constraints
Verify Requirements	Performed a structured walkthrough
Validate Requirements	Performed a structured walkthrough

Barb's BA Themes

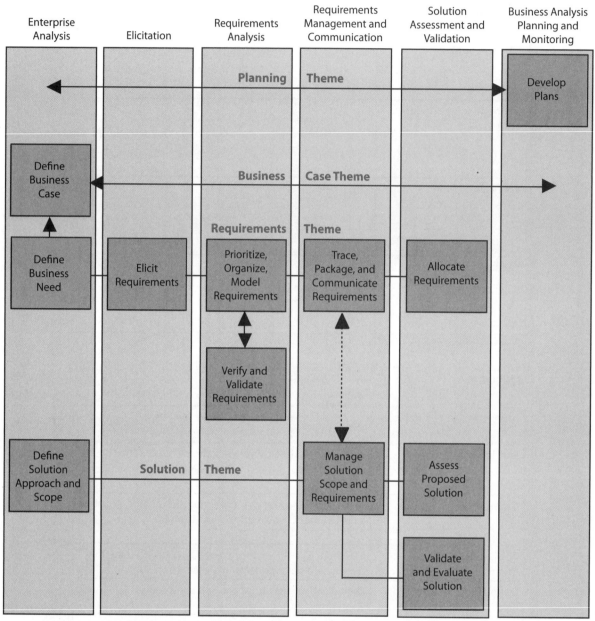

It should come as no surprise that Requirements Analysis touches all the major themes of business analysis. During Business Analysis Planning and Monitoring, a requirements management plan is created that details how requirements will be managed, described, stored, and changed. All of the work included in the Requirements Analysis knowledge area is completed according to the requirements management plan. The business analysis plan describes the approach to be used in creating the analysis deliverables.

The Business Case Theme crosses Requirements Analysis because every requirement must be reviewed for its relationship to the business case. Requirements that do not support the business case should not be approved or included in the solution design. Understanding the business case also helps the team prioritize and validate requirements. Some requirements will bring more business value than others and, as such, should be implemented early in the project if the solution is delivered in phases.

The Requirements Theme is the most important theme in this knowledge area because the tasks describe how we capture and document the requirements, and ultimately have them reviewed for correctness.

The Solution Theme crosses Requirements Analysis because you must always ensure that all requirements are within solution scope and that no requirements are missed.

Things to Know about Requirements Analysis for the Exam

- The tasks in this knowledge area are rarely performed in sequential order, but are usually done concurrently.
- Requirements Analysis tasks are usually done as part of a project, but can also be performed outside of project work.
- You can analyze as-is requirements and to-be requirements. To-be requirements describe the solution.
- Requirements are developed iteratively; when one requirement changes, its relationship to other requirements may also change. Therefore, requirements need to be reanalyzed throughout the project or initiative.
- Organizing requirements can be done in many different ways. Be sure you know the "requirements modeling concepts" and "requirements classifications" defined in the *BABOK®* *Guide* and discussed in the Organize Requirements task in this chapter.
- Don't let a different name for an activity in an exam question confuse you. Structured walkthroughs can be referred to as reviews, requirements reviews, design reviews, or inspections. A deliverable is the same thing as an artifact.
- Many of the techniques in this knowledge area are both "thinking" tools (analysis) and documentation tools. It is important for you to understand the analysis value of each technique in addition to knowing what the resulting deliverable looks like.
- Some techniques may not produce a formal deliverable, but rather a business analysis work product. A work product is something you use to analyze, such as notes or rough sketches of diagrams that are not usually presented to a stakeholder.
- The purpose of documenting requirements is to communicate them. Regardless of the technique, requirement type, diagram, model, etc., if your deliverable makes sense to your audience and they agree it is correct, then it is correct (even if you didn't use perfect notation).
- Know the importance of *just enough documentation*—Just enough documentation as is necessary to communicate accurately. Don't include any more or any less.

REQUIREMENTS ANALYSIS TASKS

The tasks in Requirements Analysis are the fundamental analytical work of the business analysis profession. These tasks are performed over and over again at different levels of detail, at different points of the project, and for different types of requirements.

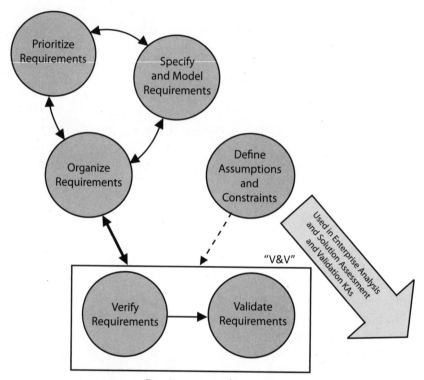

Requirements Analysis Tasks

The first three tasks of this knowledge area (Prioritize Requirements, Organize Requirements, and Specify and Model Requirements) are performed concurrently and iteratively. As requirements are identified, their relationships to existing requirements are also analyzed. The Verify Requirements and Validate Requirements tasks can be performed on interim requirements whenever the business analyst or team wants to confirm the requirements development work is moving in the right direction. Verification and validation are also performed when the requirements are complete, to ensure they are of the highest quality and bring business value to the organization. Verification and Validation will trigger changes to requirements, resulting in additional analysis.

The Define Assumptions and Constraints task is generally done at the same time as the Prioritize, Organize, and Specify and Model Requirements tasks, but the output of this task is not requirements. Assumptions and constraints are not typically put through the Verify and Validate processes but are used to review requirements. Assumptions and constraints are inputs to the Enterprise Analysis tasks of Define Solution Scope and Define Business Case. They are also used to assess the solution in the Solution Assessment and Validation knowledge area.

Prioritize Requirements (6.1)

The goal of the Prioritize Requirements task is to make sure the analysis and implementation teams focus on the most important requirements that will bring the most value to the organization.

Everyone agrees we should satisfy the most important requirements, but which requirements are the most important? Which requirements will bring the most value to the organization? This is where opinions differ and where you will use all of your communication, facilitation, and negotiation skills to bring the team to consensus. In a change-driven development approach, requirements are prioritized based on implementing the highest-value and most time- and cost-efficient ones first.

This is a challenging task because, as the business analyst, you don't have the authority to make prioritization decisions yourself. You must help stakeholders agree on priorities. Watch out for exam questions with answer choices implying that you set the priority.

Prioritize Requirements		
Inputs	**Techniques**	**Outputs**
Business Need (5.1)	Decision Analysis (9.8)	Requirements [Prioritized] (6.1)
Business Case (5.5)	Risk Analysis (9.24)	
Stakeholder List, Roles, and Responsibilities (2.2)		
Requirements		
Requirements Management Plan (2.5)		

BA's Responsibilities in Prioritizing Requirements
- Understand each requirement and its importance to the business
- Understand the relative feasibility and cost of implementing each requirement
- Identify prioritization conflicts and facilitate resolution
- Facilitate a discussion with business domain SMEs and implementation SMEs to come to consensus about the priority of each requirement
- Facilitate development of a phased/iterative approach to solution development and implementation

What Do You Need to Successfully Prioritize Requirements?
The most obvious inputs to Prioritize Requirements are requirements! Notice that any type of requirement can be an input here: business requirements, stakeholder requirements, etc. These requirements can be in any state (e.g., unconfirmed, confirmed, unapproved, approved, prioritized, etc.). This means that any requirement can be prioritized at any time. It also allows for a requirement that has previously been prioritized to be re-prioritized later in the project. As work on a project progresses, things change and priorities may need to be reconsidered. You also need to make sure the priorities correctly align with the business need and business case. You need to know which stakeholders have authority to make prioritization decisions and you need to refer to the requirements management plan that describes how your team planned to conduct prioritization activities.

Factors Used to Prioritize Requirements

Requirements are evaluated and prioritized based on the *business value* of each requirement. The business value is measured by analyzing the cost and benefit of each requirement. *Technical risk* and *implementation difficulty* must also be considered. A requirement that is easy to implement may be prioritized higher than a more difficult one.

As the liaison and facilitator on the team, you should make sure stakeholders understand the time and cost to satisfy each requirement and its *likelihood of success*. When the business stakeholders understand the complexity of the implementation, it may be easier to achieve stakeholder agreement regarding modification of their requests: decreasing the scope of the solution, increasing the time allowed, or obtaining additional resources. If stakeholders have impossible demands, you will work with the project manager and the project sponsor to deal with the situation. You must also watch out for the solution team unrealistically estimating the difficulty of the change in order to influence the prioritization.

Other technical factors that impact priority include *dependencies* on other requirements. For example, a reporting requirement cannot be implemented before the data on the report is available from a database or file. *Relationships between requirements* may influence the team's prioritization decisions in cases where implementing related requirements together would be more efficient and/or less costly.

When there is *urgency* about a requirement, it will be prioritized as high as possible. Urgency can be driven by an external constraint such as *regulatory or policy compliance* or by an internal constraint such as a product launch date. You should clearly understand the reason for the urgency and the ramifications of missing the desired date. You must communicate honestly with stakeholders about the ability of the team to implement the solution in the requested timeframe.

> | Factors Used to Prioritize Requirements |
> | --- |
> | • Business Value (cost-benefit) |
> | • Business or Technical Risk |
> | • Implementation Difficulty |
> | • Likelihood of Success |
> | • Stakeholder Agreement |
> | • Regulatory or Policy Compliance |
> | • Relationships between Requirements |
> | • Urgency |

 The Prioritize Requirements task is often performed concurrently with Define Solution Scope (in Enterprise Analysis). When defining scope, the team is deciding which requirements should be included in the solution scope. This is prioritization.

Techniques to Prioritize Requirements

Your requirements management plan should include a description of how requirements will be prioritized. Prioritization is a collaborative decision making process with domain SMEs and implementation SMEs contributing the factors needed for the group to come to decisions. Project managers and business analysts help the team weigh those factors and come to consensus. Prioritization decisions are usually approved by the sponsor. There are many ways to prioritize requirements.

Decision Analysis (9.8)

The decision analysis technique is used to quantify the value of requirements. Knowing the cost and benefit estimates for a particular requirement will help the stakeholders make more informed decisions about prioritization. Implementation SMEs provide time and cost estimates based on the description of each requirement. The more detailed the requirement, the more accurate the estimate.

Risk Analysis (9.24)

The risk analysis technique is used to identify and assess the risks associated with each requirement. Requirements that address a critical business risk will be prioritized higher than those that do not. Requirements whose implementation will pose a serious technical risk may be prioritized lower than those that do not.

Timeboxing/Budgeting

Before conducting a prioritization workshop, implementation SMEs estimate the time and cost to complete each requirement. With this information, a timeboxing approach starts with a specific implementation timeframe or budget. The team must choose which requirements can and should be included, given time and cost constraints. Used in many of the change-driven software development approaches, this technique causes the stakeholders to pick the most important requirements, effectively marking them as the highest priority. Let's look at a couple of variations of the timeboxing technique.

All In Approach   The business analyst asks the group to begin with the assumption that the requirements and stakeholder requests are "all in," meaning they are all of high priority and they are all within scope. Then the group looks for one requirement they all agree could be put off until later. If the solution will be implemented in phases, the requirement is moved to a later phase or it may be rejected by the team. This less important requirement is removed from the list or marked as a low priority. The group then looks at the remaining requirements and tries to find another one that could be put off until later. This process continues until the group can't agree on any more low-priority requirements. This approach is used when there is a short list of high-level requirements to be considered. It is impractical when the team is dealing with a very large number of detailed requirements because it is difficult to consider too many items at once.

All Out Approach   The "all out" approach works in the opposite way from the "all in" approach. The team begins by assuming all of the requirements are outside of scope. The group then identifies one requirement they all agree should be within scope. That requirement moves inside the scope (or is marked as the highest priority). The group then continues to identify requirements they all agree are within scope. This continues until the group can't agree on any more high-priority requirements. The remaining requirements are moved to a future phase or project, or are rejected by the team.

Selective Approach   A third option to reaching stakeholder agreement on high-priority requirements is to start with a budget or end date and determine which requirements can be completed within the time or budget constraints. This approach may be used in conjunction with either the all in or all out approach to prioritizing requirements.

 During a group session, a simple "in/out" table may be used to document agreements.

Item	In Scope	Out Of Scope
Login ID security for workers	X	
Ability to report hours		X
Ability to change phone number and e-mail address	X	

Documenting Priorities (MoSCoW Analysis)

Regardless of the approach used, requirements priority should be documented and reviewed for adjustments at the end of each phase or iteration. When requirements are documented in text, some teams use MoSCoW analysis to indicate priorities. The capital letters stand for Must, Should, Could, and Won't. For example:

- The system *must* provide a secure login for active employees.
- The system *should* allow employees to update their own phone numbers.
- The system *could* include a notification e-mail to the employee's manager when the phone number has been changed.
- The system *won't* allow employees to update their own department code or job title.

When using this approach, be sure to get agreement about the meanings of the words *should* and *could*.

Documenting Priorities (High/Medium/Low)

Another technique for documenting priorities is to assign each requirement a high, medium, or low prioritization or use a numeric scheme (e.g., 1 for highest priority, 10 for lowest).

Requirements Prioritization			
ID	Feature	Business Priority (H,M,L)	Technical Priority (H, M, L)
F459	The system shall provide a unique login ID for each worker.	Medium	High
F593	The system shall provide a place for workers to report their hours on each project.	High	Low

Requirements Prioritization Example

Technical Priority   Typically, business priority is determined first. Business people tell us how important each requirement is to them. Technical priority, provided by the implementation SMEs, is based on time and cost estimates and implementation constraints. When the technical priority is added to the discussion, decisions about priorities may change. Sometimes the decision about which requirement to address first becomes much easier. In the preceding example, the login is a high priority to the implementation team, because they don't want an employee doing anything without first logging in. This is a good example of how the technical priority will sometimes override the business priority. The system can't have workers report hours without a login ID.

As a tree cannot bear fruit without first developing roots and a trunk, an information system needs architecture or infrastructure like roots and a trunk (databases, networks, communications) before it can produce reports and features. These technical priorities or constraints are often unknown to domain SMEs. As a business analyst, your job is to help the domain stakeholders understand why some requirements *must be* completed before others. This will help them determine where each request falls in prioritization and why its priority may be different than they first proposed.

EXERCISE Review the following case study and suggest how stakeholders might prioritize the stakeholder requirements. Then decide in which phase each requirement should be implemented.

This project was initiated to give employees more control over their home office equipment and decrease the role of the Human Resources department in equipment management. Currently, HR is acting as the "middleman," accepting requests from employees in locations around the world for new equipment and repairs, and forwarding the requests to vendors. A secure website will be developed to allow employees to make such requests electronically.

The stakeholders have identified the following facts regarding equipment purchases:
- HR receives 4,000 requests for new PCs each year.
- The procurement department chooses a limited number of approved PC models each year based on volume purchase agreements with vendors. This information is not currently stored in a database accessible from the employee website.
- HR receives 500 requests for new printers each year.
- HR receives 400 requests for PC repairs each year.
- Ordering a new PC involves selecting a vendor, processing the payment, receiving the PC, recording the PC serial number, and shipping the PC to the employee. Observation of this process revealed it takes an HR administrator an average of eight hours per PC.
- Employees occasionally call HR to check on the status of their new PC.

Stakeholder Requirements	Business Priority (H, M, L)	Estimate (in days)	Phase
An employee can request a new PC via the website.		5	
An employee can check the status of a new PC order via the website.		1	
An employee can record receipt of the new PC via the website.		1	
An employee can review PC brand and model options via the website.		10	
An employee can request a new printer via the website.		5	
An employee can request a repair via the website.		3	

SAMPLE ANSWER

Stakeholder Requirements	Business Priority (H, M, L)	Estimate (in days)	Phase
An employee can request a new PC via the website.	H	5	1
An employee can check the status of a new PC order via the website.	L	1	1
An employee can record receipt of the new PC via the website.	M	1	1
An employee can review PC brand and model options via the website.	Reject	10	
An employee can request a new printer via the website.	M	5	2
An employee can request a repair via the website.	M	3	2

New PC orders, which are the highest-volume transaction and take eight hours each, should be the highest priority. The organization will get the biggest value from decreasing the time required for this process. By having employees record the receipt of their PC, HR could have PCs sent directly to employees, saving time and shipping costs. Since employees only occasionally call to check the status of their orders, providing status information on the website is a low priority. However, enabling the employee to access status information won't take long and could easily be done with other components of phase 1, since the information will be available at that time. The volume of requests for printers and repairs are lower, so those are also lower priorities, although a good business analyst would ask questions about how long each process takes, and if there are any other factors that might influence the priority. Enabling an employee to review PC brand and model options doesn't sound like a worthwhile requirement at all, since the procurement department limits the choices and this data is not currently accessible. This could be a costly change.

Summary

Prioritizing requirements is extremely important and can be very difficult for stakeholders. Considering a phased implementation helps ease this process, because the business will receive part of their solution sooner. Often it is difficult for stakeholders to envision an interim solution resulting from a phased implementation, but if you can help them understand they will receive some of their most important requests sooner, they are likely to agree. Business analysts must consider the numerous factors that contribute to prioritization decisions and help stakeholders come to good decisions.

Be prepared for questions about determining the priority of specific requirements. The business analyst does not *decide* on priority; he or she *facilitates* the prioritization process to help stakeholders reach consensus.

Organize Requirements (6.2)

Have you ever tried to review requirements that were not organized? Even a small requirements package that is poorly presented is time-consuming to review. You find yourself flipping pages back and forth, trying to detect a sequential flow, or looking for the definition of a term you don't know. An organized approach to capturing, analyzing, and presenting requirements is a timesaver for both the author of the requirements (the business analyst) and the reviewers (all of the stakeholders).

Organizing requirements is challenging, because requirements are complex and come in many different sizes and shapes. Some are textual paragraphs, some are copies of screens or reports, and some are diagrams. If this work is new to you, consider an analogy: mementos. Imagine going into the attic of an old home where a family kept all of their photos and scrapbooks and trying to organize all of the items you find. Some photos are black and white, some are color, some are big, and some are small. Some photos are labeled with the date and names of the people in the photo. There are birth and death certificates, graduation programs, baptism records, marriage licenses, and bank records, along with the photos. Your goal might be to write a family history. How do you put all of the pieces together in a cohesive way?

Deciding how best to organize requirements is similar to this challenge. As the number of requirements grows, a system for organizing them becomes more and more important. This task addresses the important activity of developing a structure within which to keep track of your requirements. Ideally, you will develop this system of organization *before* you start eliciting and collecting requirements. A good system will allow you to "file" each requirement as you receive it, making it easy to refer back to each one as you need it.

Organize Requirements		
Inputs	**Techniques**	**Outputs**
Organizational Process Assets	Business Rules Analysis (9.4)	Requirements Structure (6.2)
Requirements [Stated]	Data Flow Diagrams (9.6)	
Solution Scope (5.4)	Data Modeling (9.7)	
	Functional Decomposition (9.12)	
	Organization Modeling (9.19)	
	Process Modeling (9.21)	
	Scenarios and Use Cases (9.26)	
	Scope Modeling (9.27)	
	User Stories (9.33)	

BA's Responsibilities in Organizing Requirements
- Understand why a requirements structure is important to organize requirements of different types, levels of detail, and modeling concepts
- Understand the range of modeling techniques and be able to choose the appropriate one(s) for each requirement
- Be aware of the organization's standards and templates for organizing requirements
- Be able to organize requirements according to the agreed-upon standard
- Use organizational standards and give feedback for future improvements to the standards
- Develop templates and a requirements structure for the team (senior business analysts)

What Do You Need to Successfully Organize Requirements?

If your organization already has a standard "filing system" for requirements, you'll want to use it. This system includes any requirements templates or requirements management software tools, part of your organizational process assets. If your organization does not have a standard system for organizing requirements, you need to develop one for yourself. The size and complexity of your business solution will help you determine how sophisticated your system should be. You'll need to refer to your solution scope to make sure the filing system will accommodate the type of requirements you need. For example, if your solution scope includes purchasing a software package, your requirements structure must include a template for assessing potential vendors. Stated requirements are an input here, only to help you develop a system that will be appropriate for this particular assignment. You may review the available *stated* requirements to see how they will fit into your system, although you could develop this system before you have any requirements to organize.

Approaches to Organizing Requirements

As you are thinking about how you will organize requirements, you need to think about the *levels of abstraction* of requirements. Level of abstraction is the opposite of level of detail. Consider looking at a building. When you are close to it, you see all of its details like the number of floors and windows. If you were in an airplane, flying over it, you might only be able to see its roof and parking lot. This is a higher level of abstraction. If you were in a rocket ship, circling the earth, you might not see the building at all, but would see the geographic area in which it is located. The farther away you get from the details, the higher the level of abstraction.

As you know, some requirements are very high-level, while others are more detailed. Applying levels of abstraction to requirements is useful because it is easiest for reviewers to review a set of requirements that are all at about the same level of abstraction. Generally, the first requirements defined are higher-level and as you analyze and ask more detailed questions, you develop more detailed requirements.

Requirements	Level of Abstraction	Level of Detail
We need a new payroll system.	High level of abstraction	Low level of detail
The system should be able to pay workers in the 12 different countries in which we operate.	↑	↓
The system should allow employees to log in to a secure website to change their phone number.	Low level of abstraction	High level of detail

There are several approaches to organizing requirements. These are not mutually exclusive. On a large project a combination of approaches is often used. Be familiar with these three:

- Organize around modeling concepts
- Organize by requirements classification
- Organize with templates

Organizing Around Modeling Concepts   One approach to organizing requirements is to focus on a few key modeling concepts. These concepts (shown in the circles in the following graphic) represent components of the requirements included in models. Models provide a good way to represent different views and illustrate relationships between the various requirements.

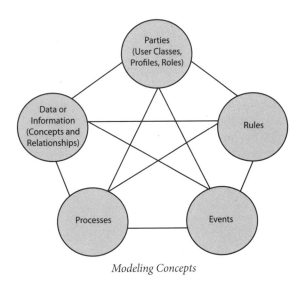

Modeling Concepts

Data, parties, rules, processes, and events each address a different view of the requirements. Together, along with the relationships between them, they provide a structured approach to analysis. If you think about each requirement in terms of these five concepts, you will most likely ask all of the important questions necessary to thoroughly understand the business need and describe the solution.

Initially it may be challenging to break down requirements into these concepts, but with practice it gets easier. Remember, the definition of analysis is breaking a whole down into its components, an essential habit for business analysts. I'll introduce the concepts here and talk more about them when we cover the modeling techniques. If you have not been exposed to these modeling concepts before, mark this section of the book to come back and review it after you have finished the chapter.

Data is information or concepts (named with nouns) that may be stored in databases, files, on forms, in spreadsheets, or even in desk drawers. These concepts have relationships to other concepts that are also important requirements. Information or data needs impact *processes* and *rules*; you will need to think about how the data is collected and where it is stored.

Processes are activities of the business (named with verbs). Processes, (also referred to as procedures or tasks) describe the work performed in the business domain. Examples of processes include Add New Worker, Release Worker.

Rules are policies, guidelines, regulations, etc., that constrain processes. Businesses have lots of rules. Business analysts identify rules by listening to how the stakeholders talk about exceptions, making decisions, checking for validity, and correctness. Decisions all involve rules, such as All job applications must include a résumé.

Events happen outside of the solution and cause the business to do work. Events may occur inside or outside the organization. For example, Candidate Submits Application.

Parties include any person or group involved with the business area being studied. You must be aware of all of the parties involved with the solution and attempt to include representatives from each in your stakeholder list. External parties like customers or vendors may have input into the new solution. Internal parties are specified in *user classes*, *roles*, or *profiles*. A class or role describes a group of users who have common needs from the solution. Customer service representatives are a class of users. A profile describes the characteristics of a group. The customer service user profile might include a description of the work environment. "Customer service personnel wear headsets and are constantly in conversation with customers. Their screens should allow simple point-and-click queries into customer and order data."

Each of these concepts is related to the others. Whenever you are learning about the business, you should be listening for these five concepts. Once you get into the habit of doing this, it will become easier for you. As you listen to domain stakeholders, you will immediately hear the concepts. You will find all five modeling concepts in this short description: "When an employee (a party) requests a new PC (an event), the HR department (another party) asks for manager approval (another party and a process). The PC must be ordered from an approved vendor (another party and a business rule), so the order (data) is sent to (a process) the selected vendor (another party)."

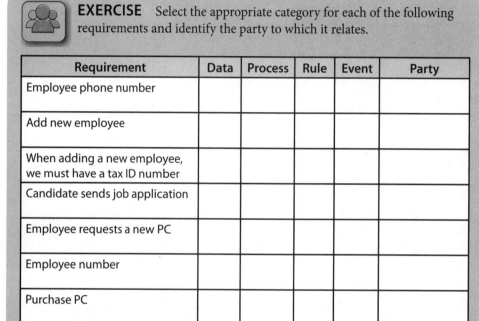

EXERCISE Select the appropriate category for each of the following requirements and identify the party to which it relates.

Requirement	Data	Process	Rule	Event	Party
Employee phone number					
Add new employee					
When adding a new employee, we must have a tax ID number					
Candidate sends job application					
Employee requests a new PC					
Employee number					
Purchase PC					
PCs can only be purchased from approved vendors					
Candidates must provide a work history with their application					

ANSWER

Requirement	Data	Process	Rule	Event	Party
Employee phone number	X				Employee
Add new employee		X			Employee
When adding a new employee, we must have a tax ID number			X		Employee
Candidate sends job application				X	Candidate
Employee requests a new PC				X	Employee
Employee number	X				Employee
Purchase PC		X			Employee, Vendor
PCs can only be purchased from approved vendors			X		Vendor
Candidates must provide a work history with their application			X		Candidate

Organizing by Requirements Type   Many business analysts use requirements types (also referred to as categories or classifications) as a way to organize their requirements. Typical classifications are business requirements, functional requirements, and technical requirements. The *BABOK® Guide* includes sample classifications in the introduction chapter, with the disclaimer that there is currently no industry standard classification scheme.

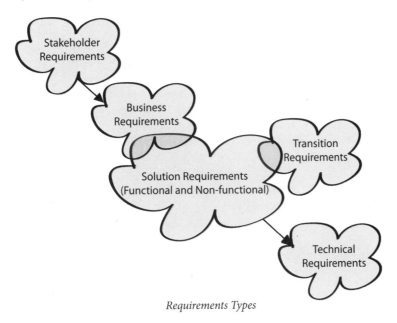

Requirements Types

There are other ways to categorize requirements, but these classifications are commonly used to make requirements more manageable. Think of the requirements classifications as starting with requests, or stakeholder requirements, and ending with technical requirements that are usually developed by technical implementation SMEs. In between, the business analyst differentiates between business requirements (things that are important to the business, independent of technology), solution requirements (the descriptions of what the solution should do and look like), and transition requirements (descriptions of how to smoothly implement the solution). Solution requirements are further detailed into functional and non-functional requirements. Functional requirements are behaviors of the solution. Non-functional requirements relate to quality of service.

Let's look at more detailed definitions of each requirement type. You must be able to define each of these classifications and be able to recognize examples of each for the exam.

Stakeholder Requirements are features and capabilities requested by specific stakeholders. For example, "Employees should be able to access the website from any device (e.g., PC, tablet, phone)." A request for a feature or capability may come from an individual stakeholder or a stakeholder group.

Business Requirements are typically data, processes, or rules that are needed for ongoing business operations, whether or not there is an automated system to support them.

Core business needs, such as being able to pay your workforce, are *ongoing* business needs. Over time, the way the business accomplishes the work may change. The company may buy a payroll software application, and then a few years later, outsource payroll processes to a servicer as needs grow. Regardless of how payments are made, the need continues to exist. Business requirements for Workforce Tracking include processes like Add New Employee and data elements like employee name and address. These are core business needs, things that are necessary to run the business regardless of the type of technology used to support them.

Business requirements also describe why the project has been initiated. Business requirements should be maintained as assets in a requirements repository because they can be reused on future projects. (We'll talk more about repositories in the Requirements Management and Communication chapter.)

Solution Requirements describe what the solution should do and look like. For example, a web page will allow workers to send a request for a benefit change.

Solution requirements describe how the work will be accomplished from the perspective of the business. They may include the software, hardware, forms, and procedures used to support the business. Solution requirements may be used as system documentation for ongoing maintenance and enhancements. They may be divided into functional and non-functional requirements (or other categories as needed).

Transition Requirements are descriptions of how best to implement the solution with the least amount of business interruption. For example, communicate in advance with HR administrators that they will have to start responding to worker requests via e-mail.

Transition requirements are only needed to implement the new solution. They are temporary requirements that will probably not be needed after the project is closed.

Technical Requirements, also referred to as technical specifications, are generally developed by a technical stakeholder such as an architect or lead designer, not by a business analyst. Business

© 2012 RMC Publications, Inc • 952.846.4484 • info@rmcproject.com • www.rmcproject.com

analysts are often asked to review technical requirements for conformance with the business and solution requirements.

 Technical requirements are not defined in the *BABOK® Guide*, but you must be aware of their existence and purpose. Be sure you understand the WHAT vs. HOW distinction when answering questions about requirements categories. *What* the business needs vs. *how* the business accomplishes it differentiates business requirements from solution requirements. But when you talk about solution design, *what* the solution does (the look and feel of the solution) differentiates solution requirements from technical requirements that describe *how* the solution is built. Keep in mind your perspective.

 There are gray areas in any requirements classification scheme. A particular requirement (e.g., customer e-mail address) could be considered a business requirement because it is needed by the business stakeholders, a functional requirement because it is needed for a computer system, or a technical requirement because it will be stored in a database. Don't let a rigid understanding of the classifications confuse you on a question. Also remember that each of these categories may contain the five requirements concepts (data, processes, parties, events, and rules).

Organizing with Templates   A template is a structured way of capturing and organizing requirements to ensure consistency and completeness. If all of the business analysts in your organization use the same templates, your requirements will all "look" similar, making it easier for stakeholders to review requirements from different business analysts or projects. See the following example.

Template for a Business Process Requirement	
Name of Process	Add New Employee
Number	P1.2
General Description	When a candidate is hired, he or she is added to the HR system by an HR administrator prior to the employment start date. All of the data fields in the new employee record are added to the employee database.
Performed By	HR application by an HR authorized administrator
Reviewed By	HR Manager
Data Used by the Process	Employee name, address, phone number, e-mail address, start date, tax ID number, job code
Business Rules Involved	The employee tax ID must not already exist in the database. A unique employee number will be assigned once the employee is added.
Technology Used	The HR system is a purchased application supported by the vendor.

Templates are organizational process assets. At the end of your assignments, you should make suggestions for how the templates could be improved.

Techniques to Organize Requirements

To select the best modeling and analysis techniques to use, you need to be aware of the many options available. You will rarely use all of these techniques on a single project. Instead, you will decide which one(s) best support the analysis work you are performing. In this task, you select which techniques you are going to use. You actually use these techniques in the next task, Specify and Model Requirements.

We'll discuss several of these techniques in the next chapter. This is just an introduction to help you start thinking about all of the options you have. Your analysis activities have already been outlined in your business analysis plan. Some decisions about which techniques to use may have already been made.

Technique	Usage in the Organize Requirements Task	Where Technique Is Discussed in This Book
Business Rules Analysis (9.4)	Decide how business rules will be identified and documented.	Requirements Analysis: Specify and Model Requirements (6.3)
Data Flow Diagrams (9.6)	Decide if data flow diagrams will be helpful.	Requirements Analysis: Specify and Model Requirements (6.3)
Data Modeling (9.7)	Decide if data modeling is necessary.	Requirements Analysis: Specify and Model Requirements (6.3)
Functional Decomposition (9.12)	Decide if a functional decomposition diagram would be useful for organizing business processes or solution components.	Enterprise Analysis: Define Solution Scope (5.4)
Organization Modeling (9.19)	Decide if organization modeling would be helpful.	Solution Assessment and Validation: Assess Organizational Readiness (7.3)
Process Modeling (9.21)	Decide how processes will be identified and documented.	Requirements Analysis: Specify and Model Requirements (6.3)
Scenarios and Use Cases (9.26)	Decide if use cases are appropriate for this project.	Requirements Analysis: Specify and Model Requirements (6.3)
Scope Modeling (9.27)	Use your knowledge of the solution scope to design a requirements structure.	Enterprise Analysis: Define Solution Scope (5.4)
User Stories (9.33)	Decide if user stories are appropriate for this project.	Requirements Analysis: Specify and Model Requirements (6.3)

Don't worry if you don't yet know how to make these decisions. As you learn about each technique you will be better able to choose the best techniques for each assignment.

Summary

Requirements must be presented in a consistent, organized fashion for easy review. To support this presentation, business analysts develop a system of organization, follow it, and improve it over time. As you are specifying and modeling requirements, you may revisit this task to make adjustments to your filing system or to consider other techniques. Organizing requirements helps to put them into a structure that is easy to review, update, and maintain.

Specify and Model Requirements (6.3)

This is it! You have now reached the most complex part of business analysis: specifying and modeling requirements! People who don't understand business analysis call this task "documenting requirements." But to understand business analysis is to see this task as much more than simply "documenting." Specifying and modeling requirements requires critical thinking and results in a clear understanding of the true requirements along with the best presentation format(s) for communicating with stakeholders. There are two important goals here: making sure the requirements have been accurately represented, and communicating about requirements with stakeholders so everyone understands the requirements in the same way. Your requirements specifications or models will be correct if your audience understands them.

TRICKS OF THE TRADE® Specifying requirements refers to stating the requirement or documenting it. Many teams use the word specification rather than requirement. To remember this task, think of *specifying* as meaning "to write a requirement in a sentence" and *modeling* as meaning "to draw a requirements diagram."

The result of this task is usually something tangible, a deliverable presented in a format that can be reviewed and approved by stakeholders. You'll notice this task has more techniques than any other. Many of the techniques are not referenced in any other tasks, because these techniques were specifically created to specify and model requirements.

Specify and Model Requirements		
Inputs	**Techniques**	**Outputs**
Requirements Structure (6.2)	Acceptance and Evaluation Criteria Definition (9.1)	Requirements [Analyzed] (6.3)
Requirements [Stated] (3.3)	Business Rules Analysis (9.4)	
	Data Dictionary and Glossary (9.5)	
	Data Flow Diagrams (9.6)	
	Data Modeling (9.7)	
	Functional Decomposition (9.12)	
	Interface Analysis (9.13)	
	Metrics and Key Performance Indicators (9.16)	
	Non-functional Requirements Analysis (9.17)	
	Organization Modeling (9.19)	
	Process Modeling (9.21)	
	Prototyping (9.22)	
	Scenarios and Use Cases (9.26)	
	Sequence Diagrams (9.28)	
	State Diagrams (9.29)	
	User Stories (9.33)	

BA's Responsibilities in Specifying and Modeling Requirements

- Analyze business needs and stakeholder requests, to thoroughly understand the ramifications of each
- Understand the current business environment and be able to assess the impacts of change
- Describe solution characteristics in enough detail for implementation SMEs to create a technical design
- Periodically learn about and try a new technique in conjunction with a well-understood one to improve your analysis skills and increase the number of tools available to you for future work

What Do You Need to Successfully Specify and Model Requirements?

You created a requirements structure or filing system in the last task and decided which techniques you will use so now you are ready to analyze the *stated* requirements from your elicitation sessions. You will analyze these requirements as you specify and model them. The resulting requirements are in a different *state*; they are *analyzed* requirements.

Ways to Specify Requirements

The most common ways to specify requirements are:

- Textual sentences
- Matrix and table formats
- Models and diagrams

Let's discuss these in more detail. Then we will look at techniques in which each of these formats is used.

Textual Sentences

Textual sentences are the easiest format in which to write requirements, but they can also be the most ambiguous. They are the most difficult to organize and categorize because people write at different levels of detail and complexity. Achieving consistency is also difficult, as you see in the following examples:

R1 The system should allow employees to update their own phone numbers.

R2 Upgrade the payroll system to handle global employees.

R3 The system must provide a secure login for active employees.

R4 The system shall include a notification e-mail to the employee's manager when the phone number has been changed.

When requirements are specified in text, each sentence or requirement is usually named or numbered with a *unique identifier*. This unique identifier (ID) is a tag, name, or number that is used when referencing the requirement.

Matrices and Tables

Matrices and tables are easier to review and maintain than textual sentences. In this format, requirements are broken into core concepts and can be described more fully with consistent details. These details are referred to as *requirements attributes*. The *BABOK*® *Guide* includes many examples of requirements attributes. For example, the *author* of each requirement may be the stakeholder who originally requested it, and the *owner* of the requirement may be the department or group who will maintain the requirement within the solution after implementation. Deciding which requirements attributes to use is done during Business Analysis Planning and Monitoring.

 See Element 2.5.4.3 in the Plan Requirements Management Process task in the Business Analysis Planning and Monitoring chapter for a list of attributes and their definitions.

In the following table, some of the requirements attributes are listed at the top of the columns.

Requirement	Unique ID	Author	Complexity	Ownership	Priority	Risks	Source	Stability	Status	Urgency
Track home office equipment	F1	Smith	4	Fac	3	R1	HR	L	I	M
Allow employee to report to more than one manager	F2	Dinkins	8	HR	2	R23, R12	HR	H	I	L
Allow worker to report work by hour, day, or project assignment	F3	Smith	2	HR	4	R12	HR	L	I	M
Allow worker to change phone number, e-mail address, or mailing address	F4	Smith	1	HR	2	R26	HR	H	I	H

Requirements Table

Models and Diagrams   Models and diagrams represent requirements in pictures or graphics. You have heard the saying, "A picture is worth a thousand words?" Here is the perfect example.

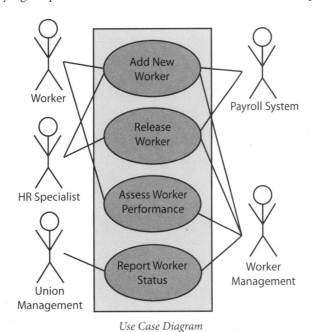

Use Case Diagram

Diagrams are meaningful and useful because graphic components (shapes) are used to represent specific concepts. The use case diagram we used to Define the Solution Scope (task 5.4) is a meaningful graphic depiction of the high-level requirements of the solution. When a reviewer understands the shapes, he or she can quickly understand the message being communicated by the picture. These shapes are called notations. The American National Standards Institute (ANSI) first published diagramming notation standards for flowcharting. Other organizations also publish diagramming and notation standards, so be aware there are differences. For each technique we discuss, I will alert you to important notation issues.

A model is a collection of artifacts that together define a business domain or solution. It is made up of diagrams, tables, and descriptions to give a complete view of a set of requirements. A model might include the deliverables of several different techniques. A model might include an entity relationship diagram, a workflow diagram, and a list of business rules.

Techniques to Specify and Model Requirements

The following techniques are all well-established, tested ways to perform analysis. You have probably used several of them, or seen them used by other analysts. Many of these techniques overlap and some of them have very specific applications. As you learn about each technique, think about when it might have been helpful on projects you have worked on. Exam questions will test your understanding of how each technique assists with analysis.

Acceptance and Evaluation Criteria Definition (9.1)

For requirements to be acceptable to stakeholders, they must be defined clearly and in a testable form. For a requirement to be testable, it must be specified in detail with a clear description of how the solution will support it. The acceptance and evaluation criteria definition is used to define this acceptance criteria. As requirements are being modeled and specified using the following techniques, each one must be evaluated for its applicability to the business need and its feasibility in the solution. We need to know what our requirements will be evaluated against.

Business Rules Analysis (9.4)

Business rules are the constraints, or guidelines, upon which the business makes decisions. These rules are critical in understanding how work is currently done and how it might change in the future. Whereas data and process requirements are relatively stable in most organizations, some business rules change frequently. This volatility makes them expensive requirements to automate. You need to identify which rules are most volatile, and help the solution team create a solution that allows them to be easily maintained.

Let's look at some examples of business rules.

Rule Number	Business Rule
BR1	An employee must declare a primary country of residence for payroll tax deduction processing.
BR2	Every worker must provide his or her legal name, primary residence address, government tax identification number, and primary citizenship.
BR3	All country-specific tax withholding laws will be obeyed unless exceptions have been legally approved.
BR4	Each employee is assigned an employee number for tracking within the organization. This number will be assigned sequentially by the HR system at the time of employment.
BR5	If an employee is married, he or she must provide the spouse's name and tax ID.

To identify existing business rules, listen carefully to your stakeholders for decision words like "choice," "option," "validate," or "qualify." "If... then..." statements also describe rules. Some business rules are high-level and can be broken down into more detailed rules.

Business rules analysis is a very important, but sometimes overlooked, technique. As you learn about rules in the business, ask questions to confirm the existing rules are clear, correct, and necessary, and that they are being applied consistently. Inconsistent or incorrect enforcement of rules may be the root cause of the problem you are seeking to address. Often these problems can be easily fixed through clearer communication with the employees who enforce the rules.

Business rules are often the competitive advantage of an organization. Think about the banking industry. The data collected and managed for a checking account at a bank is probably the same for most banks. Also, the processes the banks perform (accept deposits, cash checks, reconcile accounts) are likely similar. What distinguishes one bank from another, then, are the rules. One bank might offer free checking if your balance is above $5,000. Another bank might offer free checking if you also open a savings account. This shows how important the business rules are to a business.

Analyzing and specifying business rules is valuable to domain SMEs because it illuminates their current business practices and provides requirements for the solution design. If a business rule can be automated by a software system, its enforcement will be consistent. Understanding the rules allows the analyst to create meaningful warning and error messages in software. Every rule that will be enforced by the software must have exception-processing requirements so the software developers can build in helpful user messages.

Rule Number	Business Rule	Error or Warning Message
BR6	Employees must have a valid login ID and password to use the website.	"If you do not have a login ID and password, contact HR at 800-123-4567."
BR7	PCs are purchased from approved vendors.	"Your request specifies a vendor not on the approved vendor list. Please choose an approved vendor or contact HR for a special order."
BR8	The employee's manager must approve the purchase of a new PC.	"Your request has not yet been approved by your manager." OR "Your request has been denied by your manager."

When discussing business rules with your stakeholders, it is important to ask whether each rule is *mandatory* or is a *guideline*. Can the rule be overridden? If so, how? When software systems are built to enforce mandatory rules, the user will not be able to override the rules. When a rule is a guideline, you may design a supervisor override or pass code to bypass the rule when appropriate.

Characteristics of Business Rules   Expect to see a question about the following characteristics of business rules.

Structural or **operative** refers to the nature of the rule. The easiest way to learn this distinction is to focus on the word structure. A *structural* rule is created because of the nature or structure of something the company cannot change. For example, every human being has a unique fingerprint. This is a structural rule a company cannot override. If the company can change a rule, it is *operative*. For example, PCs must be ordered from an approved vendor *unless* a special request is approved. Operative rules drive the way the business *operates*. Operative rules often have exceptions.

Volatility describes the likelihood the rule will change. Operative rules change frequently, so you should ask the stakeholders how often and in what ways the rules might change. "Free shipping with orders over $100" is a rule that may change frequently, because the dollar amount in the rule is volatile. Some business rules have *expiration dates* or expiration conditions (e.g., once we reach a certain level of revenue, the rule is bypassed). Some regulations and laws have expiration dates for compliance.

Specifying Rules   Business rules can be specified and modeled using various formats:
- Decision tree
- Decision table
- Workflow models (Technique 9.21)
- Scenarios and Use cases (Technique 9.26)
- User stories (Technique 9.33)

You should be able to interpret a decision tree and a decision table.

Decision Tree   A decision tree is a diagram that shows decisions and the results of those decisions. It is used for simple business rule chains.

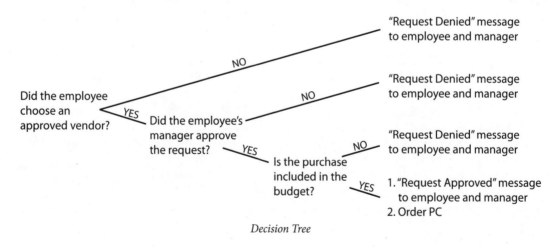

Decision Tree

Decision Table   A decision table shows the conditions about which a decision is made, along with the conclusion. Ideally, each row in the table describes a complete rule.

Condition 1		Condition 2		Conclusion
Age of employee (in years)		Number of years of employment		Retirement eligibility
Over	62	Over	25	Full
Over	62	Between	10 and 25	Partial
Over	62	Under	10	None
Less than or equal to	62	Over 25	25	Partial
Less than or equal to	62	Under	25	None

EXERCISE   Review the business rules below. Can you see any ambiguity? What follow-up questions would you ask?

Business Rules Worksheet		
Rule ID	**Business Rule**	**Follow-Up Questions**
BR9	Each employee must have one home address.	
BR10	An employee is allowed only one pay increase per year.	
BR11	A promotion must be approved by an HR manager.	
BR12	An employee is allowed to change his or her phone number online.	
BR13	An inquiry from an employee to the payroll department will be answered within two business days.	

SAMPLE ANSWER

Rule ID	Business Rule	Follow-Up Questions
BR9	Each employee must have one home address.	What if an employee has two homes? Can an employee use a post office box rather than a home address?
BR10	An employee is allowed only one pay increase per year.	For a calendar year or fiscal year? Does every employee get a pay increase each year? Are there any exceptions?
BR11	A promotion must be approved by an HR manager.	How is the approval secured? What if the HR manager does not approve? Is there more than one HR manager? What if they disagree?
BR12	An employee is allowed to change his or her phone number online.	Why not his or her e-mail address? Which phone number: cell phone, home phone, office phone? What does *online* mean?
BR13	An inquiry from an employee to the payroll department will be answered within two business days.	What types of inquiries are included? Within two business days—does this mean Monday through Friday? Are holidays or vacation days considered business days? What happens if the inquiry is not addressed within two days?

Thorough analysis usually requires more elicitation. You ask these follow-up questions of your stakeholders, refine the wording of each rule, and have them reviewed again. This is an iterative process of asking questions, drafting requirements, thinking about completeness and clarity, and then asking more questions!

Data Dictionary and Glossary (9.5)

This technique should be used on every project and assignment. Getting clear agreement on terms is a fundamental part of requirements analysis. Both glossaries and data dictionaries serve to define terms and facilitate consistent language in requirements analysis. A *glossary* usually includes the term or acronym and its definition, and may include examples or aliases. A *data dictionary* contains more specific data elements with detailed characteristics of each element. Glossaries and data dictionaries capture agreements and serve as references for requirements consistency.

We communicate requirements with words, we design solutions with words, and we plan with words. On diagrams and models, a few key words are used to communicate. An experienced business analyst understands the importance of reaching clear agreement about the definitions of key words with all stakeholders. Documenting these definitions at the beginning of a project or assignment (and as new terms are discovered) helps the team and all stakeholders use consistent terminology and quickly identify and deal with differing interpretations.

Definitions of key business terms are considered requirements. They are maintained in a glossary and reused by other, related projects. The unique identifier of each term is the term itself. Many words have very similar meanings, making a clear definition critical. Notice the terms from our case study defined below. Are these terms defined differently in your organization?

Glossary of Business Terms	
Term	**Definition**
Consultant	A person who is employed by an outside company and is assigned to review our company's processes and recommend improvements. A consultant usually does not perform day-to-day business operational work.
Contractor	A person who is employed by an outside company and is assigned to work on one or more of our projects as a part- or full-time team member. A contractor is expected to follow company standards and procedures while performing his or her assignments.

When your solution involves the collection, storage, or manipulation of data, a data dictionary is a useful way to inventory the pieces of information needed, along with their characteristics.

Data Dictionary							
Composite Name	**Seq**	**Primitive Name**	**Aliases**	**Description**	**Value/ Meaning**	**Optional?**	**Repeats?**
Policy Number	1	Original contract year	Year	Last two digits of year when the policy was originally sold	2-digit year	N	N
	2	Policy type	Product type	The type of policy	A=auto H=home	N	N
	3	Sequence number		Unique number assigned to policy	7-digit number assigned sequentially by the system	N	N
Customer Street Address	1	Street number		The location identifier on a street	6 characters (numbers or letters)	N	N
	2	Street direction		Direction of the street if it is part of the proper name of the street	1 character N, S, E, or W	Y	N
	3	Street name		Name of the street	30 characters	N	N
	4	Street type		Description used after the street proper name	10 characters (Blvd, Ave, Street, Hwy, Parkway, Lane)	Y	N

Notice the columns in the previous example. A *composite* data element is made up of *primitive* elements. A primitive element is at the lowest level of detail. Composite data elements include a sequence number to show the order of the primitive data elements. Each data element may have one or more aliases if the organization uses multiple names for the same data. Data dictionaries also include the value or meaning of each data element. This can indicate the data type (e.g., character or numeric), list of valid codes, and default value. It also may indicate the optionality of the data element (Is it mandatory?) and repetitions (Can there be more than one value?).

APPLY YOUR KNOWLEDGE If you have never used a data dictionary, use the following table to list a few data elements from a simple software system you use (e.g., personal finance, or address book). See how many of the cells you can fill in. For the ones you don't know, develop a question you would ask the vendor to elicit this detail.

Data Dictionary							
Composite Name	Seq	Primitive Name	Aliases	Description	Value/ Meaning	Optional?	Repeats?

© 2012 RMC Publications, Inc • 952.846.4484 • info@rmcproject.com • www.rmcproject.com

When you purchase a software application, ask the vendor to provide a data dictionary so you can see how the information is stored in the software.

Data Flow Diagrams (9.6)

Data flow diagramming (DFD) is another well-established analysis and design technique. Its structure and components guide analysts to think carefully about every process within the solution scope and make sure all inputs are available. There are very strict rules for data flow diagramming that ensure consistency and completeness.

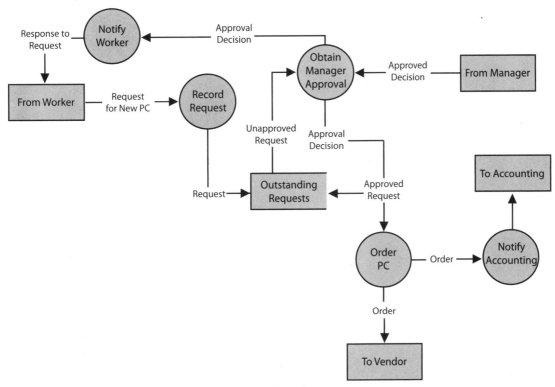

Data Flow Diagram for Order New Computer

Data flow diagrams use four symbols. A process is shown inside a circle, data flows through arrows, parties (*external entities*) are shown as rectangles, and data stores are shown as partial rectangles (see below).

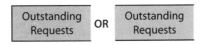

Data Stores

Know the Rules for Data Flow Diagramming

1. Inputs (data) must either come directly from an outside party or be created by another process. There are three sources from which data flow inputs can be drawn:
    - Parties or externals of the process (represented by rectangles)
    - Other processes (represented by circles)
    - A data store (information that is sitting in the business waiting to be used; this could be in a file, database, or just in someone's brain) represented by a "three-sided rectangle" or two parallel lines

2. Every process must have at least one input and one output. In data flow diagramming, a process is defined as an *activity that transforms data*. Every process has data coming in (inputs) which are transformed into outputs. These outputs may become inputs to other processes.

3. Every output must flow to an external, another process, or a data store (to be stored for future use). Arrows show the movement of data.

 Data flow diagrams are powerful because they can be used to show business models that are independent of technology. They can also be used at various levels of abstraction to show detailed solution and technical requirements.

 Review the *BABOK® Guide* discussion of the data flow diagramming technique (9.6) now.

APPLY YOUR KNOWLEDGE   If you have never used data flow diagrams, practice drawing one for a process in your business. Ask someone familiar with the process to review your diagram and see if it looks correct to them.

Data Modeling (9.7)

Data is information that is important to the business. Data modeling is a technique for identifying, analyzing, and presenting that information. You must understand the importance of data modeling and be able to "read" or review various types of data models. There may be up to three questions on the exam about data modeling.

You will always know when stakeholders are talking about data, because they will use nouns such as customer, employee, vendor, product, service, contract, policy, or account. Business people use information to perform their work. To truly understand the business, you must understand the information being used.

EXERCISE   Can you think of information that is important in a payroll system?

Data Used in a Payroll System

ANSWER

- Employee: employee name, phone number, address, country code, e-mail address, location, pay rate
- Deductions: country tax withholding rate, local tax withholding rate, number of dependents, retirement withholding rate, benefit deductions
- Work: week-ending date, regular hours worked, overtime hours worked, vacation hours used, supervisor approval

TRICKS OF THE TRADE® Data modeling is not the same as database design. Data modeling looks at business information. Database design involves software-specific tables, files, and fields. There is a myth that you don't need any data requirements unless you are designing a new database. This is far from true. Every business uses data, and understanding the data is a core aspect of understanding the business. An experienced analyst always performs some data analysis to understand this important component of the solution.

Ask Questions   One of the benefits of using a structured data modeling technique is that it helps you ask excellent questions when eliciting data requirements and analyzing the data.

Following are questions you might ask about our Workforce Tracking case study project.
- What is a *Worker*?
- How many *Workers* do you keep track of?
- What information about *Workers* is important?
- How do you tell one *Worker* from another?
- How do you currently keep track of *Worker first name*?
- Can a *Worker* have more than one first name?
- Does every Worker have a First name?
- What type of data is *First name* (text or numeric)?
- How do you use the *Worker first name*?

There are two diagrams used to model data: the entity relationship diagram (ERD) and the class diagram.

Entity Relationship Diagram   The entity relationship diagram has been in use since the 1970s and is universally accepted as an effective method of analyzing and representing data. It is also a great technique to use for business rules analysis. This industry standard is based on mathematical rules that help you ask consistent, detailed questions about the data.

Here is an example of data modeling using an ERD. If you need help understanding it, see the explanations of the components following the example.

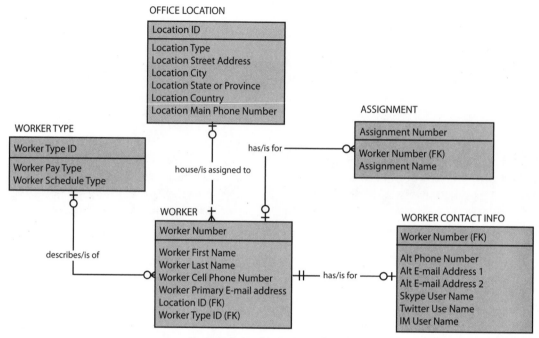

Entity Relationship Diagram (ERD)

Data Modeling Component	Definition	Notation
Entity	A class of information used by the business (nouns) For example: Worker, Worker Type, Office Location	Rectangle or box
Attribute	Individual data elements that further describes each entity For example: Worker First Name, Worker Last Name, Worker Cell Phone Number	Listed inside each entity box
Unique identifier (ID)	Data element(s) that allow identification of each entity occurrence For example: Worker Number allows the business to keep track of worker's information	The attribute(s) that uniquely identifies the entity will be highlighted in bold or be inside its own box within the entity box
Data Relationship	Shows how one entity relates to another	A line linking two entities
Cardinality*	Numerical characteristics of each attribute and relationship. There are three main cardinalities: uniqueness, minimum number, and maximum number.	Attribute cardinalities may not be shown on the diagram. Relationship cardinalities are shown by symbols at the end of each line.
Foreign Key (FK)	An attribute that is shared by two entities because it specifies their connection	(FK) after the attribute name in the related entity

Quantities are referred to as cardinalities in data modeling. Cardinality is a mathematical term meaning the number of elements in the set.

© 2012 RMC Publications, Inc • 952.846.4484 • info@rmcproject.com • www.rmcproject.com

When reviewing an ERD, the entities and attributes are fairly easy to understand. The tricky parts of the diagram are the relationship lines and their symbols. Here are some hints to reading the relationships.

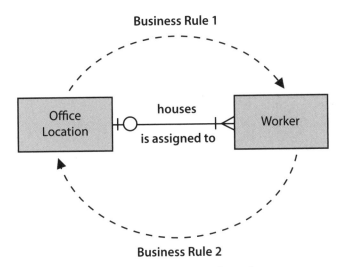

Simple Example of a Data Relationship

Each relationship line represents two distinct business rules. The symbols at the ends of the line show the cardinality of each of those business rules. The names of the entities in combination with the relationship name and cardinalities should make a cohesive, true sentence about the business. In the previous ERD example, Rule 1 can be read as: An office location houses one to many workers. Rule 2 states: A worker is assigned to zero or one office location(s). Regardless of the position on the diagram, relationship names and symbols are read clockwise from one entity to the other. (Beware: Some data modeling tools are not sophisticated enough to manage the clockwise rule.) Entity names are always singular; the cardinalities define if a plural usage is correct, as in Rule 1: An office location houses one to many workers.

Be sure you know relationship cardinality notations for the exam:

Relationship Cardinality	Diagram Notations
Optional	A zero or small open circle is drawn on the relationship line.
One or mandatory	A small line is drawn on the relationship line.
Many or more than one	A *crow's foot* or large black dot is drawn on the relationship line.

You must understand why a "many-to-many" relationship is a poorly defined business rule and know how to resolve it. A relationship between two entities is "many-to-many" when both ends of the line show a crow's foot. This relationship needs to be further analyzed and clarified by an additional entity. For example, a product can be purchased by many customers and a customer can purchase many products. This "many-to-many" leaves the data model without any indication of which customer purchased which products. Resolving this many-to-many relationship with an entity called Purchase Order would solve this modeling problem.

Review the *BABOK® Guide* discussion of the data modeling technique (9.7) now.

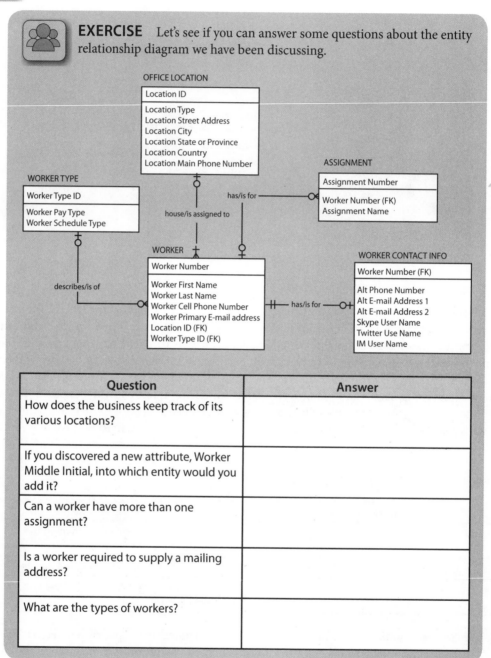

EXERCISE   Let's see if you can answer some questions about the entity relationship diagram we have been discussing.

Question	Answer
How does the business keep track of its various locations?	
If you discovered a new attribute, Worker Middle Initial, into which entity would you add it?	
Can a worker have more than one assignment?	
Is a worker required to supply a mailing address?	
What are the types of workers?	

ANSWER

Question	Answer
How does the business keep track of their various locations?	Location ID
If you discovered a new attribute, Worker Middle Initial, into which entity would you add it?	Worker
Can a worker have more than one assignment?	Yes
Is a worker required to supply a mailing address?	No
What are the types of workers?	Can't be determined from the diagram

Details Behind an ERD   For each data element or attribute that is represented in the model, you can ask the stakeholders several questions, such as: How many of this data element do you have? How do you uniquely identify each piece of data? Is the data element mandatory or optional? What are its characteristics, such as length, type, and most importantly, valid values? Asking these questions helps you to understand the business needs in detail and often leads to additional questions and the discovery of additional requirements. It is a good practice to involve your stakeholders in brainstorming sessions to identify data elements. If you just ask them for a list of data elements, they may not understand what you are looking for, but once you help them get started they will be able to give you most of them. Continue to ask follow-up questions to make sure they didn't forget to name any elements.

The information can be captured in a table like the following.

Attribute Details							
Entity	Attribute Name	Alias	Description	Valid Value/ Meaning	Is it unique?	Is it optional?	Can there be more than one?
Worker	Worker number	Employee ID	Unique number assigned to each worker	7-digit number assigned sequentially by the system	Y	N	N
	Worker first name		Legal first name of worker	20 characters	N	N	N
	Worker last name		Legal family or last name of the worker	30 characters	N	N	N
	Worker cell phone number	Mobile number	Number at which the worker can be contacted at any time	12-digit number with country code first	Y	Y	N
	Worker primary e-mail address		E-mail address assigned by the company	30 characters	Y	N	N
	Location ID	Office	Place where the worker works	7-digit number assigned sequentially by the system	N	Y	N
	Worker type ID	Worker type	Indicates whether the worker is an employee, contractor, or consultant	E = employee C = contractor N = consultant	N	N	N

Notice, the attribute details table is very similar to a data dictionary. They both list data elements and detailed information about each data element. The data dictionary technique does not include an ERD, so it doesn't include relationships. You would not use both an attribute table and a data dictionary on the same project.

© 2012 RMC Publications, Inc • 952.846.4484 • info@rmcproject.com • www.rmcproject.com

EXERCISE List data elements your business might need for ordering a new computer.

Entity	Attributes

SAMPLE ANSWER

Entity	Attributes
Vendor	Name, address, phone, website
Employee	Name, employee number, phone, mailing address, e-mail
PC	Model, serial number, type, brand
Purchase order	Number, date, amount, estimated shipment date

EXERCISE Draw a data model for the previous exercise. Include data elements your business might need for ordering a new computer.

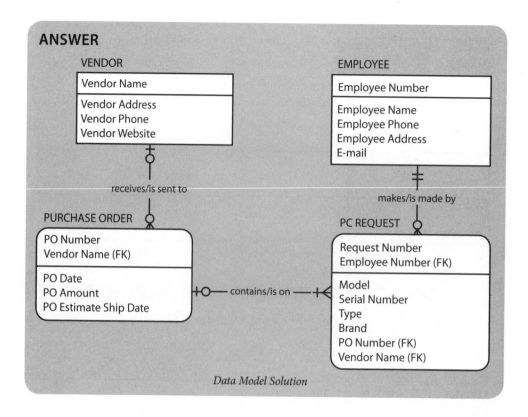

Data Model Solution

Class Diagram   A class diagram is another technique for modeling data. It was invented as part of the Object-Oriented software development methodologies (OO). The notation and analysis rules are defined in the Unified Modeling Language (UML), which is administered by the Object Management Group (OMG). Considered by many business analysts to be more technical than an ERD, it is used when required by the organization's methodology or implementation standards.

The major difference between an ERD and a class diagram is the addition of *behaviors* (also referred to as *methods* or *operations* in the class diagram model). *Classes* are very similar to entities, and both diagrams use attributes for data elements. They also both show data relationships and cardinalities.

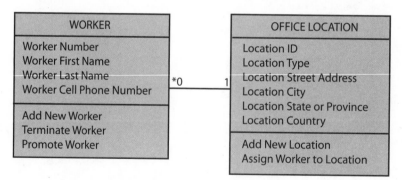

Two Simple Classes Class Diagram

Classes are shown as boxes, and relationships are lines between the boxes. *Behaviors* are shown below the attributes and represent operations that can be executed for each class. These behaviors are included specifically for communicating with software developers. You probably won't be asked about behaviors since the business analysis focus on this technique is on data. Both entity relationship diagrams and class diagrams are primarily used to ensure thorough analysis and for communicating with implementation SMEs.

 A class diagram uses UML, so the cardinality notations are different from an ERD. For example, "many" is usually represented by an asterisk rather than by a crow's foot. When a business rule is one and only one, the diagram simply lists the number 1 next to the line. In the previous example, a Worker is related to one and only one Office Location. An Office Location is related to between zero and many Workers.

 Metadata is a term with which you should be familiar. It means "data about data." Is this a new term for you? Data models document metadata. They don't include actual pieces of information. Data or information are the actual values important to the business. An example should help.

Data	Metadata
John	First name
Smith	Last name
jsmith@abc.org	E-mail address
555-123-4567	Phone number

Let's say customer information is important to our business. Rather than writing requirements for every single customer, we instead describe the actual data with a data model or metadata (data about data). For example, Metadata = first name, last name, e-mail address, phone number; Data = John Smith, jsmith@abc.org, 555-123-4567. It is easy to see that writing requirements for every single customer would be enormous, but when we define the customer *metadata*, requirements can be defined once for all customers. Metadata is an academic term; you'd probably never use it when talking with a business stakeholder, but its definition might appear on your exam.

Functional Decomposition (9.12)

Functional decomposition is the breaking down of a whole into its parts. This highly analytical technique, which was discussed in the Enterprise Analysis chapter, can be used for many tasks in business analysis. When specifying and modeling requirements, functional decomposition is performed at a detailed level on business processes, procedures, tasks, or even software components.

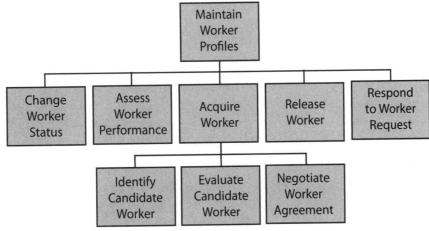

Decomposition Diagram of Business Processes

The decomposition diagram is very popular because it is easy for reviewers to understand. Notice the diagram does not show or imply any sequence. These processes may be performed in any order. This is a major difference from process models or data flow diagrams that include arrows and show the flow of work or data. A decomposition diagram is simply a list of processes and their sub-processes. Although this diagram is very powerful and useful, it does not give details about the processes. Each process should have more detailed information presented in a table or document supporting the diagram. In a sophisticated modeling tool, the user would be able to double-click on the process box and open a detailed window with the process characteristics. When we discuss the organization modeling technique, you will see that the decomposition diagram is also used to create organization charts.

Interface Analysis (9.13)

This technique was discussed in the Elicitation chapter as a method for identifying and understanding interfaces between people, systems, and organizations. When you document interfaces, you are specifying and modeling requirements. The user interfaces such as screen prototypes, report layouts, and data transfer descriptions we looked at earlier are solution requirements.

Metrics and Key Performance Indicators (9.16)

This technique was discussed in the Enterprise Analysis chapter as a method for measuring business process performance, looking for process improvements, and estimating the business value of the solution. When specifying and modeling requirements, you may need to measure the time and cost of a current business process to determine if an improvement to its efficiency or effectiveness will meet the business objectives.

Measuring can be as simple as using a stopwatch to see how long it takes for an end user to enter data on a screen. It may involve counting the number of pages of a report and multiplying by the number of copies of the report that are distributed to calculate paper costs. Measuring allows you to consider common improvement opportunities like automation or simplification of work, improvement of access to information, reduction of complexity, increase in consistency of behaviors, and elimination of redundant work.

Non-functional Requirements Analysis (9.17)

Non-functional requirements describe the environment within which the solution must function, and are often referred to as quality-of-service requirements. They describe things like the speed or performance of the software application and the security aspects of the solution. Non-functional requirements are extremely important, but often are not identified until the end of analysis. You should be listening for non-functional requirements during all of your requirements elicitation sessions. (You may hear analysts refer to non-functional requirements as the "bilities," because many of them end in those letters.)

Non-functional requirements are typically needed when the solution includes a software component. They are usually specified in sentences, as shown in the following table.

Examples of Non-functional Requirements
• Performance (speed and quantity)
• Security
• Compatibility
• Usability or Operability
• Reliability
• Portability
• Configurability
• Maintainability

© 2012 RMC Publications, Inc • 952.846.4484 • info@rmcproject.com • www.rmcproject.com

Unique ID	Non-functional Requirement
NF1	The worker website should be available 24 hours a day, 7 days a week, except during scheduled maintenance work. Downtime should be limited to 2 hours per week.
NF2	The website should operate within the current and previous two versions of the following Internet browsers: Internet Explorer, Google Chrome, Mozilla, and Firefox.
NF3	Users must be required to change their passwords at least once every six months.
NF4	The web page should open within 20 seconds on a standard DSL connection.

Organization Modeling (9.19)

An organization model is a collection of diagrams, descriptions, and characteristics of the organization. When specifying requirements, a clear understanding of the job titles and roles of the stakeholders and how they are involved with the business processes will be critical for you and your team to design a solution that will best meet their needs. You will see this technique again in Solution Assessment and Validation as a method for capturing information about the organization and its readiness to transition to the solution.

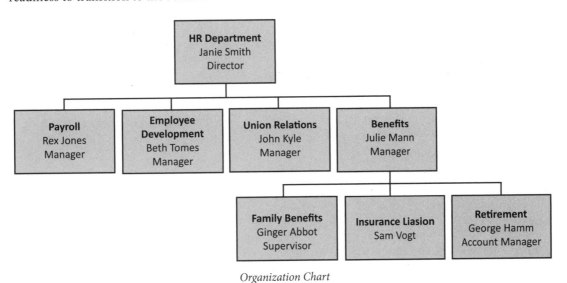

Organization Chart

Do you remember what this type of diagram is called? Functional decomposition!

Process Modeling (9.21)

Process modeling shows how work is performed in a business domain. As we have discussed, processes are the verbs or action words of our businesses that transform data. Many symbols and concepts are used in process modeling.

A process is initiated by an *event*. The analyst follows the activities of the business that are performed in response to the event. Candidate Applies for a Job is an event that causes the HR department to perform several processes. These processes are also known as *responses* to the event. Events are also referred to as *triggers* because they cause a process to start.

Event or Trigger	Processes (also known as responses to the event)
A candidate applies for a job	Accept application Review application Hire candidate Reject candidate Notify candidate of decision

Asking detailed questions about each process allows the analyst to get a detailed understanding of the business.

Sample questions to ask include:
- How do you currently perform the process?
- Are there sub-processes within a larger process?
- How many times do you do it (daily, weekly)?
- What information do you need to do it?
- What causes you to do it?
- What happens after the process is complete?
- Who performs the process?
- Who receives the output of the process?
- Where is the process performed?
- What do you think would improve the process?

Process modeling results in a diagram (and supporting details) of the business activities that are performed, in the sequence they are performed, along with decision points. The model may also show who performs each process.

Workflow diagramming is a popular way to visualize a process. You will also hear it called *flowcharting*, process modeling, or *process mapping*. A workflow diagram of a process delineates beginning and ending points (also referred to as *terminal points*), and shows *how work gets done, who does it, what decisions are faced*, and *how exceptions are handled*. To describe the same process with textual sentences would take hundreds of words.

The following example uses *swimlanes*—rows across the page representing parties involved with the process. This style of diagram shows how departments or groups interact with each other to accomplish the process. Swimlane diagrams are most useful to show handoffs and communications between roles and/or organizations (internal or external). These diagrams can be high-level or very detailed, depending on your need.

Boxes represent activities, diamond shapes represent decisions, and arrows show sequence. You may draw a diagram of the current (as-is) process or a recommendation for a future (to-be) process. These diagrams are relatively easy to follow, so business stakeholders are usually comfortable reviewing them and giving you feedback to clarify your understanding. The implementation SMEs use these diagrams to understand the desired solution design.

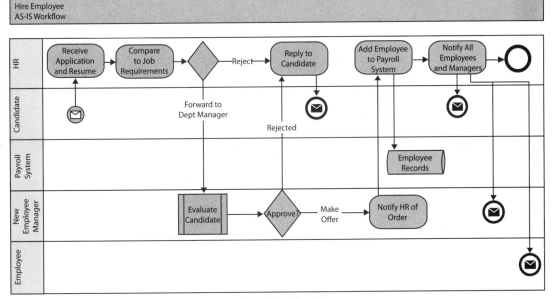

Hire Employee Workflow Diagram

This diagram is drawn using Business Process Modeling Notation (BPMN), which is a relatively new standard for process modeling, supported by the Object Management Group (OMG). It uses the traditional ANSI symbols and adds a few more. The circles are start or end events. The envelope represents a message. You probably won't see these symbols on the exam, but you might see a reference to BPMN.

EXERCISE Read the following interview with a stakeholder who describes the Transfer Employee process. Use the swimlanes in the worksheet to draw a workflow diagram of the process.

Interview notes:
"Our company philosophy is to encourage employees to work in different departments to learn about all aspects of the business. Of course their current and future managers must agree to the transfer before we respond to any employee request. The process is pretty simple; we update the employee records database with the new department code and an effective date. We also send out a notice to the related employees and managers to notify them of the change. If the transfer request is not approved by either manager, we ask the manager to document the reason and this becomes part of the employee's permanent HR file. Sometimes a transfer is requested by a manager who thinks his or her employee (and the organization) would benefit from the change."

Workflow Diagram

| Transfer Employee |
| AS-IS Workflow |

HR	
Current Employee Manager	
Payroll System	
New Employee Manager	
Employee	

SAMPLE ANSWER

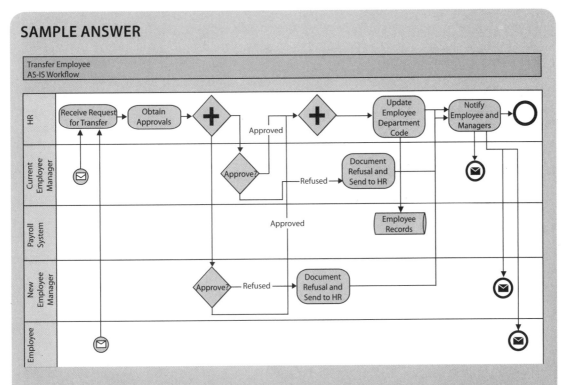

If you struggled with this exercise, you need more practice. Any process can be diagrammed, so start with something simple like paying a utility bill or getting cash from your bank. Ask co-workers if you can review their diagrams to see more examples.

Were you able to use the symbols we discussed earlier in this chapter? This graphic uses a symbol from BPMN that may be new to you. The plus signs inside the decision diamonds indicate parallel gateways used to split and merge the workflow. (You probably won't need to know these symbols for the CCBA® exam.)

 There are numerous process modeling notations: American National Standards Institute (ANSI), Value Stream Mapping (from Lean), Supplier-Input-Process-Output-Customer (SIPOC) (from Six Sigma), Business Process Modeling Notation (BPMN) from OMG. Be comfortable reviewing different notations. ANSI is similar to BPMN, with a smaller subset of icons. These notations are slightly different from each other—use your experience and logic to interpret the variations.

Prototyping (9.22)
This technique was discussed in the Elicitation chapter as a method for eliciting stakeholder and functional requirements. Can you see how this commonly used technique is also useful in the Specify and Model Requirements task? It allows the analyst to do several tasks at once: elicit, specify, model, document, and present requirements for confirmation.

Scenarios and Use Cases (9.26)
Scenarios and use case techniques were developed as part of Object-Oriented software development methodologies (OO). *Use cases* represent goals of the system, and *scenarios* represent the various paths the business may follow to achieve a goal. Many people refer to scenarios as *alternate paths*

through the use case. The notation and analysis rules are defined in UML. Use cases are mainly used in plan-driven development approaches. Change-driven approaches make use of user stories (discussed later in this task).

A *use case model* includes a use case diagram (or list) and detailed descriptions of each use case. The use case model was developed to be business-friendly and allow business stakeholders to show their desired functionality to the technical developers. The use of simple shapes like the stick figure and oval make the model less technical and easier to review.

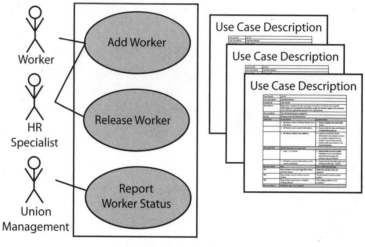

Use Case Model

Use Cases   Each use case represents a goal of an actor. As such, they are named from the perspective of the primary actor and are named with a verb-noun combination describing the action (verb) and the data or information (noun). Use case names are important because they are the primary component of the use case diagram and are used by the team to talk about the requirements. The name should reflect the goal of the actor, and should not be a technical name. For that reason, "Add New Worker" is a better name for the first use case than "Add Record to Database."

Examples of use cases:
- Apply for job
- Update mailing address
- Assess worker performance
- Report worker status

This diagram, like the context diagram we discussed in the Define Solution Scope task in Enterprise Analysis, shows boundaries or scope. It also shows how users will interact with the system and gives initial information about transition requirements. Notice on this diagram how the job of each actor is partially defined by the use cases to which it is attached. If the worker does not currently perform this function, we know the transition to this solution will require adjustments to job definitions, as well as training and procedure changes.

This is another example of two business analysis tasks that are performed concurrently. When you are Defining the Solution Scope (using a use case diagram) you are also Specifying and Modeling Requirements because the scope includes high-level requirements. This diagram could also be used to define more detailed requirements at a lower level of abstraction for a subset of the solution.

There are two specialized associations in a use case diagram that may be used for business analysis: *extends* and *includes*. The "extends" association shows an alternate flow or scenario. An "includes" association shows that one use case is used as a part of another use case. These *stereotypes* (relationships *between* use cases) are primarily used by software designers and developers, but you should be familiar with the terms just in case an exam question uses them.

APPLY YOUR KNOWLEDGE   Draw a use case diagram for a software application used in your company. How many different actors are involved? Did you include users and other systems that interface with the application? Present your diagram to someone who uses the application and ask if you missed anything.

Use Case Descriptions   Each use case is detailed in a description of how the solution should be built. Use cases typically describe an online screen or web page. The screen prototype is generally developed concurrently with the use case description. Use case descriptions are usually formatted using a standard template.

The following is an example of a use case description for Add New Worker.

Use Case ID	UC101	
Use Case Name	Add New Worker	
Created by	John Smith	
Description	Whenever a worker joins the company we need to record his or her payroll information, set up payroll and benefits, assign the worker a login to the network, and notify the appropriate people in the organization.	
Pre-Condition	The HR Administrator is logged in.	
Actors	Primary actor: HR Administrator	
Basic Path	Actor Action	System Action
	1. HR Admin selects Add New Worker from the menu.	2. System displays the add profile screen.
	3. HR Admin enters worker information.	4. System edits the data and displays a confirmation pop-up.
	5. HR Admin confirms the addition.	6. System records the worker information and activates worker by creating a login ID for the worker to access the network. 7. System adds new worker to the payroll database.
Alternate Path	Worker data does not pass edits.	
	1. Steps 1-3 as above.	2. System finds an error in edits, highlights errors, and displays appropriate message (see business rules list below).
	3. HR Admin corrects information on the screen as directed.	4. System checks the edits again and continues with step 4 above.

Business Rules	Rule	Error or Warning Message
BR1	New workers must have legal first names and last names.	"Both first and last name are required."
BR2	New worker's tax ID number must be unique.	"Tax ID already used by another worker."
BR3	New workers must have a complete mailing address.	"The mailing address is not complete."
Post-Condition	HR Admin signs out of system.	

Use Case Description

Typical components of a use case description:
- Name and unique identifier
- Precondition
- Primary actor
- Basic or "happy" path (a path is made up of sequentially numbered steps describing how the function is performed)
  - Actor actions
  - System actions
  - Business rules related to each step
- Alternate paths
- Business rules with related error or warning messages
- Post-condition(s)

Sequence Diagrams (9.28)

Sequence diagrams are used in software design and development to show how different software components (objects or classes) interact with each other via messages. They are developed from use cases and scenarios to communicate to the implementation SMEs how the solution should be built. They represent system interactions.

This example will help you understand the technique.

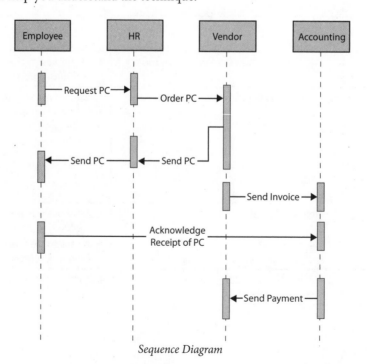

Sequence Diagram

The rectangles on top of the diagram are the objects or classes. The vertical dotted lines are referred to as their *lifelines*. Each interaction between the classes is shown by a horizontal arrow from one lifeline to another with a label describing the interaction (also called a *message*).

Sequence diagrams are used to communicate with software architects. Few business analysts use them. If the term comes up on your exam, it will most likely be used as a distracter answer.

State Diagrams (9.29)

A state diagram is an analytical technique used by analysts and developers to identify business processes or to double-check the completeness of existing process models. The state diagram focuses on business objects or entities and their life cycle conditions (or *states*) to confirm completeness when designing a solution. Working with state diagrams is referred to as performing *state transition analysis*.

State transition analysis is usually performed for high-level business objects or key data concepts such as product, order, vendor, employee, contract, and policy. The analyst and domain SMEs examine each object and list its states or life cycle phases. Think of life cycle phases in terms of a human life cycle: people are born, grow up, live, and eventually die.

The employee is an important business object in the Workforce Tracking case study. An employee is "born" when he or she applies for a job. The object might be referred to as a Candidate at this point. The Candidate "grows up" when he or she is hired and becomes an Active Employee. While the employee "lives" in the organization, he or she might go through other states such as "On Leave" or "On Probation." And eventually, when the employee leaves the company ("dies"), he or she is "Retired" or "Terminated."

Notations for drawing a state diagram include the commonly used UML Activity Diagram notation. States are usually drawn as ovals or roundtangles (rounded rectangles). Transitions are shown on arrows.

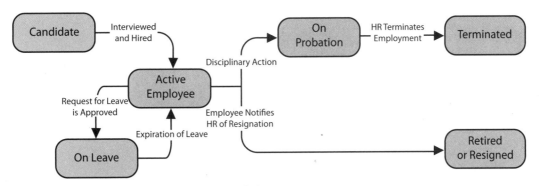

Simple State Diagram

When working with stakeholders to identify states, ask questions about how the object comes into being and the stages it moves through. The great thing about this technique is it reminds us to include the very beginning and very ending of each object in the analysis, to make sure we haven't missed anything.

TRICKS OF THE TRADE® Performing state transition analysis is extremely useful, but the resulting diagram may not be. A state diagram (also referred to as a state machine diagram or state transition diagram) is rarely a requirements deliverable presented to business stakeholders. It is most often used by analysts to double-check their other models.

Once the states are identified, this technique helps the analyst to ask questions about how the object gets from one state to the next. These transitions often describe business processes that are performed in the business domain. In our example, to move a Candidate to an Active Employee requires a process called Add New Employee. Each transition should be compared to the existing process model to make sure nothing has been missed, or it can be used to identify and name processes at the beginning of process modeling.

User Stories (9.33)

A user story is a brief description of a feature or function needed by a stakeholder. User stories were described in Enterprise Analysis as a technique for defining the solution scope. If you created user stories to define the solution scope, you have already specified many of your requirements.

#0023	Employee Login	Estimate	5
As an employee, I want to login to change my profile			
Require username + password			

User Story Card

The main purpose of writing a user story is to describe the requirement in just enough detail for a developer to estimate the time required to build it. User stories are brief descriptions intended to remind the team to have a conversation about the requirement. Once the estimates are assigned, the stakeholders can prioritize all stories based on their expected business value and expected cost. The highest priority stories will be assigned to the first *sprint*, or iteration.

 Epic is a new term used in many change-driven approaches. An epic is a collection of related user stories.

Summary of Techniques

The long list of techniques for this task reflects its importance! The *BABOK® Guide* includes the techniques most commonly used to Specify and Model Requirements.

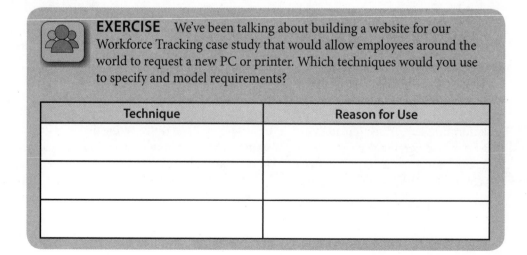

EXERCISE We've been talking about building a website for our Workforce Tracking case study that would allow employees around the world to request a new PC or printer. Which techniques would you use to specify and model requirements?

Technique	Reason for Use

SAMPLE ANSWER

Technique	Reason for Use
Prototype the web pages	Show stakeholders what the solution would look like.
Data Modeling (draw an entity relationship diagram with a detailed list of attributes)	Make sure all the information needed to process the request is known and will be stored in a database or file.
Business Rules Analysis	List all the rules used to determine if the employee request is approved.
Non-functional Requirements Analysis	Tell implementation SMEs the expected number of requests, and how fast the users expect the website to respond.
Scenarios and Use Cases	Describe how the employees will use the web page to enter their requests and how the software should handle errors or exceptions.
User Stories	In a change-driven approach, user stories would start a conversation with the business SME. Then the implementation SMEs would build the solution as the domain SMEs provided feedback.

Did you choose some other techniques? There isn't really a wrong answer to this question; it doesn't hurt to try a technique and see if it helps with the analysis or communication of the requirements.

Summary

Specifying and modeling requirements is the heart of analysis. Sometimes people say business analysis is both art and science. Well, this is the *science*. It is important that you feel comfortable with structured analysis techniques. The value of using structured techniques is the ability to look at the problem or potential solution from different perspectives. This task involves thinking about the *stated* requirements from different perspectives, asking more questions, and producing deliverables that represent *analyzed* requirements to the stakeholders for review and for development of the solution.

Define Assumptions and Constraints (6.4)

This task describes the importance of acknowledging and reaching agreement about things the team assumes, but does not know, to be true, and limitations, or constraints, placed upon the solution. Assumptions and constraints are as important as requirements when designing a solution to a business need. Assumptions and constraints can be identified at any time during the project and should be captured as they are identified. They often become apparent as stakeholders voice concerns during requirements elicitation. "The system must run on our existing PCs" is an example of a constraint. The purpose of documenting assumptions and constraints is to alert the implementation SMEs about the limitations on their solution design.

Define Assumptions and Constraints		
Inputs	**Techniques**	**Outputs**
Stakeholder Concerns (3.3)	Problem Tracking (9.20)	Assumptions and Constraints (6.4)
	Risk Analysis (9.24)	

BA's Responsibilities in Defining Assumptions and Constraints
- Understand the purpose of identifying and documenting assumptions and constraints
- Facilitate discussion of each assumption and constraint to make sure it is accurate, well stated, and agreed upon
- Identify and alert the stakeholders to any assumptions or constraints that may limit the ability of the solution to meet the business need.

What Do You Need to Successfully Define Assumptions and Constraints?

Assumptions and constraints are often identified during elicitation events with stakeholders. You may recall that there were two outputs of elicitation: requirements and stakeholder concerns. These stakeholder concerns are used to find assumptions and constraints. Have you ever thought about this? When a stakeholder is worried about something related to the business problem or potential solution, you need to find out what he or she is worried about and why. Many of these worries are well-founded because stakeholders know about the day-to-day operations of the business and may be aware of something that could prevent the solution from being successful. You need to use your questioning and listening skills to get to the root cause of the worry or concern and find out what the underlying assumptions and constraints are. Here we are again performing two business analysis tasks at the same time: Conduct Elicitation Activity and Define Assumptions and Constraints.

Communicate about Assumptions and Constraints   Assumptions and constraints are challenging to identify and describe. Every project or assignment has some underlying assumptions and constraints, whether or not they are discussed or documented. For example, if you are asked to analyze a change to a software data entry screen, there are implicit assumptions, such as, "The change will not alter the underlying architecture of the software application." There are often unspoken constraints as well, such as, "This change must not negatively impact the speed at which a user can enter data." An experienced business analyst always verifies assumptions and constraints with knowledgeable stakeholders.

Know the following definitions for the exam:

Assumption   Something that is assumed, but not proven, to be true, usually during the life of the solution.

> **Example Assumption:**
> Employees will have access to the HR website from wherever they work.

Business Constraint   A limitation on the business need/solution design.

> **Example Business Constraint:**
> Contract workers should only be able to access the equipment tracking portion of the system.

Technical Constraint   A limitation or boundary beyond which the technology or technology budget cannot reach. The team must design a solution that works within the technical constraints.

> **Example Technical Constraint:**
> The system must work on all the Internet browsers supported by the company.

Project Constraint   A limitation on the project. Project managers use the term constraint when referring to the project budget and time limitations.

Many constraints and assumptions can be rephrased into requirements or risks.
> Constraint: Our employees only have access to a standard Internet browser.
> Requirement: The system must support our standard Internet browser.
> Risk: Employees can't access website due to browser problems.

Deciding whether to formally document assumptions and constraints is a judgment call made by the project manager and business analyst based on their knowledge of the business domain and the solution. On small assignments, you may not document assumptions and constraints but you still need to be aware of them.

Techniques to Define Assumptions and Constraints

Problem Tracking (9.20)
The problem tracking technique is used to identify and verify assumptions and constraints during the project work. Problems related to assumptions and constraints are usually referred to as *issues*. Issues include assumptions or constraints that have not yet been confirmed with the appropriate stakeholder or that conflict with other information you have received. Issues must be recorded, tracked, and resolved.

Risk Analysis (9.24)
The risk analysis technique is used to assess assumptions and constraints identified on the project. It is important for you to recognize that assumptions and constraints are risks. Using risk analysis, the team evaluates the impact of acting on inaccurate assumptions, thereby minimizing the risk those assumptions bring to project success. You should help the team analyze the positive or negative effects of changing existing constraints.

Summary

It is interesting to note that assumptions and constraints are not used as inputs to any other tasks in this knowledge area. (They are inputs to the Define Business Case task in Enterprise Analysis and to the Assess Proposed Solution task in Solution Assessment and Validation.) Whether or not they are formally documented, assumptions and constraints continue to exist even after the solution is implemented, and the success of the solution depends on their ongoing accuracy. Unless they are officially removed, constraints must always be adhered to and are frequently referenced during solution design and development. As time passes, some of these assumptions and constraints may change, resulting in a new business need.

Verify Requirements (6.5)

Verifying requirements makes sure the requirements meet the standards of the organization and ensures a quality solution will be built. When working with testers and quality assurance professionals, you may hear the phrase "V and V." The two Vs stand for verification and validation, extremely important activities for assuring quality in our requirements and the resulting solutions.

It is important to understand the difference between verification and validation and to understand how they are used together to ensure the highest quality solutions. A quality solution is one that operates as expected and meets our original business need as articulated in the business case.

There are three business analysis tasks that start with Verify or Validate. The Verify Requirements task answers the questions: Are the requirements of the highest quality? Do they meet the organization's standards for documenting requirements? Do they meet the characteristics of excellent requirements?

The Validate Requirements task answers the questions: Do the requirements describe a solution that will bring business value? Will the solution meet the project objectives and solve the original business problems?

After the solution is built, we will Validate the Solution. In other words, we will confirm that the solution did, in fact, do what it was intended to. This task is in the Solution Assessment and Validation knowledge area.

Some teams verify and validate requirements at the same time, but proper practices require verification to be performed first. During either type of review, your reviewers will point out ambiguous requirements and find missing components. You should encourage reviewers to find as many problems as possible during both verification and validation. The more requirements problems found (and corrected), the better the resulting solution will be.

Look at the following example. The business case states a new furnace is needed and the value will be energy and cost savings. Requirements are developed. Now it is time to make sure the requirements meet the need.

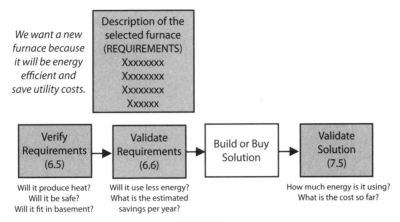

We want a new furnace because it will be energy efficient and save utility costs.

Description of the selected furnace (REQUIREMENTS)
Xxxxxxxx
Xxxxxxxx
Xxxxxxxx
Xxxxx

Verify Requirements (6.5)

Validate Requirements (6.6)

Build or Buy Solution

Validate Solution (7.5)

Will it produce heat? Will it be safe? Will it fit in basement?

Will it use less energy? What is the estimated savings per year?

How much energy is it using? What is the cost so far?

V&V tasks

Verify Requirements		
Inputs	**Techniques**	**Outputs**
Requirements [Any Except Stated]	Acceptance and Evaluation Criteria Definition (9.1)	Requirements [Verified] (6.5)
	Problem Tracking (9.20)	
	Structured Walkthrough (9.30)	

BA's Responsibilities in Verifying Requirements

- Understand the purpose of requirements verification (are the requirements RIGHT?)
- Schedule and conduct walkthroughs in accordance with the business analysis plan
- Schedule and conduct additional walkthroughs as needed
- Accept suggestions and criticisms with grace, thanking the reviewers for helping to improve the quality of the ultimate solution

What Do You Need to Successfully Verify Requirements?

It would be a waste of time to verify requirements that had not yet been analyzed, confirmed, or approved. Stated requirements are a starting point and, as such, are not expected to conform to the standards of well-documented requirements.

The easiest way to verify requirements is to have a standard your organization uses to evaluate all requirements. The standard may be represented in a checklist used by reviewers to confirm compliance with the organization's standards for requirements. There are several quality characteristics that are important for requirements:

- Cohesive
- Complete
- Consistent
- Correct
- Feasible
- Modifiable
- Unambiguous
- Testable

Reviewers will look for clear, understandable deliverables that describe the solution. They will make sure connections between requirements are accurate and look for missing requirements.

Techniques to Verify Requirements

Acceptance and Evaluation Criteria Definition (9.1)
Ideally, your organization has acceptance criteria already defined to help reviewers verify requirements. These criteria, more specific than the quality characteristics listed above, set a standard that requirements must meet before they are handed over to the implementation SMEs and used for technical design. If your organization doesn't currently have a standard, begin to develop checklists to provide to reviewers when they verify your requirements.

Problem Tracking (9.20)
Problems found during verification are added to the issue log if they cannot be immediately resolved.

Structured Walkthrough (9.30)
Structured walkthroughs are also known as requirements reviews or design reviews. A review of a document, model, diagram, or other deliverable is *human-based testing*. Walkthroughs are one of the foundations of quality assurance. When another person reviews a requirements deliverable, he or she asks questions that may reveal ambiguity and uncover missing requirements. Another set of eyes looking at a product always improves its quality. These quality improvements are much easier to fix in a requirements deliverable than to fix in a constructed solution. If the solution is built incorrectly, costs to repair it are high. The more problems we find and resolve with the requirements, the fewer problems we have with the final solution.

Any activity that checks on an interim or final deliverable is a verification or validation activity. Although it is true that the more your organization reviews and checks things, the higher the quality of the product you will deliver, reviews can be time-consuming and costly, so they must be done efficiently.

Know the Steps to Conducting a Structured Walkthrough
To conduct an effective review, you must follow the process outlined here. This process makes the best use of reviewers' time and results in the most quality improvements to the deliverable. Reviewers may include domain SMEs, implementation SMEs, testers, or peers (other business analysts).

Determine the purpose of the walkthrough (interim or final) and the participants. The author of the deliverable is always present and may act as the facilitator or moderator.

1. Deliver materials to be reviewed to participants at least 48 hours before review.
2. Confirm individual reviews have been done before start of working session.
3. Conduct working session.
4. Record feedback/questions/corrections/issues.
5. Update materials and re-review if necessary.

Accepting Feedback   It is important for business analysis professionals to have humility. As the author of the requirements, you must welcome questions, suggestions, criticism, and improvement ideas for the requirements. It will be difficult, but you must put away your ego and not allow your feelings to be hurt during a walkthrough. This is not about criticizing you; it is about improving the quality of the requirements and, ultimately, the solution. Being honest about your abilities and mistakes is a characteristic of ethical behavior.

© 2012 RMC Publications, Inc • 952.846.4484 • info@rmcproject.com • www.rmcproject.com

EXERCISE Review the to-be workflow for Worker Requests New Equipment. Then develop a list of questions/concerns that you would discuss with the author during a walkthrough.

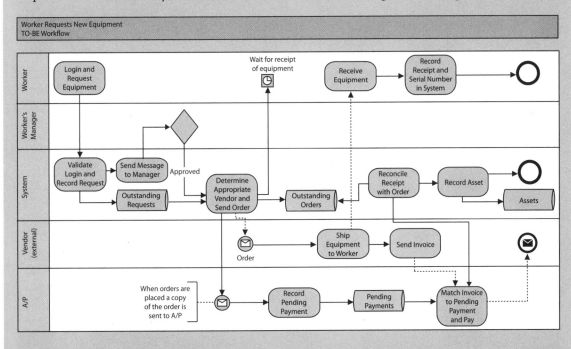

Questions and Comments to Discuss During the Walkthrough

SAMPLE ANSWER

- What if the worker login does not work?
- If the manager rejects the request, is there an appeal process?
- What is the process if a request is rejected?
- The gateway or decision diamond in the manager lane should be labeled.
- How long will the worker wait for the equipment?
- How will the system decide which vendor to order from?
- What prompts the worker to record receipt of the equipment?
- Is the worker notified if the request is approved?
- Is the worker notified if the request is rejected?
- How do outstanding orders get deleted?
- What if an invoice doesn't reconcile?
- What if a shipment goes to the wrong place?

When an individual reviews a document, he or she will find inconsistencies, errors, or ambiguities. When the group then discusses the document and each participant shares his or her findings, the group as a whole will often come up with even more quality improvements. This illustrates the value of a review as a collaborative group activity.

Summary

The output of verification is requirements [verified]. Verification is the first V in "V and V" because we first make sure the requirements meet the organization's standards and are consistent and clear. The next task, Validate Requirements, will check to see whether the solution, as described in the requirements, will bring business value to the organization.

Validate Requirements (6.6)

Validating requirements is another important part of Requirements Analysis. We need to make sure our solution requirements will bring value to the organization *before* we use the requirements to build the solution. Value does not only mean money! Do the requirements, which we verified in the previous task, describe a solution that will solve the business problem? Keep in mind that the requirements alone don't bring a lot of value to the organization—it is the solution that will bring business value, and the requirements describe the solution. This task requires you and your team to step back from the detailed analysis work and look at the requirements from the perspective of the business.

 A hint to remember: VALidate = VALue. We are now answering the question: Will the solution we have described in the requirements give value to the business?

Validate Requirements		
Inputs	**Techniques**	**Outputs**
Stakeholder, Solution or Transition Requirements [Verified] (6.5)	Acceptance and Evaluation Criteria Definition (9.1)	Requirements [Validated] (6.6)
Business Case (5.5)	Metrics and Key Performance Indicators (9.16)	
	Prototyping (9.22)	
	Risk Analysis (9.24)	
	Structured Walkthrough (9.30)	

BA's Responsibilities in Validating Requirements

- Understand the purpose of requirements validation and how validating requirements is different from requirements verification
- Schedule and conduct walkthroughs in accordance with the business analysis plan
- Schedule and conduct additional walkthroughs as needed
- Trace each requirement back to the business objective it will satisfy

What Do You Need to Successfully Validate Requirements?

To validate the requirements, we need to go back to the original business case and make sure our detailed work supports the high-level objectives. Validating the requirements must be done before the solution is built. Our requirements must describe the solution design in enough detail that it can be envisioned and its business value estimated. Defining measurable evaluation criteria of how it will address the business need, and determining the business value requires forecasts and estimates. Assumptions and constraints are also used to validate the requirements.

Validation Is a Major Milestone

Validating the requirements is a major milestone of a project. We step back, review the original business case, and confirm that we have designed a solution that will realize the benefits predicted. The team must take an objective look at the solution design and confirm that the organization should move forward to build it. Reevaluating decisions based on current information prevents the organization from wasting resources or missing a different opportunity. If the analysis and requirements took a couple of months or longer, the team should reconsider the project based on the current environment. Is this still the most important project? Is the original business case still valid?

Validating the requirements requires reviewers to look at each requirement and make sure it is necessary and critical to the success of the solution. Traceability can help with this work. Each requirement should be traced back to the original business objective that it supports. I will show you examples of how to document traceability in the next chapter, Requirements Management and Communication.

Techniques to Validate Requirements

Acceptance and Evaluation Criteria Definition (9.1)

This technique is used to set the criteria upon which the requirements will be validated. Your organization should have quality standards for validation. A common standard is that every requirement must trace back to an original business need.

Metrics and Key Performance Indicators (9.16)

The metrics and key performance indicators technique was discussed in the Enterprise Analysis chapter as a method for measuring business process performance, looking for process improvements, and estimating the business value of the solution. If performance metrics were estimated in the business case, they should be reviewed here against the description of the solution. For example, the original business case may have estimated a savings of three hours on each PC request for the HR team, since the PC will now be shipped directly to the employee from the vendor. To validate the solution requirements, the reviewers should assess whether that estimated savings will be realized through the proposed solution.

Prototyping (9.22) and Structured Walkthroughs (9.30)

Prototyping and walkthroughs are additional ways to confirm that the requirements reflect the desired solution. In change-driven software projects, requirements are validated by having software developers build a part of the solution (or a prototype or simulation). Reviewers (domain SMEs and end users) can look at the solution and determine if it will solve their problem and bring them value. Adjustments are made to the solution to improve the expected value. Structured walkthroughs focus on evaluating the solution design to validate the requirements.

Risk Analysis (9.24)

The risk analysis technique can help you identify and assess the risks associated with each requirement. Here the team is looking at the probability and impact of identified risks to the requirements and how the occurrence of these risks could affect the value of the solution.

Summary

This task is the final opportunity to make sure the requirements are complete before the implementation stakeholders use them to build the solution. Of course, validation of requirements doesn't have to be performed on the entire requirements package at once. In change-driven approaches, user stories are validated as they are completed and the solution, or at least parts of it, gets built right away. Regardless of the approach, every requirement should bring value to the organization, and the business analyst is responsible for making sure it will!

——— SUMMARY OF THE REQUIREMENTS ANALYSIS KNOWLEDGE AREA ———

Well, you made it through Requirements Analysis! This is the biggest chapter, so you are now more than halfway through this book! This is the heart of business analysis! Don't be discouraged if you didn't recognize all of the techniques. Few business analysts have used all of them. Look at this as your opportunity to learn some new ways of analyzing requirements. Review your list of unfamiliar techniques from the checklists in the Tricks of the Trade® Chapter (page 12) and practice using them on a current project. The tasks and techniques in this chapter provide many different ways of solving a problem or understanding a complex process. Whenever you feel stuck, try another technique and it will probably help you see the situation from a new perspective.

APPLY YOUR KNOWLEDGE

1. Draw a *decomposition diagram* of major processes within your company or department. Ask a co-worker to review it for accuracy.
2. Draw an *organization model* of your company or another organization you know. Are there clear reporting lines? Volunteer organizations often have unclear reporting lines; presenting a graphic of the communication challenges can help improve the organization.
3. Draw a *workflow diagram* of your personal process for paying bills or for filing your tax return to practice workflow diagramming.
4. Make a list of data elements or draw a simple *data model* of your family finances.
5. Review public websites for their *non-functional requirements*. How well does the site perform (on different browsers, with different applications open)? How is the security designed? How reliable is it? As a user, what recommendations would you make?
6. Imagine a website to support your hobby or interest. Write some *user stories* for the features you would request. Remember to use the three Cs.

Before taking the practice exam, I recommend that you read the Requirements Analysis chapter of the *BABOK® Guide* (Chapter 6), and the descriptions of the key techniques of this knowledge area (in Chapter 9 of the *BABOK® Guide*):

- Business Rules Analysis (9.4)
- Data Dictionary and Glossary (9.5)
- Data Flow Diagrams (9.6)
- Data Modeling (9.7)
- Metrics and Key Performance Indicators (9.16)
- Non-functional Requirements Analysis (9.17)
- Organization Modeling (9.19)
- Process Modeling (9.21)
- Scenarios and Use Cases (9.26)
- Sequence Diagrams (9.28)
- Structured Walkthrough (9.30)
- User Stories (9.33)

Practice Exam

1. Which techniques would be MOST useful for designing a new business process?

   A. Data dictionary, interface analysis, and process modeling
   B. Business rules analysis, data flow diagrams, and metrics and key performance indicators.
   C. Business rules analysis, process modeling, and state diagrams
   D. Business rules analysis, functional decomposition, and process modeling

2. The BEST way to prioritize requirements is to:

   A. Ask the business stakeholders to put them in order of importance.
   B. Use your knowledge of the business to put them in order of importance.
   C. Ask the implementation SMEs to put them in order of priority.
   D. Facilitate a discussion between the business and implementation SMEs to get agreement on priorities.

3. A structured walkthrough is also known as:

   A. A requirements review.
   B. A SWOT analysis.
   C. Observation.
   D. Benchmarking.

4. You have studied a business process using observation and need to document the process. It involves three departments and several tasks. Which of the following is the BEST presentation technique to use?

   A. A textual description of the process
   B. A swimlane workflow diagram
   C. An entity relationship diagram
   D. A context diagram

5. Requirements MUST be:

   A. Formally documented in a requirements package.
   B. Fully analyzed.
   C. Completely detailed.
   D. Communicated verbally to save time.

6. A key component of any set of requirements is:

   A. The glossary of terms and definitions.
   B. The table of contents for the requirements package.
   C. An index referencing the most commonly used phrases.
   D. The revision log.

© 2012 RMC Publications, Inc • 952.846.4484 • info@rmcproject.com • www.rmcproject.com

7. A data dictionary is:

    A. A database of information about corporate customers.
    B. Rarely used in business analysis.
    C. A list of data elements with their descriptions.
    D. An artifact created and maintained by the project manager.

8. A use case diagram includes:

    A. Actors, use cases, and associations.
    B. The software, interfaces, and screen design.
    C. Users, stakeholders, and use cases.
    D. Features to be included in the system.

9. A business analyst produces many things. Which of the following describes a result used for analysis but NOT formally presented to a stakeholder?

    A. Formal deliverable
    B. Elicitation plan
    C. Requirements workshop agenda
    D. Work product

10. In the Workforce Tracking System, a stakeholder requests each employee's eye color be recorded and stored. This requirement:

    A. May not be correct.
    B. May not be feasible.
    C. Is ambiguous.
    D. Is incomplete.

11. Once requirements have been reviewed and approved by business stakeholders and solution architects, they can be referred to as:

    A. Stated requirements.
    B. Refined requirements.
    C. Verified requirements.
    D. Functional requirements.

12. A high-level, informal, short description of a feature that provides value to a stakeholder is called a:

    A. Use case.
    B. User story.
    C. Prototype.
    D. Sprint.

13. The main purpose of writing a user story is:

    A. To confirm the stakeholder's verbal description of a business process.
    B. To confirm the business analyst understands the business process.
    C. To describe the requirement in just enough detail for a developer to estimate time and cost required to build it.
    D. To allow the architect to design the solution components to work together.

14. While talking with business domain SMEs about the impacts of the solution on their personnel, which diagram may be MOST helpful?

    A. Use Case Diagram
    B. Data model (ERD)
    C. SWOT diagram
    D. Context diagram

15. UML stands for:

    A. Unexpected Management Landmines.
    B. Unspecified Modeling Losses.
    C. Unambiguous Measurable Legitimate.
    D. Unified Modeling Language.

16. A swimlane style workflow diagram should be used:

    A. When there are handoffs and communications between several roles and departments or organizations.
    B. When the process is extremely complex with numerous business rules.
    C. When management is opposed to the change and needs to understand the ramifications.
    D. Only for documenting as-is processes.

17. When building a to-be workflow diagram, all of the following are included EXCEPT:

    A. Who will do the work; job descriptions are the business stakeholder's responsibilities.
    B. Business rules that should be followed; they should be included in the employee procedure manual.
    C. Exception or error processing; it will be handled as it occurs by the workers.
    D. A detailed description of why the change is being made, and the ultimate goal.

18. A state diagram is useful for:

    A. Showing the geographic locations of the enterprise.
    B. Showing the stated business rules of the business domain.
    C. Showing the key stakeholders and their locations.
    D. Showing the key states of a particular business object.

19. To double-check your process model, it is BEST to use:

    A. A SWOT diagram.
    B. A UML activity diagram.
    C. A state diagram.
    D. A decision table.

20. Generally speaking, which parts of speech correlate to which requirements modeling concepts?

    A. Nouns are data and verbs are processes.
    B. Nouns are processes and verbs are data.
    C. Nouns are business rules and verbs are processes.
    D. Nouns are stakeholders and verbs are business rules.

21. If one requirement will provide higher business value than a second requirement:

    A. The first requirement must be assigned a higher priority.
    B. The second requirement must be assigned a higher priority.
    C. The second requirement should be postponed to the next phase or iteration.
    D. The first requirement may be assigned a higher priority.

22. The components of a data model include:

    A. Entities, attributes, and relationships.
    B. Processes, functions, and use cases.
    C. User stories, entities, and attributes.
    D. Data elements, attributes, and fields.

23. Into which classification does this requirement fit? "The users will require training on the new software prior to implementation."

    A. Business requirement
    B. Transition requirement
    C. Functional requirement
    D. Non-functional requirement

24. A decomposition diagram cannot show:

    A. Business processes.
    B. Sub-processes.
    C. Sequence.
    D. Business functions.

25. The main input to Define Assumptions and Constraints is:

    A. The business need.
    B. Stakeholder requirements.
    C. Stakeholder concerns.
    D. The business case.

26. To validate requirements, they must be:

    A. Verified.
    B. Approved.
    C. Technical.
    D. Stated.

27. To validate requirements, you must review:

    A. The business case.
    B. The solution design.
    C. The transition plan.
    D. The requirements management plan.

28. Techniques useful for validating requirements include:

   A. Acceptance and evaluation criteria definition and metrics and key performance indicators.
   B. Data modeling and scope modeling.
   C. Requirements workshops and observation.
   D. Decision analysis and acceptance and evaluation criteria definition.

Answers

1. **Answer** D
   Explanation Process modeling is the first technique you would think of. Functional decomposition is useful for breaking down processes. Business rules analysis is necessary to make sure the redesigned process enforces the correct rules. The other techniques might be used but are not the most useful.

2. **Answer** D
   Explanation Many factors go into requirements prioritization. Although the business stakeholders are the ultimate decision makers, their priorities might change when they find out the cost/time to implement a particular requirement. To properly prioritize, the team must consider business value, cost, time, technical constraints, and alignment with enterprise goals and enterprise architecture, so they need the input from business and implementation SMEs.

3. **Answer** A
   Explanation SWOT analysis is a competitive marketing technique for identifying strengths, weaknesses, threats, and opportunities. Observation is watching business stakeholders to learn the business. Benchmarking is measuring against competitive organizations to compare performance. A requirements review is another name for a structured walkthrough.

4. **Answer** B
   Explanation A visual presentation is usually better than a textual description, because it can be shown with fewer words and is easier to review. An entity relationship diagram is a data modeling tool. The context diagram is used to show solution scope. A swimlane workflow diagram is best, since there are three departments involved. A swimlane workflow diagram shows handoffs between groups.

5. **Answer** B
   Explanation Requirements do not need to be formal on some projects and may or may not be presented in a package. On change-driven projects, they may be communicated verbally, but they may also be documented on informal tools like flip charts, whiteboards, wikis, etc. Not every requirement needs to be completely detailed. You need *just enough* detail to confirm understanding and communicate to the solution team. The only answer where MUST is appropriate here is that requirements must be fully analyzed.

6. **Answer** A
   Explanation Although all of these may be important in certain requirements packages, the most important from this list is the glossary of terms. If reviewers do not have a clear understanding of the terms used in the requirements diagrams and text, they will not have a clear understanding of the requirements.

7. **Answer** C
   Explanation A data dictionary is a list of data elements with their descriptions. It is frequently used by business analysts as part of a requirements set because the data elements are important needs of the business.

8. **Answer** A
   Explanation The use case diagram is defined by the UML standard and can be used to scope the software or system being built. It does not show screen design or specific features, but instead shows use cases, which are goals of actors, and associations between the actor and the system.

9. **Answer** D

   Explanation Elicitation plans and agendas should be reviewed by stakeholders to get their agreement, and as such are considered deliverables. A work product is a document, diagrams, or notes used by the business analyst during analysis. If any part of the work product is to be presented to a stakeholder, it is refined into a deliverable, such as a workflow diagram.

10. **Answer** A

    Explanation A data element like employee eye color is a requirement. It could be considered unambiguous, feasible, and complete (we understand what is meant by eye color and we could store it in a database). But is employee eye color necessary for Workforce Tracking? Hopefully you would ask the stakeholder, "Why do you need eye color?" or "What will you do with this piece of information?" to assess if it is correct.

11. **Answer** C

    Explanation Stated requirements have not yet been analyzed or refined. Refined is not a requirements state in the *BABOK® Guide*. Functional requirements are behaviors of the solution and may exist in any state. Requirements that have been reviewed and approved by business stakeholders and solution architects are verified requirements.

12. **Answer** B

    Explanation A use case is a detailed description of a goal of software from the point of view of an actor or user of the system. A prototype is a mockup or layout of a screen, report, or other solution component. A sprint is an iteration, release, or phase of a change-driven project. A user story is an informal, short description of a feature.

13. **Answer** C

    Explanation Confirming descriptions and understanding of business processes should be done before user stories are created, as part of business modeling. The overall solution design/ architecture should also be done before the first sprint or iteration (during planning). User stories are brief descriptions used by developers to create an estimate. After estimates have been created, the stakeholders can prioritize all stories based on their expected business value and expected cost. The highest priority stories will be assigned to the first sprint or iteration.

14. **Answer** A

    Explanation A data model, ERD, or SWOT diagram doesn't show users. A context diagram shows external agents or parties, not employees working inside the business domain. A use case diagram shows a system and the actors or users who have access to it. The association lines show how each actor will interact or use the system. A use case diagram can be very useful when working with business SMEs, determining how a system change is going to impact their employee procedures.

15. **Answer** D

    Explanation Unified Modeling Language (UML) is supported by the Object Management Group which also supports Business Process Modeling Language (BPMN). UML supports Object-Oriented software analysis, design, and development.

16. **Answer**   A

Explanation   Very complex processes may be better presented with a traditional flowchart, a decision tree, or a decision table. If management is opposed to the change, a better presentation might be a business case or impact analysis. Swimlane diagrams can be used to document both as-is and to-be processes. Swimlane diagrams are useful to show handoffs and communications between roles and/or organizations (internal or external). Both internal and external parties can be shown as swimlanes.

17. **Answer**   D

Explanation   This question may be difficult because it is important to communicate (and usually document) all of these components. A workflow diagram should include as much detail as necessary about who will do the work, how it will be done, decisions and rules to be followed, and exception processing/error handling. The workflow diagram may be used by the solution builders to create the solution and/or by the business workers who will support and implement it. The reason for the change and the goal of the project are usually included in the business case and may be reiterated in transition requirements and communications. They are not depicted in a workflow diagram.

18. **Answer**   D

Explanation   The state diagram focuses on business objects or entities and their life cycle conditions or *states*. The diagram is useful for thinking about how a business object changes and what causes it to change or *transition*. These transitions often describe business processes.

19. **Answer**   C

Explanation   SWOT is a competitive analysis tool that includes strengths, weaknesses, threats, and opportunities. A UML activity diagram shows how software will be developed. A decision table shows business rules. A state diagram focuses on business objects or entities and their life cycle conditions or *states*. The diagram is useful for thinking about how a business object changes and what causes it to change or *transition*. These transitions often describe business processes.

20. **Answer**   A

Explanation   Data components describe people, places, or things that are important to the business (nouns). Processes are activities of the business (verbs).

21. **Answer**   D

Explanation   Business value is only one of the factors used to determine priority. If the second requirement is less expensive to implement, it may be assigned a higher priority and be implemented first.

22. **Answer**   A

Explanation   Processes, functions, use cases, and user stories describe the work performed by the business. You recognize them because they are named with verbs. Field is a technical term for a data element that resides in a database or file. Data components are named with nouns; a formal data model includes entities, attributes, and relationships.

23. **Answer**   B

Explanation   Transition requirements describe tasks that must be performed to ensure a smooth implementation of the solution into the business domain.

24. **Answer** C

Explanation A decomposition diagram can be used to show the breakdown of functions, processes, organizational units, goals, and many other items. It does not show sequence.

25. **Answer** C

Explanation Stakeholder concerns are used to identify assumptions and constraints. Assumptions are things which are given to be true and constraints are limitations on the solution design. If a stakeholder has a concern about a particular aspect of the solution, that concern should be investigated. If it is found to be valid, it will either become a requirement, an assumption, or a constraint.

26. **Answer** A

Explanation Requirements should be verified before they are validated. Verification checks the requirements for correctness and conformance to standards. Validation checks the requirements for business value.

27. **Answer** A

Explanation The solution design and transition plan are parts of the requirements. The requirements management plan describes where requirements will be stored and how they will be managed. The business case contains the business need and justification for the project. This allows you to make sure the requirements will bring the expected business value.

28. **Answer** A

Explanation Data and scope models are parts of requirements. Requirements workshops and observation are elicitation techniques. Decision analysis is the financial analysis used to compare costs and benefits. Acceptance and evaluation criteria definition is used to describe the criteria upon which the requirements will be validated. Metrics and key performance indicators are used to determine the appropriate measures against which the solution design will be evaluated.

CHAPTER 6

Requirements Management and Communication

Aligned with the BABOK® Guide Chapter Four

The Requirements Management and Communication knowledge area is focused on maintaining requirements integrity and communicating about the requirements. While the other knowledge areas describe how to discover and analyze requirements, this area tells you how to manage them once you've got them. This work includes managing requirements and their links to other project elements (traceability), maintaining requirements during and after implementation so they can be used again on future projects, and packaging and communicating requirements to stakeholders for confirmation of accuracy and approval.

The tasks in this knowledge area are not performed in any particular order and are done iteratively throughout the life of a project. Some of them are also done outside of project work. They are performed in conjunction with tasks from many other knowledge areas. Approximately 24 exam questions will reference this knowledge area.

QUICK TEST

- Baselining
- Conflict and issue management
- Derivation (Backward traceability)
- Allocation (Forward traceability)
- Traceability relationship
- Lineage
- Dependency
- Link
- Product roadmap
- Vision document
- Impact analysis
- Requirements coverage
- Requirements allocation
- Configuration management system
- Coverage matrix
- Ongoing requirements
- Satisfied requirements
- Requirements package
- Request for Information (RFI)
- Request for Proposal (RFP)
- Request for Quotation (RFQ)
- Requirements structure
- Deliverable
- Business requirements document (BRD)
- Software requirement specification (SRS)

Requirements Management and Communication in Action

I was a business analyst on a project for a government transportation agency. The agency worked with many companies purchasing fuel, vehicles, insurance, and parts. They referred to these companies as *vendors*. The main project objective was to simplify vendor payment processing (thereby saving payment processing time and decreasing the number of errors). The solution approach involved the development of a custom software application and related procedure changes. The high-level requirements included the creation of a vendor database, electronic processing of vendor payments, and reporting on budgeted vs. actual vendor expenditures.

We created a context diagram to show the solution scope and interfaces. The context diagram and descriptions of the goals, assumptions, stakeholders, and other scoping information were presented to the sponsor for approval. We used a requirements tool to capture requirements and manage traceability. Since many of the vendors supplied multiple government agencies, one of our goals was to consolidate vendor information for use by all of these agencies. In order to achieve this goal, we elicited requirements from several of the agencies. We developed data flow diagrams and data models, and created a requirements package. We reviewed the requirements with our key stakeholders and obtained approvals as specified in our software development methodology and requirements management plan. As the solution was designed and built, changes to the original requirements were always compared to the solution scope and managed through the change control process. Whenever a requirement changed, its traceability was reviewed and updated. Traceability matrices were used to make sure all of the business requirements were addressed in the solution requirements. At the end of the project, the requirements were carefully documented and stored in a shared directory for future use on other projects.

EXERCISE   There are five tasks in the Requirements Management and Communication knowledge area: Manage Solution Scope and Requirements, Manage Requirements Traceability, Maintain Requirements for Re-use, Prepare Requirements Package, and Communicate Requirements. Can you identify the five tasks in the previous story?

Requirements Management and Communications Knowledge Area Task	Work Performed in the Story
Manage Solution Scope and Requirements	
Manage Requirements Traceability	
Maintain Requirements for Re-use	
Prepare Requirements Package	
Communicate Requirements	

ANSWER

Requirements Management and Communications Knowledge Area Task	Work Performed in the Story
Manage Solution Scope and Requirements	Got approval of the scope from the sponsor and approval of the requirements from the key stakeholders Referred back to the context diagram when new requirements were identified Note: Creating the context diagram is part of defining solution scope, a task performed in Enterprise Analysis. The solution scope is *managed*, not *defined*, in Requirements Management and Communication.
Manage Requirements Traceability	Traced business requirements to solution requirements Updated traceability when requirements changed
Maintain Requirements for Re-use	Knowing vendor information would be shared by other agencies on future projects, elicited requirements from other stakeholders, stored requirements for re-use
Prepare Requirements Package	Presented the scope diagram and documents to the sponsor Developed data flow diagrams and data models and produced the requirements package for key stakeholders Note: Did you realize there were two requirements packages in this story? • The scope diagram and documents (for the sponsor) AND • The data flow diagrams, data models, and other requirements (for key stakeholders)
Communicate Requirements	Presented the context diagram and descriptions of the goals, assumptions, stakeholders, and other scoping information to the sponsor for approval Reviewed requirements with key stakeholders

Barb's BA Themes

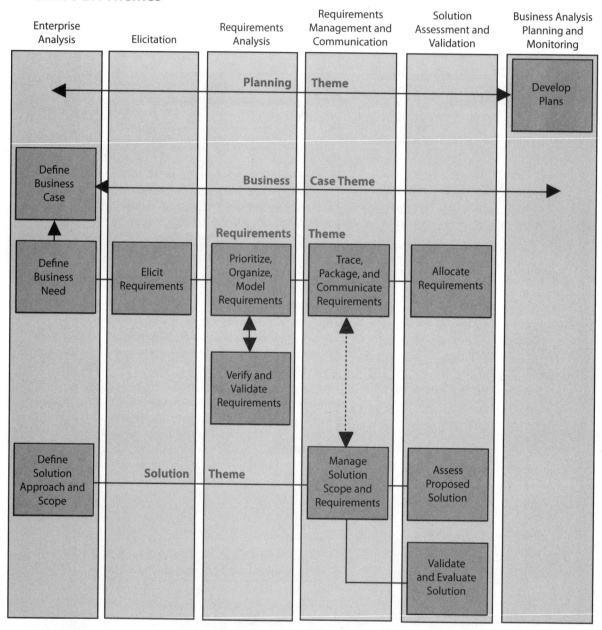

The Requirements Management and Communication knowledge area could be considered the hub of business analysis work. The tasks in this knowledge area are performed frequently and help to direct the business analysis work. The Planning Theme provides guidelines for the work performed in this knowledge area via the requirements management plan and the business analysis communication plan. The Business Case Theme reminds us that our goal, as always, is to meet the business need as defined in the business case.

Requirements Management and Communication is the knowledge area where the Requirements Theme and the Solution Theme converge (notice the dotted line between the two themes). The Manage Solution Scope and Requirements task acts as a director of requirements, making sure they are within scope, conflicts are resolved, and eventually the requirements are approved. Every requirement must pass through this director before it can be implemented. Requirements are also traced, packaged, and communicated in this knowledge area.

Things to Know about Requirements Management and Communication for the Exam

- These five tasks may be performed many times on a project, even on a small assignment.
- Manage Solution Scope and Requirements (4.1) is a big task that includes several elements—study it well.
- When requirements are traced, the link may be referred to as a relationship, connection, allocation, derivation, lineage, or dependency.
- Know all of the states of requirements; several new ones are introduced in this chapter (communicated, traced, approved, maintained, reusable, satisfied, ongoing).
- Packaging is an optional task; requirements are packaged only if it will better facilitate communication. A requirements package can include one or more requirements or requirements deliverables.

Introduction to the Tasks of Requirements Management and Communication

The tasks in Requirements Management and Communication are an odd collection of work. They include work that is often performed at the beginning of a project or new assignment (reusing requirements from other projects), throughout assignments (packaging and communicating requirements), all the way to work that is done after a solution is implemented (maintaining requirements for re-use). Remember when I warned you that business analysis work is not sequential? This chapter really proves it!

When you study the tasks in this chapter, it is best to think about requirements as individual components that are all at different stages of development. Some are still unrefined [stated], some have been analyzed, and some have been verified and validated. In this chapter, you'll learn about even more states of requirements. Requirements will become *approved*, *communicated*, *traced*, *maintained*, and *reusable*. Most of these tasks change the *state* of the requirements. These states show how requirements are evolving as the work described here is completed. Focus on learning the requirements states and the tasks will be easy to understand.

REQUIREMENTS MANAGEMENT AND COMMUNICATION KNOWLEDGE AREA TASKS

Manage Solution Scope and Requirements (4.1)

Scope is one of the most complex and difficult concepts of business analysis (and of project management as well). We looked at the solution scope in Enterprise Analysis. Let's review it again as part of the Solution Theme.

The Solution Theme

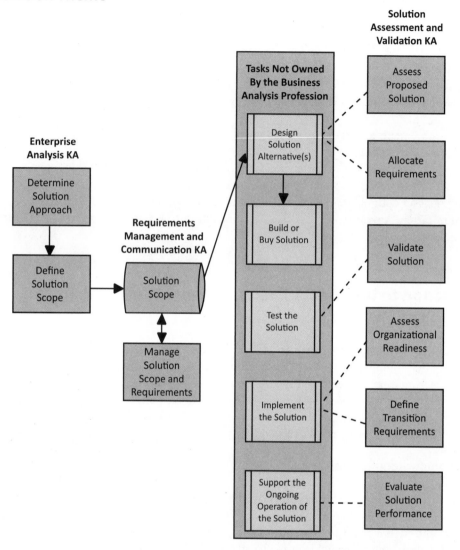

As you have already learned, solution scope is *born* in Enterprise Analysis. Determine Solution Approach and Define Solution Scope are the tasks in Enterprise Analysis that refer to solution scope. These tasks are completed at the beginning of analysis work to give us boundaries within which to analyze. They define the type of solution desired and describe high-level features of the solution. But the solution scope is not *approved* in Enterprise Analysis. Approval of the solution scope takes place in this knowledge area task, Manage Solution Scope and Requirements. Why? The answer goes to one of the most important concepts in business analysis: don't jump to a solution before you really understand the problem. The analysis required to define a solution scope (in Enterprise Analysis) is relatively high-level. Until we get into the details (in this task), we can't know for sure that the solution will work.

Often a project is initiated because someone has an idea for a solution. The idea is agreed to and funded before the organization really analyzes it and confirms that the idea will, in fact, solve the problem, is feasible, and is acceptable to all parties involved. The *BABOK® Guide* is saying, in effect: We know you have a good idea (solution approach and solution scope), but let's make sure it is a *really* good idea by analyzing it before we get approval and start working on it! One of the inputs to this task is requirements, specifically stakeholder, solution, and transition requirements. These are more detailed than business requirements and allow us to better understand how the solution should be built. Until we have the details, we can't feel comfortable recommending approval of the solution scope.

The Manage Solution Scope and Requirements task, shown in the center of the Solution Theme graphic, is performed numerous times as we learn more and spend more time analyzing the initiative and its requirements. Think of this as the "director of requirements," as every requirement must be addressed in this task. There are several important elements of this task: requirements conflicts are resolved, requirements are compared to the solution scope to make sure they are in bounds, and requirements are approved and baselined. Changes to requirements are also considered in this task. Can you see that the Manage Solution Scope and Requirements task is really the "director" of requirements management?

Once the solution scope is approved, one or more solution designs will be created by implementation SMEs. When we move into Solution Assessment and Validation, the solution scope will be used by implementation SMEs and testers to design, build, test, and implement the solution.

Manage Solution Scope and Requirements		
Inputs	**Techniques**	**Outputs**
Requirements Management Plan (2.5)	Problem Tracking (9.20)	Requirements [Approved] (4.1)
Solution Scope (5.4)		
Stakeholder List, Roles and Responsibilities (2.2)		
Stakeholder, Solution, or Transition Requirements [Communicated](4.2)		
Stakeholder, Solution, or Transition Requirements [Traced] 4.5		

BA's Responsibilities in Manage Solution Scope and Requirements
- Resolve requirements conflicts between stakeholders
- Make sure all requirements are within the solution scope boundaries
- Initiate the change control process to review requests that are outside of scope
- Obtain approval and signoff of solution scope and requirements from appropriate stakeholders
- Baseline requirements after approval

What Do You Need to Successfully Manage Solution Scope and Requirements?
The requirements management plan developed in Business Analysis Planning and Monitoring describes how you will manage the solution scope and requirements. In addition to the description of the solution scope, stakeholder, solution, and transition requirements created in Requirements Analysis are managed in this task as the project progresses. You are communicating with and getting approval from key stakeholders, so you will utilize your stakeholder list, also created in Planning, to ensure you include all of the right people.

The Director of Requirements

As noted earlier, this task could really be considered the director of all requirements work. You are performing this work whenever you look at a requirement to make sure it is within the scope boundaries. You are also performing this work whenever you see two conflicting stakeholder requirements and you work with the stakeholders to get a resolution. And, when you get a requirement approved, you are managing solution scope and requirements.

As you read and learn about this task, you may wonder why it isn't called Get Approval of the Requirements, or Resolve Requirements Conflicts. Some might argue this is the most important task in the entire *BABOK® Guide*, since it involves resolving conflicts and obtaining approval of the requirements! You might also ask why this task isn't placed in Enterprise Analysis, right after the Define Solution Scope task. Don't you resolve conflicts and get the scope approved after you define it? These are very good questions and demonstrate your deepening understanding of the business analysis discipline.

Even though you may have formal signoff on your solution scope and requirements, throughout the life of the project you will be constantly revisiting the scope and requirements and confirming the approvals. Let me say that again, because it is very important: The solution scope and requirements will be continually reviewed, revised, adjusted, and reapproved as we develop more detailed descriptions of the solution components and begin to build the proposed solution.

Manage Solution Scope and Requirements is an ongoing, iterative process of learning more and revisiting the requirements. There are only two things in business analysis that we *manage*: our own performance (you'll see this in Business Analysis Planning and Monitoring) and requirements.

 Any changes to scope and requirements need to go through the integrated change control process and be approved by the project manager. Right? Well, it depends! One of the most challenging collaborations between the project manager and the business analyst is scope management. When an adjustment to the scope is discovered, does it require a change control request, or is it just a more detailed understanding that can be incorporated into the original understanding? Only a trusting, collaborative project manager/business analyst team can easily navigate these difficult questions.

For example, if a report is being built to show payroll amount by month, and the end user requests a year-to-date total be added to the report, is this a scope change? This is a judgment call that you make based on your knowledge of the change. If your developer can easily add this calculation to the report, you might just go ahead and authorize it without involving the project manager or change control process. On the other hand, if the calculation is complex and will require significant programming time, you would recommend a change request be submitted. A good rule of thumb is: if the change will take less time than the change control approval process, authorize it!

The Sub-Tasks

The Manage Solution Scope and Requirements task includes four important sub-tasks that are not covered anywhere else in the *BABOK® Guide*. Let's take a close look at these sub-tasks.

Resolve Requirements Conflicts   Whenever you have more than one stakeholder interested in a solution, you will probably have some requirements conflicts. Requirements conflicts occur when stakeholders have different opinions, ideas, and needs. Conflicts are important to identify, and sometimes challenging to resolve, but they are a crucial part of the analysis process. Often the discussion about the conflict reveals a new approach to the requirements that is even better than the original one.

Business analysts are excellent facilitators and communicators. We use our communication skills to identify and resolve requirements conflicts. Think about all the techniques we use to elicit requirements: interviews, observation, focus groups. Sometimes we use several different techniques, because we are trying to learn everything we can about each requirement. The more we learn about the requirements of each of our stakeholders, the more likely we are to find conflicts. The more conflicts we find, the better job we have done in elicitation! Ideally we will bring the stakeholders to consensus. Do you remember the definition of the word consensus? Consensus means each party has an opportunity to influence the decision and each party agrees to or "buys into" the final decision.

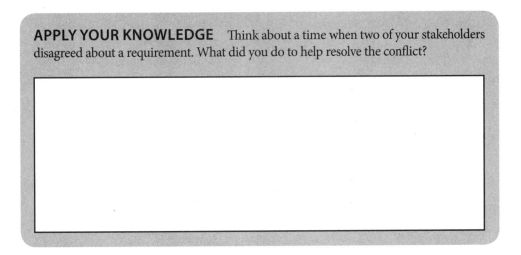

APPLY YOUR KNOWLEDGE   Think about a time when two of your stakeholders disagreed about a requirement. What did you do to help resolve the conflict?

Manage Solution Scope

A second sub-task of Manage Solution Scope and Requirements is making sure all of the requirements are within the solution boundaries. This activity requires constant vigilance, because as stakeholders describe detailed requirements, they will often talk about business processes outside of the solution scope. You must always be listening for the boundaries of your assignment. There will be interfaces to outside processes and parties you also need to address, but don't let the stakeholders lead you to requirements that are outside the approved scope. This will prevent you and your team from ever finishing your work.

Obtain Requirements Approval

The third sub-task is presenting the requirements for review to stakeholders with the authority to approve them. This presentation is done as specified in the business analysis communications plan, in conjunction with packaging requirements and communicating requirements (the last two tasks in this knowledge area). To obtain approval, we need to clearly present the requirements to the stakeholder with approval authority. Signoff or approval can be obtained in any number of ways. Follow whatever standard is used by your organization and keep a record of the approval. Plan-driven approaches to software development usually require a physical or electronic signature. Change-driven approaches usually allow a verbal approval.

Baseline Approved Requirements

Baselining refers to saving or freezing requirements at approval so that changes to requirements requested later in the project can be compared to this saved "baseline." This comparison helps to prevent scope creep. New requirements or changes outside the approved baseline must be evaluated for their impact using the change control process.

Baselining and tracking changes to requirements can be difficult if you are not using a requirements management tool (most requirements analysis tools can save a version of a requirement and track changes for you). When requirements are documented in a text document or spreadsheet, the entire file may be saved as the baseline.

Baselining Example   This is a simple example to illustrate the process of baselining and changing requirements after approval. Imagine in our Workforce Tracking case study we ask the HR administrator to tell us what information she needs for a new employee. We document her requirements, she reviews the list (below) and approves it, so we *baseline* it.

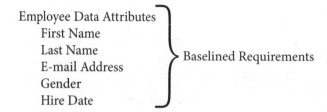

A couple of days later, she calls and says she realized she forgot to mention a couple of other pieces of information she needs. She also wants to change the name of one attribute from Hire Date to Start Date.

These are additional requirements. Now we need to:

1. Make sure they are within the solution scope. (Why would we need a termination date for a new employee?)
2. Determine whether they conflict with any other requirements. (If other stakeholders use the term Hire Date, changing the name to Start Date might cause a conflict or confusion. Any conflict or confusion must be investigated and resolved.)
3. Determine if this change is going to require more analysis work. (We might have to ask for more time from the project manager.)
4. Look at the other requirements and trace these new attributes to the appropriate processes, business rules, etc.
5. Get approval of these new requirements via the change control process.

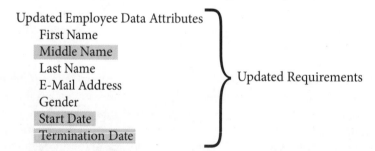

The new requirements will be highlighted because they are changes to the baseline.

Techniques to Manage Solution Scope and Requirements

Problem Tracking (9.20)

Problem tracking would probably be better named problem resolution. It is fine to track problems, but if you don't resolve them, they still exist, and may come back to haunt you! The problem tracking technique is used here to track requirements conflicts. This is also known as *issue tracking* or managing a *parking lot*. You should track conflicts related to requirements and solution design. A requirement cannot be approved until its conflicts are resolved.

As soon as a conflict is identified, it should be documented and communicated to the team. Analyzing and understanding the extent and possible ramifications of the problem help the team determine the priority of its resolution. Problems are often assigned to a specific team member to handle. The resolution is documented and the problem or issue is considered closed.

Most business analysts track requirements conflicts in a table along with other problems and issues where they record who is assigned to each problem, opening and closing dates, and the resolution. This method allows you to report statistics to the project manager and sponsor on status, including the number of outstanding problems vs. resolved problems. Documentation also prevents the team from having to revisit problems that have already been solved if the same problem is raised again later in the effort. You may choose to use a simple table like the following.

Issue Log					
Problem ID #	**Problem Description**	**Assigned to**	**Open Date**	**Close Date**	**Resolution**
121	The term Order is defined differently by the Accounting Dept. and the Customer Service Dept.	BA Barb	09/01/xxxx		
122	A change to the current website will impact the completion of another project.	Sponsor	09/10/xxxx		

Problem tracking may also include information regarding the priority of the problem and/or its potential impact on the project.

EXERCISE   There are four major sub-tasks of the Manage Solution Scope and Requirements task. What are they?

1.
2.
3.
4.

ANSWER

1. Resolve requirements conflicts
2. Make sure requirements are in scope
3. Obtain requirements approval
4. Baseline approved requirements

Summary

Managing Solution Scope and Requirements is the main director of requirements because requirements must be approved before we can use them to build a solution. On change-driven projects, this work may not be done formally or in writing, but it is done. If you think of this task as a repeated approval process, it is easy to learn its elements. How do you get approval of anything? You determine the scope, resolve conflicts between stakeholders, present the result, and ask for approval. Logically, *approved* requirements are the output of this task.

Manage Requirements Traceability (4.2)

Traceability refers to the links or relationships between one requirement and another (or between a requirement and another project component). Requirements are ultimately linked back to a business objective. There can also be links to solution components (e.g., databases, modules, or test cases). There is no limit to the number of links that may be traced on a large project.

Early in the project, the project objectives and the solution approach are determined. Based on this information, traceability decisions are documented in your requirements management plan.

During planning, when the requirements management plan is developed, you should work with your project manager, lead implementation SME, and lead tester to decide what will be traced and who will maintain this information.

Traceability decisions include which requirements will be traced to which other elements, what software tool(s) will be used to document traceability, and who will maintain the traceability. Sometimes your methodology or business analysis approach will dictate traceability, but usually you will decide which links will be useful to trace for each assignment. Understanding the value of traceability helps you make these decisions.

 When a requirement is traced to another requirement (or other element) you may see this referred to as a connection, coverage, relationship, association, allocation, derivation, lineage, dependency, or link; so many terms for one concept!

Manage Requirements Traceability		
Inputs	**Techniques**	**Outputs**
Requirements	Coverage Matrix	Requirements [Traced] (4.2)
Requirements Management Plan (2.5)		

BA's Responsibilities in Managing Requirements Traceability
- Understand the value of traceability
- Document traceability as specified in the requirements management plan
- Share traceability information with implementation SMEs and testers as needed
- Maintain traceability with requirements after implementation

What Do You Need to Successfully Manage Requirements Traceability?
Any type of requirement may be traced, so requirements are clearly an input to this task. The requirements management plan, created in Business Analysis Planning and Monitoring, documents the processes and tools that will be used to accomplish traceability.

How Do You Track Traceability?
To trace a requirement, you need to show how it is related to another requirement or another project component (e.g., solution component or test case). The simplest way to show these relationships or links is in a two-dimensional table. In the table below, processes are in rows and data entities are in columns. When a process uses a data entity, an X is placed in the intersecting cell of the matrix. For example, the process Add New Employee uses information about Employee, Job Description, Manager, and Pay Rate. This is a simple traceability matrix.

Process/Data (Entity)	Employee	Job Description	Manager	Pay Rate
Add New Employee	X	X	X	X
Release Employee	X		X	
Transfer Employee	X	X	X	X

Responsibility for Traceability
Since requirements can be traced to other project components, the responsibility for documenting and maintaining traceability information must be determined. In some organizations, testers trace their test cases back to requirements and use their matrices to make sure they have tested every requirement. (A test case is a specific procedure testers follow to make sure the software performs properly). Sometimes implementation SMEs trace solution design components back to requirements to make sure their design has included all of the requirements. Business analysts are solely responsible for any links between business, stakeholder, and solution requirements.

 If you have access to a requirements management tool or configuration management system, you have automated support to maintain traceability. A configuration management system is used to maintain the individual components of a system. Most software development organizations use configuration management to manage their software systems. These products offer features like backups, change logs, and tracking the relationships between components.

Tracing with Unique Identifiers
Each requirement and other traceable element should have a unique name or number. This unique identifier allows the element to be referenced in a traceability matrix without spelling out the entire element. Below is a simple traceability matrix using unique identifiers.

Feature ID	Business Objectives			
	B1	B2	B3	B4
F459	X			
F593			X	
F594	X	X	X	
F599				X

Tracing with Unique Identifiers

Traceability Provides a Double Check

Traceability is a great way to make sure we didn't miss any requirements. One of the most difficult things about developing requirements is knowing when you are done. How do you know you haven't missed anything? This fear sometimes causes us to spend more time than we should asking additional questions. Tracing requirements and their relationship to other requirements is a great way to check your work and help you find missing pieces. Whenever a row or column is empty in a traceability matrix, you may be missing a requirement.

Traceability Allows Impact Analysis

Impact analysis involves looking at the potential impact of a change. So, if our business wants to change the way it sells a product, what are all of the implications on our systems and procedures? How big a change would this be? Impact analysis is very useful for decision making, but unfortunately many organizations don't have a quick, easy way of doing impact analysis. Therefore, it is often a tedious manual process. A traceability matrix is a valuable tool for impact analysis when the requirements are correctly linked. In a sophisticated requirements management tool, the user can select a specific requirement component and create a report listing all the other requirements to which it is connected. Impact analysis may be performed during a project in conjunction with a change request, or it may be requested after solution implementation when a change to the production system is being considered.

Traceability Keeps the Team Focused

Traceability matrices can be used on any requirements components. By showing priorities and links in one place, we can easily see which requirements need most of our time and energy. If a requirement is a high priority and has lots of links, we better make sure we get it right.

The product backlog table used for solution scoping can include traceability information. This example shows the original features requested by the stakeholders, along with their priority, and shows which use cases will implement each feature. It also shows the test cases that will be used to test each feature. This is another way to document traceability.

Product Backlog Table					
ID	Feature	Business Priority	Technical Priority	Use Case ID	Test Case ID
F459	Provide a unique login ID for each worker.	High	High	UC23	TC243, TC244, TC245
F593	Provide a place for workers to report their hours on each project.	High	Low	UC39	TC33-TC53

Product Backlog Table					
ID	Feature	Business Priority	Technical Priority	Use Case ID	Test Case ID
F594	Provide a place for workers to add notes on each project.	Medium	Low	UC39	TC54

Risks may also be included in a traceability matrix to show how much risk each feature has or how many use cases address each risk. There are an infinite number of possible combinations of tracing that can be done as needed on your project or initiative.

APPLY YOUR KNOWLEDGE   Have you ever linked requirements to other requirements or to test cases? If so, you have used traceability. Describe the type of traceability you did and why.

Relationship Types

Another benefit of tracing requirements is seeing patterns or relationships that may help with solution design decisions. The *BABOK® Guide* defines several types of relationships between requirements or solution components that you should understand for the exam:

Necessity   Two requirements or solution components are so closely related that implementing one is useless without also including the other.

Effort   A related requirement is easier to implement with its linked requirement.

Value   The value of a requirement is increased when its linked requirement is also implemented.

Subset or Cover   One requirement is a subset of (or *covers*) another. For example, if your team decides to automate process 1, the three decomposed processes (1.a, 1.b, and 1.c) are subsets that should be included.

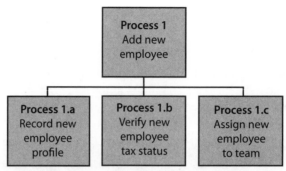

Examples of Traceability Relationship Types

Databases		
Processes	**Employee Database**	
Process 1. Add New Employee	Necessity relationship exists here. There is no point in adding a new employee without a database to store the employee information.	
Process 2. Transfer Employee	Effort relationship exists here. Although we could automate transfers without an employee database, it would be easier if the data about the employee already existed.	
Process 3. Accept Employee Profile Change	Value relationship exists here. Since employee profile information is stored in the employee database, allowing employees to update their own information will save HR time.	

Techniques to Manage Requirements Traceability

Coverage Matrix

The term coverage or traceability matrix describes manual tools used to manage traceability. "Coverage" is used because we are making sure we *covered* everything! These matrices are rarely presented to stakeholders in a requirements package as part of a formal deliverable, because they can be confusing to someone without business analysis training. However, you may want to discuss the contents of a matrix with a stakeholder, especially when you think you have found a missing requirement. The exception is when regulations stipulate traceability be reported to the regulating agency. In these cases, your traceability matrix may be a formal deliverable provided to the regulator. Note this technique is not included in Chapter 9, the Techniques Chapter of the *BABOK® Guide*.

CRUD Matrix   To get even more value out of a traceability matrix, you can embed information into the cells of the table. The example below from the Workforce Tracking case study is a very specific and useful matrix referred to as a CRUD matrix. The acronym CRUD stands for Create, Read, Update, and Delete. This matrix shows how each data element is created, read, updated, and deleted by the processes. This matrix allows you to make sure none of the data actions have been missed. See if you can interpret the information in the following matrix.

 EXERCISE   Review a section of a matrix from the Payroll Project and answer the questions about it.

ID	Process Name	Worker Data				
		Pay Rate	Benefit Type	Benefit Deduction	Tax Status	Notification e-mail Address
P1	Accept Withholding Change		R	CRUD		
P2	Calculate Worker Payment	R	R	R		
P3	Make Deposit	R				
P4	Notify Worker of Payment					R
P5	Notify Benefit Provider of Change		R	R		R
P6	Record Working Time					
P7	Change Worker Pay Rate	U				R
P8	Change Worker Deposit Instructions					R

Question	Answer
Which process creates the benefit deduction?	
The Record Working Time process doesn't use any of the data elements shown. What data is missing?	
Tax Status data isn't being used by any of the processes shown. Which ones might use it?	
The Change Worker Deposit Instructions process should update something. What data is missing?	

ANSWER

Question	Answer
Which process creates the benefit deduction?	The Accept Withholding Change process
The Record Working Time process doesn't use any of the data elements shown. What data is missing?	Hours worked, week ending date, employee ID
Tax Status data isn't being used by any of the processes shown. Which ones might use it?	The Accept Withholding Change process or Change Worker Pay Rate process
The Change Worker Deposit Instructions process should update something. What data is missing?	Deposit instructions (bank account number, routing number, bank account type, etc.)

Traceability Example   Let's look at a complex traceability example. A business analyst would not likely create this type of diagram for a real-world project. However, it is included here to help you better understand the concept of traceability.

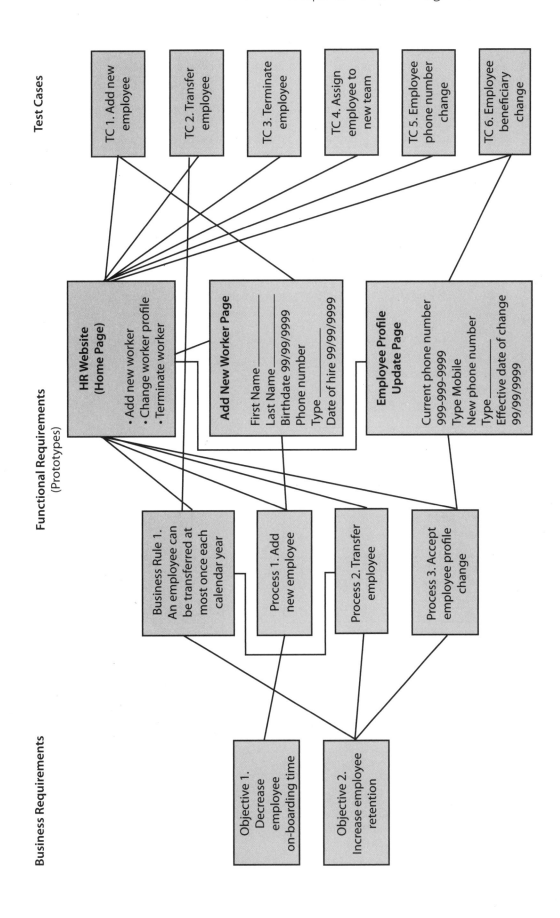

The diagram shows requirements from the Workforce Tracking case study. There are two objectives, one business rule, three business processes, three functional requirements (prototypes) and six test cases. Lines connecting the boxes represent the links. Notice the types of links or relationships included:

Business objectives	are traced to	Business processes
Business processes	are traced to	Prototypes (functional requirements)
Business objectives	are traced to	Business rules
Business rules	are traced to	Business processes
Business rules	are traced to	Prototypes
Prototypes	are traced to	Test cases
Prototypes	are traced to	Other prototypes

 EXERCISE   Answer the following questions about the traceability example.

Question	Answer
1. Which business objective is impacted by process 1?	
2. Which business objective is constrained by business rule 1?	
3. Which business objective is allocated to the Add New Worker Page (prototype)?	
4. Which test case(s) will validate that business objective 1 has been accomplished?	
5. Can we verify that business rule 1 has been implemented?	
6. In the future, if business rule 1 is changed, which process(es) will be impacted?	
7. Which process(es) is validated by test case 4?	
8. Which objective looks like the most expensive to implement?	

ANSWER

Question	Answer
1. Which business objective is impacted by process 1?	Objective 1
2. Which business objective is constrained by business rule 1?	Objective 2
3. Which business objective is allocated to the Add New Worker Page (prototype)?	Objective 1 via process 1
4. Which test case(s) will validate that business objective 1 has been accomplished?	Test case 1 via Add New Worker Page via process 1
5. Can we verify that business rule 1 has been implemented?	No. It is linked to the home page, but we don't see a screen prototype for the transfer function
6. In the future, if business rule 1 is changed, which process(es) will be impacted?	Process 2
7. Which process(es) is validated by test case 4?	We can't tell here, but it doesn't seem to be directly related to any of these processes
8. Which objective looks like the most expensive to implement?	Objective 2 is linked to two processes, (and one business rule) which are linked to two prototypes, which are linked to all of the test cases, so it seems to be the most expensive one

The *BABOK® Guide* uses lots of terminology to describe traceability. These are not difficult concepts, you just need to learn the terms. Let's use the previous traceability example to define them.

Forward Traceability refers to following the links from one requirement forward (from business to solution to technical requirements). Questions 1 through 3 in the exercise above asked you to perform forward traceability. See, it is so easy you didn't even know you were doing it! Think of forward traceability as moving from business objectives to business and stakeholder requirements (the beginning of the project) forward to the solution requirements and so on. Forward traceability allows you to confirm that each business objective has been addressed in the solution and will be tested. Forward traceability is also referred to as *allocation*. You should be able to answer the question: "How is business objective 1 *allocated* to the solution components?" We'll talk more about allocating requirements to solution components in the Solution Assessment and Validation chapter.

Backward Traceability refers to following the links from one component backward (from the solution components to technical requirements to solution requirements and ultimately to business requirements and objectives). Questions 4 and 5 in the exercise above asked you to perform backward traceability. This process ensures that every solution component is *derived* from a business objective. This helps prevent gold plating (adding features into a solution that were not approved). Backward traceability is also known as *derivation* or *lineage* (because it shows how components descended from others). For example, you may have to determine, "How was the prototype Add New Worker *derived* from the business objectives?" In other words, why did we need a data entry screen to add new workers? Because one of our original business objectives was to decrease HR costs and improve efficiency.

Here are a couple of additional exercises to build your understanding and confidence regarding traceability.

 EXERCISE   Using the diagram on page 247, complete the coverage matrix below showing how the processes are allocated to the prototypes. Put an X in the cells of the table where the requirements are related.

	HR Website (Home Page)	Add New Worker Page	Employee Profile Update Page
Process 1. Add New Employee			
Process 2. Transfer Employee			
Process 3. Accept Employee Profile Change			

ANSWER

	HR Website (Home Page)	Add New Worker Page	Employee Profile Update Page
Process 1. Add new employee	X	X	
Process 2. Transfer employee	X		
Process 3. Accept employee profile change	X		X

 EXERCISE   Based on your results, do you think there are any missing processes or prototypes?

Possible Missing Processes	Possible Missing Prototypes

© 2012 RMC Publications, Inc • 952.846.4484 • info@rmcproject.com • www.rmcproject.com

ANSWER

Possible Missing Processes	Possible Missing Prototypes
Terminate Worker	Transfer Employee
	Terminate Employee

 EXERCISE Build a CRUD matrix using the data elements listed below. Remember, CRUD stands for Create, Read, Update, and Delete.

Employee Data Elements	First Name	Last Name	Birth Date	Phone Number	Phone Type	Date of Hire	Effective Date of Phone Number Change	Tax ID Number	Number of Dependents
Process 1. Add New Employee									
Process 2. Transfer Employee									
Process 3. Accept Employee Profile Change									

ANSWER Did you struggle with filling in the matrix? You really need a detailed understanding of the processes to be able to answer these questions. On a real project, you would have that information along with access to stakeholders to ask follow-up questions. As you can see, this technique causes you to ask many more detailed questions. This is the true value of traceability.

Employee Data Elements	First Name	Last Name	Birth Date	Phone Number	Phone Type	Date of Hire	Effective Date of Phone Number Change	Tax ID Number	Number of Dependents
Process 1. Add New Employee	C	C	C	C	C	C		These seem like they should be Create but they are not shown on the prototype? Need follow up.	
Process 2. Transfer Employee	R	R		U	U	R	U		
Process 3. Accept Employee Profile Change	RU	RU		U	U		U		U, but not on prototype. Needs follow up.

EXERCISE Based on your analysis, do you think there are any missing data elements or processes?

Possible Missing Data Elements	Possible Missing Processes

© 2012 RMC Publications, Inc • 952.846.4484 • info@rmcproject.com • www.rmcproject.com

ANSWER

Possible Missing Data Elements	Possible Missing Processes
Employee Number or ID	Add Worker Dependent Information
Middle Name	Terminate Employee
Gender	
Department Code or Manager Name	
Last Transfer Date (needed to enforce Business Rule 1)	

EXERCISE What follow-up questions need to be answered?

ANSWER

1. Can an employee change his or her name? What if it was entered incorrectly?
2. Can an employee change his or her birth date? What if it was entered incorrectly?
3. Does a user enter the date of hire or does the system fill it in based on the current date? Can it be changed?
4. When an employee is transferred, does his or her phone number always change?

Summary

Even though you may not have access to a requirements management tool, you can use traceability matrices and unique requirement identification numbers to keep track of relationships and perform impact analysis. Traceability matrices are useful for assessing the impact of changes during the project, and help with change control. If you have good documentation and a user asks for a change, you can easily determine and report on the complexity and ramifications of the change.

Deciding which requirements to trace is difficult for new business analysts. As an experienced practitioner, you should help new business analysts make these decisions. Rarely do we have time to trace every requirement. Choosing a few key relationships increases the completeness of your requirements without jeopardizing the time schedule of the project.

Outputs of this task are described as *traced* requirements or solution components. At any time in the project, these requirements may be traced to additional components, or tracing may be adjusted due to other requirements changes.

Maintain Requirements for Re-use (4.3)

It is important for analysts and the entire organization to recognize that requirements are valuable assets and should be kept up-to-date as the business changes. Business domain SMEs, business analysts, implementation SMEs, and other team members spend many hours creating accurate, useful requirements. It is wasteful not to save them after the completion of the initiative. The core business requirements of an organization will continue to be relevant and can be used on future projects, thereby saving time for future teams. In this task, you save requirements for re-use after solution implementation.

Maintain Requirements for Re-Use		
Inputs	**Techniques**	**Outputs**
Requirements	None	Requirements [Maintained and Reusable] (4.3)
Organizational Process Assets		

BA's Responsibilities in Maintaining Requirements for Re-use
- Review existing requirements from prior projects and reuse the ones which are inside the scope of your current assignment
- Be able to use the organization's requirements repository
- Ensure new requirements are documented to enable future re-use
- Identify requirements conflicts with existing requirements

What Do You Need to Successfully Maintain Requirements for Re-use?
Requirements that will be maintained by the organization for long-term use must conform to organization standards. The standards for maintaining and reusing those requirements are documented in the organizational process assets.

TRICKS OF THE TRADE® A requirements asset management plan is the key to getting a handle on managing and re-using your organization's requirements. This plan is generally an organizational process asset of the company managed by the PMO or Business Analysis Center of Excellence. Think about corporate assets such as furniture or equipment. Each piece of furniture is tagged with a unique number or code so the organization can track where it is being used, its age, its original cost, and its current value. At any point in time, the organization can report on the total number of pieces of furniture, the location, and the current value of each piece. Similar to managing other corporate assets, requirements should be uniquely named or numbered and stored in an accessible, safe place for easy retrieval.

Requirements Repository
The requirements repository is a requirements management tool where the requirements will "live." This repository can be as simple as a hard drive on your network, or a wiki, it can be stored in a cloud, or it can be a complex, intelligent database that manages the flow of requirements in and out.

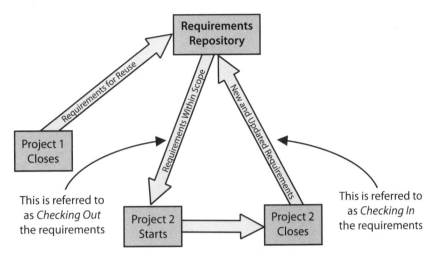

Requirement Check In/Check Out

Ideally a requirements repository is available for any business analyst to view. Whenever you start a new assignment or want to learn about a new business domain, you can start with existing requirements. An authorized user is allowed to *check out* any requirements for use on a project. When you are done with your work, you check the requirements back in, and if any of them changed, the change is recorded and logged. This check in/check out system lets other people know who is working on each requirement and quickly highlights overlapping projects and possible requirements conflicts from one project to another.

Regardless of the technology, the requirements repository has two major benefits.

Ease of Accessibility
The requirements repository should be accessible to new teams as they are defining their solution scope and high-level requirements. Requirements should be easy to find and named in a logical fashion.

Accessibility Example
Let's look at the Workforce Tracking case study again. When a project is initiated, the business analyst can look at existing requirements in the repository and identify those that might be useful on this new project. Using the Check In/Check Out diagram, let's say Project 1 successfully created a website that allows workers to update their phone numbers and addresses. Project 2 will build on that system and add functionality for workers to request new equipment for their home offices. Many of the requirements created for Project 1 will be useful on Project 2 without any changes. For example, we will use data elements like Worker First Name, Last Name, Phone, and e-mail address to allow the worker to request equipment. These data elements can be reused, as can the employee database itself. For Project 2, we will need another set of data elements describing equipment options and to allow a worker to request equipment. These data elements will be new requirements that we will elicit, analyze, confirm, and implement, and then add into the repository for use by future projects.

Identification of Requirements Conflicts
The requirements repository is also used to identify and resolve requirements conflicts. The identification and resolution of these conflicts before the solution is built is a significant time saver.

Requirements Conflict Example
Glossary terms and their definitions are stored in our requirements repository and can be reused. As the analyst, I select the term Worker from the

repository to use in my new requirements package. But when I review the definition, I realize that Workers are defined as employees. What about consultants or contractors? Consultants and contractors can also request equipment, so my definition of Worker is broader than just employees. To resolve the conflict, I talk with stakeholders who use the current website and determine how the change (to include contractors and consultants in the definition of Worker) will impact them. This might highlight a problem with the current solution approach. Maybe we can't use the existing website. Finding a conflict like this early in the project is a great way to avoid the wasted time and effort of building a solution that will conflict with existing systems.

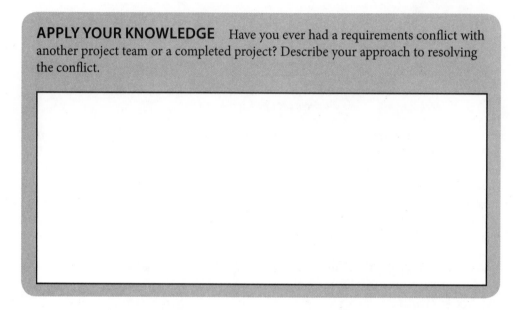

APPLY YOUR KNOWLEDGE   Have you ever had a requirements conflict with another project team or a completed project? Describe your approach to resolving the conflict.

A couple of terms in this task are a little confusing:

Ongoing Requirements   *Ongoing* requirements should be managed as an asset because they could be reused on future projects. These requirements can be thought of as needs that must be met on a continual basis, such as business rules and processes, quality standards that apply to all work of the organization, and requirements relating to long-term contract commitments of the organization.

Satisfied Requirements   Requirements that have been met by the solution are considered *satisfied*. Some of these requirements will become managed assets because they can potentially be used on future, similar efforts. Other satisfied requirements will not be *ongoing*, like employee training on the new system. Once the training is complete, this transition requirement is no longer needed.

TRICKS OF THE TRADE®   Requirements states can be confusing because a requirement may be in more than one state at a time. For example, a requirement can be *satisfied* and *ongoing* at the same time. Carefully read the adjectives before and/or after the word *requirements* when answering exam questions to be sure you know what state(s) the requirement is in.

Summary

The result of this task is maintained and reusable requirements. Requirements are not typically changed by this task; they are stored in a repository and made available for use on future projects.

Prepare Requirements Package (4.4)

A requirements package is nothing more than a group or set of requirements. A requirements package is built because you want to communicate the requirements to someone. During a medium- to large-size project, you may build several requirements packages for different purposes or to present to different stakeholders.

Deciding whether or not to package requirements, when to package, and what to package depends on several factors:
- To whom are you presenting?
- What format does your audience prefer?
- Will your audience read the package on their own, or attend a presentation to be led through it?
- What is the goal of presenting the requirements? Feedback? Confirmation? Approval?
- How formal does the package need to be? Will it include an executive summary, table of contents?
- Is it being sent to outside stakeholders such as regulatory agencies or vendors?

This task describes the decisions about the structure and contents of requirements packages.

Prepare Requirements Package		
Inputs	**Techniques**	**Outputs**
Business Analysis Communication Plan (2.4)	Requirements Documentation	Requirements Package (4.4)
Organizational Process Assets	Requirements for Vendor Selection	
Requirements		
Requirements Structure (6.2)		

BA's Responsibilities in Preparing the Requirements Package
- Ensure that requirements are documented in a manner that is understandable to the appropriate stakeholder groups
- Assemble related requirements into a package for review
- Prepare requirements to be included in RFIs, RFPs, or RFQs for vendor packages

What Do You Need to Successfully Prepare the Requirements Package?
The business analysis communication plan, developed as part of Business Analysis Planning and Monitoring, specifies who needs to review each requirement, and may specify packaging information. As part of organizational process assets, your organization may have templates for packaging requirements. You are going to need the requirements to package!

The requirements structure, an output of the Organize Requirements task of Requirements Analysis (page 169) will give you direction for creating requirements packages for your project. It includes the types of requirements (e.g., business, functional, non-functional), and the format(s) in which they were specified and modeled.

Presenting the Requirements to Your Stakeholders

Some business analysts have gotten a negative reputation for creating huge requirements documents and/or packages that take hundreds of hours to put together and review. This is a reputation you do not want! Your goal should be to present the necessary information in the clearest, most concise method possible. You also must communicate what you hope to gain from the audience (e.g., approval or feedback). Your requirements documentation should be easy for you to update when necessary. Before approval, requirements are fluid and refined frequently. The cost to refine and correct requirements at this point should be relatively low.

Deciding how best to present requirements is deciding how best to communicate with your stakeholders. If your department always uses an object-oriented approach to software development, you should learn to develop object models as your deliverables. If formal requirements package presentations are the norm, you should develop strong documentation skills to create them. You should also be able to make recommendations on the most appropriate presentation format when the team doesn't have an established structure or approach. Your recommendations will be based on your stakeholder analysis and your understanding of the needs of the project.

Requirements Presentation Formats for Software Projects

The formality of the presentation and the format of the written documentation will be different for each situation. In traditional software development plan-driven approaches, requirements are documented in formal packages with executive summaries, tables of content, and detailed descriptions. In change-driven approaches, requirements are discussed with the team, summarized in a product backlog list or in a user story, and built quickly for review. All of these approaches are valid ways to present requirements and get confirmation

Requirements Presentation Formats for Other Projects

In engineering or architecture projects, requirements are packaged and presented using drawings or blueprints, along with textual descriptions. They may also be represented in models of the building or product being designed. For business process improvement projects, packages include diagrams like value stream maps, workflow diagrams, and business process models, along with employee procedure documents.

EXERCISE How much detail would be necessary in a requirements package for each of the following situations?

Situation	Requirements Package
A consulting company is bidding on a contract to write a large custom software application for one of their customers. The consulting company has elicited requirements and is now ready to present a recommendation to their potential customer.	
The business analyst on a virtual team needs to get requirements signoff on a minor interface change from a small number of stakeholders. The stakeholders have reviewed earlier drafts and are already familiar with the requirements.	

Situation	Requirements Package
This is a process improvement project where the current business processes have been observed and diagrammed for future use. Many stakeholders are involved, each owning a few of the processes on which he or she is an expert.	
This software development project is using a change-driven approach like agile. The team will be meeting to prioritize the backlog of stakeholder requirements.	

SAMPLE ANSWER

Situation	Requirements Package
A consulting company is bidding on a contract to write a large custom software application for one of their customers. The consulting company has elicited requirements and is now ready to present a recommendation to their potential customer.	Extremely formal, professionally published and bound book with a table of contents, index, exhibits, and footnotes.
The business analyst on a virtual team needs to get requirements signoff on a minor interface change from a small number of stakeholders. The stakeholders have reviewed earlier drafts and are already familiar with the requirements.	An e-mail message asking for approval of the requirements with requirements document files attached.
This is a process improvement project where the current business processes have been observed and diagrammed for future use. Many stakeholders are involved, each owning a few of the processes on which he or she is an expert.	A separate requirements package for each stakeholder with his or her process workflows included. OR A complete requirements package with a list of the process names for each stakeholder, including hyperlinks so the reader can jump directly to any page.
This software development project is using a change-driven approach like agile. The team will be meeting to prioritize the backlog of stakeholder requirements.	A product backlog spreadsheet with a list of user requests and columns labeled: Requested by, Priority, Estimated Cost, Iteration or Phase. User stories on index cards may describe the features.

Techniques to Prepare the Requirements Package

Requirements Documentation

There are some requirements packages that have been defined by methodologies and standards organizations. The most well-known is the business requirements document (BRD), which is used by hundreds of organizations. A BRD is a collection of business requirements, packaged together for review and approval. For software development projects, a software requirements specification (SRS) is often used. Variations include a functional requirements document (FRD) or a functional spec (specification). For strategic or enterprise-level initiatives, the package might be called a *vision document* or strategic plan. You can also think of a business case as a requirements package because it contains requirements packaged for presentation to stakeholders. When an organization develops a product for sale to their customers, they might refer to the package as a *Product Roadmap*. When an organization is thinking of purchasing a product or service, it might prepare a *Request for Proposal* (RFP). (See more on this below). The way you package requirements and the name of the package is entirely dependent on your audience needs.

Packaging Requirements for Vendor Selection

Many business needs are best addressed by purchasing a product or service from another company. Selecting a vendor for a significant purchase is an analysis activity and, as such, is well performed with the involvement of a business analyst. There are many different roles/professions involved in the selection process. Procurement professionals are experts at developing pricing models. Lawyers are experts in contract law. Business analysts are the requirements experts. We are the professionals who elicit the internal requirements, write the requirements section of the contract, and confirm to the project manager and/or procurement manager that the vendor solution meets those requirements. As the business analyst involved in a vendor assessment, you need to understand your role and its relationship to the other professionals involved, and to work with those professionals to ensure a thorough assessment is completed.

Contracts for large purchases and ongoing services are very complex. There are many laws governing the way contracts should be written and lawyers work to mitigate risks by documenting contingencies in the contract. You can assist your legal team by providing requirements and ongoing business risks related to the vendor's product. Terms and conditions are specified in the contract for the payment schedule, the product delivery, and the ongoing support aspects of the work.

Because the solution includes a component that will be purchased from or developed by an outside company, requirements packaging is more structured and formal. There are three common packages that are prepared for outside vendors:

Request for Information (RFI)
This is often the first step in a vendor assessment process, where the team is looking for vendors who are interested in working on the solution. It includes a general description of the proposed solution with high-level requirements. The RFI is sent to several vendors who offer products that might fit the needs of the initiative.

Request for Proposal (RFP)
This is a more detailed and formal package, including specific functional and non-functional requirements. The proposals received from the vendors in response to this request may include building custom software or customizing an existing software package, training on the application, installation support, and ongoing customer service.

Request for Quotation (RFQ)
This is a less formal request for pricing of a product or service.

Vendor Assessment Criteria   When selecting a vendor, there are two questions to answer:

Is the Vendor an Organization You Want to Have a Relationship With?   Vendor experience and reputation are useful indicators of future performance. To select the best vendor for your need, you should learn as much about the vendor's organization as you can. You can request background information about the vendor in the RFP, or this research can be done by contacting current customers of the vendor, reading industry reviews and surveys, and meeting with individuals who work for the vendor. Performing a vendor assessment can be a big project; your team must decide which factors are most important and focus on those. For example, if you are purchasing a software application for a highly regulated product where regulations change frequently, you will be looking for a vendor who is in close contact with the regulators as decisions are being made and can respond quickly to regulation changes. If you are contracting for a customer support call center, you will be looking for a vendor with high-quality employee training and development along with low employee turnover. If you are purchasing a product that requires the vendor to provide a long-term maintenance contract, you will be looking for a vendor with strong financial stability and longevity. There is a technique in the *BABOK® Guide* Chapter 9 called Vendor Assessment (9.34), which is not referenced here.

Does the Product or Service Meet Your Needs?   Having clear, well-defined requirements is the best way to assess a vendor's product or service. When you and your team know what you need, it is easy to evaluate a vendor's product for compliance with your requirements. The product's reputation and market position may also be important factors for your stakeholders, but don't allow these factors to override the requirements match. Rarely does a vendor solution perfectly meet every need. Gap analysis (discussed in the Enterprise Analysis chapter) is performed to determine the missing pieces and help your team decide which vendor offers the product closest to your needs. If custom products will be built by the vendor to meet your requirements, assessing the product involves assessing the skills of the vendor's implementation team. How have their products been developed in the past? Are current customers happy with the results? Have their time estimates been accurate?

Know the Best Practices for Vendor Assessment

Know what you are looking for before you go shopping! Have you ever gone to the grocery store without a list? Did you spend more money than you planned? Did you end up with items you really didn't want or need, and forget some items you meant to purchase? You may experience the same problem if you start talking with vendors before doing requirements elicitation and analysis.

- Create an objective priority list of your requirements before you look at the solution (in the Prioritize Requirements task in Requirements Analysis). Decide which of your requirements are "must haves" (vs. "nice to haves"). When you compare your list to a vendor solution, eliminate the vendor packages that are missing your "must have" requirements.
- Consider several vendors. Don't buy from the first company you meet, or the nicest salesperson. Conduct an objective evaluation to make sure all of your needs will be met.
- Assess the product and the vendor. Carefully review the product or solution being offered and asses the vendor itself. Is the company reliable? Financially stable? Ethical? Available?
- Research existing customers of each vendor to determine their satisfaction with the product and the ongoing service.
- Work with your legal team to contractually specify customization, implementation, training, and any other promises made during the negotiation process.

APPLY YOUR KNOWLEDGE   Use your personal experience to learn more about this technique. Think about a major purchasing decision you have made (e.g., car, house, private school, or college). Answer the following questions.

Purchased Item or Service: _____

How did you make the decision to purchase the item?	
How many people were involved in the purchase?	
How many different vendors did you consider before the purchase?	
Did you buy new or used?	
Did you have any customization done?	
Was there a contract? How did you negotiate the terms?	
How did you evaluate the vendor? Did you ask friends? Conduct research? Consider brand reputation?	
Did the purchase and acquisition go smoothly?	
A few months after the purchase, did you have any buyer's remorse? Why?	
What would you do differently before your next purchase?	

Summary

The result of the Prepare Requirements Package task is a requirements package. This is the most visible work a business analyst produces. This deliverable will be used to communicate requirements and often to obtain approval of the requirements.

Communicate Requirements (4.5)

This task is all about outgoing communications to the stakeholders. It is probably one of the tasks most frequently performed by a business analyst! We are constantly communicating with stakeholders about requirements. In Enterprise Analysis, we communicate about the business case and solution scope. When we Conduct an Elicitation Activity, we typically paraphrase requirements back to the stakeholders to confirm understanding and to uncover additional requirements. In Requirements Analysis, communication is needed to prioritize and finalize requirements. When we ask for approval, (in Requirements Management and Communication) we are communicating requirements. In Solution Assessment and Validation, communication is focused on assessing the solution requirements and identifying transition requirements. The list goes on and on. Be sure to remember that you can communicate requirements with or without a requirements document or package. Exam questions in this area are easier, because communicating is something we do constantly. Be careful when you see words like *always* or *never*. There are very few things we *always* do or *never* do. Correct answers will describe honest and ethical communication. As you will read in the Underlying Competencies chapter of the *BABOK® Guide* (if you haven't already done so), these are important behavioral characteristics of business analysis professionals.

Communicate Requirements		
Inputs	**Techniques**	**Outputs**
Business Analysis Communications Plan (2.4)	Requirements Workshops (9.23)	Requirements [Communicated] (4.5)
Requirements	Structured Walkthroughs (9.30)	
Requirements Package (4.4)		

What Do You Need to Successfully Communicate Requirements?

Created in the Business Analysis Planning and Monitoring knowledge area, the business analysis communication plan outlines what information should be communicated, to whom, how often, and in what format. This plan specifically describes when and how requirements will be documented and signoff requested.

If a requirements package was created in the previous task, it is an input here, as it documents the requirements to be communicated. Remember, however, that requirements can be communicated with or without a requirements package.

Communication Methods

Business analysts communicate with stakeholders about requirements for various reasons, using the communication method most appropriate for the situation. Communication methods include formal and informal communication, in written and verbal formats.

	Verbal	**Written**
Formal Communication	Presentations Meetings	Requirements deliverables Requirements packages
Informal Communication	Scheduled or unscheduled conversations/discussions During elicitation sessions During status meetings	Flip charts, whiteboards E-mails, unrefined notes Meeting minutes Hand-drawn sketches, diagrams, or prototypes

Know the Reasons for Communicating Requirements

There are many reasons to communicate requirements. The most common are:
- To confirm the business analyst's understanding of the requirements
- To bring stakeholders to a common understanding
- To instruct the implementation SMEs about what to build
- To inform business stakeholders and end users about the implementation plan (transition requirements)
- To inform other parts of the organization about the upcoming change
- To inform other project teams about interfaces or overlaps with their projects

Best Practices for Making a Formal Presentation

Occasionally you are called upon to give formal presentations of requirements, proposed solutions, business cases, or implementation plans. You should be aware of the critical success factors for giving an excellent formal presentation:

- Be extremely-well prepared
- Practice with trusted colleagues and get feedback
- Know your audience
- Do not use emotions as justification
- Clearly explain alternative solutions that you considered
- Listen to questions/criticism and respond objectively
- Give listeners time to understand your recommendation
- Ask for approval (when appropriate)

Techniques to Communicate Requirements

Requirements Workshops (9.23)

Requirements are often communicated during a requirements workshop. Most sessions will be started with a brief review of the project objectives and scope to ensure the discussion is kept within the solution boundaries. This technique was covered in the Elicitation chapter.

Structured Walkthrough (9.30)

Requirements are often communicated during a structured walkthrough. The moderator or author will present an introduction to the deliverable being reviewed and how it fits into the overall solution. The reviewers will provide feedback on the requirements based on their perspectives and knowledge. This technique was discussed in the Requirements Analysis chapter.

Summary

When this task is complete, the requirements are unchanged, except they now have been *communicated*. The same requirements may be communicated many times and for many reasons!

— SUMMARY OF REQUIREMENTS MANAGEMENT AND COMMUNICATION —

Requirements Management and Communication describes the work necessary to *manage* and *communicate* requirements. To successfully manage requirements, we have to document how they are related to other requirements (tracing), we have to make sure they are approved (manage to the scope), and we have to carefully store them (maintain for re-use). To communicate them, we have to present them to our stakeholders in a useful format (which may include packaging) and then listen and respond to their feedback (communicate).

EXERCISE   There are many different adjectives used to describe requirements. You must be able to define these *states* or conditions of requirements. It may help you to think of these as the life cycle or life stages of the requirements. Define each, and keep in mind that several of these definitions overlap.

Requirement Type	Requirement State
Requirements [Maintained]	
Requirements [Satisfied]	
Requirements [Ongoing]	
Requirements [Communicated]	
Requirements [Traced]	
Requirements [Approved]	
Requirements [Reusable]	

ANSWER

Did you notice that requirements that are maintained, reusable, and ongoing are very similar? These terms are used interchangeably. Be sure to understand how they differ from *satisfied*.

Requirement Type	Requirement State
Requirements [Maintained]	These requirements will be managed and survive past the end of the project.
Requirements [Satisfied]	These requirements were met by the project solution.
Requirements [Ongoing]	These requirements will survive past the end of the project and be maintained or managed.
Requirements [Communicated]	These requirements have been presented to someone in some format (verbally, written, packaged, formal presentation, etc.)
Requirements [Traced]	These requirements are linked to other requirements.

Requirement Type	Requirement State
Requirements [Approved]	These requirements have been signed off.
Requirements [Reusable]	These requirements will be maintained or managed as assets for use on future projects.

 Before taking the practice exam, I recommend that you read the Requirements Management and Communication chapter of the *BABOK® Guide* (Chapter 4).

Practice Exam

1. After a project is closed, the requirements:

   A. Will be immediately used on another project.
   B. Should all be archived.
   C. Should be stored based on the requirements management plan.
   D. Are virtually useless.

2. Why must requirements be documented?

   A. Most methodologies require formal requirements documents.
   B. To maintain a requirement in a repository and reuse it, the requirement must be documented.
   C. Requirements do not need to be documented when using a change-driven approach like agile or Scrum.
   D. Most solution teams are remote, so requirements must be sent to them in documents.

3. Requirements asset management refers to:

   A. Requirements to support the Corporate Asset Management System.
   B. The process of saving and reusing requirements.
   C. The management of people who know how to manage requirements.
   D. The management of stakeholders who provide requirements.

4. Which of the following types of requirements will NOT be maintained after a project is complete?

   A. Throw-away prototypes and as-is workflows
   B. Business and non-functional requirements
   C. Throw-away prototypes and business requirements
   D. As-is workflows and functional requirements

5. The knowledge area that includes getting approval of the requirements is:

   A. Requirements Analysis.
   B. Enterprise Analysis.
   C. Requirements Management and Communication.
   D. Solution Assessment and Validation.

6. Your project involves several hundred stakeholders and the solution must meet regulatory standards. Which of the following would BEST describe your requirements package?

   A. Informal style with a few pages of textual requirements
   B. Informal style with a list of stakeholder requests sorted by the requestor's name
   C. Formal style with application regulations copied into the document
   D. Formal style with textual requirements and footnotes to the applicable regulations

7. You have created a beautiful requirements package with headings, sections, and page references, but your reviewers complain it is too long to review. What should you do?

   A. Go to the sponsor and ask him to encourage the reviewers to read the package.
   B. Tell the stakeholders to just sign-off on the package. They can trust that you got it right.
   C. Set up individual meetings with each stakeholder to walk through the package with each one.
   D. Break the package into smaller pieces, and send pieces to the appropriate reviewers.

8. A _____ is an agreed-upon set of requirements that will be used to keep the project work in scope.

   A. Baseline
   B. Business requirements document (BRD)
   C. Requirements package
   D. Coverage matrix

9. Which of the following is a true statement about baselined requirements?

   A. Baselined requirements cannot be changed.
   B. Baselined requirements define the scope of the solution.
   C. Baselined requirements are primarily used to obtain user sign-off.
   D. Baselined requirements only include solution requirements (functional and non-functional).

10. An example of a requirements conflict is:

    A. One stakeholder performs a calculation using MS Excel, while another performs it using MS Access.
    B. One stakeholder wants requirements elicited during a requirements workshop, while another prefers individual interviews.
    C. One stakeholder wants the new system implemented in his department without employee training, while another wants her employees trained before rollout.
    D. One stakeholder defines Order as approved for shipping, while another defines Order as a customer request.

11. The Add Profile web page supports the Maintain Profile Information business process, which will impact the objective of Increase timeliness of product information by 10%. This is an example of:

    A. Derivation or backward traceability.
    B. Allocation or forward traceability.
    C. Impact analysis.
    D. Requirements coverage.

12. To determine the potential size and cost of a change, use:

    A. Forward traceability (allocation).
    B. Impact analysis.
    C. Change control process.
    D. Conflict management.

13. The business analyst's role in vendor contract development is:

    A. Accountable—the busines analyst makes sure the contract is correct, and complete and approves it
    B. Responsible—the business analyst makes sure the contract is correct and complete and provides it to the project manager and sponsor for approval
    C. Consultative—the business analyst provides requirements to be included in the contract
    D. Informed—the business analyst should receive a copy of the contract once it is signed

14. RFP stands for:

    A. Request for proposal.
    B. Requirements for proposal.
    C. Requirements functional proposed.
    D. Request for process.

15. Requirements traceability refers to:

    A. Tracing a requirement from one stakeholder to another.
    B. Tracing the work flowing through the business area.
    C. Tracing a requirement to related requirements.
    D. Tracing a requirement to the stakeholder who requested it.

16. In which task are requirements approved?

    A. Manage Solution Scope and Requirements
    B. Define Solution Scope
    C. Allocate Requirements
    D. Validate Requirements

17. Another word for deliverable is:

    A. Artifact
    B. Work product
    C. Model
    D. Diagram

18. A vision statement describes:

    A. The sponsor's specific objectives of a project.
    B. The user's view of the software interfaces.
    C. The business view of the future state.
    D. The solution team's specification of what to build.

19. To successfully communicate requirements, you ALWAYS need:

    A. Requirements, a business analysis communication plan, and a requirements package.
    B. Requirements in a requirements package.
    C. Strong presentation skills and a business analysis communication plan.
    D. Strong communication skills and requirements.

20. What type of requirements CANNOT be communicated by a business analyst?

    A. Requirements that have been packaged
    B. Requirements that have not been stated
    C. Requirements that have been validated
    D. Stakeholder requirements

21. A RFP (request for proposal) includes:

    A. Traceability.
    B. Stakeholder register.
    C. Requirements.
    D. Sign-off.

22. An example of derivation or backward traceability is:

    A. Real-time tracking of product locations will be accomplished by the implementation of a bar code scanner.
    B. A bar code scanner uses a light sensor to read and record a product location.
    C. We must have real-time product location information to better serve our customers.
    D. The new bar code scanner addresses the objective of real-time tracking of product locations.

© 2012 RMC Publications, Inc • 952.846.4484 • info@rmcproject.com • www.rmcproject.com

Answers

1. **Answer**   C
    Explanation   Research shows that reusing requirements components increases productivity. The requirements management plan should include a description of where requirements will be stored and which requirements should be maintained for use on future projects. Maintaining a repository of requirements is costly, so only valuable assets should be included. Although the requirements may not be reused immediately, they should still be maintained.

2. **Answer**   B
    Explanation   This may be tricky because it is a myth that requirements are not documented when using a change-driven approach. Although the requirements may be documented on a sticky note or a whiteboard, they are documented. To maintain a requirement and reuse it on future projects, it must be documented.

3. **Answer**   B
    Explanation   Requirements management never refers to the management of people. Requirements should be considered corporate assets because they are valuable. They represent important information about the business and can be reused on future projects. As such, they should be stored in a central location and be available for other projects to use.

4. **Answer**   A
    Explanation   Business and functional requirements are generally reusable on future projects. Non-functional requirements can also be used again on enhancement projects. As-is workflows are usually replaced by to-be workflows (which become the new as-is workflow after implementation).

5. **Answer**   C
    Explanation   The solution scope and high-level requirements are defined in Enterprise Analysis. Detailed requirements are analyzed in Requirements Analysis. The solution is assessed and validated in Solution Assessment and Validation. Approved requirements are the output of the task Manage Solution Scope and Requirements in the Requirements Management and Communication knowledge area.

6. **Answer**   D
    Explanation   As soon as you know your solution is regulated by a government or industry organization, you should consider a formal style for your requirements package. Compliance with regulations and making sure your implementation SMEs build according to regulations usually necessitate more formality and a formal approval process. The requirements package should include all requirements, including adherence to regulatory standards.

7. **Answer**   D
    Explanation   Individual meetings might work if you have a very small number of stakeholders, but usually this is not practical. Breaking up requirements into small, easy-to-review, pieces increases the likelihood your stakeholders will give you meaningful feedback. You should strive to have reviewers only review the requirements for which they have expertise or involvement.

8. **Answer**   A
    Explanation   Did you should struggle between Baseline and BRD? A BRD may include a subset of requirements or may include approved changes to the baseline. The correct answer is baseline. Baselining is only done to manage scope creep.

9. **Answer**   B

   Explanation   The baseline can be changed by using the established change control process. Any types of requirements can be baselined. They are signed off, but obtaining sign-off is not the primary purpose of baselining. The primary purpose is to prevent scope creep. Baselined requirements define the scope of the solution.

10. **Answer**   D

    Explanation   Different procedures used in the current or as-is process are not viewed as a requirements conflict (MS Excel vs. Access) unless the solution design elements preferred are different (in the to-be process). Preferences about elicitation techniques may reflect learning style or communication differences, but both preferences can be accommodated. During rollout, different stakeholders may have different needs that can be accommodated (like training), and if so, there is no conflict.

11. **Answer**   A

    Explanation   Forward traceability starts at high-level requirements and follows links to solution components. Impact analysis assesses the impact of a change and uses tracing links. Requirements coverage refers to making sure each high-level requirement will be satisfied. This is performed using forward tracing. Backward traceability means we can look at a solution component (like a web page) and follow its links back to their origin (business process and objective).

12. **Answer**   B

    Explanation   Impact analysis involves identifying the impacts of a potential change. This will be performed in conjunction with a change control request to provide the information needed by the decision maker to approve or deny the change. Forward traceability may be used to perform impact analysis.

13. **Answer**   C

    Explanation   Business analysts usually don't have the legal knowledge or expertise to be accountable for the entire agreement, but they should definitely be consulted (not just informed after the fact).

14. **Answer**   A

    Explanation   The acronym RFP stands for request for proposal.

15. **Answer**   C

    Explanation   Traceability describes the links between requirement components. For example, a process requirement like Accept Order is related to (linked or traced to) data requirements like Order Number or Order Date. Tracing also shows how requirements are implemented into the final product.

16. **Answer**   A

    Explanation   The Manage Solution Scope and Requirements task includes approval of requirements.

17. **Answer**   A

    Explanation   An artifact or deliverable is something that will be presented to a stakeholder. A work product is created by a business analyst (or anyone) as he or she is analyzing and is not usually presented to others. Models and diagrams can be deliverables, artifacts, or work products.

18. **Answer**   C
    Explanation   A vision statement describes the desired future state of a product or solution. The vision may describe a result that involves many projects. It is not specific enough to state measurable objectives. Software interfaces and technical specification should support the vision, but they are much more detailed.

19. **Answer**   D
    Explanation   A requirements package is an optional input to the Communicate Requirements task. You don't always use a formal presentation; you may e-mail a deliverable to a stakeholder. You must have some requirements to communicate and communication skills.

20. **Answer**   B
    Explanation   Any type of requirement can be communicated by a business analyst as long as it has been stated by someone. Requirements do not have to be packaged or validated to be communicated.

21. **Answer**   C
    Explanation   To a business analyst, requirements are the most important part of an RFP. When asking vendors to propose a solution they must be provided with excellent requirements. Traceability is rarely complete or included at this point. The stakeholder list or register is not included, because names of employees may be confidential and you don't want vendors contacting the stakeholder directly. Stakeholder or user roles or profiles should be part of the requirements along with their security requirements. Sign-offs are an internal process and not normally included.

22. **Answer**   D
    Explanation   Backward traceability means we can look at a sole component (like a bar code scanner) and follow its links to their origin (real-time tracking objective).

CHAPTER 7

Solution Assessment and Validation

Aligned with the *BABOK® Guide* Chapter Seven

Solution Assessment and Validation is critical, since achieving the right solution is the ultimate goal of all business analysis work. This knowledge area includes the work necessary to ensure the solution truly meets the business needs and is the best solution for the organization.

Designing, developing, building (or acquiring), and testing the solution are the responsibility of other team members. Your job is to perform due diligence to make sure the proposed solution meets each approved requirement, and to work closely with the team to make sure the solution will bring value to the business. After the solution has been built or acquired, you will make sure it works as needed and help to plan the implementation or transition into production. You will see approximately 24 questions on this knowledge area on the exam.

Q U I C K T E S T

- Verify solution
- Validate solution
- Allocate requirements
- Service-Oriented Architecture (SOA)
- Enterprise architecture
- Organizational readiness
- Change management
- Implementation strategy
- Cutover
- Pilot
- Parallel processing
- Release planning
- Cultural assessment
- Technical assessment
- User acceptance testing (UAT)
- Post-implementation assessment
- Lessons learned
- Test case
- Test plan
- Quality control
- Quality assurance
- Opportunity cost
- Sunk cost
- Commercial Off-the-Shelf (COTS)
- Design
- Mitigating action
- Defect

Solution Assessment and Validation in Action

One of my assignments was to build an annual inventory software system for a group of automobile assembly plants. I was responsible for the entire solution: analysis, design, coding, testing, and implementation. My domain stakeholders were engineers and plant supervisors. Instead of manually counting component parts sitting on an assembly line, our new software would read the engineering database and match individual orders with their required parts. By analyzing each order, the software would count the number of parts that were "in-process" and produce a complete inventory report.

Our team considered several technical design options and we learned a lot about engineering as we assessed each approach! Once we decided on the approach, we had to make sure the software would satisfy all of the original requirements. The system had to produce the inventory report by a particular time on a specific date to coincide with the external audit, and the report had to list each part number, name, and quantity. The date of implementation was dictated and the system would only run once per year at each location.

We did a lot of planning for using the software at the first plant. A full system test was conducted a few weeks before the first run. (As you know, software testing is not part of the role of a business analyst, but I was also the tester!) I was involved in planning for the testing, and was responsible for reviewing the test results and resolving defects. I reviewed the test reports with the engineers to make sure they were completely accurate. I built an hour-by-hour implementation schedule for the first production run to ensure we could meet the mandated audit date and time. I met with the plant manager and the head of manufacturing to be sure they felt confident with the new system. I also wrote detailed instructions for how to run the system, since I knew it would only be used once per year and didn't want to rely on anyone's memory.

During the first production run, I made sure the inventory counts were accurate. I met with the external auditor, showed her the inventory report, and explained how we calculated the totals. She was satisfied and signed off on the accuracy of the inventory!

Then it was on to the next plant. Before beginning the second implementation, I met with key stakeholders to debrief them and look for system improvements. We made a few adjustments, enabling our second implementation to proceed even more smoothly.

EXERCISE There are six tasks in the Solution Assessment and Validation knowledge area: Assess Proposed Solution, Allocate Requirements, Assess Organizational Readiness, Define Transition Requirements, Validate Solution, and Evaluate Solution Performance. Can you identify the six tasks in the previous story?

Solution Assessment and Validation Knowledge Area Task	Work Performed in the Story
Assess Proposed Solution	
Allocate Requirements	
Assess Organizational Readiness	
Define Transition Requirements	
Validate Solution	
Evaluate Solution Performance	

ANSWER

Solution Assessment and Validation Knowledge Area Task	Work Performed in the Story
Assess Proposed Solution	Spoke with engineers and team about options
Allocate Requirements	Made sure the selected solution would satisfy the original requirements
Assess Organizational Readiness	Spoke to the plant manager and manufacturing manager to make sure they had confidence in the new system
Define Transition Requirements	Created an hour-by-hour implementation schedule and documented the instructions for running the system
Validate Solution	Reviewed testing reports for accuracy
Evaluate Solution Performance	Debriefed stakeholders after first production run to evaluate performance and made adjustments before the next implementation

Barb's BA Themes

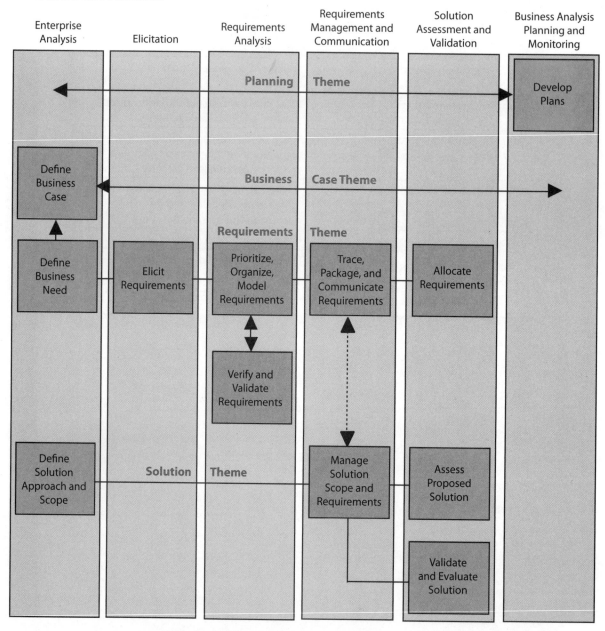

The Solution Assessment and Validation knowledge area involves each of the business analysis themes. As always, all of our work should be completed according to the business analysis plans. And, everything we do should support the original business case.

In the Requirements Theme, we confirm that all of the requirements will be met by the solution. We do this by tracing each requirement to the piece of the solution (solution component) that satisfies the requirement. This is referred to as allocating requirements, a special type of tracing.

The Solution Theme is the primary focus of this knowledge area. We start by considering the solution approach and scope developed in Enterprise Analysis. The solution scope is considered part of the high-level requirements, which are further elaborated (specified and modeled), in Requirements

© 2012 RMC Publications, Inc • 952.846.4484 • info@rmcproject.com • www.rmcproject.com

Analysis. In the Manage Solution Scope and Requirements task (in Requirements Management and Communication) you are always monitoring the detailed requirements to make sure they are within scope and they are approved. The team develops solution alternatives, decides which one is best, and makes sure all of the requirements are met by the solution design. Tasks in this knowledge area look at the completed solution and confirm that it truly brings value to the organization. In addition, we make sure the organization is ready for the change and document the implementation plans and transition requirements.

Things to Know about Solution Assessment and Validation for the Exam

- Several tasks in this knowledge area are performed concurrently with tasks in other knowledge areas. For example, while you are eliciting requirements, you are also assessing the organization's readiness for a change. Don't be lured into thinking that Solution Assessment and Validation tasks are only performed at the end of a project.
- Carefully review questions that include the word *design*. Business analysis work includes the design of functional behaviors like screen design (prototyping), but designing the solution architecture is usually done by an implementation SME (a business architect). Business analysts *facilitate* agreement about the design and review it to make sure it satisfies the requirements.
- Solution components are things like hardware, software, process changes, and personnel changes. All of these components work together to address the business need.
- The introduction to the *BABOK® Guide* suggests that the most likely starting task for business analysis is either Define Business Need (in Enterprise Analysis) or Evaluate Solution Performance (here in Solution Assessment and Validation). Work may start here because a problem with an existing solution or system is driving the need for change.

Introduction to the Tasks of Solution and Assessment Validation

As you begin to read about solution assessment and validation, you may feel like there is a gap between the Requirements Management and Communication knowledge area and this knowledge area. We were just communicating and managing requirements, and now we are suddenly validating the solution! When was the solution created?

Let's look more closely at the Solution Theme. The gap you noticed is filled by tasks that are not owned by the business analysis profession and, as such, are not included in the *BABOK® Guide* or our Themes graphic. The following graphic shows how these "missing" tasks would fit into our Solution Theme. If we were to name these "missing" tasks, they might be called Design Solution Alternatives, Build or Buy the Solution, Test the Solution, Implement the Solution, and Support the Operation of the Solution. Business analysts support, review, assist, facilitate, and communicate about the solution, and they work with the other stakeholders to bring the solution to completion and transition it into the business.

In addition to the tasks specifically identified in the Themes graphic, this knowledge area includes tasks to make sure the business organization is ready for the solution to be implemented and to develop transition requirements for the implementation.

The Solution Theme

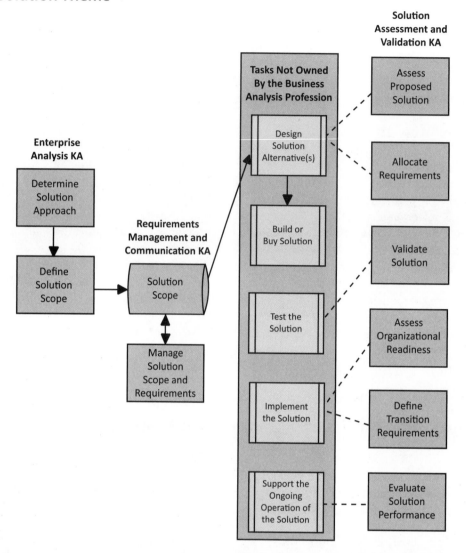

Solution Assessment and Validation tasks are grouped together in this knowledge area because they describe work that supports the implementation SMEs responsible for testing and implementing the solution. It is more important for you to understand the work described by each of these tasks *independently* than to understand how these tasks are dependent on each other. If you were to draw a data flow diagram of the tasks in this knowledge area, you would see that very few of the outputs are used by other Solution Assessment and Validation tasks.

© 2012 RMC Publications, Inc • 952.846.4484 • info@rmcproject.com • www.rmcproject.com

--- SOLUTION ASSESSMENT AND VALIDATION TASKS ---

Assess Proposed Solution (7.1)

A "proposed solution" is an idea for a business change to address a need (problem or opportunity). It may be carefully thought-out and documented in a blueprint, architecture plan, software specification, or some other technical design document. It may just be an idea someone suggested that hasn't really been analyzed or detailed yet. To assess a proposed solution is to review the solution description or design and determine if it would best meet the business need. This is a business analysis activity, because the designer of the solution may be a technical stakeholder who is not directly involved with the end users and the business requirements. Your job is to look at the proposed solution from all perspectives.

The placement of this task in the Solution Assessment and Validation knowledge area can be a little tricky to understand. As you already know, tasks in business analysis are not sequential and are often performed iteratively. This task can be performed immediately after the solution scope is defined (in Enterprise Analysis) or any time there are decisions to be made about solution options. No matter how good your team has been at imagining a solution scope, once you get into detailed requirements, you will have a clearer perspective of the need and may see alternate solutions.

Some projects start with the Assess Proposed Solution task. Have you ever been given an assignment that started out with a proposed solution? "Barb, we're going to buy XZY software package. You're assigned to be the business analyst on the project!" In a situation like this, you are immediately assessing a proposed solution, while also eliciting requirements and trying to backtrack to understand the original business need that prompted this idea.

Assess Proposed Solution		
Inputs	**Techniques**	**Outputs**
Assumptions and Constraints (6.4)	Acceptance and Evaluation Criteria Definition (9.1)	Assessment of Proposed Solution (7.1)
Requirements [Prioritized and Approved] (4.1, 6.1)	Decision Analysis (9.8)	
Solution Option(s)	Vendor Assessment (9.34)	

BA's Responsibilities In Assessing the Proposed Solution
- Work with implementation SMEs to identify and present solution options to business domain stakeholders
- Collect technical estimates from the implementation stakeholders
- Facilitate agreement on evaluation criteria
- Facilitate assessment, ranking, and decisions about each option
- Facilitate the selection of the "best" solution

What Do You Need to Successfully Assess the Proposed Solution?
The most important input to this task is a solution option. You can't assess if you don't have a proposal! These usually come from implementation SMEs. To assess each option, you and your team need to review the approved, prioritized requirements, along with assumptions and constraints, to determine how well each solution option meets the acceptance criteria.

TRICKS OF THE TRADE® Determine Solution Approach (in Enterprise Analysis) sounds very similar to the task Assess Proposed Solution in the Solution Assessment and Validation knowledge area. The difference is in the level of detail. In Enterprise Analysis, we are looking at a high-level view of business needs and capabilities (business requirements). In Solution Assessment and Validation, we are looking at the detailed options for a solution (stakeholder and solution requirements).

Solution Design

Understanding the business problems, opportunities, and environment will allow you to help your team design a solution. Don't be afraid of the word *design*. To design is to plan, imagine, architect, or sketch out a solution. Ideally, the solution design is developed collaboratively, with all key stakeholders having input. For example, you may design a screen prototype (with your end users) and then the implementation SMEs will design the software system needed to display and process the screen functions. No one expects you to be a database designer or architect. Think of your work as *facilitating* the design. Facilitation is used by business analysts to help stakeholders discuss possible solutions and determine which one is the best.

Assessing Each Solution Alternative

Often there are several solution options that could address a business need, so this task may be performed multiple times on a single project or initiative. Teams without business analysts sometimes jump on an idea that initially sounds good and start building. On change-driven projects, the assessment is performed on a high-level idea or a prototype of part of the solution. On plan-driven projects, a more formal assessment of all the requirements is conducted, to avoid the solution being partially or completely built before someone realizes the flaws. This is a costly way to assess a potential design. A little time evaluating saves lots of time and money later! You need to make sure each solution proposal is assessed thoroughly before too much money is spent building it.

Each solution idea is reviewed and evaluated against several criteria. Does it support the business case? Does it accomplish the project objectives? Does it meet business requirements? Is it feasible? You will help the team carefully and objectively assess each suggestion to make sure all approved requirements will be met by the solution.

As part of the evaluation of each proposed solution, the team needs to make a high-level estimate of time and costs. These estimates should include not only the development and materials costs, but also transition, change management, and interface costs. Ongoing maintenance costs must be considered as well. Do you remember the cost-benefit analysis discussion in the Enterprise Analysis chapter? In some organizations, the Assess Proposed Solution task is performed during Enterprise Analysis and becomes part of the business case.

Which proposed solution is the "best?" A decision is made by looking at all the factors surrounding the business need, the business environment, the solution characteristics, and the anticipated value the solution will bring. Often options are ranked according to agreed-upon criteria.

Adding Capabilities

Sometimes, additional capabilities that were not originally requested, or were ranked as low priorities, will be considered at this point because they are easy to add to the solution without incurring additional cost. The design may be adjusted to allow for ease of future changes. You must work closely with your project manager, domain SMEs, and implementation team to make sure you don't jeopardize the time or cost constraints of the project or initiative by adding these capabilities.

Service-Oriented Architecture   Service-oriented architecture (SOA) is an important software design approach that increases the quality and maintainability of technology systems and decreases the time required to make additions and enhancements. If your organization is using SOA, you must make sure that every solution design fits into the architecture plans. An SOA approach includes the construction of small, reusable components that are shared throughout the enterprise. SOA recognizes that many of the same services are needed in multiple departments and divisions throughout the enterprise. When a service needs a change, the reusable component only needs to be changed and tested once before it becomes effective for all uses.

EXERCISE   Review the features and proposed design below. Assess the potential solution and develop a list of questions or comments for follow-up. Then create a list of criteria to evaluate the proposed design.

Exercise Case Study
Problem Statement: We need a solution to keep worker information up-to-date. With so many people working in so many different locations, it is difficult to add new workers and maintain worker profiles. We must also make sure the employee paychecks are deposited correctly and benefits information is current.

Primary Objective (from the business case): Decrease HR costs by 15 percent in two years by streamlining the Workforce Tracking system.

Specific Features Needed:
1. Allow candidate workers to apply for a position online from anywhere in the world.
2. Allow workers (employees, consultants, or contractors) to change their phone number, mailing address, e-mail address, bank account number for direct deposits, and tax information online from anywhere in the world.
3. When employee information is added or changed, it should automatically be sent to all of the involved parties (government taxing authority, benefit providers, payroll system) to be updated. The employee should be notified when the change has been completed.

Current (As-Is) Process:
In North America, applicants can apply online and the headquarters' HR managers are notified of new applications. Outside North America, local hiring managers accept applications, screen them, and forward them to headquarters' HR. They may be e-mailed (scanned and attached as a document), mailed, or faxed. The application forms are not consistent from one country to another.

Solution Proposal:

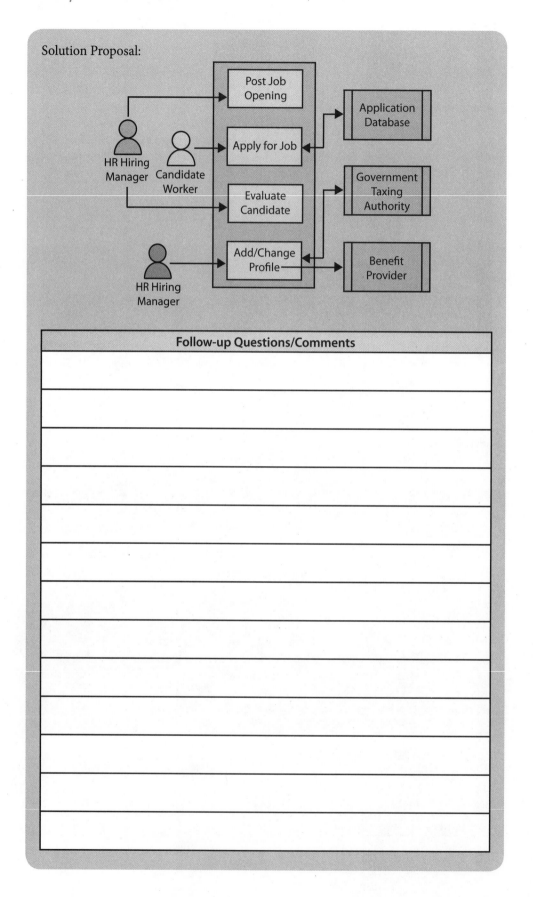

Follow-up Questions/Comments

Possible Evaluation Criteria

ANSWER

Follow-up Questions/Comments
1. "Post job openings" functionality was not mentioned in features.
2. How will HR know when a candidate has applied? E-mail?
3. What screening is currently done, and how will it be done in the new system?
4. Don't other people, such as functional managers, get involved with hiring? Will managers be able to review the applications online?
5. Payroll system was mentioned in features but is not shown here.
6. Isn't the application database needed to evaluate a candidate?
7. Where is the HR or worker login process? Does it already exist?
8. Can existing employees use this system to apply for a different job?
9. Should application forms be standardized for all countries?
10. What is the purpose of the arrow going from Application Database back to Apply for Job?
11. What is the purpose of the arrow going from Government Taxing Authority to Add/Change profile?
12. Does the candidate or worker receive confirmation that his input (application or profile change) has been received?

Possible Evaluation Criteria
Cost of website development
Expected performance (speed) of the website
Will it encourage more candidates to apply for jobs?
How much HR time will be saved?

Although the previous graphic is not created with a standard diagramming method, I'll bet you were still able to review and assess it. A solution can be represented in many different ways, and can still be intelligently reviewed by a business analyst or other stakeholders! You can always learn and ask questions, even if you don't completely understand the technical design.

Sometimes a proposed solution looks good at first glance, but when you closely examine it against the requirements, you begin to find holes or inconsistencies. Become a critical reviewer, looking for problems at this stage, rather than after the product has been built. Imagine problems or challenges that might arise for the end users.

Techniques to Assess Proposed Solution

Acceptance and Evaluation Criteria Definition (9.1)

Acceptance and Evaluation Criteria Definition helps the team decide how to evaluate the solution options. What criteria are most important to the stakeholders and how does each option meet the criteria? Each solution option is compared to the desired criteria and the options are ranked numerically. The option with the highest ranking is usually chosen. Acceptance and evaluation criteria must be defined before assessing a solution to make sure the criteria are not biased toward one proposal.

	Evaluation Criteria			
	Easy to Maintain (1 is Most Difficult, 10 is Easiest)	**One Year Payback 0 = No 10 = Yes**	**Estimated Useful Life**	**Total**
Proposed Solution 1	6	10	2 years	18
Proposed Solution 2	5	0	15 years	20*** (highest score)
Proposed Solution 3	3	0	5 years	8

Example of Solution Assessment

Decision Analysis (9.8)

When stakeholders come from different business domains, there may be competing or conflicting criteria upon which the solution could be evaluated. The assessment of solution options and the selection of the best one often utilizes decision analysis.

This is a good time to review the financial analysis terms we learned in the Enterprise Analysis task, Define Business Case (page 81).

EXERCISE

Financial Analysis Term	Definition
Return on Investment (ROI)	
Discounted Cash Flow	
Net Present Value (NPV)	
Internal Rate of Return (IRR)	
Payback Period	

ANSWER

Financial Analysis Term	Definition
Return on Investment (ROI)	ROI attempts to measure the profitability of an investment by calculating the amount of benefits received in relation to the amount of cost (investment). The higher the ROI, the better.
Discounted Cash Flow	Discounted cash flow is used to estimate the attractiveness of an investment by predicting how much money will be received in the future and discounting it to its current value.

Financial Analysis Term	Definition
Net Present Value (NPV)	NPV is the present value of the total benefits (income or revenue) minus the costs over many time periods. Calculating the NPV of each proposal provides a means for the organization to compare options and select the best one. Generally, if the NPV is positive, the investment is a good choice unless an even better investment opportunity exists. The option with the greatest NPV is typically selected.
Internal Rate of Return (IRR)	This is another measure of the return based on company cash flow and used to compare investment options.
Payback Period	This term refers to the length of time it takes for the organization to recover its investment in the solution and start generating net benefits.

Vendor Assessment (9.34)

If a solution option is a vendor-supplied product or service, it must be evaluated not only for its ability to meet requirements, but also for its ongoing support and maintenance costs. Every solution (including those built internally) will have ongoing maintenance costs, but vendor-supported products pose a different risk. Your organization will be dependent on an outside company to fix problems and add functionality needed in the future. Decision analysis looks at ongoing maintenance charges and contractual future rate increases when calculating ROI. You must also determine acceptable vendor response times and assess long term vendor stability. Refer back to the Requirements Management and Communication chapter (Prepare Requirements Package task) to review best practices for Vendor Assessment.

Summary

The result, or output, of this task is an assessment of the proposed solution(s). Each option is objectively assessed using agreed-upon evaluation criteria and measured against the criteria. Stakeholder buy-in will increase when you show them that multiple options have been considered and that the chosen solution best supports their needs.

Allocate Requirements (7.2)

This task includes two types of requirements allocation. First, to be sure all approved requirements will be fulfilled, each requirement is mapped to the part of the solution that satisfies it. Together, these solution components define the whole solution. Solution components can include hardware, software, business process changes, business rule changes, organization changes, etc. Allocating each requirement to a component of the solution is a great double check on the solution design.

A second allocation is related to development of the solution. The solution may be broken into releases or phases for development and implementation, and the requirements allocated to each release. This allows pieces of the solution to be created (and possibly implemented) earlier rather than doing everything all at once. In change-driven projects, development iterations may be as short as two weeks, and a release to production will include several iterations.

Both of these allocations are shown in a traceability matrix or other cross-reference between the requirements and the solution components. It is important to realize that these are two different allocation activities.

Allocate Requirements		
Inputs	**Techniques**	**Outputs**
Solution [Designed]	Acceptance and Evaluation Criteria Definition (9.1)	Requirements [Allocated] (7.2)
Requirements [Prioritized and Approved] (4.1, 6.1)	Business Rules Analysis (9.4)	
Solution Scope (5.4)	Decision Analysis (9.8)	
	Functional Decomposition (9.12)	
	Process Modeling (9.21)	
	Scenarios and Use Cases (9.26)	

BA's Responsibilities in Allocating Requirements
- Make sure each approved and prioritized requirement is satisfied by the solution
- Alert stakeholders to unsatisfied requirements or solution components that are unnecessary
- Facilitate stakeholder agreement on the release plan

What Do You Need to Successfully Allocate Requirements?
Notice the input solution [designed] is not an output of any task in the *BABOK® Guide*. We saw in the Solution Theme graphic on page 280, that designing the solution is not business analysis work. It comes from outside the business analysis profession. We make sure the solution design supports the solution scope and requirements. Notice also that we only allocate requirements that have been prioritized and approved.

Allocating to Solution Components   Solution components can be any parts of the solution that support a requirement. Components of software solutions include screens, reports, databases, programs, modules, etc. Hardware components include servers, mobile devices, network cards, scanners, etc. Not all projects formally allocate each requirement to a solution component, but by doing so, you can be sure that all of your requirements are included in the design. You can also make sure the implementation SMEs are not building features that were not requested. This can be a useful way to oversee implementation SMEs who do not work for your company (e.g., vendors or contractors).

Allocating to Releases   Requirements are allocated to releases so the development team can concentrate on one small piece of the solution at a time. This allows for faster development and adjustments as the end users see the solution being built. Any type of requirement can be allocated to releases or phases. Often stakeholder requirements are allocated so each stakeholder can see when his or her request is scheduled to be completed and implemented.

Coverage or tracing is another name for this allocation work.

Requirements Allocated to Phases			
Stakeholder Requirements	Business Priority (H, M, L)	Estimate (in days)	Phase
An employee can request a new PC via the website.	H	5	1
An employee can check the status of a new PC order via the website.	L	1	1
An employee can record receipt of the new PC via the website.	M	1	1
An employee can review PC brand and model options via the website.	Reject	10	
An employee can request a new printer via the website.	M	5	2
An employee can request a repair via the website.	M	3	2

Solution Adjustments   As the solution design becomes clear and the team sees exactly how the solution will change the business, adjustments may be made to the solution, or requirements may be reprioritized. Imagine you decided to build a swing set for your children. You sketched out a design and made a list of the materials you need. Then you went into the backyard to assess your solution design. You might make some adjustments to your design as you consider exactly where and how the swing set will fit. If the ground is not level, you may need longer poles on one side.

Adjustments may be needed if component parts of the solution are unavailable. Adjustments may also be made because of dependencies that dictate the order of the solution development. For example, if a software feature can only be used on the latest version of the operating system, but the department is currently using an older version, that feature is *dependent* on the implementation of the latest version of the operating system. This may cause the feature to be assigned a lower priority and/or moved to a later release, after the operating system implementation is complete. This release planning allows the team to decide which solution components will be built first.

As mentioned earlier, additional capabilities that were ranked as low priority may be reconsidered at this point, because they are easy to add to the solution without incurring additional cost. A good business analyst is always on the lookout for these bonuses; requirements that can be completed earlier and at a lower cost than originally estimated. These are usually minor adjustments. Significant changes must be reviewed in the change control process.

 In plan-driven approaches, the words release, phase, and iteration are used somewhat interchangeably to mean a set of functions that are built at the same time. In change-driven approaches, release indicates the set of features that will be implemented together, while sprint or iteration indicates the set of features which will be built together.

Techniques to Allocate Requirements

Acceptance and Evaluation Criteria Definition (9.1)

During release planning, a minimum set of requirements may be needed to make a release worthwhile to the business. This minimum set of requirements is acceptance criteria for a release. For example, a minimum acceptance criterion for your children's swing set is that it must have at least one play component. In other words, from the perspective of the children, just putting up the frame in phase 1 isn't "worth it" to them. We need to include at least one swing or a slide to make it worth having.

Business Rules Analysis (9.4)

Since business rules are part of many requirements, the business analyst must also allocate each rule to a solution component. This ensures we haven't forgotten to include a business rule in the solution. For example:

Business Rule	Solution Component	Notes
Each employee must have a unique employee ID.	Add New Worker screen	The system will assign a unique employee ID to each new worker.
Each employee must provide his or her tax ID number.	Add New Worker screen	The system will not add a new employee without a valid tax ID number.
Each employee must provide legal proof of his or her country of residence.	HR Admin—manual procedure	The HR Administrator will copy an acceptable legal document and file it with the employee's job application.

Decision Analysis (9.8)

Decision analysis should be used to compare the financial impact of different allocation options being considered. The change-driven approach determines the value of individual requirements and puts the highest value requirements into the earlier iterations.

Functional Decomposition (9.12)

Functional decomposition can be used to visually show the solution components for allocation to the releases. Implementation SMEs may provide a decomposition diagram of the solution design for your review.

Process Modeling (9.21)

Business processes are requirements, and another important part of solution allocations. You must make sure that each and every business process within scope is allocated to a specific solution component. You also need to make sure domain SMEs understand how their processes are allocated to solution releases if a phased implementation is planned. Process modeling was discussed in detail in the Requirements Analysis chapter.

Scenarios and Use Cases (9.26)

As we discussed in the Requirements Analysis chapter, a use case is a goal of the system as defined by an actor. Each use case has a primary or "happy" path that describes the most common steps to accomplish the goal. Alternative paths or scenarios include exceptions to the primary path or instructions for how the system should handle errors that may occur along the way. These paths can each be considered separate functions. As separate functions, they may be assigned to different phases of the solution.

When determining what will be included in each release of the solution, use case paths (aka scenarios) may be referenced. A use case primary path may go into an early release, since it is the most common transaction. Alternate paths may be allocated to later releases depending on their frequency of occurrence.

For example, in the use case Add New Worker, the primary path might be adding a worker in the United States, since this is where the majority of employees are added. Therefore, it might be assigned to phase 1. The scenario of Add New Worker in Europe might be assigned to phase 2.

EXERCISE   Review the requirements and solution components below. Can you allocate each solution component to a requirement? Are all of the requirements satisfied? Are all of the solution components necessary?

Project: Build a place for my children to play.

ID	Requirements		ID	Solution Components
R1	Safe for children over 3 years old		A	Ladder
R2	Slide for children under 36 inches tall		B	8-foot-high plastic slide
R3	At least two swings (one that can be used by an adult)		C	2–3 plastic swing seats and chains
R4	Platform from which to jump (with a soft landing)		D	1 long pole for top of frame
R5	Weatherproof		E	4 poles for sides of frame
			F	Cement to secure poles in ground
			G	Park bench

Complete the following matrix by allocating each solution component to the appropriate requirement.

Allocation Matrix	
Requirement	**Solution Component(s)**
R1	
R2	
R3	
R4	
R5	

ANSWER

Allocation Matrix	
Requirement	**Solution Component(s)**
R1	F
R2	A, B, D, E
R3	C, D, E
R4	
R5	B, C (plastic is weatherproof)

Are all the requirements satisfied? If not, which requirements are not satisfied?

Are all the solution components necessary? If not, which components are not necessary?

Could this solution be built in phases? If so, complete the sample plan below.

Sample Release Plan	
Solution Component	**Phase**
A	
B	
C	
D	
E	
F	
G	

ANSWER

The requirements are not all satisfied. The swing set materials do not include a platform for jumping or soft landing material (requirement R4).

The park bench (G) does not seem to be a necessary solution component. This is an additional capability (place for adult supervision nearby) that was not requested in the original requirements.

What about the poles? Which requirement do they satisfy? ALL of them. The poles are the infrastructure components needed to support the solution, so they are necessary and must be mapped back to at least one of the requirements. This is an example of a dependency. We can't build a swing set without the poles. As long as each solution component satisfies at least one requirement, it is not necessary to allocate it any further, unless your methodology requires it.

Could this solution be built in phases? Yes. Phase 1 could be the frame (poles), the ladder, and the slide, and phase 2 could be the swings.

Sample Release Plan	
Solution Component	**Phase**
A	1
B	1
C	2
D	1
E	1
F	1
G	None

Summary

Even if you have been doing business analysis work for a long time, you may never have allocated requirements formally, using a table or cross-reference. But, as an excellent business analyst, you always made sure the solution met the business needs by reviewing the solution design and making sure it covered everything. Think about one of your past solutions. Did it meet all of the requirements? If it did, you were successful in allocating requirements!

Assess Organizational Readiness (7.3)

Determining whether an organization is ready for a change is not easy. It requires the business analyst to understand the organizational culture, the operations, the impact on individual stakeholders, and the physical logistics of implementing the change. Business analysts assess the environment, specifically the stakeholders, to determine their readiness for a change. If the business is not ready to accept a change, the initiative will be a failure even if the solution is properly built.

The Assess Organizational Readiness task is closely tied to the next task, Define Transition Requirements, and the two tasks are often performed concurrently. The less ready an organization is for a change, the more transition requirements will be necessary. When impacted stakeholders are geographically dispersed, formal change communication plans must be developed.

Assess Organizational Readiness		
Inputs	**Techniques**	**Outputs**
Solution [Designed]	Acceptance and Evaluation Criteria Definition (9.1)	Organizational Readiness Assessment (7.3)
Enterprise Architecture	Data Flow Diagrams (9.6)	
Solution Scope (5.4)	Focus Groups (9.11)	
Stakeholder Concerns (3.3)	Interviews (9.14)	
	Organization Modeling (9.19)	
	Problem Tracking (9.20)	
	Process Modeling (9.21)	
	Risk Analysis (9.24)	
	Survey/Questionnaire (9.31)	
	SWOT Analysis (9.32)	

BA's Responsibilities in Assessing Organizational Readiness

- Determine the impact of the change on all stakeholder groups with special emphasis on operational support and hands-on users
- Determine the organization's ability to adopt the solution
- Work with the sponsor and key stakeholders to discuss and resolve concerns about readiness

What Do You Need to Successfully Assess Organizational Readiness?

To assess organizational readiness we need to anticipate how the solution will fit into the current organization (enterprise architecture) and determine the changes that will be necessary to successfully implement and operate it. The solution scope shows us the interfaces so that we can make sure all interfacing stakeholders are ready for the change. We also need to address any stakeholder concerns that were voiced during elicitation sessions.

 We talked about enterprise architecture in the Enterprise Analysis chapter. It is also used here, and again in the Business Analysis Planning and Monitoring chapter. It is important that you understand the purpose of an enterprise architecture and can recognize some of its potential components. If you don't feel comfortable with this concept, go back to the Enterprise Analysis chapter, page 60 to review it. It is included as an input to Assess Organizational Readiness because it is important to know the structure of the organization when you are determining whether the stakeholders are ready for the change.

Are We Ready for the Solution?

This task describes how we determine if our business stakeholders are ready to adopt the solution. We look at the impact of the change on the stakeholders to decide if they will accept the change, and think about how best to smooth the transition for each stakeholder group. Will stakeholder processes change when the solution is implemented? Will work be performed at different times or in different locations? Will stakeholders be interacting with different customers or co-workers? And most importantly, how do the impacted stakeholders feel about the change?

The amount of time needed to perform the Assess Organizational Readiness task depends primarily on the type of solution. If a network server is to be replaced with an identical model, brand, and size, the impact to the organization should be minimal, so the organizational readiness assessment will be relatively insignificant. When we are implementing a brand new process, the assessment could take a few weeks.

Don't assume that a small software change will only have a small impact. Imagine rearranging data entry fields on a screen used by thousands of people every day. To the software developer, this may be an insignificant change, but to a thousand users, it may be enormous. In addition to the impact on the business stakeholders and end users, consider the impact on the operational and support personnel. Will the solution require regular maintenance? Who will perform the maintenance? Who will troubleshoot problems? If the solution is provided by an outside vendor, who will be the ongoing liaison to the vendor?

Assessing Readiness   There are several factors we can use to assess readiness. The most important determinant in a successful implementation of a change is the attitude of the people who will be dealing with the change. If the stakeholders are looking forward to working with the new solution, their positive attitude will help them to work through any temporary inconveniences and be patient with the learning curve. If your stakeholders have a negative attitude toward the change, they could make it worse by complaining, resisting, and even sabotaging the change. A cultural assessment is usually done informally from the beginning of the project, as you get to know the stakeholders and you get a sense of their feelings about the change. The stakeholder concerns expressed during elicitation sessions probably gave additional insight into stakeholder attitudes toward the change. Now is the time to make sure these concerns are addressed.

In addition, a *technical assessment* is a more objective evaluation of how well the stakeholders are prepared to use the solution. Do they have the knowledge and expertise to use the new technology or processes? You need to consider each task or function performed by stakeholders and how it might change. Even activities not directly impacted by the solution may experience subtle changes.

Techniques to Assess Organizational Readiness

Acceptance and Evaluation Criteria Definition (9.1)
When considering the organization's readiness to accept the solution, you need to make sure the established acceptance criteria are agreed upon by all the key stakeholders. Setting realistic user expectations is a big part of a successful change. For example, a vendor Commercial Off-the-Shelf (COTS) software package may be your best solution, but it may not meet every requirement. Your implementation SMEs may have to develop procedures for functions that are not provided. We learned in the Enterprise Analysis chapter that identifying and filling the gaps between the solution and the original requests is gap analysis. As the liaison between the business and implementation stakeholders, your role as a business analyst is to help the team determine what is acceptable and which parts of the solution include gaps that require further development or customization.

Data Flow Diagrams (9.6) and Process Modeling (9.21)
Both of these techniques may be used to graphically illustrate the organizational or procedural changes that will be necessary to successfully implement the solution. Workflow swimlane diagrams will probably be the most useful diagrams, since they show the stakeholder groups involved as well as the flow of work. These techniques were discussed in detail in the Requirements Analysis chapter.

Focus Groups (9.11), Interviews (9.14) and Surveys/Questionnaires (9.31)

It is important to elicit stakeholder attitudes about the implementation of the solution. Are any stakeholders worried about the success of the change? Are any stakeholders resistant to making changes in their day-to-day procedures? As discussed in the Elicitation chapter, each of the elicitation techniques provides the analyst a unique forum from which to ask questions and get responses from stakeholders.

Organization Modeling (9.19)

Organization modeling may be used to identify the stakeholders who will be impacted by the solution, their physical locations, their work environments, and other factors that will impact readiness and solution success. An organization model is a collection of diagrams, descriptions, and characteristics of the organization. It may include an organization chart showing individuals and their reporting structure along with job descriptions. It may also include a location map or list of physical locations where the organization resides, as well as strategic planning components such as the corporate vision or mission statement.

Read the *BABOK® Guide* description of Organization Modeling (9.19) now.

Problem Tracking (9.20)

Problem or issue tracking can be used to document problems found during the organizational readiness assessment and help determine how each problem will be handled. Issues identified throughout the project need to be resolved before implementation.

Risk Analysis (9.24)

Can you imagine how risk analysis applies to the Assess Organizational Readiness task? Risks will be identified as you consider how ready the organization is to accept the change. Resistance to adopting the solution is, in and of itself, a risk! Risks related to organizational readiness can be managed just like any other risks. The list of these risks is important to review with your team and sponsor before the final implementation decision is made and a date is set. See page 83 in the Enterprise Analysis Chapter to review an example of a risk management plan.

SWOT Analysis (9.32)

Do you remember what SWOT stands for? S-strengths, W-weaknesses, O-opportunities, T-threats. This technique was discussed in the Enterprise Analysis chapter as a way to brainstorm about competitive opportunities. It is also useful for assessing organizational readiness. SWOT analysis gives you a clear assessment of the impact of the change, and the readiness of the organization to embrace it.

Force Field Analysis

Force field analysis is a structured analysis and presentation technique that can be used by one or more people on the team to better understand the impacts of a change. Many business analysts use this technique in group sessions to facilitate discussion on the change and develop ideas for better managing the change.

Read about Force Field Analysis in Task 7.3 now. Note this technique is not included in Chapter 9, the Techniques Chapter of the *BABOK® Guide*.

APPLY YOUR KNOWLEDGE   Think about the last time one of your work tools was changed (e.g., a word processing software upgrade, a new copy machine, an updated e-mail system). Were you notified of the change before it happened? Were you ready for the change? How long did it take for you to adjust to the change? What would have made the transition easier for you?

What if the Organization Is Not Ready?

Organizational readiness assessment may lead you to conclude that the organization is not ready to transition to the new solution. You may feel this concern early in the project. As soon as you have concerns, speak to your project manager or sponsor. Being honest and open about the likelihood of failure is an important responsibility of a business analyst. The earlier your team discusses this potential problem, the more time you will have to prepare the organization for the change or discuss other options with your sponsor. This may lead to revisions in the solution scope, or it may lead the team to create an early release of less disruptive functionality.

Summary

You bring value to your stakeholders when you clearly understand the ramifications of a proposed change. Assisting the organization to smoothly implement changes will allow it to better achieve its goals. An excellent business analyst proactively considers the difficulties each stakeholder might experience in adjusting to a change. By realistically addressing these challenges, the solution will be accepted and implemented more effectively.

Define Transition Requirements (7.4)

It is great when the project team builds a high-quality solution, but how do we incorporate it into the business without interrupting critical workflow? We need to intentionally plan and manage the transition. This is referred to as *organizational change management*. The things we need for this change are referred to as *transition requirements*. Transition requirements describe the work needed to ensure a smooth transition or implementation of the solution into the business. Developing transition requirements involves stakeholder analysis, planning, and communication, just like the other types of requirement.

As you assess the organization's readiness to accept the change, you can define the transition requirements. (Notice there are concurrent tasks here!) Transition requirements include rollout plans, employee training programs, change communication, operations turnover, and anything else needed to ensure a smooth transition.

Define Transition Requirements		
Inputs	**Techniques**	**Outputs**
Solution [Designed]	Business Rules Analysis (9.4)	Transition Requirements (7.4)
Organizational Readiness Assessment (7.3)	Data Flow Diagrams (9.6)	
Solution [Deployed]	Data Modeling (9.7)	
Requirements [Stated]	Organization Modeling (9.19)	
	Process Modeling (9.21)	

BA's Responsibilities in Defining Transition Requirements
- Work with business stakeholders to determine transition needs
- Document data conversion rules
- Facilitate and document decisions about the rollout plans, implementation dates, and organizational change management plans
- Assist business domain stakeholders and change management professionals to develop a comprehensive communication plan for the change
- Work with the project manager to prepare operations and support personnel for the change

What Do You Need to Successfully Define Transition Requirements?
The organizational readiness assessment is a key input to defining transition requirements. Different stakeholder groups may require different transition requirements. You will utilize elicitation to discuss transition needs (stated requirements) with stakeholders.

To plan for the conversion from an old system to a new one, you will need to understand the currently deployed solution (the old one) and the new solution design. Your transition requirements will include an implementation strategy and may include data conversion requirements.

Organizational Change Management
The term organizational change management generally refers to change within an organization—focusing on people and the way they get work done. Poor change management can sabotage a great project and slow or stop adoption of a new process. The challenges of change are often underestimated. Be sure to think carefully about this important step in the business analysis process.

The discipline of organizational change management has become more widely recognized as organizations have become larger and more complex. Organizational change management specialists usually report to the Human Resources department.

Find out if there is anyone in your organization who is formally trained in organizational change management and ask for their assistance on your projects. If your organization doesn't have this expertise, get some training or consider bringing in a consultant to help with major changes.

Plan Ahead for Transitions

Experienced business analysts think about transition issues from the very beginning of solution design. How will we help the business change the way they do work to make the best use of this new solution? How much support will the employees or customers need once the change has been made? Will employees need training on the new system? Will procedures be changed? When will the implementation be least disruptive to the ongoing business operations? How will the solution be supported after implementation? Do operational support people need training or new procedures? The goal is to be proactive and prepare people so they know what to expect when the change occurs.

Understanding transition issues could lead to an adjustment to the solution design (when it is identified early), to the solution itself (when the solution is already built), or a change to the organization to better accommodate the new system.

Transition requirements are usually formally documented on medium to large projects. You should work with the project manager to develop an implementation plan that meets project requirements and supports all stakeholders. Traditionally, the project manager plans for the transition of the final product to the support team, while the business analyst works with the business stakeholders to plan the transition within the business areas.

Implementation Strategies

An implementation strategy describes how the solution will be incorporated into the business. Various strategies and options should be considered. Factors that will influence the decision include business risks, the number of stakeholders, and the size of the change. Let's look at some commonly used implementation strategies.

Cutover   An implementation date/time is selected, and on that date, the old process stops and the new process starts. This is the fastest approach and often the most risky. This strategy requires significant testing and a back-out plan in case of unexpected problems.

Phased Rollout Various locations or stakeholder groups receive the new solution at different times. This reduces the impact of the change, as there are fewer stakeholders for the implementation team to support on the new system simultaneously. It can be costly because it requires the organization to run both the old system and the new one. Rolling out a solution can be difficult if the various groups share data.

Parallel Processing   This option involves running both the new and old systems in parallel for a period of time. Although this is the safest option, it is the most expensive because it requires duplication of effort for the business and operational support.

Pilot   A pilot is usually a small-scale implementation used as a test of the solution. It may refer to a small part of the solution or a small part of the business. A pilot can be used prior to any of the other implementation strategies.

EXERCISE   Review the following scenarios. What implementation strategy would you recommend for each scenario?

Scenario	Implementation Strategy
Your team's solution is a replacement of the corporate payroll system. There are 20,000 employees who are paid weekly in seven different countries. The payroll system has automated interfaces with several government taxing authorities and benefit providers.	
Your team's solution is a minor adjustment to an informational website available to your external customers.	
Your team's project is to support the sales of a new product to existing customers. The sales force has already accepted hundreds of pre-orders and is anxiously waiting for the ordering/shipping process (and the inventory) to be ready.	
Your team's solution is a business process change, involving about 400 employees. Each employee must be trained on the new process, which involves complex decision making.	
In the Workforce Tracking case study, the new website for ordering equipment will be available January 1 while HR will continue to accept phone orders for three months.	

SAMPLE ANSWER

Scenario	Implementation Strategy
Your team's solution is a replacement of the corporate payroll system. There are 20,000 employees who are paid weekly in seven different countries. The payroll system has automated interfaces with several government taxing authorities and benefit providers.	Phased rollout to each country or region
Your team's solution is a minor adjustment to an informational website available to your external customers.	Cutover during lowest web usage time of day and monitor customer service for any problems
Your team's project is to support the sales of a new product to existing customers. The sales force has already accepted hundreds of pre-orders and is anxiously waiting for the ordering/shipping process (and the inventory) to be ready.	Cutover using new orders as the pilot to test the system and adjust as necessary.
Your team's solution is a business process change, involving about 400 employees. Each employee must be trained on the new process, which involves complex decision making.	Phased rollout. Develop training materials. Identify or hire instructors for each country or region and schedule face-to-face training classes. Can this be rolled out slowly?
In the Workforce Tracking case study, the new website for ordering equipment will be available Jan. 1 while HR will continue to accept phone orders for three months.	Parallel processing

Implementation Plan

Implementation plans should include as much detail as is needed for the project. For a small maintenance change, there probably will not be a written plan, just a date of implementation. For a large, corporate-wide implementation, the organizational change management plan might be larger than the requirements! Business analysts are good at planning and facilitating, and these are two key skills needed for smooth implementations.

Remember our case study solution design of allowing workers around the world to request new equipment via a website? Review the following proposed implementation plan.

Example Implementation Plan		
Date	**Event**	**Notes**
December 1	E-mail blast is sent to all registered workers of the corporate system notifying them of the new website. (As-is procedures may be used in parallel with the new website for the next three months to ensure a smooth transition and no interruption of service.) Transition schedule to be provided in the e-mail message.	E-mail should be brief and have a link to more information with screenshots and new procedures.
December	Approved vendors and servicers are contacted by their procurement specialist and informed of the new procedures for employees to order new PCs.	Vendors and servicers have already been notified that this change is coming.
January 1	Website is live.	Website will include FAQ and Contact Us page.
January 2	E-mail blast to workers with link to new website.	Include April 1 deadline for phone requests to purchase PCs.
January–March	HR continues to accept equipment orders over the phone, but encourages workers to try the website.	
January 29	Website maintenance is performed based on feedback from early adopters.	Issues/changes will be prioritized using the problem tracking system.
March 15	Final e-mail blast reminding workers of the April 1st change.	

APPLY YOUR KNOWLEDGE   What else would you do in your organization?

Data Conversion

When a solution is implemented, it often requires that information (data) from an old system be moved into the new system. If an electronic data store (e.g., database or file) is one of the solution components, data from an existing source may need to be loaded or converted into the new format. This is referred to as data conversion. When a software application is purchased from a vendor, data conversion may be performed by the vendor or by implementation SMEs in your organization. Either way, the conversion rules should be documented to ensure data integrity. For example, in the old system, a month was stored as a three-character abbreviation. In the new system, it will be stored as a two-digit number; the day of the month will be either 1 or 15. A data conversion program will change each occurrence of "date" based on this conversion rule. Conversion rules are transition requirements.

Conversion Rules
If day of month is less than 15, convert to 1. If day of month is greater than 14, convert to 15. Convert character month to numeric.

Conversion Examples		
Old System Month	Old System Day	New System Date
JAN	12	01/01
FEB	2	02/01
MAR	30	03/15
APR	3	04/01

You should be familiar with the acronym ETL. *Extraction*, *Transformation*, and *Load* is related to data conversions and transmissions. To extract data is to pull it out of an existing source. Transformation refers to any reformatting or conversion needed to prepare it for use in the new system. Load means to put it in the new storage location. This acronym is used by implementation SMEs working on electronic data transfer, data warehouse, and business intelligence systems.

Techniques to Define Transition Requirements

EXERCISE   You have already learned about all of the techniques referenced in this task. Based on what you know about each technique, how do you think each might be used to Define Transition Requirements?

Technique	How It Could Be Used to Define Transition Requirements
Business Rules Analysis (9.4)	
Data Flow Diagrams (9.6)	
Data Modeling (9.7)	
Organization Modeling (9.19)	
Process Modeling (9.21)	

ANSWER

Technique	How It Could Be Used to Define Transition Requirements
Business Rules Analysis (9.4)	• If business rules are changing as part of the solution, stakeholders may need training and communication on the new rules. • There may be rules about how the transition will be performed. For example, when data is converted from an old system to a new system, there are often conversion rules. These should be included in the transition requirements.
Data Modeling (9.7)	• As-is and to-be data models could be compared to assess the changes to information in the business and in existing data stores (databases or files). • A data model of a vendor application package could be used to define the data conversion process.
Data Flow Diagrams (9.6) Organization Modeling (9.19) Process Modeling (9.21)	• As-is and to-be diagrams and models could be used to show the changes to the business and to develop employee training materials. They also could be used to develop the communication plan for the change.

Hopefully you are feeling comfortable with the idea that a technique can be used in many different ways, in many different situations. The more comfortable you are with the flexibility provided by these techniques, the more effective your analysis work will become.

Summary

The transition requirements created in this task are not related to the stated requirements for the solution. They involve answering the questions such as "What needs to be done before implementation?" Transition requirements may include:

- Develop employee training materials
- Create or update employee procedure manuals
- Assist with job description changes
- Facilitate/determine the best timeframe for change
- Determine the best implementation strategy (e.g., cutover, pilot, parallel)
- Define data conversion rules
- Develop communication plans for before, during, and after the change
- Monitor early usage of the solution to recommend adjustments

Almost every stakeholder involved in the project will be impacted by the change. Thinking about how each stakeholder group will be impacted and how you can make the transition easy for them is the goal of this task. Transition requirements are generally transitory requirements, meaning they will not be kept in the reusable requirements repository after the project is complete, as they are usually unique to the current change. Keeping them as examples for future projects, though, can be very helpful.

Validate Solution (7.5)

This is your last chance to make sure the solution satisfies the business need before it is implemented! Validating the solution includes a final test, or "dress rehearsal," before release or delivery. For a final time, the business analyst asks questions like: "Does the solution meet the business needs?" This is where we find out whether we really solved the business problem. A solution that satisfies requirements but doesn't help users is a failure. (With an excellent business analyst on the team, this should never happen!) This task includes assessing the level of quality of the solution, identifying defects, and creating mitigation strategies, or "workarounds" for defects that will not be fixed before implementation. On software projects, this work is often referred to as User Acceptance Testing (UAT).

Validate Solution		
Inputs	**Techniques**	**Outputs**
Solution [Constructed]	Acceptance and Evaluation Criteria Definition (9.1)	Identified Defects (7.5)
Requirements [Prioritized and Validated] (4.1, 6.6)	Problem Tracking (9.20)	Mitigating Actions (7.5)
	Root Cause Analysis (9.25)	Solution Validation Assessment (7.5)

BA's Responsibilities in Validating the Solution

- Work with testers to review the solution to make sure that it will bring business value to the stakeholders
- Work with regulators, if they will be reviewing or auditing the solution for compliance
- Identify, document, and find the root cause of defects
- Work with the implementation SMEs to help correct defects
- Develop mitigation strategies for the defects that may not be corrected before implementation

What Do You Need to Successfully Validate the Solution?

To validate the solution, we use the constructed solution and compare it to requirements. Notice the states of the requirements used here: prioritized and validated. Since we have already validated the requirements (in other words, we know that they describe a solution that will provide value to the business), we can simply compare these requirements to the resulting solution.

Who Validates the Solution?

In the Requirements Analysis chapter, we discussed the words verification and validation. Do you remember the difference? We are making sure the solution has value. How can you make sure the solution you have built brings value? Business analysis work includes the verification and validation of requirements (because requirements are our deliverables), and *validation of the solution*. Testers and implementation SMEs *verify* the

> **Remember:**
>
> Does it work = Verify
> Does it add value = Validate

solution, since they have built it and the test cases. This will be easy to remember if you truly understand the use of the words verify and validate.

Task	Who	Knowledge Area
Verify Requirements	BA	Requirements Analysis
Validate Requirements	BA	Requirements Analysis
Verify Solution	Testers and Implementation SMEs	Outside of Business Analysis
Validate Solution	BA	Solution Assessment and Validation

Testers and implementation SMEs use quality control and quality assurance methods to verify the solution. If a component of the solution is hardware or equipment, quality control processes will be used to make sure the component operates as needed. If a component of the solution is software, standard software testing practices will be used by testers. If a component of the solution is a business process change, the new process will be tested by walking through the process. Interfaces to other systems will also be tested to ensure accurate transfer of information.

 The terms quality control and quality assurance tend to be used interchangeably in business analysis.

 If an exam question deals with verifying or testing the solution, assume an implementation SME or the tester is doing it, not the business analyst.

How Do We Validate?

The core business analysis responsibility is to make sure the solution brings business value to the organization as defined in the business case. Business analysts work with testers and implementation SMEs to perform validation. You may review test results to compare them to the requirements. You may run tests yourself to increase your confidence that the solution will bring business value. You may work with end users to execute user acceptance testing (UAT) to make sure the end users see business value.

When solution defects are identified, you should analyze each one, helping to prioritize their resolution. Because you thoroughly understand the original business need and the current business environment, you will be able to determine the significance of the problem and its impact on the business. Low-priority defects may not be fixed until after implementation if you and the team can agree on workarounds or mitigating actions. If a problem is significant to the business operations, implementation of the solution may be delayed until the problem is resolved.

User acceptance testing (UAT) is typically the last phase of software testing. Its purpose is to ensure the product complies with business requirements. A business analyst usually works with the stakeholders to assist with this testing. This may involve a dry run of the solution along with training on its use. A senior business analyst should be aware of all testing phases and terminology. (See the definitions at the end of this task.)

Techniques to Validate the Solution

Acceptance and Evaluation Criteria Definition (9.1)

Acceptance and evaluation criteria definition is used here to evaluate the solution and determine if it will be acceptable to the stakeholders. At this point we are evaluating the completed, constructed solution, not just a design or description of it.

Problem Tracking (9.20)

Problem tracking or defect tracking refers to a formal process by which problems are identified, recorded, researched, and (hopefully), resolved! Rarely is a solution built perfectly. As the solution is reviewed, tested, and validated, problems will be discovered. A problem tracking process details the steps to report, analyze, and resolve each problem. The business analyst plays an important role in problem tracking and resolution.

Problem tracking software is commonly used to manage defects. The software will assign a unique number to each defect and allow users to enter information about the defect and its resolution. Typically, the quality assurance group will be responsible for managing the problem tracking system since the system continues to be used after implementation for ongoing maintenance of the solution. When problems are reported, many characteristics of the problem may be documented for use in resolution and follow up.

Know the Steps of Problem Tracking

1. Identify the problem.
2. Report the problem in the problem tracking system.
3. Assess the problem to find the root cause.
4. Rank the problem priority/severity.
5. Determine the cost and time to solve.
6. After correction, retest.
7. Close the problem in the problem tracking system.
8. Update lessons learned to minimize errors of this type in future projects.

 Read the *BABOK® Guide* description of the Problem Tracking technique (9.20) now. Pay attention to the list of characteristics of the problem that may be identified.

Root Cause Analysis (9.25)

When a problem is found, the team not only works to determine how to fix the problem, but also seeks to determine why the problem occurred. Root cause analysis is used to find the cause of the problem and record lessons learned. Understanding how a defect was introduced into the solution allows us to modify our requirements process and decrease the likelihood that similar defects will be created in the future. Root cause analysis was discussed in detail in the Enterprise Analysis chapter (Define Business Need, page 57). If necessary, go back and review the Five Whys.

 Are you familiar with testing terminology? In the following table are terms used by quality assurance professionals and testers with which you should be familiar.

Term	Definition	Check if Unfamiliar
Inspection	This involves looking at a product or part of a product for compliance with standards and requirements. This term may be used interchangeably with review or walkthrough (the Structured Walkthrough technique (9.30) was discussed in the Requirements Analysis chapter).	
Unit Testing	Unit testing involves testing a small piece of the solution (sub-program, sub-routine, module), referred to as a unit. A unit is a small piece that can be tested independently. This is typically the first phase of testing. It finds initial problems that are easy to fix.	
Black Box Testing	The phrase black box is used when the tester defines the inputs and expected outputs of a test without knowing how the software will accomplish the transformation. Contrast this with white or glass box testing where the tester understands the software code being tested and designs test cases to exercise specific lines of code.	
Integration Testing	Integration testing involves testing sub-assemblies or a few units linked together. These integration tests are looking at how the individual units that have already been tested will work together. Units may pass data to each other or trigger work in each other. This is usually the second level or phase of testing, because the integrations are tested before the entire solution is put together.	
System Testing	System testing involves putting together the solution or system and testing it as a whole. This testing looks for how well the overall system meets the requirements and the business needs.	
Regression Testing	Regression testing refers to retesting a unit, sub-system, or system that has already been tested and then changed. Changes may be related to defect correction or change control requests. Regardless of the reason for the change, retesting is critical to making sure the change did not negatively impact the existing functionality.	
Performance Testing	Does the product perform as expected? Non-functional requirements and project objectives should include very specific criteria upon which the end product is measured. The product will either pass or fail based on measurements against the success criteria.	
Audit	An audit is a review for standards compliance, regulatory compliance, financial accuracy, or any other review conducted by an internal or external auditor.	
Test Case	The Institute of Electrical and Electronics Engineers (IEEE) defines this as a specific test with predefined inputs and expected outputs. It includes a test procedure detailing the steps required to execute the test.	
Test Plan	The IEEE defines this as an overall strategy document for testing the product and all related interfaces. It includes things like resources needed, testing environment, risks and priorities, items out of scope, and test data sources.	

Summary

When your organization has a quality assurance or testing department, validating the solution may simply involve reviewing and evaluating test results produced by the testers. If your organization relies on business analysts to also perform testing, be careful answering questions on the exam, since testing work is not part of the business analysis work as defined in the *BABOK® Guide*. The business analysis responsibility is to be sure the constructed solution performs as users expect and brings value to the organization.

Evaluate Solution Performance (7.6)

This is it! We are at the last task of business analysis. Well, maybe. It is time to evaluate the performance of the solution we have helped to create. The team has delivered a solution to the business and now we assess how we did. Did we deliver something that is really useful and helpful? Did we solve the original problem? Did we create any new problems? Did we meet the original project objectives? Is this a success or a failure?

But this task can also be the first task of business analysis!

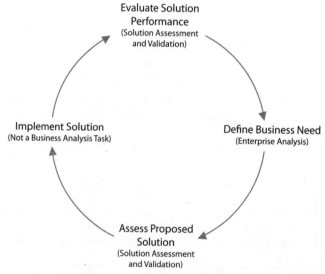

Where Does Business Analysis Start (Or End)?

Business analysis work usually starts with a business need (Define Business Need) and ends with an evaluation of how well the solution meets the need (Evaluate Solution Performance). Alternatively, you might start with Evaluate Solution Performance if you are asked to observe an existing business system and you identify a need for improvement. You could also start by evaluating a suggestion for a change (Assess Proposed Solution) made by a stakeholder.

Regardless of when you do it, performance is evaluated on a solution that has been deployed and used in its business environment. This work is also referred to as *post-implementation assessment* or post-implementation review. Seeing how the solution works in the actual day-to-day operations of the business gives the truest picture of its effectiveness. Often the team will wait to evaluate performance for a few days or weeks after implementation to make sure the business stakeholders and users have time to learn the new system and get comfortable with new features.

Much can be accomplished by conducting a post-implementation assessment. You can:
- Determine if the business objectives were met
- Determine if the solution needs any adjustments or refinements
- Continue to strengthen relationships within the business by showing you care about ongoing operations
- Identify needs for future projects

Evaluate Solution Performance		
Inputs	**Techniques**	**Outputs**
Solution [Deployed]	Decision Analysis (9.8)	Solution Performance Assessment (7.6)
Business Requirements	Focus Groups (9.11)	
Identified Defects (7.5)	Observation (9.18)	
Solution Performance Metrics	Survey/Questionnaire (9.31)	

BA's Responsibilities in Evaluating Solution Performance
- Compare actual solution performance to original project objectives to evaluate success
- Confirm that the domain SMEs, customer, and sponsor are satisfied with the solution
- Address areas of the solution that are not meeting expectations

What Do You Need to Successfully Evaluate Solution Performance?
To evaluate the performance of a newly-deployed solution, we need to review the deployed solution operating in the business environment. We can evaluate how well the solution is meeting the business requirements based on previously established performance metrics and identified defects.

How Is the Solution Performing?
In developing the business case, we estimated the expected benefits of the solution by performing cost-benefit analysis. Now we can measure and compare the actual benefits to our estimates. For example, if we estimated we could save one half hour per transaction, after implementation we can time actual transactions, compare their duration to the metrics gathered before implementation, and report that we actually saved three quarters of an hour per transaction!

 Be sure you understand the difference between Validate Solution and Evaluate Solution Performance. Validation happens before implementation, and is focused on making sure the solution is going to work as expected. We estimate the expected value of the solution, but we can't be sure it will deliver as expected. (And during validation, we still have the opportunity to "bail out" if our solution is determined to be flawed.) Evaluate Solution Performance requires a different mindset. It is performed after implementation and is focused on measuring the effectiveness of the solution in the business environment. How well does the solution satisfy the original needs? Only after the solution has been incorporated into the business, and users have been trained to use the new system and adjusted to the changes, can we really determine the value brought to the business.

Solution Replacement or Elimination
As you review this task in the *BABOK® Guide*, you may be surprised to find a section about replacing the solution. Didn't we just build and implement it? The *Guide* includes this section to complete the life cycle of a solution. Any product or solution will eventually become obsolete or ineffective. During solution design and development, you should think about how long a solution will be useful and begin to plan for its eventual replacement or elimination. There are many things to consider when analyzing solutions at the end of their life. Among other things, the business analyst will ask: Is it still

providing the benefits for which it was developed? What is the cost of maintaining it, vs. replacing it? The decision to replace a system often involves financial analysis. What would it cost to fix the system compared to the cost to replace it. A couple of terms to know here: *opportunity cost* is the value that could be gained by pursuing other opportunities. *Sunk cost* is the amount you've already spent on the solution, which should not be included in any analysis of future decisions.

Techniques to Evaluate Solution Performance

EXERCISE You have already learned about all of the techniques referenced in this task. Based on what you know about each technique, how do you think each might be used to Evaluate Solution Performance?

Technique	How It Can Be Used to Evaluate Solution Performance
Decision Analysis (9.8)	
Focus Groups (9.11)	
Observation (9.18)	
Survey/Questionnaire (9.31)	

ANSWER

Technique	How It Can Be Used to Evaluate Solution Performance
Decision Analysis (9.8)	Once the solution is in use, you can measure its financial performance and compare it to the anticipated benefits described in the business case.
Focus Groups (9.11)	Focus groups are usually for outside customers. You could use this technique to find out how your customers or other stakeholders like the change you have made.
Observation (9.18)	Watching your stakeholders, especially end users and operational support people, is a good way to determine how the new solution is working.
Survey/Questionnaire (9.31)	Typically used for large groups of stakeholders, this is another elicitation technique you could use to find out how well stakeholders believe the new system is working.

APPLY YOUR KNOWLEDGE   Think about a situation when you really wanted a change and you got it. Did it meet your original expectations? In what ways was it better than you expected? In what ways was it worse?

Summary

If you and your team worked well together and followed your organization's processes, this should be the most rewarding part of business analysis work. You get the opportunity to see the results of your efforts. By evaluating the solution after it has been in use for a while, you get a realistic measure of the benefits being gained from the change. Of course, you also need to be prepared to hear about the problems or challenges your stakeholders are experiencing. Be open, listen, take notes, and be positive about potential enhancements that may be prioritized in the future. Celebrate with your team and record lessons learned for your next business improvement opportunity!

── Summary of Solution Assessment and Validation ──

Solution Assessment and Validation is all about the solution—choosing the best solution from proposed ideas, and making sure the solution satisfies approved requirements, works as planned, and brings business value. It also includes the work necessary to help the organization accept and incorporate the change into its day-to-day business practices.

EXERCISE Which of the tasks in Solution Assessment and Validation can be performed before the solution is built?

Solution Assessment and Validation Task	Yes/No
Assess Proposed Solution	
Allocate Requirements	
Assess Organizational Readiness	
Define Transition Requirements	
Validate Solution	
Evaluate Solution Performance	

ANSWER

Solution Assessment and Validation Task	Yes/No
Assess Proposed Solution	Yes
Allocate Requirements	Yes
Assess Organizational Readiness	Yes
Define Transition Requirements	No
Validate Solution	No
Evaluate Solution Performance	No

EXERCISE Describe each of the solution states used in this knowledge area.

Solution [Constructed]	
Solution [Designed]	
Solution [Deployed]	

ANSWER

Solution [Constructed]	The solution has been built, so it can be tested. It may or may not be deployed and be in use yet.
Solution [Designed]	The solution has been specified by a technical or implementation stakeholder to describe how it will be built.
Solution [Deployed]	The solution has been built and implemented, so it is being used by the organization for ongoing work.

Before taking the practice exam, I recommend that you read the Solution Validation and Assessment chapter of the *BABOK® Guide* (Chapter 7), and the descriptions of the key techniques of this knowledge area (in Chapter 9 of the *BABOK® Guide*):

- Acceptance and Evaluation Criteria Definition (9.1)
- Organization Modeling (9.19)

Practice Exam

1. Transition requirements include:

   A. Training, organizational change, and rollout plans.
   B. Data, process, and business rules.
   C. Business and stakeholder requirements.
   D. Use case descriptions and user stories.

2. Who is responsible for designing the solution?

   A. The business analyst
   B. The sponsor and project manager
   C. The business SMEs and the business analyst
   D. The business and implementation SMEs

3. The solution has been completed and tested. The project manager has asked you to show it to the business stakeholders before implementation. One of the key stakeholders finds a serious problem. What should you do?

   A. Tell the stakeholder you will develop a workaround for him.
   B. Tell the project manager the implementation must be delayed.
   C. Talk with the development team and ask them to make a change.
   D. Assess the impact of the problem.

4. As a business analyst collects information about how the business does work, determines the best time for a process change, and analyzes the ability of workers to adapt, he or she is preparing to develop:

   A. Business requirements.
   B. Stakeholder requirements.
   C. Transition requirements.
   D. Non-functional requirements.

5. A test case is:

   A. A non-functional requirement describing performance requirements.
   B. A business requirement describing how the work is performed.
   C. A scenario or script describing how to look for defects.
   D. A strategic plan describing how the solution will be validated.

6. There are several types of testing. Testing performed to ensure compliance with requirements and business needs is called:

   A. User Acceptance Testing.
   B. Regression testing.
   C. Solution validation.
   D. Systems testing.

7. Solution Verification is performed to:

    A. Ensure the requirements describe a solution that will bring business value to the organization.
    B. Ensure the solution will bring business value to the organization.
    C. Ensure the solution meets the requirements specified.
    D. Ensure the requirements conform to standards for quality set by the organization.

8. While talking with business domain SMEs about the impact of the solution on their personnel, you are eliciting:

    A. Business requirements.
    B. Stakeholder requirements.
    C. Non-functional requirements.
    D. Transition requirements.

9. The difference between a system and software is:

    A. A system may include software, hardware, processes, and people.
    B. A software application dictates how the system operates.
    C. There is no difference.
    D. A system describes software that is purchased rather than being built as part of the project.

10. One way to assess a proposed solution design is to:

    A. Trace the project objectives to the solution components.
    B. Find out the estimated cost of the solution.
    C. Perform root cause analysis on the original business problem.
    D. Use business rules analysis to decide between multiple proposals.

11. The purpose of assessing a proposed solution is to:

    A. Determine which requirements are satisfied by each solution component.
    B. Determine if stakeholders will accept the proposed solution.
    C. Determine the value that will be delivered by the solution.
    D. Determine how the proposed solution will be rolled out to the business.

12. Given the following solution design options, which one is BEST?

    A. The solution design that delivers the highest ROI
    B. The solution design that most closely meets the requirements
    C. The solution design that costs the least to develop
    D. The solution design that will be easiest to implement

13. A couple of months after your project is complete, you go out to the business stakeholder's location to check on their operations. The purpose of this visit is:

    A. Post-implementation assessment.
    B. Observation.
    C. Lessons learned.
    D. Project closing.

14. Your initial testing identified several defects that the solution team has addressed. Your next step is to:

    A. Perform user acceptance testing: show the solution to your key stakeholders.
    B. Perform unit testing: make sure each component of the solution behaves as expected.
    C. Identify the root cause of each problem and the individual responsible.
    D. Perform regression testing: make sure the changes didn't negatively impact another part of the solution.

15. Your requirements are complete and have been approved. The solution team is building the solution. A quality assurance expert joins the team to prepare for testing and finds problems with the requirements. You should:

    A. Explain that the requirements have been approved by the stakeholders and no further changes are allowed.
    B. Discuss each of the concerns, analyze and use the change control process to assess the changes, and assign priorities.
    C. Ask the solution team to stop building until the quality concerns are corrected in the requirements documents.
    D. Ask for the quality assurance expert to be removed from the team and prepare for testing yourself.

16. A key input to Assess Proposed Solution is:

    A. Proposed solution.
    B. Solution scope.
    C. Elicitation results.
    D. Transition requirements.

17. When you make sure each requirement is addressed in the solution design, you are performing:

    A. Allocate Requirements.
    B. Verify Requirements.
    C. Validate Requirements.
    D. Validate Solution.

18. To assess organizational readiness for the solution, you should:

    A. Perform stakeholder analysis to identify all stakeholders.
    B. Plan the rollout of the solution including schedules, training, and conversions.
    C. Assess the cultural environment of the business and its ability to absorb change.
    D. Perform root cause analysis of the business problem and/or understand the business opportunity.

19. Which of the following is an example of a transition requirement?

    A. A state transition diagram
    B. An employee training plan
    C. An as-is workflow diagram
    D. A business case

20. To validate the solution, you need:

    A. Requirements and the solution scope.
    B. Requirements and the solution design.
    C. The business case and the deployed solution.
    D. Requirements and the solution.

21. The solution, the business requirements, identified defects, and solution performance metrics are all inputs to:

    A. Evaluate Solution Performance.
    B. Determine Solution Scope.
    C. Validate Solution.
    D. Problem Resolution and Tracking.

22. A business analyst is involved with defect:

    A. Identification and reporting.
    B. Identification, analysis, and resolution.
    C. Research and resolution.
    D. Awareness only. Defects are managed by quality assurance professionals.

23. Vendor assessment is typically performed:

    A. In the Determine Solution Scope task, during Enterprise Analysis.
    B. During detailed requirements analysis.
    C. During the planning of the business analysis approach.
    D. While assessing proposed solutions.

24. Enterprise architecture is an input to:

    A. Assess Organizational Readiness.
    B. Determine Solution Scope.
    C. Plan Business Analysis Approach.
    D. Assess Proposed Solution.

25. The two most likely starting points for business analysis work are:

    A. Define Business Need and Assess Proposed Solution.
    B. Define Business Need and Evaluate Solution Performance.
    C. Assess Capability Gaps and Evaluate Solution Performance.
    D. Assess Capability Gaps and Assess Proposed Solution.

Answers

1. **Answer** A

   Explanation   Transition requirements describe the things necessary to ensure a smooth change. They describe how best to implement the solution into the business. They may reference data, processes and rules but are not the descriptions of these requirements components. They are usually tactical, specific, and more detailed than business or stakeholder requirements. Use Case descriptions and user stories describe the solution itself, not how it will be implemented.

2. **Answer** D

   Explanation   The solution design must be a joint effort between the business and the implementation SMEs. The business SMEs understand the need, and the implementation SMEs understand what is feasible. The business analyst is a facilitator in this process, helping both sides to better understand each other and come to a design agreement that meets all needs.

3. **Answer** D

   Explanation   It is possible that a serious problem might affect your implementation schedule. You may need to develop a workaround or request a change. However, before doing any of these, you need to assess the impact in order to determine the best course of action.

4. **Answer** C

   Explanation   The key words here are "determines the best time for a change" and "the ability of workers to adapt." Transition requirements describe how and when the solution will be rolled out to minimize the business disruption.

5. **Answer** C

   Explanation   A test case is not a requirement, but rather a method of making sure requirements have been correctly built into the solution. The test case is an individual scenario or script describing how to test a particular function.

6. **Answer** A

   Explanation   Solution validation is accomplished via UAT, but is not considered a testing type. Regression and systems testing look for defects. Only UAT assesses compliance and conformance. This type of testing should answer the question: "Does it work well for the business?"

7. **Answer** C

   Explanation   Ensure the requirements describe a solution that will bring business value to the organization is Requirements validation. Ensuring the solution will bring business value to the organization describes solution validation. Ensuring requirements conform to standards is requirements verification. Solution verification ensures the solution meets the requirements specified.

8. **Answer** D

   Explanation   Transition requirements describe how to smoothly implement the project results (solution) into the business with minimum business interruption. They may include training plans, job description changes, employee procedure changes, data conversion specification, and an implementation schedule.

9. **Answer**   A
   Explanation   The difference between these terms is very important in business analysis. Software is just one of the many solution components that may solve a business problem. A system is a group of interacting, interrelated, or interdependent elements forming a complex whole. The system describes how the entire business area operates with its technology, its people, its policies, and its procedures. Business analysts always need to consider the entire business system, not just the software.

10. **Answer**   A
    Explanation   Finding out the estimated cost of the solution is useful, but a low-cost solution that doesn't meet business needs is a bad solution. Root cause analysis is typically used at the beginning of analysis to find the root cause of the business problem and assist in the development of proposed solutions. Business rules analysis is also used before the design, to help understand the business needs. Assessing the proposed solution determines how well the proposed solution meets the stakeholder and solution requirements. The best approach is to review the project objectives, and make sure they are accomplished by tracing them to specific solution components.

11. **Answer**   C
    Explanation   Determining which requirements are satisfied by each solution component is called allocating requirements. Determining if stakeholders will accept the proposed solution and how it will be rolled out are assessing readiness and developing transition requirements. Assessing a proposed solution means to evaluate it and decide if it is the best solution for the business needs. This is done by determining the value of the solution to the business and comparing the value expected to the original project objectives. If the objective was to cut costs and the proposed solution will increase revenue, there is not a match.

12. **Answer**   B
    Explanation   This is a tough question because the best answer would be the solution design that best meets the project objectives. However, on the exam, you must select the BEST choice of those presented. You would recommend the design that most closely meets the requirements, because using excellent business analysis practices, the project objectives would be supported by the requirements (and traced to them). Although the other answers seem to be good reasons for selecting a design, if they don't deliver on the objectives and requirements they will not be considered a success by the sponsor and stakeholders.

13. **Answer**   A
    Explanation   You may use observation to see how things are going, but your purpose is to evaluate how well the solution is working and met the original project goals. You may get some lessons learned while you are there, but your focus is on measuring the performance of the transition and implementation of the solution.

14. **Answer**   D
    Explanation   Unit testing happens much earlier, as each unit is built. UAT should be conducted after the high-priority problems have been fixed and retested. Regression testing means to retest. Whenever a change is made to a product, it should be retested to make sure the problem has been corrected, and no new problems have been introduced. Complex solutions are sensitive to change, so it is common for a developer to fix one problem while inadvertently causing another.

15. **Answer** B

    Explanation Although it is unfortunate that the quality assurance expert joined the team late, you should welcome his or her feedback at any point. When he or she has discovered an erroneous or missing requirement, the change control process should be followed to assess the impact of the change and have it prioritized by the business stakeholders. While a change at this point might result in rework, allowing the entire solution to be built incorrectly will be more costly in the long run.

16. **Answer** A

    Explanation Solution scope describes the boundaries of the solution but does not contain a detailed description of it. Elicitation results become stated requirements. They are not approved yet, so they are not ready to be compared to a proposed solution. Transition requirements describe how the solution will be smoothly rolled out to the business. When a task name starts with Assess, a key input will be the thing being assessed. In this example, Assess Proposed Solution needs the proposed solution as an input. Don't overthink questions.

17. **Answer** A

    Explanation The key to answering this question is looking at the verbs. To validate is to make sure the requirements or solution provide business VALUE. To verify is to make sure the requirements meet standards and are correct. To allocate requirements is to make sure that each requirement is satisfied by a component of the solution.

18. **Answer** C

    Explanation Stakeholder analysis is performed during planning (generally before elicitation of requirements). Rollout plans are transition requirements that are developed after the organizational readiness has been evaluated. Analyzing business problems and opportunities is performed during Enterprise Analysis.

19. **Answer** B

    Explanation A state transition diagram is used to show requirements of a business concept or object and how it changes over time. An as-is workflow shows a current business process. A business case describes the rationale (financial and other) for making a change. An employee training plan is a transition requirement, because it will help the organization accept and successfully work with the new solution.

20. **Answer** D

    Explanation Having the business case will also be useful to make sure the solution meets the original objectives, but the *BABOK® Guide* doesn't list business case as an input. Validation is performed before the new solution is deployed. You can't validate the solution without the solution! You need the requirements [validated] because the solution will bring value (validate) if it meets the validated requirements.

21. **Answer** A

    Explanation Problem resolution is a technique, not a task, so it does not have inputs. The solution, identified defects, and solution performance metrics are not inputs to Determine Solution Scope because the solution has not yet been created. Validate Solution doesn't use metrics. The solution, the business requirements, identified defects, and solution performance metrics are all inputs to Evaluate Solution Performance.

22. **Answer** B
   Explanation Quality assurance professionals usually keep track of defects and problem tracking and reporting, but business analysts, like all team members, identify, analyze and resolve defects whenever possible.

23. **Answer** D
   Explanation This is a tough question. There are two places in the *BABOK® Guide* where Vendor Assessment is listed: Enterprise Analysis and Solution Assessment and Validation. (In Enterprise Analysis, it is part of Define Business Case, not Determine Solution Scope.) The placement in these two knowledge areas implies you do it before the project starts and/or at the end. In reality, it is done as soon as the team knows a purchased solution is a possibility. It must also be done to assess the solution options.

24. **Answer** A
   Explanation Enterprise architecture is needed to Assess Organizational Readiness because you are looking at the organization's structures, personnel, policies, locations, and culture to determine how well the organization will be able to absorb the change.

25. **Answer** B
   Explanation Business analysis work is usually started because of a business problem or opportunity (business need) or because an existing production system is not performing well.

CHAPTER 8

Business Analysis Planning & Monitoring

Aligned with the *BABOK® Guide* Chapter Two

Business Analysis Planning and Monitoring is the first knowledge area in the *BABOK® Guide* and it is the last knowledge area discussed in this book. I have presented this knowledge area at the end because it is a good review of everything you have learned so far. If you are reading this book in order, you already know most of the business analysis tasks, and there are only a few new concepts for you to learn. Business Analysis Planning and Monitoring involves planning the work that is performed in all the other knowledge areas. This is a challenging knowledge area, because most business analysts don't do formal planning. When you are answering exam questions, assume proper planning has been done. Since business analysis work is complex, involves many people, and is critical to the success of any project or assignment, it must be carefully planned. There will be about 30 questions on the exam dealing with planning.

QUICK TEST

- Plan-driven
- Change-driven
- Methodology
- Lean
- Six Sigma
- Level of formality
- Work breakdown structure (WBS)
- Work package
- Expert judgment
- Rolling wave estimation
- Analogous estimation
- Parametric estimation
- Bottom-up estimation
- Three-point estimation
- Delphi estimation
- Variance analysis

- Traceability
- Baseline
- Dispersed teams
- Collocated teams
- Attitude
- Influence
- Authority
- Template
- Deliverable
- As-is vs. to-be
- Requirements attributes
- Variance analysis
- Onion diagram
- Stakeholder matrix
- Critical path
- Stakeholder register

Business Analysis Planning and Monitoring in Action

I was assigned to a project to develop a new product for sale to our external customers. The project manager asked me to estimate how long it would take for me to perform my tasks. To provide an accurate estimate, I performed business analysis planning. I thought about how the team would go about designing, building, marketing, and supporting the new product. This organization typically used a plan-driven approach to product development. People from many departments were involved: marketing, IT, production, and customer service. I decided to elicit requirements through individual interviews, since each stakeholder's viewpoint was different and they had different needs. I decided to document the requirements in our office automation system (using documents, spreadsheets, and graphics) because all of the stakeholders had access to it. My stakeholders were in different locations, so we would work via phone, e-mail, and shared documents. Since it was a relatively small team, I planned to communicate individually with each stakeholder about his or her needs and to report progress on a weekly basis. My project manager used my estimates and the estimates from the other team members to build a comprehensive project plan. I planned to document requirements in text format, as most of the business domain stakeholders preferred textual requirements, and I decided to incorporate tables and diagrams to make the requirements easier to review. The IT group wanted data and process models, so I planned to use modeling to communicate the functional requirements.

Knowing we would upgrade this new product every couple of years, it was worthwhile to archive the requirements after my work was done, to use them as a starting point for the future upgrade projects. Since we didn't have a requirements management tool or repository, I kept the requirements documents on a shared server in my department.

I measured my performance according to my plan by tracking my time each week against my estimates. I assessed the quality of my work by having someone else review the requirements, checking for completeness. I also assessed my effectiveness by recording the questions I was asked by implementation SMEs to clarify the requirements, and by the number of problems found during testing. Ultimately I got feedback about my work from our customers as they began to use our new product.

EXERCISE   There are six tasks in the Business Analysis Planning and Monitoring knowledge area: Plan Business Analysis Approach, Conduct Stakeholder Analysis, Plan Business Analysis Activities, Plan Business Analysis Communication, Plan Requirements Management Process, and Manage Business Analysis Performance. Can you identify the tasks in the previous story?

Business Analysis Planning and Monitoring Knowledge Area Task	Work Performed in the Story
Plan Business Analysis Approach	
Conduct Stakeholder Analysis	
Plan Business Analysis Activities	
Plan Business Analysis Communication	
Plan Requirements Management Process	
Manage Business Analysis Performance	

ANSWER

Business Analysis Planning and Monitoring Knowledge Area Task	Work Performed in the Story
Plan Business Analysis Approach	Considered how the work should be done, decided on a plan-driven approach
Conduct Stakeholder Analysis	Identified departments involved (Marketing, IT, Production, Customer Service) and their locations, conducted interviews
Plan Business Analysis Activities	Planned to document requirements in text and models
Plan Business Analysis Communication	Chose to work with stakeholders via phone, e-mail, and shared documents, reported progress on a weekly basis
Plan Requirements Management Process	Planned to use documents and diagrams, saved files for re-use on a shared directory
Manage Business Analysis Performance	Tracked time by week against estimates, recorded questions and problems found with requirements, received customer feedback on the new product

Barb's BA Themes

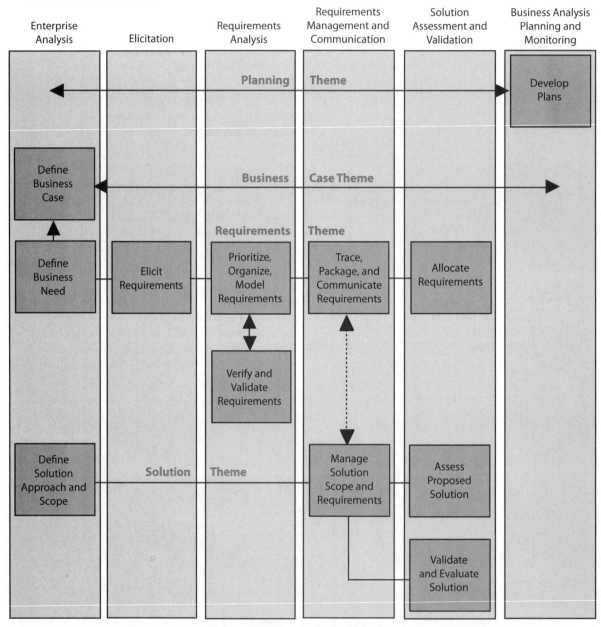

Planning is so important that it is the first theme. The plans created in this knowledge area are used to guide the performance of all of your business analysis work. Planning is always the first step when you encounter a new business analysis challenge. It will entail different levels of formality depending on the project or initiative.

You can't really plan if you don't know what the assignment is, so the Business Case Theme is needed as an input to the planning process. The business need is the only input into the Business Analysis Planning and Monitoring knowledge area that comes from another knowledge area. As you recall, business need is an output of Enterprise Analysis. You can get started planning even if you only have a brief description of the business need. Sometimes planning and enterprise analysis are done concurrently. As you and your team are determining the solution approach and defining scope, you are also planning how you will go about developing the detailed requirements. When you define the business case (in Enterprise Analysis), you will need a cost estimate from planning.

The outputs of planning are used to guide the performance of all of your other business analysis work. Your business analysis plans describe how you will perform the tasks in the Requirements and Solution Themes.

Things to Know about Business Analysis Planning and Monitoring for the Exam

- Business analysts are responsible for planning their own work and managing their time and performance. When you work with a project manager, your plan will become part of the overall project plan.
- You should always plan, even for small assignments. But you don't always have to *document* your plan. When you are acting as the project manager *and* business analyst, you will plan both the project and business analysis work. But remember that exam questions will ask about business analysis planning, not project planning.
- Although you should plan at the beginning of each assignment, replanning is necessary whenever circumstances change or you learn more about what is needed.
- Planning requires you to make lots of decisions: With whom will you work? What elicitation techniques will you use? How much time do you need? Etc.
- When answering questions about the other knowledge areas, remember that the questions assume your work has already been planned and you always follow the plan.
- Know the names and components of each plan: the business analysis plan, the business analysis communication plan, and the requirements management plan.

Introduction to the Tasks of Business Analysis Planning and Monitoring

The tasks in Business Analysis Planning and Monitoring are very closely related and frequently performed concurrently. They have been broken out and described as separate tasks to help you understand the specific steps of planning that result in the most effective business analysis work. Within this knowledge area, at least three plans will be developed: a business analysis (work) plan, a business analysis communication plan, and a requirements management plan. These plans may be formal, documented plans, or they may be informal and undocumented. Either way, you need to plan for all three activities!

 You need to be aware of the differences between project management and business analysis, particularly with regard to planning. You should know that a project plan consists of a series of management plans, including the business analysis plans.

Review of Risk

Before getting into the specifics of planning, let's review risk. You will see risk analysis as a technique in several of the planning tasks. An important part of planning is thinking about risks. Risks (threats and opportunities) are unplanned events that can negatively or positively impact an initiative, project, or ongoing business. Use the following review exercise to be sure you understand the concept of risk analysis and the terminology used to discuss risk management before you study planning.

EXERCISE   See if you can define each of the risk response strategies and risk tolerance terms from the Risk Analysis technique in the *BABOK® Guide*. You may see a couple of these on your exam.

Risk Response Strategy	Definition
Accept	
Avoid	
Enhance	
Exploit	
Mitigate	
Share	
Transfer	

Risk Tolerance	Definition
Neutrality	
Risk averse	
Risk seeking	

© 2012 RMC Publications, Inc • 952.846.4484 • info@rmcproject.com • www.rmcproject.com

ANSWER

Risk Response Strategy	Definition
Accept	"If it happens, it happens."
Avoid	Eliminate the threat of a risk by eliminating the cause.
Enhance	Increase the expected time, quality, or monetary value of an opportunity by increasing its probability of occurrence.
Exploit	Increase the opportunity by making the cause more probable.
Mitigate	Reduce the impact of a risk, or the probability of it occurring.
Share	Work with a third party to increase the opportunity.
Transfer	Assign the risk to a third party by subcontracting or purchasing insurance.

Risk Tolerance	Definition
Neutrality	The benefits of a risk response must equal or outweigh the costs in order to justify the decision
Risk averse	Unwilling to accept risk
Risk seeking	Willing to accept risk to increase the benefits

BUSINESS ANALYSIS PLANNING AND MONITORING TASKS

Plan Business Analysis Approach (2.1)

The word *approach* is used here in the same way it was in Enterprise Analysis (in Determine Solution Approach). The *approach* is a high-level plan—a broad look at how business analysis work will be accomplished. Planning the approach to business analysis is the starting point for developing your plans. You begin by looking at the business need and the environment in which you will be working. This high-level plan or approach will be detailed in the subsequent three tasks of this knowledge area.

Plan Business Analysis Approach		
Inputs	**Techniques**	**Outputs**
Business Need (5.1)	Decision Analysis (9.8)	Business Analysis Approach (2.1)
Expert Judgment	Process Modeling (9.21)	
Organizational Process Assets	Structured Walkthrough (9.30)	

BA's Responsibilities in Planning the Business Analysis Approach
- Assess the complexity of the project, type of solution, and development approach
- Decide how formal your business analysis planning needs to be
- Decide on a plan-driven or change-driven approach to business analysis (or combination)
- Find out what templates, standards, and tools are available for use on this assignment

What Do You Need to Successfully Plan the Business Analysis Approach?
To be able to plan, you need to know *what* you are planning, so the business need is an important input. It may be brief and high-level, but it will give you an idea of the type of analysis work that will be needed. In addition, you will use organizational process assets like lessons learned and standard business analysis practices to determine the best business analysis approach for this assignment. And the most important input you have is expert judgment, yours and that of your colleagues. Every assignment is unique, so you won't be able to follow the exact same process you used on a prior project, but you will use your experience and the experience of others to come up with a general roadmap for your business analysis work.

> **EXERCISE**   If you were assigned as the business analyst on a project to update the payroll system in your organization, what kinds of things would you consider as you planned the effort? Who would the stakeholders be? What kinds of requirements would you use? What activities would you perform? Use your *expert judgment* to make a list.

SAMPLE ANSWER

Even with only a brief description of a business need, your expert judgment will enable you to list items such as the following:

- There are stakeholders in human resources, accounting, and management, and every employee is a stakeholder. Most likely, a taxing authority will also be involved.
- This is a high-risk business process, since payroll involves money and the welfare of the company's employees.
- Business rules and data are going to be important requirements modeling concepts. (Note: Do you remember the other modeling concepts? Refer back to the Requirements Analysis chapter if you do not.)
- Satisfying this business need will likely entail a software change that will require functional and non-functional requirements, along with software testing coordination.
- This work may require a significant communication effort (remember transition requirements?) if the employees will experience a change in their payment timing or amount.
- You will have to learn the old system (as-is) to help design a new one (to-be).

You probably came up with many more items. Your business analysis experience (expert judgment) gives you lots of ideas about what you will have to consider to be successful. You would probably discuss your plan with other experienced professionals. Their expert judgment should also be an input to your planning.

Approaches to Business Analysis

The most important terms to learn in this task are *plan-driven* and *change-driven* approaches. You first learned about these approaches in Chapter 2, Business Analysis Key Concepts. Let's review the differences in these approaches.

Plan-Driven   Plan-driven approaches refer to traditional methodologies and processes like waterfall or a structured project management process. They are typically used on projects that require formal approvals and checkpoints. Projects that have a high level of risk are candidates for the plan-driven approach because formal planning includes more focus on minimizing risk. The solution is clearly and completely designed before it is built, to allow the team maximum control over the solution components.

Change-Driven   Change-driven approaches refer to newer processes like agile, Scrum, and Extreme Programming (XP). They focus on rapid delivery in short iterations and use a more exploratory approach to solution design. Business analysis deliverables are less formal than on plan-driven projects. Solution components are prioritized and built in iterations. Remaining requirements are reprioritized as the solution is developed. Changes to requirements are expected and accepted as part of the regular work.

These approaches describe two ends of a spectrum. Most project teams use an approach somewhere in the middle, combining the best practices of each as they apply to the solution being developed. (In the Business Analysis Key Concepts chapter of this book, I recommended you read the descriptions of plan-driven and change-driven approaches in the *BABOK® Guide*. If you have not yet read this, do so now.)

What Approach Will You Use?

Change-driven and plan-driven approaches generally refer to software development and project management methodologies, but they can easily be used to describe business analysis work as well. Business analysis professionals should be able to work in varied environments, using either approach, so be prepared to answer questions about how you would tailor your planning to specific situations. For example, you would allow additional time for formal requirements documentation when using a plan-driven approach.

TRICKS OF THE TRADE® Most business systems use software or some type of technology, so most solutions have at least one technology component. If you don't have software development experience, try to learn as much as you can about how software is designed and developed. Think about a software application you use (e.g., online banking, e-commerce) and how you have seen it change over time. Were the changes major, well-planned releases (probably plan-driven) or small, evolving enhancements (probably change-driven)?

Choosing the Best Approach

There are many factors to consider when you are deciding on a business analysis approach. How complex are the business need and the solution to be built? How many stakeholders will be involved? Who are they? What is the anticipated timeframe of the work? What requirements tools and templates (organizational process assets) are available in your organization?

When you are using a plan-driven approach, most of the requirements will be gathered in an early phase of the project, before the solution is designed and built.

When you are using a change-driven approach, only high-level requirements will be gathered and prioritized upfront. The highest-priority requirements will be detailed and implemented in the first phase or iteration. Requirements analysis will be performed at the beginning of each iteration.

Plan-driven projects will use more formal communications, while change-driven approaches rely on informal, collaborative communications.

Do not jump to a decision on an approach before thinking through the implications. Just because your solution is a software package, and your development team is very excited about using Scrum, that doesn't mean the business analysis work must follow the same approach. For example, if your software solution supports a medical device that is highly regulated and can affect a person's health, your requirements will need to be formally documented (plan-driven) and the testing team will follow a very structured quality assurance process. On the other hand, just because your implementation SMEs are used to a very structured project management process, that doesn't mean your requirements can't be lightweight and agile (change-driven).

The decisions you make about your business analysis approach will drive your more detailed planning activities (in the next tasks).

When you answer situational questions on the exam, determine whether a plan-driven or change-driven approach is being described. You should be able to figure out which approach is being used by focusing on key words in the question, such as the following.

Key Words Describing a Change-Driven Approach	Key Words Describing a Plan-Driven Approach
Informal	Formal
Short iterations or sprints	Phases
Feedback on a working solution	Formal approvals
New product development	Regulatory compliance
Agile, lightweight	Structured walkthrough

Other Types of Projects   Not every project involves software development. Business analysis work is also performed on process improvement projects. You must be familiar with the terminology and concepts of Lean and Six Sigma processes used on business process improvement projects. The term "lean" comes from the concept of lean manufacturing, which is over 100 years old. The principle behind lean is to remove waste from a process. Think about Henry Ford and the invention of the assembly line. The assembly line efficiently moved the product being built (the car) to the people who were skilled at adding each part, eliminating the time wasted when workers moved around the plant, building each car individually. Six Sigma practices also came out of the manufacturing industry, as organizations began to focus on quality improvement techniques. It uses very precise measurements to find defects and fix the processes that are causing the defects.

How Will Your Team Prioritize Requirements?

During planning, decisions are made regarding how requirements will be prioritized. Business analysts do not determine priorities, we facilitate these decisions. You determine how you will facilitate prioritization based on your knowledge of the project and your stakeholders. Do you anticipate that prioritization will be difficult because you have stakeholders from a number of different areas with different needs? Do you anticipate requirements priorities will change as stakeholders begin to see how the solution will impact their day-to-day work? Your prioritization approach will be refined in the Plan Requirements Management Process task.

There were several techniques suggested for prioritizing requirements in the Requirements Analysis chapter: decision analysis, risk analysis, MoSCoW analysis, and timeboxing. As you plan, consider whether any of these techniques will be useful on your project.

 Expect to see a situational question about conflicting stakeholder priorities. How would you handle a situation where one stakeholder wants requirement A while another demands requirement B? Correct answers include: facilitate a discussion about the business value of each requirement, determine the estimated cost to satisfy each requirement and compare the cost to the expected benefits, and find out if one requirement is dependent on the other. Having a predefined prioritization process helps to resolve conflicts in a consistent way. Resolving conflict is part of the Manage Solution Scope and Requirements task in Requirements Management and Communication.

How Will You Manage Requirements Changes?

Another aspect of planning is deciding how you will handle those inevitable requirements changes. In project management, requirements change management is referred to as change control or integrated change control.

The fact that requirements change frequently is a challenge for business analysts. The change management approach is outlined here and documented as part of the requirements management plan (created in the Plan Requirements Management Process task in this chapter). You must understand why and how requirements change and be prepared to manage this fluid asset.

The volatility of requirements is dependent on the product or solution being built. If the product is fairly well understood and similar products have been built before, requirements can generally be defined and "frozen," or baselined, with few changes made during the building process. For example, if your payroll application is upgraded to a new release by the vendor every couple of years, you probably have a pretty well-defined process for managing each upgrade. But when you are building a solution that is not well understood or has never been built before (e.g., creating a website for accepting job applications), it is difficult for stakeholders to articulate the requirements they want, and it is common for them to change their minds once they see the product coming together.

Why do requirements change?
- The product is new, complex, or difficult to imagine or envision
- The project timeline is long, and business needs change before the product is built
- Stakeholders don't clearly understand their problem or potential solution
- Stakeholders are missed during initial requirements discussions
- The business analyst misunderstood the requirements during elicitation

All of these situations should be considered during planning, with the goal of mitigating the risks related to requirements volatility.

Knowing how much you expect requirements to change may help you decide on your approach. For example, if you are assigned to help design and build a new web ordering system and your stakeholders are not experienced with this type of system, you can expect lots of changes as they begin to learn about all the options available in web applications. This type of project lends itself well to a change-driven approach, where small pieces of the system are built and reviewed before requirements for the next piece are elicited. Alternatively, if you are working on a solution that must conform to regulations, where requirements will not change and must be met, you will use a plan-driven approach.

You should include stakeholders in this planning activity as much as possible. If you ask for their opinions on the initial decisions, you will probably get more cooperation as the project progresses.

Techniques to Plan the Business Analysis Approach

Decision Analysis (9.8)
Financial analysis is an excellent technique to help decide on a business analysis approach. Plan-driven approaches generally involve more overhead. Change-driven approaches work best when the team is collocated, but outsourcing may be a more cost-efficient choice. If your organization has historical data about the success of different business analysis approaches, that data can help solidify your decision on which approach to use. In my experience, companies should do more financial analysis before deciding on an approach. An agile approach sounds faster and cheaper than a plan-driven approach, but it doesn't always work out that way.

Process Modeling (9.21)
Process modeling is a good technique to help you organize your business analysis approach and lay out your next steps. You can draw a workflow diagram showing how the business analysis work will be accomplished and how team members will be involved. (Process Modeling was discussed in the Specify and Model Requirements task in the Requirements Analysis chapter.)

Structured Walkthrough (9.30)

To get feedback on your plans, you may use a structured walkthrough. The more people who review your plans, the better the plans become. Especially on high-risk, high-priority projects, spending time reviewing plans pays off in the long run. (Steps for conducting a structured walkthrough were discussed in the Verify Requirements task in the Requirements Analysis chapter.)

 EXERCISE Plan the business analysis work described in the following case study. Note: You will use the plan as a basis for other exercises later in this chapter.

Project Worker Profiles

Objective Increase employee satisfaction with Human Resources (HR) support by 10 percent by the end of the next calendar year.

Background Information There are about 20,000 employees worldwide. This project has been initiated because of complaints by employees and managers about the HR department. The sponsor wants to quickly put some important improvements in place.

Upon meeting with the HR director, you determine that her systems and infrastructure have been ignored for several years and are outdated. Her employees are doing the best they can, but there are too many manual processes, since the systems don't support the current needs. Employees complain about slow responses to questions about benefits and payroll tax changes. Suggestions include building a worker profile website where employees can update their own profiles, improving communication with benefit providers, and more automation for country-specific tax regulations.

The director wants a recommendation from you on what changes would most likely increase employee satisfaction with the HR department. First, you must decide on a general approach to finding out what employees want. Describe your approach. (In other words, you need to find out from 20,000 employees what changes in HR would make them more satisfied! What will you do?)

Business Analysis Approach

How will you prioritize requirements?

> **SAMPLE ANSWER**
>
> **Business Analysis Approach**
>
> This is a low-risk, low-complexity business analysis assignment where the sponsor wants a quick response, so a change-driven approach seems appropriate. But before you jump to that conclusion, think a little further about the situation. You will probably use a questionnaire (elicitation technique) because of the large number of stakeholders (20,000). When you use a questionnaire, the questions must be reviewed carefully (a formal deliverable). Also your director wants a recommendation, which will probably be a pretty formal deliverable. This is a good example of an assignment where you will combine the change-driven and plan-driven aspects to customize your approach. The questionnaires will be formally reviewed and approved before they are sent to employees. The results will be tabulated and presented to the sponsor in a formal report with recommendations.
>
> **How will you prioritize requirements?**
>
> A small team will develop and review the questionnaires. The responses from employees will be prioritized based on the number of responses for and the estimated cost of each feature.

Summary

The emphasis of this task is on deciding on your business analysis approach and setting yourself up to work on your detailed plans. You'll use the approach (developed here) in the next few tasks to end up with three plans: a business analysis plan, a business analysis communication plan, and a requirements management plan. The decisions made in this task will impact your work throughout the entire initiative.

Conduct Stakeholder Analysis (2.2)

Conduct Stakeholder Analysis is a fancy way of saying "get to know the people on your team!" Stakeholder analysis is an important part of planning because people are the most critical part of business analysis work. Stakeholders with positive attitudes toward the work being done will be strong assets to the team. Stakeholders who are reluctant or negative will require more time and communication.

There will be several questions about stakeholder analysis on the exam, although they won't always use the term stakeholder analysis. Any questions about communication, elicitation, or working with your team will assume you have performed stakeholder analysis. This means you have gotten to know as much about your stakeholders as possible and have thought about how best to work with them. Whenever you answer questions about stakeholder relationships, remember that successful business analysis involves developing honest, trusting relationships with all of your stakeholders. The more you trust each other, the better your work will be. The more you know about the people you are working with, the more effective you will be.

Conduct Stakeholder Analysis		
Inputs	**Techniques**	**Outputs**
Business Need (5.1)	Acceptance and Evaluation Criteria Definition (9.1)	Stakeholder List, Roles and Responsibilities (2.2)
Enterprise Architecture	Brainstorming (9.3)	
Organizational Process Assets	Interviews (9.14)	
	Organization Modeling (9.19)	
	Process Modeling (9.21)	
	RACI Matrix	
	Requirements Workshops (9.23)	
	Risk Analysis (9.24)	
	Scenarios and Use Cases (9.26)	
	Scope Modeling (9.27)	
	Stakeholder Map	
	Survey/Questionnaire (9.31)	

BA's Responsibilities in Conducting Stakeholder Analysis

- Identify all the stakeholders who will impact or be impacted by the solution
- Assess each stakeholder or stakeholder group for their interest, influence, and attitude about the solution
- Determine the best communication method(s) for each stakeholder or group
- Work with the project manager to facilitate agreement on each stakeholder's role and responsibilities on the project

What Do You Need to Successfully Conduct Stakeholder Analysis?

A good understanding of the business need will enable you to identify stakeholders who are impacted by the solution. Enterprise architecture includes valuable information about people, roles, and relationships within the organization. Organizational process assets may include policies and procedures for working with stakeholders.

EXERCISE   How many of the stakeholder types can you list? If you don't remember them all, refer back to the Business Analysis Key Concepts chapter for the complete list.

ANSWER

Business Analyst
Customer
Domain SME (subject matter expert)
End User
Implementation SME
Operational Support
Project Manager
Regulator
Sponsor
Supplier
Tester

Stakeholder Identification

Making a list of all of the stakeholders and stakeholder groups who will impact or be impacted by the solution is a key success factor for business analysis. This may sound easy, but it is not. Even in a small organization, making sure you identify all the people who may be impacted by your work requires you to understand how their jobs are related. For example, if you are helping to change a report that is distributed to three different departments, you need to identify the people in each department who use the report. You also need to find out if another department gets a copy of the report through an informal or undocumented process ("Oh, I also e-mail a copy of that report to John on Fridays.") For each stakeholder group, you need to identify at least one person who will represent the group during your elicitation and design sessions. You also need to make sure you identify a stakeholder representing each of the interfaces (such as external organizations). Even if you don't think an interface is going to change, you should have a stakeholder on your list who supports the interface because after the solution is completed, you will want to make sure their business functions still operate as expected.

Stakeholders' Authority, Attitude, Influence, and Impact

In business analysis literature, you will see lots of descriptions of how stakeholders are involved with the solution. Some of the differences between these descriptions are subtle. Read questions and answer choices carefully. Stakeholder *authority* generally refers to their explicit or official involvement with the solution. For example, which stakeholder has the authority to approve the business requirements? *Attitude* is personal, and not always expressed openly. For example, if a stakeholder doesn't think the sponsor is the right person to be making decisions about this solution, he or she probably won't announce his or her attitude to the team, but may let you know with nonverbal communication. *Influence* can be formal or informal. For example, a stakeholder who has been with the company for a long time might wield more influence simply because she has so much experience, even though she is not in a position of authority. *Impact* usually refers to how the solution will affect each stakeholder after implementation. Often, an end user is not actively involved in the project, but is significantly impacted because his day-to-day procedures will change after implementation. Be sure you understand what is meant by stakeholder authority, attitude, influence, and impact!

 If you have project management experience, be careful answering questions about stakeholders. *Power* is not one of the characteristics used to describe stakeholder involvement in business analysis.

Building Relationships with Stakeholders

If most of your business analysis work is done within the same organization, you will likely work with many of the same stakeholders on numerous initiatives. If you are frequently working with new people, as most consultants do, you need to use your relationship-building skills. Good relationships are built on trust, so act with integrity at all times and enjoy getting to know different types of people.

Techniques to Conduct Stakeholder Analysis

Acceptance and Evaluation Criteria Definition (9.1)
Part of stakeholder analysis is determining who will be approving your work and what criteria they will use to make the approval decision. You will also consider how stakeholders will assess proposed solution designs and validate the solution.

Brainstorming (9.3)
This versatile technique can be used to identify stakeholders and their roles and requirements.

Interviews (9.14)
Interviews are the most direct way to get to know people. Talk with them! Don't forget that an interviewee may be able to help you identify other stakeholders!

Organization Modeling (9.19)

You need to know how each stakeholder fits in the organization in order to determine how each one may be impacted by the solution. This information may be available in your organization's enterprise architecture—organization charts, job descriptions, and other company documents.

Process Modeling (9.21)

Process models from previous projects will be useful to identify stakeholders involved in the processes within your scope. If existing process models are not available, you may perform some high-level process modeling to better understand the processes you will be studying, and to identify additional stakeholders.

RACI Matrix

A RACI matrix is a technique for documenting decisions about which stakeholders will do what work. Project managers use this technique to keep track of the involvement of stakeholders with their project. You can use this to document and confirm who will be involved with the solution. I rarely recommend memorization, but you do need to memorize the words represented by the RACI acronym: responsible, accountable, consulted, and informed.

Requirements Workshops (9.23)

Requirements workshops are useful for getting to know stakeholders and helping them get to know each other. Discussion may also help identify additional stakeholders.

Risk Analysis (9.24)

During the Conduct Stakeholder Analysis task, risk analysis is performed to identify the risks associated with stakeholders involved in the project. As you are getting to know each stakeholder and stakeholder group, you should be noticing areas of concern—these are risks. You may choose not to write down these assessments, as they may be politically sensitive or unsubstantiated. You may just have a "gut feeling" that a particular stakeholder is going to be difficult to work with. These risks will be inputs into your communication strategy and timelines. Address them as specifically as you can with your project manager. Plan extra time to work directly with unsupportive stakeholders to make sure they know their opinions are being considered.

Scenarios and Use Cases (9.26)

Scenarios and use cases can also help to identify involved stakeholders. Remember the actors (stick figures) on the use case diagrams? They represent roles.

Scope Modeling (9.27)

Scope models show interfacing systems and point out stakeholders. Do you remember the context diagram? Refer back to the Enterprise Analysis chapter (Define Solution Scope, page 67) to review this technique.

Stakeholder Map

Stakeholder maps are diagrams or tables that show stakeholder involvement with a project or solution. They can be used to help you think about which stakeholders need more frequent communication. Examples include stakeholder matrices and onion diagrams.

 Read the *BABOK® Guide* description of RACI matrices and stakeholder maps (Conduct Stakeholder Analysis Task, Element 2.2.5.2 and 2.2.5.3) now. Note: These technique are not included in Chapter 9, the Techniques chapter of the *BABOK® Guide*.

APPLY YOUR KNOWLEDGE   Have you ever used a RACI matrix, stakeholder map, or onion diagram before? If not, create one for a project on which you are working. Do you see the value of analyzing stakeholders in this way?

Survey/Questionnaire (9.31)

When you are working with large stakeholder groups, surveys or questionnaires may be used to learn characteristics of the group and information about how best to communicate with them.

Summary

EXERCISE   When you first meet a stakeholder, what do you try to learn about him or her?

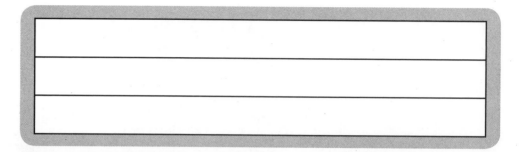

SAMPLE ANSWER

- Name, nickname, phone, e-mail address, physical office location
- Title, department, type of work performed, professional background, employment history, industry expertise
- Personal information (e.g., marital status, family background, hobbies and interests) although this information may not directly relate to the project at hand, it will help you to know your stakeholders on a more personal level
- Project knowledge and role: How much does he or she already know about the project or solution? Does he or she have any concerns, fears, or expectations about the change? Does he or she have approval authority?
- Preferred methods of communication and presentation, preferred time of day or day of week for meetings

When you have completed this task, you will have created a stakeholder list, including roles and responsibilities. It may look something like the following sample.

Sample Stakeholder List				
Name	**Title**	**Department**	**Contact Information**	**Role**
John Smith	New Employee Administrator	Human Resources	jsmith@xyz.com	John will be responsible for new employee on-boarding
Jane Jones	Sales Manager	Sales	jjones@xyz.com	Jane will represent new employees' needs, because she just started with the company last month
Heidi Vann	HR Specialist	Human Resources	hvann@xyz.com	Heidi will represent existing employees' concerns

Identifying all the people who might influence your work or be impacted by your work is a critical step in planning. You need to know who you will be communicating with, how best to communicate with them, and their level of involvement on the project. Your stakeholder list can include details about each stakeholder or stakeholder group, such as contact information, job title, role on the project, and areas of requirements expertise. Many project managers refer to this list as the *stakeholder register*. Be sure to consult with your project manager when developing this list, since you will be working with many of the same stakeholders. You and your project manager may decide to create one shared list, or each keep your own unique information. The stakeholder list, roles, and responsibilities is an important input to many other business analysis tasks. It is essential to identify and learn about as many stakeholders as possible early in the project. Missing stakeholders now may cause problems, changes, and rework later!

Stakeholder analysis is an ongoing task; you will continue to learn more about each stakeholder throughout the project.

Plan Business Analysis Activities (2.3)

Now you are going to get specific about the work you will do on the project. This task involves determining your anticipated business analysis activities and estimating how long each one will take. The list is referred to as your business analysis plan.

Plan Business Analysis Activities		
Inputs	**Techniques**	**Outputs**
Business Analysis Approach (2.1)	Estimation (9.10)	Business Analysis Plan(s) (2.3)
Stakeholder List, Roles, and Responsibilities (2.2)	Functional Decomposition (9.12)	
Business Analysis Performance Assessment (2.6)	Risk Analysis (9.24)	
Organizational Process Assets		

BA's Responsibilities in Planning Business Analysis Activities
- Determine the business analysis work that will be necessary to meet the business need
- Assess the risks of the solution on the business
- Determine which elicitation technique(s) will be used with each stakeholder group
- Determine what deliverables will be produced
- Estimate the time required to perform each business analysis task
- Develop a complete business analysis plan and provide it to the project manager to be incorporated into the project plan

What Do You Need to Successfully Plan Business Analysis Activities?
To develop a detailed plan, you will start with your approach (the output of the Plan Business Analysis Approach task in this chapter), and incorporate your organization standards (organizational process assets), your prior experience, and your stakeholder analysis from the previous task. The business analysis performance assessment refers to historical records and lessons learned from previous initiatives. Such information can save you time in planning, as estimates and other documentation from similar initiatives may be reused.

Determining Business Analysis Activities
It is not easy to create a list of activities you need to perform. Most business analysts use a top-down approach to identifying specific activities. The project management discipline has great techniques to help with this, one of which is the work breakdown structure (WBS). A WBS can be created as a decomposition diagram or in outline format. Work packages are used to describe deliverables and then decomposed into the activities needed to produce each deliverable. Each work package may be assigned a unique number or name for tracking purposes.

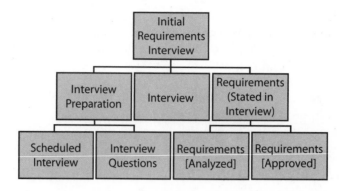

Who Will Be Involved?   The number and types of stakeholders involved with the project will be the biggest factors in developing your list of activities and estimating the time required to complete each activity. How committed are they to the project? How knowledgeable are they? We talked earlier about the importance of stakeholder relationships. You will be able to better estimate the time required to elicit requirements if you already have a relationship with the stakeholders. Plan more time for the individuals with whom you have never worked.

Requirements—What Types Are Needed?   You should think about what types of requirements are needed for your assignment. Business requirements are always needed, because they include the justification for the work and the high-level description of the problem or opportunity. Stakeholder requirements are an important part of any initiative, as they are requests that need to be refined. Functional requirements describe the solution and are usually needed, unless you are buying a product rather than building it. Non-functional requirements are needed when performance or quality constraints are important. Transition requirements are needed whenever the implementation of the solution will change the way people work.

Requirements—How Will They Be Elicited?   There is an entire knowledge area dedicated to Elicitation—let's review what we discussed in that chapter. This task requires you to plan your elicitation activities.

In planning, you decide which elicitation techniques will be used with which stakeholders. This information becomes part of the business analysis communication plan in the next task, and helps you estimate the time needed to conduct each session. You will probably use a combination of techniques (e.g., interviewing, requirements workshops, observation, and interface analysis) to elicit stakeholder requirements. You must allow time to perform all aspects of each elicitation technique you will use. Can you remember the four tasks of elicitation?

When choosing elicitation techniques, you should consider the location of team members; are they all in the same office building (collocated) or in different geographic locations? Do they work for the organization as employees, or are they outside resources?

If the end users/customers of the solution are outside of your organization, eliciting requirements from them may be more difficult. Find out what you are allowed to do. Can you select a few for a focus group? Can you conduct interviews? Does your marketing or sales department need to set up meetings for you? The more distance between the business analyst and the ultimate user, the longer elicitation will take.

Your business analysis approach may dictate some of the elicitation techniques you will use. As you might expect, change-driven approaches use less formal elicitation techniques, while

© 2012 RMC Publications, Inc • 952.846.4484 • info@rmcproject.com • www.rmcproject.com

plan-driven approaches use more formal sessions. Remember that regardless of how they are elicited, requirements are developed iteratively, so you also have to plan for follow-up sessions.

Example Business Analysis Plan   Following is a portion of a sample business analysis plan, with a discussion of each component of Elicitation.

Business Analysis Plan/Elicitation Activities			
Task	**Estimated Time**	**Number of Stakeholders**	**Total Time**
Schedule first interviews	1 hour	5	5 hours
Develop questions	2 hours	5	10 hours
Conduct interviews	1.5 hours	5	7.5 hours
Record results, analyze	2	5	10 hours
Ask follow-up questions or conduct second interview (if necessary)	1	5	5 hours
Present findings and get approval	2	5	10 hours
Total			47.5 hours

Notes on the Sample Plan

Schedule First Interviews   Why will this activity take an hour per stakeholder, your manager might ask? Setting up a meeting always takes some time. In this example, there are five people to schedule. Besides finding a place on their calendars, you may also have to reserve meeting rooms or set up the use of a collaboration tool if the stakeholders are remote.

Develop Questions   It is very important to give yourself time to plan interviews, so you can make the best use of your stakeholder's time. You may choose to develop the questions *before* you schedule so you can estimate the length of each interview.

Record Results, Analyze   Plan for adequate time after each interview to think about what you heard and to document your findings. The task Document Elicitation Results (in Elicitation) describes this work.

Ask Follow-up Questions or Conduct Second Interview   Include these in your time estimate as well, so that you can get the full benefit of each stakeholder's input.

Present Findings and Get Approval   To present your findings, you may draw a diagram, create a written document, or make a formal presentation. Allow time to incorporate stakeholder feedback before final approval.

Total   Did you notice the total estimated time in this example? Did it surprise you? Without a detailed plan, an inexperienced business analyst might say, "I've got to interview five stakeholders, so that should take about five hours." Communications about complex business requirements often take longer than we expect, so be sure to include all of the work you will perform, and take into account the complexity of the business domain.

Requirements—How Will They Be Presented?   Presenting requirements to business stakeholders for approval and to the solution team for development are important milestones in the project. There are many ways to present requirements (including tables, diagrams, and models). The presentation format(s) you will use is your planned deliverable. A business analyst has lots of flexibility in determining the best way to present requirements, and must be in sync with stakeholders on both the business and solution sides of the team. The business stakeholders may want very formal presentations, while the builders simply want you to tell them what to do. If you are working in an informal environment, requirements may be presented on a whiteboard or flip chart. If you have access to graphical or modeling tools, consider how comfortable you are using them, or whether you will require training. If the project is constrained by regulations, what presentation format is required? For example, traceability is often required by regulators. If there is significant business risk, more formal presentations and signoffs will mitigate the risks. Be sure to allocate time in your business analysis plan for requirements reviews, as well as time to incorporate the feedback you receive.

Requirements—How Will They Be Validated?   Requirements are validated by reviewing them and comparing them to the original business case. Structured walkthroughs should be planned for both interim and final deliverables. High-risk projects require more time for testing and validation activities. Your primary responsibility during testing will be problem tracking and resolution. Be sure to include time for problem resolution activities in your plan.

Transition Planning and Requirements   At the beginning of the project, you may not yet know how significant the organizational change is going to be, but try to imagine how challenging this transition will be for everyone impacted by it. You probably will be able to make some guesses about the number of people who will be impacted by the change and the significance of the rollout based on the results of your stakeholder analysis. Talk with your stakeholders about how successfully their groups have implemented changes in the past. Make notes on everything you know to help with your estimating.

How Long Will the Work Take?

Realistic estimates of business analysis tasks are an important input to the overall project planning process. You should assign an estimated number of hours to each activity on your list. The project manager needs to have an accurate picture of the time that will be required to perform all of the business analysis work, in order to include it in the project schedule. The schedule will include your work and its dependencies on the work of other team members. Business analysis tasks are usually on the *critical path* at the beginning of the project! If you fall behind, the entire project schedule will be in jeopardy.

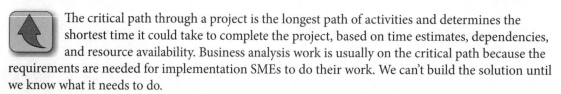 The critical path through a project is the longest path of activities and determines the shortest time it could take to complete the project, based on time estimates, dependencies, and resource availability. Business analysis work is usually on the critical path because the requirements are needed for implementation SMEs to do their work. We can't build the solution until we know what it needs to do.

Business analysis best practices support using historical data whenever it is available. If you know how long it took to perform business analysis work on a similar project, you have great data upon which to base future plans. It is always useful to track your time and compare it to your estimates. You will see the accuracy of your estimates and do a better job on future plans. We generally tend to underestimate the time it will take to accomplish a task.

In addition to time estimates, you may also request a budget for expenditures needed to support your work. Examples include the purchase of a requirements management tool, or a travel budget, if stakeholders are geographically dispersed, to accommodate observation of current processes and other face-to-face interactions.

 Senior business analysts often help less experienced business analysts with planning and estimating.

Techniques to Plan Business Analysis Activities

Estimation (9.10)

It is important to provide your project manager or supervisor with a realistic time estimate of your business analysis work at the start of each assignment. The time estimates of business analysis work are part of the overall timeline of the initiative, and may help the organization decide whether or not to proceed. There are eight different methods of estimating listed in the *BABOK® Guide*. You should know the definition of each one.

Analogous Estimation   This technique bases estimates on information from similar projects.

Bottom-Up Estimation   This technique involves creating detailed estimates for each activity or work package. The estimates are then rolled up into higher-level estimates and finally into an overall business analysis estimate. Doing this well requires an accurate WBS.

Delphi Estimation   This technique is used to achieve consensus among experts who participate anonymously. A request for information is sent to the experts, their responses are compiled, and the results are sent back to them for further review until consensus is reached.

Expert Judgment   To take advantage of expert judgment, seek input from people who have done similar work in the past.

Historic Analysis   Historical data from work done on prior projects is used to create estimates. This is similar to analogous estimating, but it can be used for estimating smaller segments of work, as well as for the overall time of the effort.

Parametric Estimation   This technique uses parameters such as hours per use case, based on history. The data can come from historical records from previous projects, industry standard metrics, or other sources. For example, you may use measures like function points or use case points. (These are industry standard measurements in software development.)

Rolling Wave Estimation   Using this technique, the business analyst estimates upcoming work with more exact detail than work planned to be done later in the project. Estimates are refined as current work is completed.

Three-Point Estimation   Using this form of estimating, the business analyst makes best case, worst case, and most likely estimates, and calculates an average. Another common approach is to provide the project manager with a time estimate range (e.g., 8 to 12 hours), for activities that are not well defined.

To help remember these definitions, note that the name of each estimation method reveals its meaning. For example, analogous means *similar* in certain respects. Parametric means to use parameters. Delphi means the top; get the top experts.

Functional Decomposition (9.12)

The work breakdown structure (WBS) is built using functional decomposition. This is a great technique for organizing your work, breaking it down, and estimating at the detailed level.

Risk Analysis (9.24)

Planning for business analysis work is difficult because you don't know how long it will take to analyze a business process until you start learning about it. As you develop your plan, you should note any risks that may impact your ability to meet the plan. For example, "If the business process for evaluating a candidate before making a job offer is more complex than we expect, my estimate for developing a workflow diagram may take longer than estimated." You may factor some of these risks into your estimates by providing ranges rather than a one-point estimate. For example, "I estimate 10 to 15 hours to model the hiring process, depending on its complexity." In Enterprise Analysis we talked about project risks and business risks. Here we are talking about business analysis risks!

 EXERCISE Let's look again at the case study exercise presented earlier in this chapter. Review the approach agreed upon below. What are the specific business analysis activities you would perform? Develop an activity list and time estimate for each activity.

Project Worker Profiles

Objective Increase employee satisfaction with Human Resources (HR) support by 10 percent by the end of the next calendar year.

Background Information There are about 20,000 employees worldwide. This project has been initiated because of complaints by employees and managers about the HR department. The sponsor wants to quickly put some important improvements in place.

Upon meeting with the HR director, you determine that her systems and infrastructure have been ignored for several years and are outdated. Her employees are doing the best they can, but there are too many manual processes, since the systems don't support the current needs. Employees complain about slow responses to questions about benefits and payroll tax changes. Suggestions include building a worker profile website where employees can update their own profiles, better communication with benefit providers, and more automation for country-specific tax regulations.

To determine what changes would most likely increase employee satisfaction with the HR department, you must decide on a general approach to finding out what employees want. The director wants a recommendation.

Agreed-Upon Approach We will develop an initial questionnaire to get a list of all of the improvement ideas from a subset of employees (about 5,000). We estimate 20 percent of employees will answer (1,000 responses).

A second questionnaire will ask all employees to rank the most frequently submitted improvement ideas. Incentives to encourage employee participation will be offered. We estimate 20 percent of employees will answer (4,000 responses).

A small team will develop and review the questionnaires. Communications with employees will be via electronic survey software and e-mail.

Activity	Time Estimate	Notes

SAMPLE ANSWER

Activity	Time Estimate	Notes
Develop initial questionnaire	2 days	
Test questionnaire on a few employees	1 day	
Refine as needed	1 day	
Work with the IT department to automate questionnaire and send e-mail to random sample of 5000 employees	5 days	Use existing survey software
Wait for response	4 days	
Compile features and rank	3 days	Spreadsheet from IT will be reviewed and sorted.
Develop second questionnaire	2 days	
Test questionnaire	1 day	
Refine as needed	1 day	
Work with the IT department to automate and send e-mail to all employees	3 days	Use existing survey software
Wait for responses	4 days	
Compile rankings and report findings	3 days	
Total Time	**30 business days = 6 weeks**	

Summary

Developing a business analysis plan requires you to think ahead about how you will accomplish your work. Thorough planning greatly increases the likelihood of success. By performing the steps of this task, you have created a business analysis plan! You will provide this plan to your project manager, who will incorporate it into the overall project plan, along with plans from other team members for their activities. Your ability to answer planning questions on the exam will depend on your ability to consider all of the factors that impact your business analysis work.

Plan Business Analysis Communication (2.4)

Creating a business analysis communication plan involves making decisions about how you will communicate with your stakeholders based on their needs and the project goals. Your plan should be as specific as possible based on your knowledge of the assignment and of your stakeholders. The two most important parts of the plan are the frequency and formality of communication.

Face-to-face communications are almost always more effective than virtual, so answer questions about planning communications with a preference to face-to-face whenever possible.

Plan Business Analysis Communication		
Inputs	**Techniques**	**Outputs**
Business Analysis Approach (2.1)	Prepare Requirements Package (4.4)	Business Analysis Communication Plan (2.4)
Stakeholder List, Roles and Responsibilities (2.2)	Communicate Requirements (4.5)	
Business Analysis Plan(s) (2.3)	Structured Walkthrough (9.30)	
Organizational Process Assets		

BA's Responsibilities in Planning Business Analysis Communication

- Determine the best communication methods for each stakeholder group
- Estimate the time required from each stakeholder and approximate dates of the elicitation so the stakeholders can plan their schedules
- Develop a general plan for the logistics of elicitation sessions (locations, budgets, attendees)
- Work with the project manager to develop a consistent approach to stakeholder communications (*frequency* and *formality*)

What Do You Need to Successfully Plan Business Analysis Communication?

As with all types of planning, you will consider many factors when deciding how best to communicate with your stakeholders. The list of stakeholders and the information you gathered during stakeholder analysis (discussed earlier in this chapter) will help you make these decisions. In addition, you will refer to organizational standards, templates, and tools that are available. You also may talk to other business analysts who have worked with specific stakeholders, to learn about what worked best for them. You will be influenced by the business analysis approach you have chosen, as well as the approach chosen by the development team. Plan-driven approaches will typically require more formal plans.

 Be careful when answering exam questions about this task. It is very similar to the Prepare for Elicitation task in the Elicitation knowledge area. The tasks involve similar work, but at different levels of detail. Plan Business Analysis Communication is performed at the beginning of the project and results in a plan for communicating with stakeholders throughout the project. Prepare for Elicitation is more detailed and is performed for each elicitation session. Examples of each task might help you here.

Task	Example
Plan Business Analysis Communication	You plan to conduct an interview with stakeholder John Smith to elicit requirements about new employee procedures because he has specific detailed knowledge that you need. You expect to conduct this interview in the first couple of weeks of the project.
Prepare for Elicitation	You contact John Smith for a convenient day and time, you reserve a conference room for the interview, and you write your interview questions.

Business Analysis Communication Plan

Your communication plan should be as detailed and specific as necessary to accomplish the needs of the project. In a plan-driven approach, the business analysis communication plan may be formal and published with the project communications management plan. In a change-driven approach, your communication plan may simply state that you will be working full-time in the conference room with your team, communicating constantly. The type of project or initiative you are involved with will also influence your communication planning. If the project is a business process improvement initiative, you will likely choose to use observation to learn the details of the current processes and procedures. If your solution is a purchased software package, you will plan time to talk with vendor representatives about the details of implementation and data conversion.

Sample Business Analysis Communication Plan Excerpt		
Stakeholder Name	Communication Strategy	Estimated Stakeholder Involvement
John Smith	Interview at least once and confirm requirements with a process model.	First two weeks of project
Jane Jones	One or two interviews to understand new employee concerns. Invite her to design walkthroughs for feedback. Involve her in solution design decisions, and work with her on organizational readiness and transition requirements.	First two weeks of project and then again during solution design
Heidi Vann	One or two interviews to learn about employee concerns. Have Heidi review the proposed solution designs because she is an expert on the current system.	Most involvement will be during design and testing phases

Cultural Differences   There can be subtle differences in stakeholders from different cultures. The *BABOK® Guide* gives four very good examples of these differences that will impact your communication planning.

 Read the culture element of the Plan Business Analysis Communication task in the *BABOK® Guide* (2.4.4.2) now.

Location   As we discussed in the Conduct Stakeholder Analysis task, the stakeholders' locations will impact your communication plan. Stakeholders who are physically located in different geographic areas will require travel and/or collaboration tools to work together. Eliciting requirements from these stakeholders will typically take more time.

Frequency and Formality   In creating the business analysis communication plan, you will have to make decisions about the frequency and formality of communications. These decisions are driven by the size of the project, complexity of the business domain or solution, impact of the solution on the business, technology experience of the team, and/or regulatory requirements. For example, mission critical projects require more frequent communications.

Techniques to Plan Business Analysis Communication

Prepare Requirements Package (4.4)
Deciding how you will document and present requirements is a planning activity. Based on your approach and your stakeholder needs, you will decide how formal your requirements need to be and how best to present them. The Prepare Requirements Package task was described in the Requirements Management and Communication chapter. Let's review the factors you will consider when deciding whether requirements should be packaged on your project.

© 2012 RMC Publications, Inc • 952.846.4484 • info@rmcproject.com • www.rmcproject.com

- To whom are you presenting?
- What format does your audience prefer?
- Will your audience read the package on their own, or attend a presentation to be led through it?
- What is the goal of presenting the requirements? Feedback? Confirmation? Approval?
- How formal does the package need to be? Will it include an executive summary, table of contents?
- Is it being sent to outside stakeholders such as regulatory agencies or vendors?

If you need to prepare requirements packages for formal review sessions, plan adequate time to prepare the packages. Projects supporting regulatory solutions may require detailed requirements packages and may have to be submitted to the regulatory agency.

Communicate Requirements (4.5)

Communicate Requirements is also a task in the Requirements Management and Communication knowledge area. How much do you remember about the Communicate Requirements task? Do you remember that the purpose of communication is to bring stakeholders to a common understanding? In planning, you determine how you will make this happen.

Structured Walkthrough (9.30)

You may choose to conduct a formal or informal review of your communication plan to make sure you haven't missed anything. A structured walkthrough is a useful technique for getting feedback on your communication plan.

EXERCISE   Let's refer again to the case study we have been working on in this chapter. Review the additional stakeholder information below and develop a business analysis communication plan.

Project   Worker Profiles

Objective   Increase employee satisfaction with Human Resources (HR) support by 10 percent by the end of the next calendar year.

Background Information   There are about 20,000 employees worldwide. This project has been initiated because of complaints by employees and managers about the HR department. The sponsor wants to quickly put some important improvements in place.

Upon meeting with the HR director, you determine that her systems and infrastructure have been ignored for several years and are outdated. Her employees are doing the best they can, but there are too many manual processes, since the systems don't support the current needs. Employees complain about slow responses to questions about benefits and payroll tax changes. Suggestions include building a worker profile website where employees can update their own profiles, better communication with benefit providers, and more automation for country-specific tax regulations.

Agreed Upon Approach   We will develop an initial questionnaire to get a list of all of the improvement ideas from a subset of employees (about 5,000). We estimate 20 percent of employees will answer (1,000 responses).

A second questionnaire will ask all employees to rank the most frequently submitted improvement ideas. Incentives to encourage employee participation will be offered. We estimate 20 percent of employees will answer (4,000 responses).

A small team will develop and review the questionnaires. Communications with employees will be via electronic survey software and e-mail.

In addition, you have gathered the following stakeholder information:
- The HR director is Jamie Smith, who is also the sponsor. She is relatively new to the organization and was hired to reduce employee complaints. She wants to quickly show improvement to her management. She is located in New York City.
- Some employees belong to a union, so any changes in their work must be approved by the union representative, Marvin Blue. His office is in Indianapolis, Indiana.
- You have a good friend, Abby Williams, who has worked for the company for 10 years. You are going to talk with her to get some insight. Abby started with the company in the United States, but now works in the Amsterdam office.
- Your office is in Minneapolis, Minnesota, and you have a travel budget for one trip on this project.

Stakeholder	Communication Strategy	Estimated Stakeholder Involvement
Jamie Smith		
Marvin Blue		
Abby Williams		
Employees		

SAMPLE ANSWER

Stakeholder	Communication Strategy	Estimated Stakeholder Involvement
Jamie Smith	Primary communication will be via phone calls and e-mail. Present approach to Jamie and include her suggestions. Communicate at least once a week on progress. Formally present the survey results in a document.	Jamie is anxious to show improvements in employee morale. Keep close contact to provide her with progress and listen for adjustments to the plan as needed.
Marvin Blue	Schedule an initial phone meeting to discuss the project with Marvin and ask for suggestions. Ask Marvin to review and approve survey questions. Formally present the survey results. Plan to travel to Indianapolis if Marvin becomes disengaged or negative toward the project.	Since Marvin must approve any changes to employee procedures, work very closely with him to understand his expectations.
Abby Williams	Since Abby and I are friends, our communications will be informal. I will call or e-mail her with questions as they come up. She will provide an international perspective.	As needed.
Employees	Formal surveys will be sent electronically with an e-mail response mechanism. Report overall results after they are approved by Marvin and Jamie.	Estimate of 20 percent response to the surveys based on past experience.

Summary

Thinking ahead about how, when, and why you will communicate with individual stakeholders and stakeholder groups will improve your business analysis work. Each stakeholder has unique characteristics, and tailoring your communications to these characteristics will make them more efficient and effective. Quality communications will build stakeholder trust and improve ongoing stakeholder relationships. For the exam, remember that communications are planned and then executed according to the plan.

Plan Requirements Management Process (2.5)

A requirements management process is a method to keep track of your requirements. This task requires you to plan what you are going to do with all of the information you elicit before you even start the process of gathering it. Think of this as a filing system for your requirements. It is a best practice to have a filing system in place *before* eliciting and to place each requirement in the appropriate spot as it is discovered. The output of this task is the requirements management plan, which describes your process.

 The *BABOK® Guide* uses the terms *requirements management process* and *requirements management plan* interchangeably.

Spending time planning requirements management before you start your work will pay off in the long run. I've seen business analysts get very excited about a new assignment and immediately start asking questions. They scribble notes and begin to collect documents and e-mails, and all of a sudden their desk is covered with random requirements that are unorganized, and all in different formats. Eventually the business analyst has to stop all work, close his or her office door (if there is one), and review each note and piece of paper to organize the requirements and determine the relationship of each requirement to all of the others. Having a filing system in place before you start working prevents this kind of delay.

Plan Requirements Management Process		
Inputs	**Techniques**	**Outputs**
Business Analysis Approach (2.1)	Decision Analysis (9.8)	Requirements Management Plan (2.5)
Business Analysis Plan(s) (2.3)	Problem Tracking (9.20)	
Organizational Process Assets	Risk Analysis (9.24)	

BA's Responsibilities in Planning the Requirements Management Process

- Determine how requirements will be documented (whiteboard, word processor, spreadsheet, requirements management tool)
- Decide which requirements attributes will be collected and maintained
- Work with the project manager on a requirements change management process
- Plan for ongoing requirement asset management
- Determine which templates, standards, and tools will be used
- Create a requirements management plan

What Do You Need to Successfully Plan the Requirements Management Process?

The business analysis approach and plans that were discussed earlier in this chapter are based on the specific needs of the initiative. These plans will help you make decisions about how requirements will be managed for this initiative in accordance with the requirements standards and tools used by the organization (organizational process assets).

Planning the Process

If you work in an organization that has a business analysis center of excellence and/or well-defined business analysis standards, you may not have to make many decisions about how you will manage requirements on the project. But for the exam, you must know how to create a requirements management process to meet the needs of your assignment. Requirements management can consume a lot of time, so you should only create processes that are necessary to ensure requirements are complete and aligned with your business needs.

APPLY YOUR KNOWLEDGE   How do you keep track of your personal financial information? Bills, check stubs, credit card statements, electronic bank statements, etc.? Did you develop the process yourself?

How Formal Should the Plan Be?

There are several factors you will consider in developing a requirements management plan. The formality of the process will be driven by your organization's culture and maturity. Are people accustomed to following structured procedures? If not, you may experience resistance to a formal process. Are requirements approved formally or informally? Stakeholders who do not understand business analysis work may not be aware of the importance of requirements reviews and confirmation.

Of course, the type of project and solution will be the biggest factors in tailoring your requirements management process. If your solution must comply with regulations, the process will, of necessity, be more formal. If your solution or product impacts a large number of stakeholders and other systems, more formality will also be advantageous and will minimize risk. The resources available to you will also help with your decision. If you are the only business analyst on a medium- to large-size project and are responsible for all of the requirements management activities, you will design a simple, easy-to-maintain process for yourself. If you have access to other resources, such as a project management office, business analysis center of excellence, outside consultants, or vendor employees, you may be able to delegate some of the requirements management work, such as requirements tracing, to others. If there are several business analysts assigned to the project, you need to design a process that allows you to collaborate and share requirements.

Repository and Traceability

The first thing you need to determine is where you are going to store your requirements. Your repository could be as sophisticated as a requirements management tool, or as simple as sticky notes or index cards. This decision will be closely tied to your decisions about which business analysis deliverables you plan to produce. These were listed in your business analysis plan. The choice of a repository may also be influenced by the formality of your requirements traceability needs.

Tracing or linking requirements serves several purposes and is usually documented in a matrix. Refer back to the Manage Requirements Traceability task in the Requirements Management and Communication chapter if you need to review this task. Most requirements management tools include a feature to trace requirements. If you don't have access to a tool, you'll have to decide how to trace and which components will be traced. Tracing requirements can be time consuming, so only plan to trace critical components or those required by regulations or standards.

Requirements Attributes

Requirements attributes are characteristics of the requirements that further describe them and provide information to help the team better analyze and implement the requirements. Attributes like author, owner, complexity, status, stability, urgency, and priority may be useful depending on the type of project and solution. During planning, you decide what attributes will be captured and documented for each requirement.

Sample Requirements Attributes Document											
Requirement	Unique ID	Author	Complexity	Ownership	Priority	Risks	Source	Stability	Status	Urgency

Requirements Attributes

EXERCISE   There are many different characteristics or attributes that can be captured for each requirement. Do you understand the purpose of each of the following attributes?

Requirements Attribute	Definition and Purpose
Absolute reference (aka, unique identifier)	
Author	
Status	
Stability	

ANSWER

Requirements Attribute	Definition and Purpose
Absolute reference (aka, unique identifier)	The absolute reference is used to name requirements and for easy reference in tables and traceability matrices.
Author	The person who told you about the requirement is considered its author. It is important to capture the name of the author when there are many stakeholders providing requirements.
Status	Status refers to the current state of the requirement. Examples of states include stated, unconfirmed, approved, verified, and satisfied.
Stability	The likelihood of change in the requirement indicates its stability. Operational business rules are more volatile than other requirements and would be assigned a low stability rating.

Requirements Prioritization

Throughout this book, I've talked a lot about prioritization. This is an important topic because stakeholders typically want more changes than our organizations have time and money to support! As a business analyst, you discuss priorities and help stakeholders figure out what they want most. Prioritization is based on the features that will bring the most business value. During planning, you should put a prioritization process in place so your stakeholders will know how and why you are building some features into their solutions but not others. You want all of your stakeholders to have input into the prioritization and to understand how decisions will be made. Creating and documenting a prioritization process will provide this transparency. The formality of the process will depend on the size and type of project, along with the business analysis approach you have chosen. Know that change-driven approaches strongly emphasize prioritization. The task in which requirements are prioritized for the project, based on this plan, is part of the Requirements Analysis knowledge area.

Requirements Change Management

Change-driven projects don't usually have a change management process, because the team can add and reprioritize requirements at the end of each iteration. Plan-driven projects, on the other hand, do use a change management process. Development of this process starts in the Plan Business Analysis Approach task. Formalizing your change management process is a significant part of the requirements management plan.

There are generally three steps in the change management process: the request, impact analysis, and approval or denial.

Know the Change Management Process
1. Someone requests a change (usually a domain SME or end user).
2. Someone assesses the impact of the change (usually a business analyst or implementation SME and the team):
   a. Estimate the cost of the change
   b. Estimate the benefits of the change
   c. Recommend an approach to the change
   d. Prioritize the change
3. Someone authorizes the change. In plan-driven projects, the sponsor usually has the final authority to approve the change.

Techniques to Plan the Requirements Management Process

Decision Analysis (9.8)
Requirements may be evaluated formally or informally, to determine whether they should be included in the current project, changed, or held for the next project or iteration. Estimating the cost and benefit of an individual change usually involves financial analysis on a smaller scale. Each requirement change should also be evaluated for impacts on other requirements, as well as impacts on stakeholders. The impacted stakeholders should come to consensus about how to address the change. Decision analysis was discussed in the Enterprise Analysis chapter.

Problem Tracking (9.20)
How will you record feedback on your requirements? Business analysts are responsible for logging and following up on requirements issues. Many organizations refer to this as an issue log or parking lot. The decision about how you will track and resolve problems must be made during planning.

Risk Analysis (9.24)
Risk analysis is used here to plan how you will manage risks associated with changing requirements. When the solution is regulated, or critical to the business, your requirements management plan for the initiative will be designed to mitigate requirements risks. The expected volume of requirements changes throughout the project will also help guide you as to the level of formality required in your risk management efforts. The project manager is ultimately responsible for managing changes to the project. The business analyst works with the project manager to support the change management process.

Summary

Requirements are very complex and can be documented and communicated in many different formats. Therefore, you must have a well-defined plan for managing them. Questions on the exam will assume every project is following a requirements management plan. The way you develop your requirements management plan will depend on your organizational standards and tools. Be sure you know all of the characteristics of a requirements management plan: repository, traceability, requirements attributes, and a change management process.

Manage Business Analysis Performance (2.6)

The name of this task could be interpreted to mean supervising or managing other business analysts. But, in fact, it refers to managing yourself! A primary responsibility of a business analysis professional is to make sure he or she is performing well. We measure our own performance, assess our effectiveness, and monitor ourselves.

We measure our performance in a quantitative way (by volume of work) and we evaluate the quality of our work. Both of these are important for business analysis success. In addition, we recommend changes to the organization's business analysis process assets (e.g., templates, tools, and standards) that will help improve the effectiveness of other business analysts.

This is an ongoing task performed within projects and outside of projects on other assignments, and not just during planning. It is not dependent on any other tasks. The concept of continuous improvement is very important to the business analysis discipline. The exam may test your awareness of this professional development focus.

Manage Business Analysis Performance		
Inputs	**Techniques**	**Outputs**
Business Analysis Performance Metrics	Interviews (9.14)	Business Analysis Performance Assessment (2.6)
Business Analysis Plan(s) (2.3)	Lessons Learned Process (9.15)	Business Analysis Process Assets (2.6)
Requirements Management Plan (2.5)	Metrics and Key Performance Indicators (9.16)	
Organizational Performance Standards	Problem Tracking (9.20)	
	Process Modeling (9.21)	
	Root Cause Analysis (9.25)	
	Survey/Questionnaire (9.31)	

BA's Responsibilities in Managing Business Analysis Performance
- Track work accomplishments and compare to established organizational standards
- Compare actual work against planned work and replan future work
- Recommend changes to the organization's business analysis templates, tools, and standards to help improve future business analysis work

What Do You Need to Successfully Manage Business Analysis Performance?
Business analysis performance metrics and organizational performance standards are actual measurements your organization has recorded on prior business analysis work. (Even if your organization does not have these, you must assume they exist for the exam.) You will also measure your performance by comparing the actual time you use to complete each task in your business analysis plans against the time estimate you provided to the project manager during planning. Comparing actual to estimated times is referred to as *variance analysis*. This is the best way for you to determine how you are doing, both in keeping the project on schedule and in the quality of your estimating. The requirements management plan may also help you assess your performance, because it will include a process for tracking changes to requirements after approval.

Manage Yourself

Business analysts should be the most efficient and effective members of the team, since we know how to improve processes! There are numerous ways we can measure our performance and compare it to our previous work. We should get faster and better at eliciting requirements, developing business cases, etc. We should also be looking for and documenting *lessons learned* to share our process improvement ideas with other business analysts.

SMART objectives were created in Enterprise Analysis to identify the success criteria for the project. These objectives are also success criteria for the project team and, specifically, for business analysis work. Most business analysts are measured on a combination of components, including:
- Quality of plans and estimates (Were our estimates accurate?)
- Quality of business cases and recommendations
- Number of requirements changes after approval
- Quality and nature of stakeholder relationships
- Success of project work (Were the project objectives met?)

You should be able to present your own performance review by reporting on the items listed above. You should be able to articulate your strengths and areas for improvement. You should also maintain a career development plan for future learning.

Even if your organization does not require it, I always recommend that business analysts keep track of what they do with their time. Writing down your tasks as you perform them keeps you focused on the most important work and allows you to learn how long it actually takes to complete a task. This will significantly improve your ability to realistically estimate time needed on future tasks. It also helps you educate your project manager and other management about the type of work needed to compile strong requirements.

Tracking can be done at a detailed level (hours) or a high level (weekly), but be sure to do it. Always note the value your work has brought to the organization. This is referred to as *performance reporting*.

Sample Business Analysis Time Tracking Report		
Name: Barb the BA **Week Ending: 3/2/xxxx**		**Project Number 19283**
Hours	Work Performed	Value to the Business
16	Interviews to learn the as-is business processes	Better understanding of business problem
8	Drafted business requirements	Better understanding of how a solution to the problem will be accepted

Techniques to Manage Business Analysis Performance

Interviews (9.14)

Stakeholders should be asked about the effectiveness of your business analysis work and asked for suggestions for improvements. Don't wait until the end of a project or assignment to get feedback on your performance; ask stakeholders how you are doing along the way.

© 2012 RMC Publications, Inc • 952.846.4484 • info@rmcproject.com • www.rmcproject.com

Lessons Learned Process (9.15)

This is a process of learning from our experiences and that of other business analysts in order to improve future performance. It is known by many other names, including debriefing, retrospective, and assessment. Lessons learned should be documented as they are discovered, and at the end of a project or initiative. The lessons learned document includes what was done right, what was done wrong, and what should be done differently on the next project. Another way of saying this is that lessons learned include the causes of the issues faced on a project and the reasoning behind the changes implemented. These lessons learned become organizational process assets, and are available for review by future teams. Reviewing lessons learned from similar projects can help you avoid repeating the mistakes of others.

Metrics and Key Performance Indicators (9.16)

Metrics should be determined by business analysis professionals because they understand how best to measure performance. Choosing a few key metrics to track and report will help the organization improve its business analysis practice. This technique was discussed in the Enterprise Analysis chapter.

Problem Tracking (9.20)

This technique can be used to track problems or other issues that need to be resolved. By tracking problems and issues with your performance as a business analyst, you will see areas for improvement, and be able to address them in your future work. As your business analysis skills improve, you will see the number of problems decrease.

Process Modeling (9.21)

Have you ever drawn a workflow diagram for your own job? Just as we are able to help organizations improve their processes by understanding the processes and capturing them in a graphic, you can assess your own work using the same technique. If you need practice with process modeling, analyze your personal work processes.

Root Cause Analysis (9.25)

This technique can be used to determine the fundamental causes of your personal business analysis performance problems, especially those that occur frequently, and help you to determine a solution. Do you remember the Five Whys?

Survey/Questionnaire (9.31)

These are good tools for collecting information from your stakeholders about the quality of your business analysis performance, including your communications and your recommendations.

> **APPLY YOUR KNOWLEDGE**   Describe how your performance is measured. How do you work to improve your performance? Think about your work last week. What value did you bring to your organization? What can you do to be more productive?

Summary

The key to answering questions about the Manage Business Analysis Performance task is to think about lessons learned. We need to honestly assess the work we do and improve our processes and skills on our next assignments. Since the business analysis profession is still relatively new, it is important for business analysts to show their commitment to continuous improvement for our organizations and ourselves. The outputs of this task are your business analysis performance assessment and improvements to your organization's business analysis process assets.

SUMMARY OF THE BUSINESS ANALYSIS PLANNING AND MONITORING KNOWLEDGE AREA

EXERCISE Review the following scenarios and think about how you would plan to perform the business analysis work for each assignment.

1. You have been assigned to an HR project to update the payroll system. The sponsor is the HR director who is very busy and only wants high-level summaries. The system must support taxing regulations in six countries where errors result in severe penalties. The software development team is offshore and outsourced. How would you approach this assignment?

2. You have been assigned to a new development project for an e-commerce website. The users have never sold their products online before, so they don't have any specific requests. The products are simple handmade wooden puzzles for children. The developers are internal employees who know the product well and are 100 percent dedicated to getting this website up and running as soon as possible. How would you approach this assignment?

SAMPLE ANSWER

1. You will have to provide very high-level summary requirements to the HR director, but very detailed requirements for the off-shore developers. Payroll is a high-risk application with heavy penalties for mistakes. This suggests the need for a plan-driven approach with formal deliverables and approvals. This is a relatively large business analysis effort, so business analysis plans should be formal.

2. This is a project where a change-driven or agile approach would work well. The developers already know about the product, and e-commerce sites are pretty standard (shopping cart, check out, credit card processing, etc.), so the developers can probably create a working system quickly. This system can be presented to the users for adjustments. You probably won't document requirements formally, but will instead facilitate the team's progress by asking follow-up questions and making sure the users are getting the basic features they need.

   Be careful not to spend more time writing requirements than absolutely necessary. If the developers are able to build a working feature that can be adjusted quickly based on user feedback, writing lengthy requirements documents is not a good use of the organization's time.

Hopefully, studying business analysis planning at the end of your exam preparation has made you feel you've come full circle. The Business Analysis Planning and Monitoring knowledge area includes two of the most important things the business analyst does: planning and assessment. Excellent business analysts do these two tasks every day. In the morning I ask myself, "What will I do today?" (Planning). At the end of the day, I ask myself, "How did I do today?" (Assessment.) By continuously planning, acting, and assessing, you see successes and failures immediately and perform continuous improvement of your processes.

 Before taking the practice exam, I recommend that you read the Business Analysis Planning and Monitoring chapter of the *BABOK® Guide* (Chapter 2), and the description of the key technique of this knowledge area (in Chapter 9 of the *BABOK® Guide*):
   • Estimation (9.10)

Practice Exam

1. Requirements traceability refers to:

   A. Tracing a requirement from one stakeholder to another.
   B. Tracing the work flowing through the business area.
   C. Tracing a requirement to related requirements.
   D. Tracing a requirement to the implementation stakeholder.

2. A WBS refers to:

   A. A work breakdown structure that describes the work required to accomplish a task or set of tasks.
   B. A work business system that describes the work performed by the business domain under study.
   C. A written business study that describes the cost-benefit analysis justifying the project.
   D. A written business specification that describes the complete requirements for the project.

3. Business analysis work is generally on the critical path of a project because:

   A. The critical path includes all of the tasks that relate to requirements.
   B. Many tasks are dependent on business analysis work.
   C. Business analysis work is the most important work of the project.
   D. These are the tasks that can be shortened if the project is behind schedule.

4. The difference between a plan-driven and change-driven approach to software development is:

   A. A plan-driven approach is more focused on risk.
   B. A plan-driven approach doesn't require a requirements package.
   C. A plan-driven approach relies on a collocated team.
   D. A plan-driven approach takes longer than a change-driven approach.

5. Variance analysis involves measuring discrepancies between planned and actual performance. To effectively perform variance analysis, a business analyst must have:

   A. Data modeling experience.
   B. Accurate measurements of performance.
   C. The ability to elicit detailed requirements.
   D. A gut-feel for how well things are going.

6. There are many ways to manage your workload. The approach used by most agile development processes is:

   A. Timebox—Set a time limit and get as much done as possible within the time allocated.
   B. Scope boundaries—Set a clear scope of work with boundaries and complete the work as described in scope as quickly as possible.
   C. Quality—Determine the desired level of quality for the work and get to that level of quality as quickly as possible.
   D. Single task focus—Work on only one task at a time until it is complete and then move onto the next task.

7. Which of the following is NOT a business analysis approach?

    A. Waterfall
    B. Lean
    C. Agile
    D. Benchmarking

8. Working in an organization with a prescribed project management methodology, business analysis planning:

    A. Is unnecessary because the methodology includes the business analysis plan.
    B. Is more significant than in an unstructured environment because the business analysis plan requires specific deliverables.
    C. Is less significant than in an unstructured environment because the business analysis planner can choose any deliverables.
    D. Is required, but should be easier because some of the business analysis work is included in the overall project plan.

9. What are the three plans developed by business analysts?

    A. Business analysis plan, business analysis communication plan, and requirements management plan
    B. Project plan, communication plan, and requirements management plan
    C. Business analysis plan, stakeholder plan, and requirements management plan
    D. Business analysis plan, business analysis communication plan, and business analysis activities plan

10. A RACI matrix shows:

    A. Requirements, attributes, concepts, and information needs.
    B. Requirements, activities, capabilities, and implementation analysis.
    C. Responsible, accountable, consulted, and informed roles.
    D. Responsible, achievable, controlled, and informed roles.

11. A matrix that shows stakeholder influence and impact is referred to as a:

    A. Traceability matrix.
    B. Requirements matrix.
    C. Power/interest grid.
    D. Stakeholder matrix.

12. Business analysis performance assessment is:

    A. An input to Manage Business Analysis Performance.
    B. An input to Plan Business Analysis Activities.
    C. An input to Assess Capability Gaps.
    D. An input to Evaluate Solution Performance.

13. A team that physically works together is referred to as:

    A. Dispersed.
    B. Outsourced.
    C. Collocated.
    D. Insourced.

14. Many factors influence business analysis planning, including:

    A. Type of project, project management tools, and work packages.
    B. Stakeholder locations, business analysis deliverables, and approved requirements.
    C. Stakeholder locations, type of project, and approved requirements.
    D. Type of project, stakeholder locations, and business analysis deliverables.

15. Information about requirements, such as the author, priority, complexity, and status are called:

    A. Requirements attributes.
    B. Requirements prioritization.
    C. Business constraints.
    D. Assumptions.

16. Developing a plan to handle requirements changes is referred to as:

    A. Change analysis.
    B. Change management.
    C. Problem tracking.
    D. Decision analysis.

17. Which plan describes the stakeholder groups and the frequency and level of formality that is appropriate for the requirements?

    A. Business analysis plan
    B. Requirements management plan
    C. Project plan
    D. Business analysis communication plan

18. Imagine you are assigned to a project with a budget of US $1 million, with a goal of upgrading a monitoring system to comply with new international shipping regulations. The business analysis approach best suited to this project is:

    A. Timeboxing.
    B. Plan-driven.
    C. Change-driven.
    D. Parametric estimation.

19. Maintaining strong relationships with stakeholders is beneficial because:

    A. Stakeholders you know will agree with you more often.
    B. Stakeholders who don't know you will try to trick you.
    C. Stakeholders who trust you will be more open about requirements.
    D. Stakeholders who you don't know are not trustworthy.

20. Which of the following estimation methods relies on expert judgment?

    A. Delphi estimation
    B. Three-point estimation
    C. Historic analysis
    D. Rolling wave estimation

21. You have been contracted to work as a business analyst in a company that uses a requirements management tool. Where would you store your requirements?

    A. On paper in a filing cabinet
    B. In the requirements management tool
    C. On a shared drive with other project deliverables
    D. As described in the requirements management plan for your project

22. To manage business analysis performance you need:

    A. Performance metrics, the solution scope, and performance assessment.
    B. Performance metrics, performance assessment, and business analysis plans.
    C. Performance metrics, business analysis plans, and organizational performance standards.
    D. Performance assessment, business analysis plans, and organizational performance standards.

23. Techniques useful for managing business analysis performance are:

    A. Process modeling, root cause analysis, and lessons learned.
    B. Process modeling, data modeling, and business rules analysis.
    C. Acceptance and evaluation criteria definition, data modeling, and root cause analysis.
    D. Brainstorming, process modeling, and business rules analysis.

24. Requirements attributes are:

    A. Approaches to eliciting requirements.
    B. Characteristics of requirements.
    C. Characteristics of a data model.
    D. The status of the requirements.

25. When you are collocated with your stakeholders working on a change-driven project, communication should be:

    A. Formal and frequent.
    B. Informal and frequent.
    C. Formal and infrequent.
    D. Informal and infrequent.

Answers

1. **Answer** C

   Explanation Traceability describes the links between requirement components. For example, a process requirement like Accept Order is related to (linked or traced to) a data requirement like Order Number or Order Date. Tracing also shows how requirements are implemented into the final product. This is referred to as allocation.

2. **Answer** A

   Explanation WBS is a well-established acronym in the project management profession and should be understood by business analysis professionals. A WBS describes the work required to accomplish a task or set of tasks. During business analysis planning, a business analyst should develop a WBS for his or her business analysis work and provide it to the project manager as an input to the overall project plan.

3. **Answer** B

   Explanation Business analysts must understand the concept of critical path and project management scheduling. This is necessary because most tasks in the project are dependent on requirements, and a delay in the business analysis work puts the project at risk.

4. **Answer** A

   Explanation Both approaches involve requirements, although plan-driven approaches typically have more formality in requirements documents. Ideally, change-driven approaches use collocated teams, but it is not a requirement of either approach. A change-driven approach is not necessarily faster, although it typically has smaller iterations or sprints, which may result in some solution components being available quickly. Plan-driven approaches like waterfall and iterative are used when risks are high and the work must be more controlled and planned.

5. **Answer** B

   Explanation Data modeling is not related to variance analysis. The ability to elicit requirements may indicate strong business analysis skills, but it doesn't help with variance analysis. Guessing or gut-feel are subjective assessments. Variance analysis is objective. Variance analysis requires a plan for expected performance and an accurate measure of actual results.

6. **Answer** A

   Explanation Agile approaches focus on short timeboxes to show value to the business as quickly as possible. To ensure a high level of quality, the work packages assigned to each timebox (aka, iteration or sprint) are small and closely monitored.

7. **Answer** D

   Explanation Benchmarking is an approach to competitive analysis used to get ideas for business improvement and to provide a basis (or benchmark) to use in measuring quality performance.

8. **Answer** D

   Explanation Whenever you are assigned to work on a project that is using a project management methodology, business analysis planning should be a little easier than in an unstructured environment because the methodology probably includes some tasks related to analysis. Business analysis planning still must be done because project management methodologies rarely include all of the necessary analysis work. Each project is unique, so the specific needs of the project will also impact the extent of business analysis planning.

9. **Answer**   A
    Explanation   Be careful not to confuse project management deliverables and business analysis deliverables. Two of the business analysis plans include the words business analysis to differentiate them from the project plans (business analysis plan and business analysis communication plan). The third plan, the requirements management plan, is shared by the project manager and business analyst, which means the project manager and business analyst need to work together to develop this plan.

10. **Answer**   C
    Explanation   No way to get around memorization here, you need to understand that a RACI matrix helps to define roles and responsibilities for project work and understand what each type of responsibility means.

11. **Answer**   D
    Explanation   The *BABOK® Guide* simply calls this the stakeholder matrix.

12. **Answer**   B
    Explanation   Business analysis performance assessment is an output of the Manage Business Analysis Performance task. It is used as an input to planning because we would like to learn from our prior experience and plan better for the next project. You can think of business analysis performance assessment as lessons learned. Capability gaps are about business needs. Solution performance is different from business analysis performance. Be careful when you read the question and answers to think about the relevant topic.

13. **Answer**   C
    Explanation   Collocated means all team members work in the same area. This makes planning for business analysis work easier. Dispersed teams have members in different geographic areas requiring special arrangements to accommodate time zones, cultural and language differences, etc. Insourced and outsourced refer to the assignment of resources or contractual arrangements for workers and don't necessarily tell you where the stakeholders are physically located. For example, an outsourced team (employees of a different organization) could work in the office next door and as such be collocated.

14. **Answer**   D
    Explanation   Project management tools and techniques are outside the scope of business analysis planning. Requirements have usually not yet been elicited, analyzed, or approved when planning is taking place. Planning is influenced by type of project, stakeholder locations, and business analysis deliverables, and moves us toward approved requirements.

15. **Answer**   A
    Explanation   Requirements attributes are characteristics of the requirements that further describe them and provide information to help the team better analyze and implement the requirements. Attributes such as author, owner, complexity, status, stability, urgency, and priority may be useful depending on the type of project and solution. During planning, the business analyst and project manager decide which of these attributes will be captured and documented for each requirement.

16. **Answer**   B

    Explanation   The *BABOK*® *Guide* uses the term change management to refer to the process of accepting and evaluating changes to requirements during the project. Be careful when answering questions about change. The question may be referring to requirements changes or organizational changes. Both must be planned and managed.

17. **Answer**   D

    Explanation   The business analysis plan lists tasks the business analyst will perform, along with time estimates for each task. The project plan is the responsibility of the project manager. The business analysis communication plan lists stakeholders and how best to communicate with each. Communicating with stakeholders includes presenting requirements in a format and level of formality appropriate to the project.

18. **Answer**   B

    Explanation   The only part of the question that is an important factor in determining the business analysis approach is the reference to regulations. Compliance projects typically are completed using plan-driven approaches because the deliverable must be formal for review by regulators.

19. **Answer**   C

    Explanation   You don't want stakeholders to agree with you just because they know you, but rather because your recommendations are sound. You also should not assume people you don't know will try to trick you or are not trustworthy. Going into a new relationship with these negative expectations will decrease your ability to build trust. Establishing a trusting relationship with stakeholders is the most beneficial, as stakeholders will be more open with you about their requirements, as well as their concerns.

20. **Answer**   A

    Explanation   Delphi estimation uses a combination of expert judgment and historical analysis.

21. **Answer**   D

    Explanation   The correct answer is to follow the requirements management plan. Even though the company has a requirements management tool, the requirements management plan for the specific project to which you are assigned is your guide.

22. **Answer**   C

    Explanation   The solution scope is not needed to assess your performance. The performance assessment is the output of this task. You need performance metrics, business analysis plans, and organizational performance standards.

23. **Answer**   A

    Explanation   Process modeling can be used to analyze your processes and find process improvements. Root cause analysis is used to determine the fundamental causes of problems, and lessons learned are used to improve future work.

24. **Answer**   B

    Explanation   Requirements attributes are characteristics of requirements, such as owner, author, priority, and volatility. The word *attribute* is also used in data modeling to mean a characteristic of an entity.

25. **Answer**   B

    Explanation   Communications on change-driven projects are less formal than on plan-driven projects. Communication is frequent because when the team is collated, they are having daily standup meetings.

CHAPTER 9

Putting It All Together

We have covered a lot of challenging material in this book. Did you do all the activities and exercises? They were specifically designed to help you get the most out of this book, and to help you remember what you have learned.

TRICKS OF THE TRADE® Did you focus on learning each task as an independent type of work? Remember, every business analysis task starts with a verb. These verbs were carefully chosen to describe the type of work involved. By understanding the verb, you will know if a task is performed on an ongoing basis (like Manage or Maintain), if a task involves evaluation (like Assess or Evaluate), or if a task involves decision making (like Determine or Prioritize). When answering a question about a task, the verb should help you remember the inputs, outputs, and stakeholders involved.

As noted in Chapter 1, in order to retain the information you've learned, you need to review it several times. Therefore, review this book again, focusing on the areas where you have identified gaps in your knowledge. You will find in a second pass through the book that you understand some topics differently than you did the first time and other concepts will stand out to you that you previously missed.

Are You Ready for the Exam?

Go back to the knowledge area tasks and technique tables beginning on page 12 of Chapter 1 where you indicated your level of experience with each. Would you change your answers now that you have studied and performed the Apply Your Knowledge activities in this book?

Here are a couple of additional exercises to review your knowledge of business analysis best practices.

EXERCISE Imagine you are conducting an interview with a business domain stakeholder about the detailed requirements for updating worker profiles. During the interview, you sketch a flowchart of the steps he describes, and you ask about how the new website will impact this processing. As you discuss the specifics of the solution, the two of you find a few problems with the solution design and come up with ways to address each issue. Which business analysis tasks and techniques have you performed?

Business Analysis Task	Knowledge Area

Techniques

SAMPLE ANSWER   You may have performed seven tasks from four different knowledge areas!

Business Analysis Task	Knowledge Area
Conduct Elicitation	Elicitation
Specify and Model Requirements	Requirements Analysis
Communicate Requirements	Requirements Management and Communication
Define Assumptions and Constraints	Requirements Analysis
Manage Solution Scope and Requirements	Requirements Management and Communication

Business Analysis Task	Knowledge Area
Assess Proposed Solution	Solution Assessment and Validation
Assess Organization Readiness	Solution Assessment and Validation

You also may have used five techniques!

Techniques
Problem Tracking (9. 20)
Interviews (9.14)
Brainstorming (9.3)
Process Modeling (9.21)
Risk Analysis (9.24)

This shows the complexity of business analysis work and the nonsequential nature of the tasks.

EXERCISE   Communicating clearly is so important to business analysis work that it is included in many business analysis tasks. Several business analysis tasks include presenting and communicating requirements. Review what you have learned about communicating requirements by completing this table.

Task	Knowledge Area	Description
Plan Business Analysis Communication		
Prepare Requirements Package		
Communicate Requirements		
Confirm Elicitation Results		

ANSWER

Task	Knowledge Area	Description
Plan Business Analysis Communication	Business Analysis Planning and Monitoring	This task includes the work required to decide which format(s) are appropriate to use in communicating requirements on a particular initiative and to identified stakeholders. Requirements should be presented in formats that are understandable for the reviewer; they must be clear, concise, accurate, and at the appropriate level of detail.
Prepare Requirements Package	Requirements Management and Communication	This task includes the work required to assemble packages of requirements for review as defined in the communication plan. Requirements must be clear, concise, accurate, and at the appropriate level of detail. Requirements documentation should be created only to the extent needed to ensure clear understanding by the team.
Communicate Requirements	Requirements Management and Communication	Communicating requirements includes presenting requirements to stakeholders for confirmation or approval.
Confirm Elicitation Results	Elicitation	This task includes making sure the information and/or requirements learned during elicitation are clearly understood and accurately represent the stakeholder requests.

In addition to these communication tasks, Oral Communications is an Underlying Competency discussed in Chapter 8 of the *BABOK® Guide*. It describes the importance of being able to develop and deliver powerful presentations by paraphrasing accurately, facilitating, and communicating priorities based on sound business rationale.

REVIEW OF TECHNIQUES   Review the techniques you are most likely to be tested on by listing at least one advantage and disadvantage of each.

Techniques	Advantages	Disadvantages
Acceptance & Evaluation Criteria Definition		
Brainstorming		
Business Rules Analysis		
Data Dictionary and Glossary		
Data Flow Diagrams		

Techniques	Advantages	Disadvantages
Data Modeling		
Decision Analysis		
Document Analysis		
Interviews		
Metrics and Key Performance Indicators		
Non-functional Requirements Analysis		
Organization Modeling		
Problem Tracking		
Process Modeling		
Requirements Workshops		
Scenarios and Use Cases		

Check your answers against the *BABOK® Guide*. Chapter 9 of the *Guide* lists advantages and disadvantages of every technique.

Are You Ready to Take Your Exam?

Do you:	✓
Know the material thoroughly and understand how to use the concepts and processes and how they work in combination with each other?	
Have experience performing work in all of the knowledge areas using most of the techniques? If you do not have experience with a particular task, spend time visualizing what it would be like if you were to perform it in your organization. Visualization will help you see the potential challenges of using business analysis practices and help you prepare for situational questions on the exam.	
Remember that business analysis work can be performed as part of a project or outside a project? Can you give examples of each?	
Know the knowledge areas and tasks of the *BABOK® Guide*?	
Have a download sheet you have practiced creating several times?	
Have a strategy for taking the exam? For example: "I will take a 5-minute break after every 50 questions because I need to let my mind rest." Or "I will answer all of the questions as quickly as possible, then take a break, and then go back to the questions I have marked for review."	
Expect there will be questions you cannot answer or even understand? This happens to everyone. Be prepared so you do not get annoyed or worse yet, doubt your abilities during the exam.	
Know where the exam site is and how long it will take you to get there? Visit the site ahead of time if you are a nervous test taker, to see the room and get comfortable with the environment.	
Feel comfortable jumping from one topic to another?	
Feel ready for the exam? Do not underestimate the physical aspects of taking an exam lasting that long. Be sure you have practiced taking an exam for 3.5 hours.	

Last Steps

- Review the first chapter of this book again to make sure you have learned Barb's BA Themes and the key business analysis concepts.
- Turn to the first page of each knowledge area chapter in this book and review the Quicktest terms.
- Practice creating your download page.
- Refer back to your study plan and make sure you have completed all of your TO DO list items.
- Do not over study. Getting completely comfortable with all of the material in this book is just not possible. It is not worth studying for hundreds of hours. It is a waste of time and will not help you on the exam.

Taking Your Exam

- You must bring your authorization letter to the test site, as well as two forms of identification with exactly the same name you entered on the exam application.
- If you experience stress when taking exams, take a few practice exams with a time limit to simulate the stress of the exam. If you deal with this stress before the exam, you will be more relaxed during the actual exam.
- Use deep-breathing techniques to help relax. This is particularly helpful if you are very nervous before or during the exam and when you notice yourself reading the same question two or three times. Breathing techniques can be as simple as breathing deeply five times, to provide more oxygen to your brain.
- Smile when taking the exam. Smiling relieves stress and makes you feel more confident.
- Do not expect the exam site to be quiet. Other people will also be taking exams nearby. Many testing sites have earplugs or headphones available if you will be distracted by noise.
- Make sure you are comfortable during the exam. Wear layered clothing and bring a sweater to sit on in case the chairs are uncomfortable.
- Bring snacks! Bring lunch! You will not be able to bring snacks into the exam room, but have them accessible outside the exam room in case you get hungry. You do not need the distraction of hunger pains when taking the exam.
- Be prepared to create your download sheet as soon as you can, possibly during the exam tutorial. This will free up your mind to handle questions once the information you are concerned about is written down. Note: The testing center will require you to exchange your used scratch paper if you need more during the exam.
- When you take the exam, you will see one question on the screen at a time. You can answer a question and/or mark it to return to it later. You will be able to move back and forth through questions during the exam.
- The exam does not adapt to your answers. This means 150 questions are selected when your exam starts, and those 150 do not change.
- Use all the exam time. Do not leave early unless you have reviewed each question twice.
- Remember your own unique test-taking quirks and how you plan to deal with them while taking the exam.
- Control the exam; do not let it control you. How would you feel if you read the first question and had no idea of the answer? The second question? And the third question? This can happen because you are just not ready to answer questions and your level of stress is not allowing you to think. So what do you do? If you do not immediately know the answer to a question, mark it for review and come back to it later. This will mean your first pass through the exam will generally be quick.

- Control your frustration and maintain focus on each question. You might very well dislike or disagree with some of the questions on this exam. You might also be surprised at how many questions you mark for review. Make sure you stay focused on the current question. If you are still thinking about question 20 when you reach question 120, there will have been 100 questions that you have not looked at closely enough.
- First identify the actual question in the words provided (it is often the last sentence), and then read the rest of the text. Note the topics discussed in the question and the descriptors (e.g., "except," "includes," "not an example of"). This should help you understand what the question is asking and reduce the need to reread questions. Determine what your answer should be, and then look at the answers shown.
- One of the main reasons people answer incorrectly is they do not read all four choices. Do not make the same mistake! Make sure you read the question and all four choices when you take the exam. This will help you select the BEST answer. If you find yourself forgetting to read all the options, start reading the choices backward (choice D first, then C, etc.).
- Quickly eliminate answers that are highly implausible. Many questions have only two plausible options and two obviously incorrect options.
- There may be more than one "correct" answer to each question, but only one "BEST" answer. Make sure you are looking for the BEST answer.
- Be alert to the fact that the answer to one question is sometimes given away in another question. Write down things you do not understand as you take the exam. Use any extra time at the end of the exam to go back to these questions.
- Attempts have been made to keep all choices the same length. Therefore, do not follow the old rule that the longest answer is the right one.
- A concerted effort has been made to use "distracters"—choices that distract you from the correct answer. These are plausible choices that less knowledgeable people will pick. Distracters make it appear as though some questions have two or more right answers. To many people, it seems as though there are only shades of difference between the choices. As noted earlier, make sure you look for the BEST answer for such questions.
- Watch out for choices that are true statements, but do not answer the question.
- Options that represent broad, sweeping generalizations tend to be incorrect, so be alert for "always," "never," "must," "completely," and so forth. Alternatively, choices that represent carefully qualified statements tend to be correct, so be alert for words such as "often," "sometimes," "perhaps," "may," and "generally."
- If a question asks you to fill in a blank space, the correct answer may not be grammatically correct when inserted in the sentence.
- You will have multiple chances to indicate that you have completed the exam. The exam will not be scored until you indicate you are ready, or your time is up. You will receive a printed summary of your test results. If you pass, the computer will print out a certificate, and you will officially be certified. If you do not pass, you will be able to retake the exam. Visit www.iiba.org for re-exam rules. You will have to pay an additional fee to retake the exam.

Conclusion

You have reached the end of the book! Congratulations! Thank you for taking this journey. I hope you will come back to RMC Project Management after you have earned your BA certification. We can help you continue your training and earn continuing development units (CDUs) to maintain your certification through our advanced learning products. Good luck, and I look forward to seeing you after the exam!

E

Elicit 100
Elicitation event 101, 142
End user 32
Enhance 331
Enterprise architecture 60, 295, 339
Entity 190
Entity relationship diagram (ERD) 189, 196
Epic 208
Estimation 66, 82, 349
Event 171
Evolutionary prototype 130, 134
Expert judgment 349
Exploit 330
External agent 71, 118, 187

F

Facilitation 100, 163, 282, 302, 380
Facilitator 115
Feature 62, 64, 76, 174
Financial analysis 78, 81, 336, 362
Flowchart 179, 200
Focus groups 56, 115, 297, 313
Forward traceability 249
Functional decomposition 56, 70, 176, 197, 291, 345
Functional prototype 130
Functional requirements 174, 346

G

Glossary 111, 184
Goals 52

H

Heterogeneous 115
High-fidelity prototype 130, 134
Historical analysis 349
Homogeneous 115
Horizontal prototyping 130
Human-to-human interface 120

I

Impact analysis 242
Impact (stakeholder) 341

Implementation SME 32, 33, 279
Implementation strategy 300
Influence (stakeholder) 341
Inspection 309
Integration testing 309
Interface 70, 72, 117, 118, 120
Internal rate of return 81
Interface analysis 70, 74, 117, 198
Interviews 122, 297, 341, 364
Invisible observation 127
Issue management 130, 211, 238, 239, 297
Iteration 208, 290, 333

J

JAD 136

K

Key performance indicator 82

L

Lean 335
Lessons learned process 365
Level of formality 78
Levels of abstraction 34, 46, 170, 189
Likelihood of success 164
Lineage 233
Link 104, 233, 240, 242
Low-fidelity 130, 132, 134

M

Machine (state) diagrams 207
Majority rules 137
Many-to-many relationship 191
Metadata 197
Metrics 82, 104
Metrics and key performance indicators 82, 198, 218, 365
Mitigate 331
Mockup 130
Model 30, 170, 171, 179
Moderator 115
MoSCoW analysis 166

© 2012 RMC Publications, Inc • 952.846.4484 • info@rmcproject.com • www.rmcproject.com